COMPRESSED VIDEO:
Operations and Applications

- Barbara T. Hakes
- Steven G. Sachs
- Cecelia Box
- John Cochenour

Printed in the United States of America

Graphics and Cover Design by Barbara Orde
Photography by Scott Forehand

The Association for Educational Communications and Technology is an international professional association dedicated to the improvement of instruction through the effective use of media and technology. Periodicals, monographs, videotapes and audiotapes available through AECT meet the needs of media and learning resource specialists, educators, librarians, industrial trainers, and a variety of other educational technology professionals.

"Great new innovations require visionary leaps of human consciousness."

Chris Whittle
Tennessee Illustrated magazine
Winter 1990

"When Edison invented electric illumination, he didn't tinker with candles to make them burn better. Instead he created something brilliantly new: the light bulb."

The Edison Project
Proposal to the New American Schools Development Corporation

"Our world demands that we invent new ways of working, thinking and learning more effectively and efficiently."

Hakes, Sachs, Box and Cochenour

Table of Contents

Foreward

In preparing this book, the authors have drawn upon their collective expertise and experience in the design, installation, and implementation of compressed video systems. Additionally, they have assembled profiles of compressed video systems being used today in public education, higher education, and the private sector. As a result, this book will serve the novice interested in learning more about compressed video, the practitioner developing a compressed video system, and the experienced professional looking for new answers to old questions.

Although not a "new" technology, compressed video has experienced renewed interest in the past two years as a result of significant technological improvements in the hardware and software used to compress and decompress the traditional video signal. Compressed video distributed over today's telephone networks presents an attractive and low-cost alternative to the more traditional methods of video signal distribution. Used in conjunction with satellite and microwave transmission, compressed video allows the broadcast of a video signal using far less space on the carrier.

Whether used for distance education and training, teleconferences, information sharing and retrieval, or as the next generation of personal communications, compressed video will continue to grow in the next decade. Knowing this, the authors have already begun collecting information on the next generation of compressed video hardware and applications, as well as additional system and application profiles for a future supplement to this edition.

This book, *Compressed Video: Operations and Applications,* serves as the single most important resource available today for individuals interested in learning how to take advantage of all this technology has to offer.

Stanley D. Zenor

Executive Director, AECT

Preface and Acknowledgements

Two-way interactive video isn't new, but how it is done has taken a new turn. As opposed to transmission of analog signals, video is now being compressed and converted to digital information which requires far less space on a carrier whether it be satellite, microwave or terrestrial lines. This compressed video (CV) can be transmitted at a variety of rates over its carrier.

We have written this book about interactive compressed video because it offers a cost-effective alternative to travel and the resulting loss of time from human resources. We have also written this book because our experience has revealed that it is a viable alternative for equalizing access to and use of information. Compressed video has the potential to be a cost-effective tool for reaching traditionally underserved populations. In this age, access to and control of information is power and bolsters self-esteem. Knowledge of how to use information management tools makes us all more competitive in this global society. Deliberately omitted are broadcast applications of compressed video. Rather, the book focuses on live, two-way audio and video uses.

As was earlier the case with CD-ROM and videodisc, people are anxious to learn more about interactive, digital, compressed video. And, like CD-ROM and other technologies, CV is advancing at such a rapid rate that this book will have a sunset very soon.

During the spring of 1991 at the University of Wyoming, we conducted a compressed video pilot to help us assess the needs for and uses of compressed video and allow us to "test drive" various vendors' compressed video equipment. In organizing the pilot, we found we had to call around to other institutions and agencies to get a profile of what was happening with compressed video in order to help us plan our own system and select our own equipment. In short, people were so busy "CVing" that they hadn't written much about it. In the process of calling other institutions we got to know many of the contributors to this book. One of those we contacted was Dr. Steven Sachs at Northern Virginia Community College. Since installing NVCC's multi-campus CV system in 1989, Steve has provided demonstrations, tours, and advice to individuals all over the country. We thought it would be useful to compile as much information as we could for the many of you who are interested in learning more about compressed video. To this end we have created this book which is divided into two parts. Part I is an overview of operations and issues related to compressed video. It is drawn from Northern Virginia Community College and University of Wyoming experiences and synthesizes what is occurring in other organizations as gleaned from Part II. Part II contains as many profiles of CV use from higher education, the private sector and the public schools as we were able to compile. We solicited user profiles from contacts made during the pilot project and we issued a call for manuscripts in the May 1992 issue of TechTrends. Although we know we have missed the inclusion of some institutions, agencies and businesses who are using compressed video, we hope this book can link you to other users for additional information in order to be able to capitalize on what other groups may have already tried or learned. We intend to publish a supplement to this book which will contain more in-depth user profiles from a greater number of groups. If we have not included your CV applications in this book, please contact us so we may add your profile to the supplement.

Many people put a great deal of effort into this book. Without their assistance we would not have made it to publication. First, our sincere appreciation goes to all the chapter authors and those who provided their profiles for Part II.

Nancy Klinck, Director of Publications at the Association for Education Communications and Technology, provided the publication guidance during the months when we were working to turn mountains of information into book form. We gratefully acknowledge her patience and good natured assistance.

A number of people at the University of Wyoming were instrumental in the production of this book. Christine Shearer asssisted with manuscript preparation. Vicki Atterbury worked on document conversion. A number of graduate students also were invaluable. Barbara Orde, a doctoral student in Instructional Technology, was responsible for the graphics and the cover design. Karen Leicht and Debra Ramirez, also Instructional Technology graduate students, provided editorial assistance and coordinated the many pieces and people involved. Scott Forehand provided photography services. Ritchie Boyd and Andy Bryson of the Center for Teaching Excellence provided on-going technical assistance with our word processing and graphics needs. Debbie Martinez also provided patient support and assistance.

Finally, each of us would also like to extend a special thanks to our friends, colleagues and particular appreciation to our spouses and families, who provided unfailing support throughout months of frantic work and pre-occupation. They truly deserve credit for this book.

We are excited about the future of this emerging technology and welcome you to join us in finding ways to harness the potential of this powerful information tool. We invite you to visit our institutions and experience our uses of compressed video. We also invite you to contribute to the supplement for this book. Please call us and we will send you guidelines for preparing a user profile.

Barbara T. Hakes, Director
  Wyoming Centers for Teaching and Learning Network
  Wyoming Center for Educational Research
  University of Wyoming
  Voice (307) 766-3146
  FAX (307) 766-6668

Steven G. Sachs, Associate Dean
  Instructional Technologies and Extended Learning
  Northern Virginia Community College
  Voice (703) 323-3371
  FAX (703) 323-3392

Cecelia Box, Assistant Professor
  Instructional Technology
  University of Wyoming
  Voice (307) 766-3337
  FAX (307) 766-6668

John Cochenour, Assistant Professor
  Instructional Technology
  University of Wyoming
  Voice (307) 766-3608
  FAX (307) 766-6668

Introduction

This book provides an overview of compressed video operations and applications. It is not an exhaustive study of the technology but rather a synthesis of information about what various institutions, agencies and businesses are doing with compressed video. It is also based on the experiences of the authors. Some of the user profiles that were included cover support systems for technologies other than compressed video. We have made no attempt to edit out information from submissions. Nor have we attempted to standardize the writing styles used by the various contributors. This book is not a scholarly treatise but rather a practical information guide. Compressed video technology is changing so rapidly that by the time readers use this book some of the information may be out-of-date.

For whom is this book written?
- For persons who know a little about compressed digital interactive video (CV) and would like to know more.
- For persons who know a great deal about CV and would like to know what others are doing.
- For anyone at any level of education, government or the private sector who is interested in using compressed video for a wide variety of applications including teaching/training, counseling, conferencing, mentoring/coaching, sharing scarce resources, advising, brainstorming, and total quality management.

How this book may be used:
- As a reference/resource guide
- As an Introductory text for instructional technology, telecommunications, information management, or instructional design.
- As a random access information tool

1

What is Compressed Video?

John J. Cochenour
Landra L. Rezabek
Coleman H. Burton

Introduction

There is a certain amount of overlap in the terminology associated with instructional video technology, and this chapter is intended to provide the reader with the information needed to discriminate among various video technologies, or at least to help readers recognize those technologies which we refer to as compressed video. In order to accomplish this goal, the chapter is divided into two sections: Section I, *Compressed Video and What's In It for Me* by John Cochenour and Landra Rezabek, and Section II, *Digital Video* by Coleman Burton. Section I is a general overview of compressed video technology including descriptions, definitions, components, options and uses that emphasize instructional applications. Section II is a reprint of a monograph produced for the Association of College and University Telecommunications Administrators in 1991. Section II provides a more technical description of compressed video systems including television fundamentals, options, features, multi-location conferencing, transmission, and set up.

Section I: Compressed Video and What's in It for Me

John J. Cochenour & Landra L. Rezabek

Compressed video is a technology that enables live, two-way auditory and visual signals to be transmitted simultaneously among sites which are equipped with specialized equipment. Using this specialized equipment, compressed video signals can be sent over fiber optic or other telephone lines, by satellite, and by microwave transmission, usually at costs substantially less than those associated with other types of live, two-way transmission. As described below, the special transmission process associated with compressed video and the resulting cost benefits make it a likely medium of choice for users interested in maintaining live, two-way visual and auditory communication while staying within budgetary guidelines. In addition, the use of compressed video offers additional presentation options that make it a flexible and viable classroom tool for distance education environments. This section briefly explains how compressed video works, describes the basic equipment and support needed, discusses ways in which the hardware may be configured, and offers options for classroom use of the technology.

How Compressed Video Works

Video is the picture portion of a televised presentation. Video is an electronic signal composed of moving frames of information and transmitted at a frequency range of 1 to 6 megahertz. Megahertz is a radio frequency term meaning one million cycles per second, so suffice it to say that video signals are transmitted quite rapidly. The term *compression* refers to the process of reducing the representation of information without reducing the information itself. Compression has the effect of lowering the time or space necessary to store or to transmit the information. Video compression involves processing the *analog* television signal digitally. Analog signals are continuous much as a clock has hands that sweep along a continuous scale or speedometers with needles that register approximate speed along a continuous scale. These devices are both analog devices and register a value analogous to the event. An analog signal can vary in strength at any moment in time, and the signal "directly and proportionately creates the display on the screen" (Tanner, 1992, p.1). A digital signal is not continuous. It is discrete — it is either there or it is not. A digital signal is really a string of digits transmitted in abrupt, distinct increments at a very high rate of speed. Currently, this digital signal can be compressed down to a very small percentage of the transmission space needed for typical broadcast quality television. Compression of digital signals is desirable because when information is converted from analog to digital it results in an enormous number of digits — more than can be delivered on a standard television cable channel. Compression allows for non-essential digits not to be transmitted thus reducing the "volume" of transmission (Johnson, 1991).

Therefore, the major difference between compressed video signals and traditional signals broadcast over the airwaves or sent over the phone lines is that the visual and auditory information delivered by a compressed video signal is "edited" during the transmission process so that it demands less "space" to send. For example, imagine that the telephone cable connecting two schools is made up of ten strands, each capable of carrying a specific amount of information. The information transmitted through the cable may normally require eight of these strands, but by using compressed video, the same amount of information could be transmitted using only two of these strands. Remember that this is only an analogy — compressed video signals are not actually transmitted in this manner — but the example underscores a critical benefit of compressed video technology. By requiring less space to transmit, compressed video signals are less costly than their non-compressed counterparts.

The compression and transmission of visual and auditory information as described can result in picture and sound signals different from the visual and audio signals most of us are used to encountering during commercial television programs. The challenge of compression is to reduce the amount of bits transmitted while still retaining a high quality video and audio signal (Tanner, 1992). Because compressed video technology only transmits new information when it is needed, motion of the screen sometimes appears jerky or after-images linger if objects move rapidly across the screen. Usually, the greater the compression, the more noticeable the picture degradation becomes, but as the techniques for compressing the video signal continue to improve, it is harder to detect signal degradation.

These slight video distortions are more noticeable if the movement takes place quickly or close to the camera and become less apparent as the motion occurs farther away from the camera. Instructors and students who use compressed video systems indicate that they soon do not notice the slightly jerky movement or the after images. Users also report that they readily learn to move away from the camera to improve the quality of the images.

Improvements in the compression algorithm (an information processing formula) of the various vendors' products allow one to adjust the time delay so that any picture degradation and audio delay are barely noticeable and produce excellent quality video. As the race among the compressed video vendors continues, improvements in how analog video information is converted to digital form for transmission and then reconverted to analog signals are occurring quarterly and both video and audio quality are improving.

Compression also causes some slight differences in audio transmission. The audio signals of some compressed video systems are somewhat delayed, causing a slight 'pause" in transmission time. No, compressed video does not result in the voice being out-of-sync with lip movements like dubbed-over foreign films. There may only be a slight pause between the time someone actually speaks and when the audio is actually heard at the distance site. Again, compressed video users indicate that they learn to adapt to this brief period quite easily and that it is not a barrier to live interactive communication.

Components of a Compressed Video System

To accomplish the transmission process described above, the sending and receiving sites making up a compressed video network must all have the same technical capabilities. The International Telegraph and Telephone Consultative Committee (CCITT) established an international standard for compressed video technology in 1990. This standard sets minimum performance levels that insures equipment compatibility, but it allows equipment variance in terms of performance and price (Johnson, 1991). Even with this standard, a great deal of variation remains among systems particularly older systems and those using satellite transmission. Compressed video consumers must be sure to work closely with vendors to make sure their system will be compatible with any other equipment to be used.

Figure 1.1
Compressed video system showing the codec at bottom left.

Each site in the compressed video network must have a compatible compressed video system complete with a codec, audio and visual receiving and transmitting hardware, and a transmission link. A codec (short for coder/decoder) is used to convert the video and audio signals to and from digital signals. This is the heart of the compressed video technology and a more detailed explanation is provided in Section II of this chapter.

The receiving and transmitting hardware varies somewhat with the application, but usually would include at least one camera, two monitors, and a microphone at each site. The video camera and microphone are used to record the visual and audio information occurring at one site. The recorded information is then processed through the codec and transmitted to the other site or sites. One monitor is used to display the information that is recorded and transmitted out, while the other monitor shows the information that is received from the other site. One monitor at each site could be used instead of two, if the users are willing to use picture-in-picture capability or a video switch for switching back and forth between the outgoing and incoming signals. Picture-in-picture capability uses an image inserted into a larger visual already displayed on the screen, a technique used frequently in news broadcasts. The video switch allows the user to choose between monitoring the signals that are being sent to or received from the other site. If budgets allow, it is usually preferred to purchase two video monitors per site, so both sending and receiving signals can be seen simultaneously.

Compressed video transmissions are normally sent "point to point," meaning that signals are sent specifically from the transmitting site to the receiving site or sites. Point-to-point transmission signals are sent to a specifically pre-determined and select locations and are not "broadcast" or "put up for grabs" as traditional television signals are. The transmission links

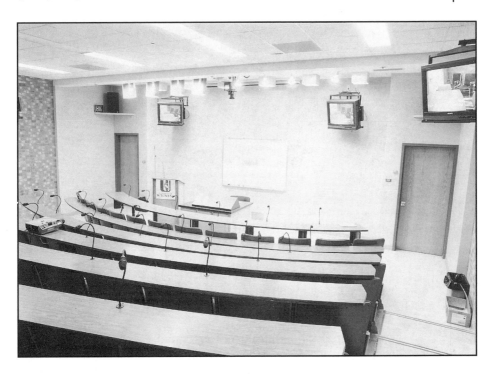

Figure 1.2
A classroom specially adapted as a fixed compressed video site

used to carry compressed video signals can be leased telephone lines, fiber optic lines, microwave transmissions, or satellite transmissions. Chapter Four provides a more detailed look at facilities and components, and some of the many options available.

Configuration Options

As mentioned above, compressed video systems can be configured in a number of ways depending upon the specific instructional or conferencing needs of the user. These configurations generally fall into three categories: custom video rooms, rollabout systems, and desktop systems. Each of the configurations include the basic technology elements mentioned above — codecs, video cameras, microphones and video monitors. In custom built settings, rooms are designed and equipment is installed in a special fixed site.

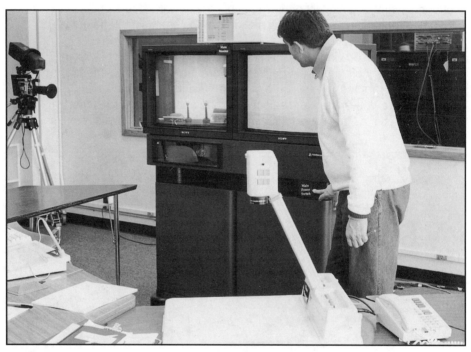

Figure 1.3
A rollabout compressed video system

Rollabout systems are those in which the equipment is mounted entirely in a cabinet that can be moved to where ever transmission facilities such as telephone or cable connections are available.

Desktop systems are also transportable, but the equipment is installed in a very limited desktop space and is intended only for individual or very small group use. Additional information on these system categories is provided in Section II of this chapter as well as in Chapters 3 and 4.

The basic compressed video system can be expanded to meet a variety of user needs and options. Additional cameras and monitors can be used to provide more complete video coverage. Such additional equipment can take advantage of split-screen viewing, multiple camera angles, and video techniques such as remote pan, tilt, zoom and focusing to enhance camera views. Switching between camera shots can be done manually, through computer programming, or by voice activation when a microphone is associated with a particular camera. As with any audio/video link, additional monitors can facilitate viewing by larger audiences and multiple microphones can be added as groups grow in size.

In addition to live audio and visual interaction, compressed video technology supports the use of a variety of instructional materials. Graphics cameras, actually just normal video cameras that frequently have special close-up lenses added, are available to use for the transmission of pre-produced or spontaneous visual aids. Most graphics cameras are mounted overhead in a special set-up and placed above a light table to enable the use of overhead transparencies and slides. Overhead-mounted graphics cameras can also be used to transmit visual information such as pictures from books or visuals drawn on paper, so users can be spontaneous in incorporating visuals.

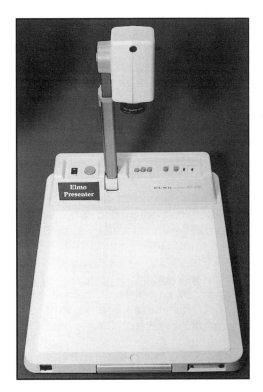

Figure 1.4
A representative graphics camera

Many compressed video systems also incorporate a video cassette recorder (VCR) to record the compressed video session or to transmit a pre-recorded tape. A fax machine can be included with a compressed video unit so that actual exchange of hard copy documents can occur during the compressed video session. Microcomputers are also being used to assist and enhance data and graphic transmission. Electronic pen pads or graphics tablets, keyboards, and infra-red or touch screen control units are

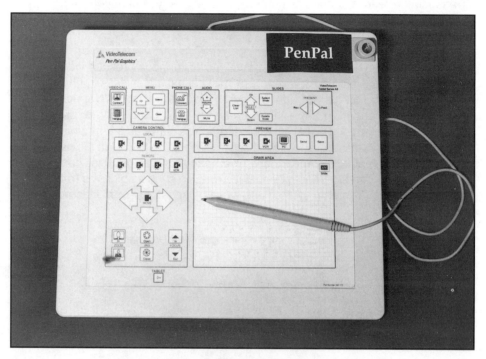

Figure 1.5
An electronic pen pad for data input

used to input information, run diagnostics, and generally, make the video conference more convenient and versatile. Additionally, information from optical disks can be transmitted by some specially-equipped compressed video systems.

A growing number of compressed video systems allow users to easily interface desired peripherals such as fax, graphics tablets, video tape, CD-ROM, and other media resources to become fully-functioning multimedia distance learning stations. Other systems require non-standard connections for interfacing these tools and can not digitize and store graphic information for use at a future time, so it is important for the user to determine desired uses for the compressed video systems and to discuss system specifications with vendors. Some vendors' products are highly integrated and function like an electronic home entertainment center while other products are not yet as well integrated and user-friendly, consisting of components from a variety of sources. Potential users also should ask vendors about provisions for up-grades to the system.

Some codecs are computer based, meaning that all upgrades or enhancements to the provision of video and audio information can be provided through a computer disc, much as the word processing package on a computer can be upgraded. Other upgrading procedures are much more complex. Also, users should be sure to ask vendors about the cost and

Figure 1.6
Keyboard and remote control also used for data input

ease of adding to or changing the basic configuration of the compressed video system. For more detailed information regarding the selection of a compressed video system, later chapters deal specifically with vendor selection, financial planning, and facilities development.

Using Compressed Video: Human Resources are the Key to Success

Human resources to conduct a compressed video session are one of the primary considerations in using the technology. Unfortunately, users usually tend to think about the technology itself and all that it can do, but often forget that the hardware is useless without capable people to make the system work. In the context of compressed video, teamwork is crucial to the success of any endeavor.

Compressed video communication often requires input from a number of human resources in order to occur effectively and efficiently. Depending on the reasons for using compressed video, the desired outcomes of the compressed video session, and the organization within which the session takes place, a variety of people impact the success of a compressed video experience. People who formally or informally make up the "team" responsible for compressed video sessions may include those from organizational management or administration, instructors, technicians, distance site facilitators, and students or participants.

For example, in the context of providing distance instruction using compressed video as the delivery system, "details" such as scheduling, registration, course credit, teacher certification, distribution of learning materials, session funding, room location, access to hardware, and a variety of other serious instructional issues must be decided. Most often, these are the arena for administrators, managers, or coordinators. Whether instruction is a semester-long college course, a three-day workshop for new corporate employees, or a one-hour lesson for third-graders, someone must make provision for this instructional endeavor which takes advantage of compressed video technology. Too often, many of these administrative and managerial details are overlooked, and pre-planning in these areas is a key.

Regardless whether a person is called an instructor, teacher, facilitator, leader, or other similar term, someone must be responsible for determining the nature of the compressed video session and for monitoring the progress of the actual session. In instructional settings, teachers may determine instructional objectives and present lessons; in distanced meetings, chairpersons may determine the agenda and keep discussions on track. Depending on the type of intended use and the desired interaction, someone must monitor and facilitate participant interaction and the progress of the compressed video session. Because users of compressed video systems are separated by geographic distance and are often using a technology new to them, facilitators should themselves first of all become comfortable with the hardware and strive to help the participants do so as well. A facilitator does not have to become a technician, and in fact, the authors believe a facilitator should not do so! But the teacher/facilitator is probably the single most critical participant in a compressed video session. If s/he thinks compressed video delivery systems will support the goals of the session and if s/he is open and willing to use the technology, the session will usually go well. If the facilitator/teacher is negative or critical, these attitudes are usually conveyed to the distant participants and a negative tone is set right away for the entire session.

In addition to knowing how to use the hardware and having a positive attitude, a facilitator must know how to generate student participation and enthusiasm. Compressed video is just one of many distance delivery systems available to support instruction and communication, so many "rules of thumb" available from distance educators and trainers will apply. For example, facilitators can do a great deal to establish a positive "climate" among distant participants by asking individuals to introduce themselves, allowing for a little personal chatter while students become used to the compressed video technology, and encouraging students to experiment with the variety of communication options available on the system. Since compressed video technology offers the opportunity for live, two-way, audio and visual interaction among participants, facilitators should take advantage of these attributes! Chapter 3 presents additional concerns for instructors using the medium of compressed video.

Technicians are other vital members of a compressed video team. As suggested above, facilitators should not be expected to know the technical details associated with compressed video systems, but they should know how to make the system do what they want it to do. Technicians will probably be in charge of much of the "hands-on" training for using the system, and it is not far-fetched to expect vendors to provide hands-on training to selected in-house technicians and instructors as well. It must be noted, however, that vendor training may not always be of the level, detail, or nature needed for a user's particular setting or application, and one should be cautious about depending entirely upon the vendor's training alone.

Technicians may or may not be needed during actual sessions. It has been the authors' experience that the more complex the system and the larger the group the more beneficial it is to have a technician present during the session. The authors have conducted distance education classes on rollabout systems with three monitors, two cameras, and remote controllers at two sites and accommodated about 40 people total quite successfully with only one instructor and without a technician. However, it is always nice to have a technician available, and most people would prefer to have a technician set up the system before a class or conference and to close it down afterwards.

Similarly, distanced site facilitators make the job of the instructor/facilitator much easier by taking care of local details. Site facilitators may proctor exams, distribute materials, troubleshoot student problems, act as local technicians, and generally help coordinate the use of compressed video systems at their location. During informal conversations with compressed video users, the authors have heard many times that the success of a session or course is very dependent upon site facilitators. In fact, administrators and instructors should note that every member of a team is just as important as another. Technicians and site facilitators work with you, not for you, and without them your life would be much more stressful. Remember that simple courtesy and interpersonal skills go a long way in promoting teamwork, especially in the context of using compressed video technology in the delivery of instruction over geographic distances.

Finally, students or participants are yet another category of team member involved in compressed video sessions. To echo the sentiment of the statement above, the authors have found that "doing with" students is much more successful than "doing to" them, particularly in the context of compressed video interaction. Compressed video technology allows live, two-way visual and auditory interaction among users if the sessions are designed in a way to encourage participants to take advantage of these attributes. Sessions where the facilitator or teacher merely talks at the distance groups would most likely be just as effective using a plain telephone with a large speaker. In order to take advantage of the compressed video technology, participants should be encouraged to communicate with each other using visual as well as verbal messages and to interact in the exchange of information . The authors have seen third graders introduced to the compressed video hardware and by the end of a two-hour session using it to interact with distanced peers because they were allowed to take ownership in the communication and learning process. An excellent discussion of student and user satisfaction with this technology is in the University of Oklahoma's profile provided by Haynes and Swisher in Part II of this book.

See Part II

Summary

This section of chapter one has provided a general introductory description of what compressed video is and how it works. It has presented some preliminary descriptions of the basic equipment requirements and configurations of compressed video systems. It has identified human resources as a factor crucial to the success of compressed video use. The question remains — so why should or would someone choose to use compressed video technology in an instructional or conferencing setting? Many of the reasons have been mentioned above, but a quick summary will close this section of the chapter.

First, compressed video provides an opportunity for live, two-way audio and video interaction among distanced locations. Second, this opportunity for high quality interaction is currently available at costs substantially less than for full-motion interaction. Third, though system configurations vary, compressed video can be extremely user-friendly and flexible. A fourth advantage is that, again depending on equipment specifications, compressed video technology can be combined with other instructional and communications media and technology and it is available in a variety of configurations. Basically, compressed video can be many things to many people who are interested in live, interactive, audio and visual interaction. This section was written to entice you to learn more about compressed video technologies, and the authors hope you will enjoy doing just that throughout the rest of this book.

Section II: Digital Video

Coleman H. Burton

Introduction

The purpose of this section is to discuss the ins and outs, whys and wherefores of transmitting full-motion, color video over conventional, commercially available digital transmission facilities. A conventional National Television Standards Committee (NTSC) television signal, such as received in the home via cable or over the air, requires six megahertz (6 million cycles per second) of analog bandwidth. Digitizing the NTSC signal produces a 90 megabit (90 million bps) bit stream. Neither the six megahertz nor the 90 megabit requirement can be handled by facilities that are economically realistic for most organizations.

Experiments based on reduced-bandwidth, digitized video had begun as early as 1970. AT&T's Picturephone enabled premise to premise audio and video "telephone calls" over the switched network. For a variety of reasons, the Picturephone was never fully successful. It used an awkward combination of analog and digital technology, and required end-to-end digital facilities between Picturephone serving offices. In 1970, digital trunking was a rarity, except between central offices in high population densities, such as New York City.

By the early 1980s, advances in micro-electronics and the widespread deployment of digital transmission facilities made transmission of digitized video viable. Micro-computers were designed to apply complex and exotic signal-processing techniques to the 90 megabit video signal to reduce (compress) the number of bits required to represent the video picture. Since the first release of video compression equipment, the speed of microprocessors has been steadily increasing, their cost has been steadily decreasing, and the mathematical algorithms used for compression have been greatly improved. All this adds up to full-motion, color, compressed video, that in the early 1980s required six to twelve megabytes per second of bandwidth to produce acceptable picture quality, now can be handled with as little as 56,000 bits per second of bandwidth, and produce acceptable picture quality.

In parallel with the development of compressed video technology, the availability of digital transmission facilities has become almost universal and affordable. DSI (1,544,000 bits per second) transmission facilities are readily available, from the major inter-exchange carriers, from nationwide fiber consortiums, and from any number of regional carriers and consortiums. Dial-up 56,000 bps service is available from the major inter-exchange carriers, and basic rate ISDN service with its two 64,000 bps B channels is available in more and more locations.

This serendipitous combination of improved electronics and available, low-cost bandwidth makes compressed video one of the "hot" telecommunications technologies for the nineties. According to a survey done by The Institute for the Future and TeleSpan Publishing Corp., in 1988 users spent $122.4 million on video teleconferencing services and equipment, $202.7 million in 1989 and project spending $335.8 million in 1990 (see Figure 1.7). The anticipated growth of video teleconferencing in the 1990s is similar to the FAX "explosion" of the 1980s.

As in the corporate world, where video teleconferencing is used to improve competitive position, so will higher education be using video teleconferencing technology to improve operations and provide a competitive advantage for institutions. Eventually, every campus telecommunications department is going to be asked about video teleconferencing, what it is and what it can do for the college or university.

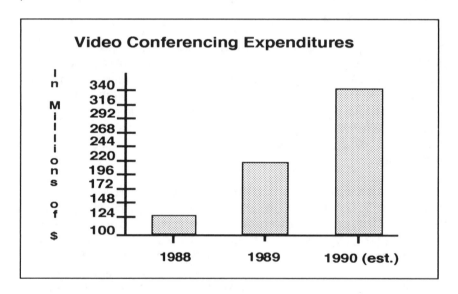

Figure 1.7

While it seems obvious, video teleconferencing is for face-to-face meetings. In the spectrum of things, video teleconferencing falls between telephone conference calls and in-person meetings. It gives a visual aspect to a meeting that an audio-only conference can't. The visual aspect includes being able to see the person(s) you are talking with, their facial expressions and body gestures and being able to view pictures, graphs, charts and other visuals simultaneously. Video teleconferencing can't provide many of the nuances that an in-person meeting provides. Nor does it allow the mini-meetings that often take place among several participants in a larger meeting. In our experience, video teleconferencing also has the potential for being embarrassing. We have had at least one occasion when a participant, who was listening to a presentation, fell asleep in full view of the other sites watching him!

In higher education, video teleconferencing technology works extremely well as a vehicle for delivering instruction. At the University of Missouri, we are using compressed video technology to deliver upper-level, undergraduate courses and graduate courses, primarily to non-traditional students. The technology has enabled us to provide course work to students in parts of the state that we would have otherwise been unable to reach. After three years of usage, the achievement of the students at the remote receiving sites has been statistically the same as the students at the originating site.

Some benefits of video teleconferencing are immediately apparent. It eliminates travel expenses such as room, board and transportation. At the University of Missouri, a four campus video teleconference saves a minimum of $180 in travel expense. Another direct benefit, that is harder to quantify is the elimination of travel time. Again, at the University of Missouri a four-campus video teleconference saves a minimum of 12 man-hours of travel time. The nature of video teleconferencing is such that the meetings must be more structured than face-to-face meetings. This results in a video teleconference being more productive for the amount of time involved. In higher education, video teleconferencing allows leveraging of the faculty, enabling them to reach more students and to reach remote geographical areas. Particularly for public institutions, this is not only a direct benefit, but a political one in relationships with the state legislature and the public. Finally, there is the intangible benefit of being perceived as a cutting-edge, high-tech organization.

Television Fundamentals

It is possible to install and operate a compressed video system without understanding how a television works. On the other hand, when a telecommunications professional, who understands voice and data, and a television professional, who understands video, get together to troubleshoot a problem, it is helpful if , there is some semblance of understanding between the two. Also, it never hurts to have a basic understanding of the technology that you are operating and managing for your campus.

A NTSC television frame consists of 525 lines, each containing 466 horizontal pixels "painted" on the picture tube by an electron gun (black and white) or three electron guns (color). New pictures are "painted" at the rate of 30 times a second. Each frame is created by two top to bottom scans that last one sixtieth of a second per scan. A single scan illuminates either the odd or even lines of the picture. Outside North America, standards known as PAL and SECAM use 625 scan lines and refresh at 25 times per second, i.e., a single scan is one fiftieth of a second. NTSC receivers are incompatible with either PAL or SECAM transmissions, and vice versa.

Simply stated, a complete television signal, such as received over the air or by cable contains three elements, video, sync and audio. In a color system, the video portion of the signal consists of chrominance and luminance information for each horizontal pixel in each scan line. Chrominance defines the intensity of each of the three primary colors (red-green-blue) needed to produce the desired color. Luminance defines brightness of the pixel. Sync consists of vertical and horizontal sync. As expected, vertical sync controls the starting point of each of the 525 scan lines, and horizontal sync controls the side to side movement of the scan. Audio is audio, and not really that much different from a FM audio transmission.

For transmission of a television signal, either over the air or by cable, the chrominance and luminance information is combined to produce what is known as non-composite video. The non-composite video is then combined with the sync information to produce a composite video signal. The composite video signal and the audio signal are then input into a RF (radio frequency) modulator which modulates the composite video and audio signals onto a carrier frequency (see Figure 1.8). The carrier frequency has a one-to-one correlation with the channel numbers on a television set or cable converter.

On the positive side, an RF signal is very easy to work with, in terms of modulation, demodulation and transmission. On the negative side, the process of modulation and demodulation reduces picture sharpness about 10%. From this standpoint, a compressed video system benefits from having the origination equipment (i.e., camera and audio) and termination equipment (i.e., television receiver) directly connected to the compressed video equipment, without intervening RF transmission.

Compressed Video Systems

The heart of a compressed video system is the codec (coder/decoder) that converts analog audio and video to a digital format. The codecs on the marketplace today fall into three general categories; low-bit rate, TI, and 45 mbps. Consideration of the 45 mbps codecs is not part of this monograph. The 45 mbps codecs provide only a 2:1 compression over the original 90 mbps digitized signal. These codecs, for all intents and purposes, maintain the studio quality image of the original signal, and they cost less then either a low bit rate or TI codec. Of course, the down side of a 45 mbps codec is that it requires a full DS3 (28 TIs) for transmission.

Combining Basic Television Signals

TI codecs generally operate at speeds of 384,000 bps to 1,544,000 bps (2,048,000 bps in Europe). Picture resolution is 480 vertical lines by 384 horizontal pixels. Refresh rate is 15 times per second; one half the NTSC refresh rate of 30 frames per second.

Low bit rate codecs generally operate at speeds of 56,000 bps to 384,000 bps. Picture resolution is 240 vertical lines by 256 horizontal pixels. Refresh rate varies among codec vendors. Some use a variable refresh rate, from 5 to 15 frames per second, while other vendors use a fixed refresh rate; 10 frames per second at lower bit rates, and 15 frames per second at higher bit rates.

For the low bit rate codecs, audio handling becomes a problem. Standard PCM audio digitizing, requires 64,000 bps - quite a problem for a

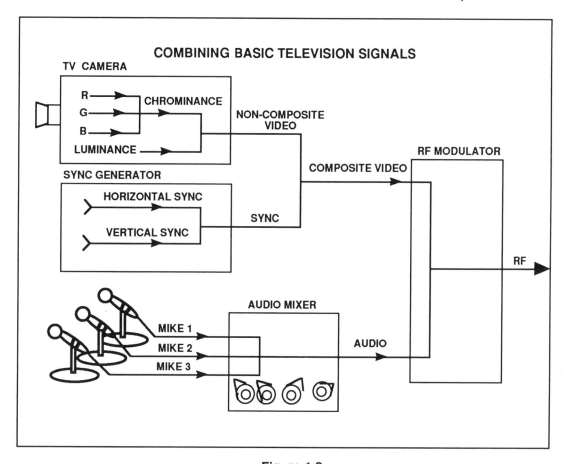

Figure 1.8

codec operating at 56,000 bps. The low-bit-rate codecs have adopted two schemes for handling audio. The first, the path of least resistance, is to transmit the audio outband, i.e., use a second transmission line to send the audio. The second, and more prevalent approach, is to use some form of low-bit-rate inband audio. Most codecs use some form of continuously variable slope delta modulation (CVSDM) to reduce the audio bit rate as low as 8,000 bps and still maintain sufficient audio quality. Still, even at 8,000 bps, quite a bit of video resolution is lost when transmitting at 56,000 bps.

The amount of motion that a compressed video codec can handle is directly related to the transmission rate of the codec—the higher the speed, the smoother the motion. Motion is in turn a function of the refresh rate of the codec. There is an interesting difference in the motion handling capabilities of fixed and variable refresh rate codecs. At some point, there will be too much motion for a codec to handle, irrespective of transmission rate. With a fixed refresh rate codec, too much motion creates a picture that appears blurred at the receive end. A variable rate codec recognizes that the motion exceeds its capabilities and slows down the refresh rate, i.e., fewer frames per second require fewer bits per second. The result at the receiving end is a "stroboscopic" effect, i.e., a person walking across the screen will appear on the left, in the middle, and then on the right, like a series of still pictures.

Viewers find either result, blurring or strobe effect, objectionable. It tends to be a subjective call as to which approach is to be preferred. The reader should not be lead to the conclusion that motion is a severe problem for compressed video codecs, and that received pictures are either blurred or jumpy. When the transmission speed of the codec is properly matched to the picture being sent, motion problems are rarely noticed. Low-speed codecs work well in a 'talking head' situation, while the higher speed codecs work well with groups of people — just don't try to transmit a basketball game.

Compressing Video

Stripping away most of the exotic technology involved, a compressed video codec is an analog to digital and digital to analog conversion device, with a special purpose computer to manipulate the digital information. Input to the codec is analog audio, analog video and sync. Under normal circumstances, sync signals are imbedded in the video signal, i.e., the codec accepts a composite video signal. An elaborate video facility may use a stand-alone sync generator to control the video camera(s) and the codec. In such a case, non-composite video and a separate sync signal are accepted by the codec.

Processing the audio is straight forward. Whereas, the video has discrete frames, of which 50 percent are thrown away at 15 frames per second, the audio is continuous. The audio side of the codec digitizes the audio according the algorithm chosen and synchronizes the time delay for which the audio processor must compensate. Failure to compensate for the video time delay would result in a loss of lip synchronization when camera subjects are speaking.

On the video side, the first step is to digitize the composite video signal into a 90 mbps format. The next step is to convert the digitized signal from raster format (odd lines followed by even lines) to a block format, which is a complete, continuous top to bottom representation of the frame.

The next couple of steps in the process are the vendor's "secret ingredient." Each vendor has their set of routines that "produce maximum picture quality for minimum bandwidth." The digitized-block format is transformed into a series of small blocks, usually 16-by-16 pixels for luminance and 8-by-8 for chrominance. The method of coding the transformed blocks has evolved over time, as the designers have become more clever and the speed of microprocessors has increased. Three techniques that have been, or are being used are: intraframe coding; interframe coding; and predictive or movement-compensated coding.

Intraframe coding is the least complicated method. Each frame is considered on a stand alone basis. The redundant information within the frame is compressed to the minimum number of bits necessary to represent the picture fully. For example, a picture of a person talking in front of a solid-color background contains much redundant information, namely the background, which is not moving, changing color or brightness. The complex portion of the picture is the person, with varying flesh tones, patterns and colors in clothing, etc. The number of bits needed to represent the background would be relatively small, while the number of bits needed to represent the person would be quite high.

Interframe coding builds upon intraframe coding. Each successive frame is compared to the previous frame and only the differences between frames are transmitted. With interframe coding, highly complex, but unmoving pictures are handled very well, giving excellent resolution. When the amount of motion present in the picture being transmitted exceeds the data rate between codecs, blurring or strobing takes place.

Predictive or motion-compensated coding is an enhanced interframe coding technique. It takes advantage of the fact, that even when a large amount of motion is involved, the picture structure from frame to frame does not change that much. What does change is the relative orientation of major blocks within the picture. The sending codec sends information to the receiving codec that a block of information that was in position (XI, YI) has now moved to location $(X2, Y2)$. The amount of motion that the predictive or motion-compensated approach can handle is directly related to the speed of the microprocessors used in the codec.

An extremely difficult situation for the codec is when the picture changes completely, such as when switching from one camera to another. Though it is very expensive in terms of bits required, most codecs handle a major picture change by going into intraframe encoding. Determining that a major picture change has occurred is a computationally intensive process.

The bit stream produced by the encoding stage is passed through one or more mathematical algorithms. The purpose of this "massaging" is to reduce the number of bits needed to represent the output of the encoding state. The process is similar to the process used to compress computer files for transmission over low speed communications facilities.

The final output of the compression stage goes into the communications controller. The communications controller multiplexes the compressed video data with the digitized audio, and frames the data to provide synchronization, control and forward error correction. The resultant data frame is then transmitted over the communications facility to the remote codec.

The remote codec reverses the process of the local codec. The received data frame is demultiplexed, with video being sent to one section of the codec and audio to another. The video section performs an inverse transform, decodes the received data, converts block data to raster format and then converts the digitized video frame to analog NTSC composite video. The audio side converts the digital audio to analog, synchronizes the audio with the video and ouputs to the audio-out connector. Sync for the output NTSC composite video signal is recovered from the input video side.

It has been implied, but not specifically stated, that compressed video codecs are full duplex devices. They transmit and receive simultaneously. This is what allows an interactive teleconference to take place. On the other hand, there is no correlation between the transmitted data stream and the received data stream. There is no reason that a codec cannot send a transmission from one video source and receive a completely unrelated transmission from another video source, i.e., used in a broadcast mode rather than interactive mode.

As noted earlier, the transform and coding techniques of the various codec manufacturers are their "secret ingredients" used to distinguish their products from others in the marketplace. The result of this is that vendor A's codec will only communicate with another vendor A codec. As long as most networks are strictly point-to-point configurations, usually operating over private or leased transmission facilities, this isn't that much of a problem. However, with the increased availability of low speed codecs that can operate effectively over the public switched network, using switched 56/64 kbps facilities, or ISDN basic rate facilities, codec incompatibility becomes an impediment to wide scale deployment of compressed video. The problem is similar to the end of the 1800s when there were competing telephone companies in a single area. If you wanted to be able to call everyone who had a telephone, you had to have a line and instrument from each of the telephone companies - which lead to the invention of the oversized desk, to hold all those telephones!

The solution to multiple telephone companies and to proprietary codecs is standards. A new worldwide standard called P X 64 (CCITT recommendation H.261) is being developed as a coding standard. Deployment of this standard will enable codecs from manufacturer A to talk to codecs from manufacturers B, C, etc. As of this writing, the complete H.261 recommendation has not been released, but enough has been released that several vendors have implemented a portion of the recommendation and demonstrated inter-manufacturer compatibility. The P X 64 algorithm is intended to apply across the entire transmission spectrum of 56 kbps to 2.048 mbps. Initial, subjective evaluation of P X 64 is that it works somewhat better at lower speeds than high speeds. So, it is expected that the TI codecs will implement both the P X 64 and a proprietary algorithm. Such codecs will automatically select their compression method based upon the far-end codec.

Options and Features

All codecs are equipped with one or more RS-232 ports to connect a control terminal or a room controller. A room controller is usually a small box containing a variety of buttons and sometimes a joy stick, and is used by the teleconference user to control the codec and possibly other aspects of the system. Programming of the codecs and diagnostic operations are accomplished through the control terminal.

A common feature of many codecs is support for multiple video sources. One source might be the normal video camera, the second a VCR and the third a still camera focused on a graphic or chart. Through either the control terminal or room controller the user can select which video source is to be encoded and sent to the far end. Similar to multiple input sources, some codecs support multiple video output connections. Since the codec is only receiving a single video picture, multiple output connectors all show the same image. Still, having multiple sources available helps in avoiding some cabling problems when using multiple monitors.

Besides composite NTSC video, many codecs support RGB video input directly from a RGB video source. Direct RGB input produces a cleaner, sharper video image than does composite video. Another feature or option, often used with RGB input is the so-called graphics option. Graphics support allows the transmission of a second video source to the far-end codec in single or freeze frame mode, at the same time the motion video is being sent. Through the control console or room controller, the user instructs the codec to transmit a graphics frame. Updating of the full motion source is suspended, and the graphics frame is sent to the far end. When the graphics frame has been sent, full motion continues. The amount of time that full motion is suspended depends upon transmission speed and frame complexity. Graphics input and output is done through separate connectors from the full motion input and output.

Graphics capability is used to display charts, blueprints, schematics, etc. so that users at each teleconferencing location can talk about and refer to a single, common document - no concerns that everyone has the same revision number. To augment this capability, many codecs support a cursor capability, enabling the user to move a cursor around the graphics frame, using a joy-stick, mouse, or tablet. Both sites see the cursor movement within the graphics frame. Some codecs go beyond the simple cursor and implement a full drawing capability, that can be seen at both sites. At least one codec contains an internal hard disk that can be used to store digitized graphics frames. These stored frames can be called up and displayed under user control - sort of a random access slide system.

Since a graphics frame doesn't have to contend with motion, the codec can produce a higher resolution image. Most low speed codecs double the number of lines and horizontal pixels for a graphics frame, and some T1 codecs double the number of horizontal pixels. This increased resolution is important when dealing with highly detailed documents.

At least one codec vendor offers an option that allows two separate video sources to be stacked either vertically or horizontally. To fit two full screens into single screen, the codec strips off the top and bottom quarter of each image when horizontally stacking, and the left and right quarters when vertically stacking.

Many codecs support what is known as the "user data" option. This option provides a point-to-point data connection through the codec. This allows data connections between sites without the need for an additional data line. Since the bandwidth for the data channel is taken from the compressed video bandwidth, picture quality will suffer when data is being transmitted. Typically, RS-232, X.35 and RS-449 interfaces are supported. The devices connected to these data channels must operate in a request-to-send, clear-to-send mode, i.e., they must transmit data in blocks, rather than continuously.

While not of much importance to college and university users, many codecs support encryption algorithms to prevent their transmissions from being intercepted by the *bad* guys. While encryption may seem a bit paranoid, intercepting compressed video transmissions that go by satellite is really quite simple, if expensive. Just as analog video is scrambled to prevent "unauthorized" reception, so is encryption of digital video, to protect government and corporate information, a prudent approach.

Most codec vendors offer package or turn-key systems that include codec, camera(s), monitor(s) and audio system. There are many features available with these turn-key systems that make use and operation of the system that much easier. Through the room controller, the user can chose to display either the incoming picture or the picture that is being sent — a real help when setting the room up for use. Some systems allow the room controller to control the camera at the remote location, including pan, tilt and zoom. Other features include audio mute and privacy, freeze frame and blank screen.

A compressed video codec and the video and audio equipment attached to it represent an impressive array of technology. When everything is working properly, it takes little effort to run the system. When something quits working, however, isolating the problem can be quite difficult. Codecs have an array of diagnostic and monitoring capabilities to help in trouble shooting. Most codecs have internal diagnostics that test the individual circuit boards and their inter-related functions. Bypass capabilities allow various portions of the codec to be bypassed to isolate failing boards within the system. To help in trouble shooting the equipment attached to the codec, the codec generates several audio tones and levels, video test patterns and full screens of various colors.

Monitoring includes several error conditions, such as loss of input signal, excessive error rate, loss of video sync, audio overload, etc. Audio levels can be monitored, both on the send and receive sides. At least one vendor supports a real-time diagnostic display that continuously updates a variety of values pertaining to the operation of the codec.

Multi-location Conferencing

As noted earlier, compressed-video codecs are inherently point-to-point devices, much like the telephone. As when using a telephone, there comes a time when it is necessary to have three or more sites participate in a video teleconference. Unlike telephone conference bridges, support for multiple location video conferences is quite new. Essentially, there are three approaches to providing multi-location video teleconferencing; "roll your own," analog bridges, and digital bridges.

Do it yourself, multi-location teleconferencing can take on several forms, depending upon the equipment available. A common method, especially for three locations, is to use the split screen capability of a special effects generator, found in many video facilities. Locations B and C send their audio and video to location A, where it is converted back to analog. The folks in location A view two monitors, one for location B and one for location C. Special effects generators are used to create two split images, A and C, which is sent to B, and A and B, which is sent to C. The participants at any location continuously see the participants at the other two locations.

While this approach works quite well, it does have some draw backs. Special effect generators are expensive and not readily available in many locations. They also require skilled technicians to operate them. Extending the configuration to more than three sites is expensive and the image size of each location gets smaller. Most of the images are compressed twice, which degrades picture quality. For three sites, four codecs are required, which is expensive. Also, care must be taken when bridging the audio to avoid feedback.

All in all, this approach is workable, but probably is only practical when the necessary video equipment already exists. To attempt building such a facility from scratch is not economically practical.

The analog switching approach is really a refinement of the above procedure. All the participating locations are terminated in a central location and their audio and video converted back to analog. Both sets (audio and video) of signals are input into the analog switcher. The switcher monitors the audio from each site and determines that one is dominant (talking the loudest). The video associated with the dominant audio is output to each codec to be transmitted back to each site. With this scheme each site sees the location that is considered dominant—a technique that promotes courtesy, since interrupting leads to chaos.

The analog switch does not suffer limitations on the number of sites handled, but does have some other drawbacks. Each site in the network requires two codecs, one on-site and the other with the switch. Bridging of audio is not handled within the switch thus requiring additional equipment, and the possible audio feedback problem remains. The image received at each site is compressed twice, unless it is from a site whose audio and video is directly connected to the analog switch.

Ideally, once a codec has compressed an image it should be delivered to the receiving sites without ever being decompressed and compressed again. This is what the digital multi-location switch does. The switch accepts the digital transmission from each site and selects the dominate site based upon audio level. The video portion of the dominant site is sent to all other sites in the teleconference. The dominant site continues to see the previous dominant site, so they don't have to view themselves after compression. The time delay in compressing is very unnerving psychologically when viewing yourself. The digital switch also handles the audio. The audio delivered to each site is the bridged audio of all sites except their own, irrespective of which site is dominant.

Besides the audio activated switching, a manual mode is available. Through the switch's room controller or console, one site is specified as the conference leader. All sites, other than the leader site see only the leader's site, irrespective of which site is talking. Video to the leader's site continues to be switched, based upon audio dominance. This switching approach is probably better suited to instructional use, than normal conferencing.

The digital switching mode has several advantages over the other two approaches. Picture quality is maintained since an image is only compressed once. The number of codecs required is the same as the number of sites involved. Codec options or features, such as user data or graphics transmission still work, which they cannot if the video is converted back to analog prior to switching.

The digital switcher does impose two limitations that the analog methods don't. The codecs and the switcher must be compatible, which essentially means they must all come from the same vendor. And all the codecs must be operating at the same speed. Using analog switching is a means for mixing codecs from different vendors and different transmission speeds. Of course, the downside of this is the loss of picture quality due to double compression.

The currently available digital switcher has several additional useful features. It can support multiple conferences simultaneously. For example, locations A, B and C could be in a teleconference at the same time as locations D, E, F and G. Needless to say, one location can participate in only one conference at a time. Through the control console, which locations (ports on the switcher) are in a conference can be programmed. While the participants in a conference all must be operating at the same speed, separate conferences may operate at different speeds.

The switcher has a single audio only port, RJ11 jack. The audio-only participant hears the audio of all other sites, just like any video site. While there is a single audio-only connection, there is nothing to prevent that port being connected to a full blown audio conferencing system.

The digital switcher can be connected to another digital switcher. With this feature and the audio-only participation feature, extremely elaborate networks can be designed to support almost any kind of conferencing or instructional scenario.

Transmission

There are a number of transmission interfaces available for both low speed and T1 codecs. For low speed codecs, V.35, dual V.35, and RS-449 interfaces are generally available. The V.35 interface is normally used to interface to 56,000 bps and 64,000 bps second facilities. If the facilities being used are point-to-point, then the codec probably will interface to a data service unit (DSU), or if a private network is being used, the codec may interface directly to a multiplexer. If switched 56,000 bps or 64,000 bps services are being used, the codec will interface to some type of data interface unit, capable of making calls over the switched network.

The dual V.35 interface is a variation of the V.35 interface . The communications processor in the codec contains the necessary logic to convert a single 112,000 bps or 128,000 bps bit stream into two parallel streams of 56,000 bps or 64,000 bps . The receiving codec recombines the two received bit streams prior to decompressing the picture . Connection alternatives for the dual V.35 interface are the same as for the V.35 interface, except that two connections are used . At the point that ISDN begins to live up to its promise, the dual V.35 becomes a natural for using ISDNs two B channels in the basic-rate interface.

The RS-449 interface is not too well known or used, but has been around since the middle 1970s. It was originally conceived of as a replacement for the venerable RS-232 interface. A major shortcoming of the RS-232 interface is that it is designed for data rates of 20,000 bps and below. The RS-449 is designed for speeds of up to three megabits per second. With this speed range, it is a natural for compressed video codecs, which may operate at speeds of 56,000 bps up to 1.5 megabits per second. For low speed codecs, the RS-449 can be used anywhere a V.35 interface is used, if the equipment connecting the codec to the network supports it. Unlike the V.35 interface, RS-449 may be used for the higher speeds supported by low speed codecs, all the way up to 3~,0(X) bps.

For T1 codecs, the available interface options are T1 and RS-119. The T1 interface will normally be connected to a channel service unit (CSU). The minimum speed for a T1 connection is 1.536 megabits per second; the remaining 8,000 bps are used for framing. When using a T1 interface, most codecs can be programmed to run at speeds less than 1.536 megabits per second. The supported speeds are the multiples of 64,000 bps, starting at 384,000 bps. This feature is an absolute necessity when using fractional T1 services.

The RS-449 interface on a T1 codec functions just like the RS-449 interface on a low speed codec. The only difference is the higher speeds supported. With a RS-449 interface it is possible to operate at speeds higher than T1 speed, provided the facilities being used can support the higher speed. The upper speed limit is constrained either by the codec's upper limit, or roughly three megabits per second, which is the RS-449 limit.

When configuring codecs in a network, timing, and data terminal equipment (DTE) and data communications equipment (DCE) relationships need careful attention. Any network to which a codec connects must have a timing source (clock). In most, but not all cases any network using facilities leased from a common carrier or inter-exchange carrier will operate off the carrier's clock. In such a situation, the codec must be configured or programmed to slave (phase lock) its internal clock to the transmission facility. A completely private network probably doesn't have an external timing source or clock. When connecting a codec to such a network, the codec may have to be configured to provide internal timing for transmitting over the network. Typically, all codecs in a network that uses any public facilities will use clocking from the network. The private network is the one that can get messy. Serious thought needs to go into clocking sources prior to attempting to connect any equipment. A network without clocking or multiple clocks does some very strange things, which can lead to premature retirement for those folks trying to diagnose the problem.

The DTE - DCE conundrum is that a DTE device must connect to a DCE device and vice versa. The DTE - DCE distinction determines which pins on the physical interface are used for what function, such as send data and receive data. If a DTE device is directly connected to another DTE device, both devices send data, and receive data on the same pin(s), the same is true for two DCE devices connected together. In either instance, not much useful work gets done.

As with the potential problem with timing, the DTE - DCE situation probably will never arise when using public network facilities. The codec (a

DTE device) will connect to a DSU, fractional T1 CSU or some type of dial-up data unit (all DCE devices). The problem is much more likely to arise in a private network, using multiplexers. Normally, the codec (DTE) will be attached to a channel card of the multiplexer (a DCE device). However, since Murphy's Law usually holds true on most college and university campuses, the codec probably will be located at the video center, which is clear across campus from the network headend and the multiplexer. A solution to this problem is a data circuit between the codec and the multiplexer. The codec connects to a DSU or DSU-like device that is in turn attached to a matched unit at the multiplexer. That unit in turn connects to the channel card on the multiplexer, and everything works like a charm - wrong!

The configuration described above is DTE-DCE-DCE-DCE, and it will not work. There are several solutions to the problem. Many multiplexers support a changeable channel card. Either through programming, dip switch setting or both, whether the card is DTE or DCE is selectable. If that is not an option, then there are "black boxes" that interconnect like devices. Finally, when all else fails, a cross-over cable can be constructed, which reroutes the signals to the correct pins - sometimes referred to as a null modem cable.

The discussion of timing, and DTE and DCE relationships is not intended to imply that there is an unreasonable level of complexity in installing codecs in a network. Ninety nine percent of the time, they can just be plugged in and they will operate perfectly. To avoid problems the other one percent of the time, careful planning and understanding will eliminate most problems.

Video Rooms

What constitutes an appropriate room for video teleconferencing is in the eye of the beholder. A complete room system can be obtained from several vendors as a turn-key system. The other end of the scale is a custom designed and installed room, designed specifically for particular uses.

Turn-key systems consist of a single cabinet containing a camera, one or more monitors, audio system and codec. Typically, the unit is on casters so that it can be rolled about and used in any room that has a communication's connection. Within reason, these units can be used in almost any room. The main consideration when using such a unit in a room is lighting and audio. Normal office lighting is usually adequate: what needs to be avoided are hot spots, such as windows - uniformity of lighting is the key. On the audio side, "hard" rooms tend to cause echo problems. A typical classroom, with its tile floor, plasterboard walls and blackboard is a "hard" room; although, it can be used with care.

Turn-key systems, depending upon their characteristics, work well for teleconferences of up to ten people at a site. In an instructional situation the typical turn key system is probably inadequate, unless the site is used strictly for reception, for a limited number of students. If a facility is to be used for both origination and reception of instructional video then it should be designed by a video professional.

Some basics for a video classroom include at least two cameras - one to cover the instructor's board or pad where notes are written and the other to cover the instructor. Ideally, there should be a third camera to cover the class. Who controls these cameras and other aspects of the room operation is a subject of considerable debate. One camp says that the instructor should be able to control the room from the podium. The other camp says that the instructor should not be concerned with operation of the room and should concentrate strictly on presentation. Ultimately, there is probably no single *right* answer.

Much of what a student watches in a video classroom will be the notes and diagrams that the instructor uses, either on a blackboard, pad, overheads, etc. The classroom must have a sufficient number of monitors, of high quality, and in the correct locations so that every student can properly read the material being presented. Figure 1.9 is a typcial custom video conference room.

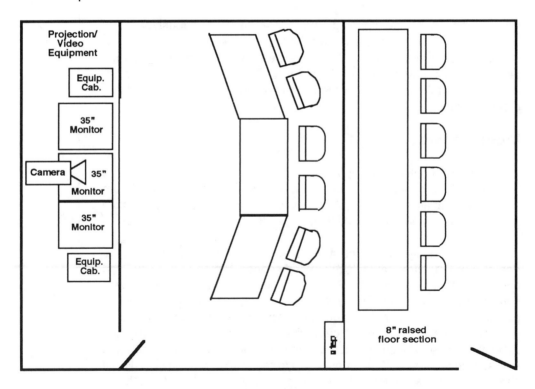

Figure 1.9
Overhead view of custom video conference room

In the audio area, there are again two schools of thought - push to talk or open microphones. Push to talk microphones are easier to control and less expensive. Depending upon the type of class being taught, push to talk does have an inhibiting influence on interaction. Open microphones demand that echo cancellation equipment be incorporated in the audio system. Placement of open microphones needs to be considered, so that the students don't cover them with their books and coats.

The most important point on putting together a custom facility is to talk to and visit other locations that have installed such rooms. Find out what they are doing with the room, why they built it the way they did, and what problems they have encountered. When you are ready to tackle your room, get the services of a professional designer, it will be time and money well spent. An improperly designed or installed video room will quickly turn people off as far as using it.

Summary

Compressed video is a hot technology and will get hotter throughout the l990s. Increased microprocessor speeds, decreasing cost and the ever increasing availability of bandwidth are all driving the usefulness and economics of the technology. The day of the true, affordable picture telephone is not that far off. In one context or another almost every college and university will at some point consider how compressed video might be used to the institution's advantage.

The underlying technology of compressed video is complex, but so is computer and telephone technology. At the practical level, implementation and operation of compressed video is no more complicated than many computer networks, and a lot less complex than some.

References

Johnson, J. T. (1991). Videoconferencing: Not just talking heads. *Data Communications 20* (15): 66-88.

Tanner, C. K. (1992). Digital compression and transmission: A primer for non-technical readers. *Specs 4*(8): 1-3.

Compressed video vendors

Compression Labs, Inc.
2600 Junction Avenue
4038
San Jose, CA 95134
408-435-3000

Datapoint Corp.
9725 Datapoint Drive
San Antonio, TX 78229-8511
V3M 5T5
512-699-7000

GPT Video Systems
737 Canal Street, Bldg. 35A
Stamford, CT 06902
703-348-6600

Hoppman Communications Corp.
4500 Southgate Place, Suite 200
Chantilly, VA 22021
703-222-0658
,
NEC America
14040 Park Center Road
Herndon. VA 22071
703-834-4400

Videoconferencing Systems
5801 Goshon Springs Road, Suite A
Norcross, GA 30071
404-242-7566

VideoTelecom Corp.
1908A Kramer Lane
Austin, TX 78758
512-834-9734

Concept Communications
1950 Stermmons Freeway, Suite

Dallas, TX 214-746-3888
214-746-3888

Eyetel Communications
522 7th Street, Suite 320
New Westminster, BC Canada

604-525-2511

Harris Corp.
Electronic Systems Sector
P.O. Box 37
Melboume, FL 32902
800-4-HARRIS ext. 2661

Image Data Corp.
1I55OIH-10 W. Suite 200
San Antonio, TX 78230
512-641-8340

PictureTel Corp.
1 Corporation Way
Peabody, MA 01960-7988
508-977-9500

Videophone, Inc.
8159 Alemda Road
Houston. TX 77054
713-741-1971

Vidicom Div.
L.D. Bevan Company, Inc.
31115 Via Colinas, Suite 301
Westlake Village, CA 91362
818-889-3653

2

Distance Education: A Framework for Compressed Video

Lawrence Silvey
John J. Cochenour

Introduction

The disciplines of instructional technology, distance education and telecommunications are relatively fledgling in nature and as such are experiencing similar growth patterns and problems that other fields of intellectual inquiry encountered during their initial stages of development. The emergence and development of compressed video is even more recent, and thus, has presented an additional set of academic opportunities and concerns which must be addressed. A difficulty most fundamental during these initial stages of development is the lack of a common body of literature and supporting research from which to educe and utilize in the academic setting, and which in part has been the stimulus for the publication of this book. Hopefully, this book will assist new users of compressed video to avoid re-inventing the wheel.

This chapter is specifically designed to present the reader with a foundation for the concepts of instructional technology, distance education and telecommunications in order that they may better understand the general framework of the field and the broad scope of intellectual possibilities available for study, application and research. It is also designed to address some of the current thinking and controversies within the discipline which may give rise to research and theory building opportunities for scholars in this field of study.

Instructional Technology Concepts

Robert Gagne' (1987) tells us that "when such a field is not old enough to be counted as a traditional discipline, the influence of certain trends can be identified and observed as they converge, while other influences remain indirect and less clearly perceivable. instructional technology is a field of this nontraditional sort" (p. 1). Periodic shifts in the field of instructional technology which include a variety of name changes, the rapid development of technology, implementation of unconventional meth-

methodologies, and the initiation of nontraditional activities have all contributed to the necessity for instructional technology scholars to concentrate their efforts in the development and learning of any art, science or technology. We must broaden the focus of our perceptions and attention, so that more and more factors can be taken into account simultaneously in order to understand and comprehend the total discipline. Although the concentration of this text is on "teletraining and compressed video," the broader concepts of instructional design, networking models, finances, evaluation, political issues, ethical and moral issues must be understood and dealt with.

The field of "instructional technology" is no longer only preoccupied with the mechanics of the technology where the bulk of the professionals are basically technicians. There has been a major shift where the leading theorists now proclaim that it is fundamental to begin "with a taxonomic framework of learning outcomes considered essential for an understanding of human learning as it occurs in instructional settings" (Gagne' & Dick, 1983, p.265). This expanded comprehensive perspective and related theory building must have had profound effects on the "technicians," since they found it necessary to be familiar with all learning theory which takes into account the "events external to the learner which are designed to support the internal process of learning" (Gagne' & Dick, 1983, p. 266). Some recent trends and developments within the field of instructional technology are an emphasis on academic areas such as "instructional theories," concepts of "cognitive psychology," "learner interaction," "instructional psychology," and "instructional design."

This movement has resulted because professionals within and related to the discipline have recognized the importance of relationships in learning theories and the behavioral sciences on the effective use of instructional technology regarding the learner. No more is it just a matter of knowing how to run a piece of equipment and how to fix it when it breaks down; it requires the development of a more theoretical base of how the technology affects the cognitive processes of the learner and how it can be used to maximize learning. Wittrock (1979) advocates that "a cognitive approach implies that learning from instruction is scientifically more productively studied as an internally, cognitively mediated process than as a direct product of the environment, people, or factors external to the learner" (p. 5). Instructional technology now demands that the professionals possess an extensive knowledge base that includes cognitive processes, learning theory, and instructional design, and then the "equipment" simply becomes an integrated part of the delivery system which affects the total learning process.

Telecommunications, including compressed video, are simply types of delivery systems which are a part of the broader spectrum of distance learning and communication in the total process of education. This technology, when incorporated into the instructional situation, should, as a general rule, be so integrated with design, method, procedure, and evaluation that it will not detract from the content or substance of the instructional materials and purpose. Once the learner becomes acquainted with the technology it should no longer be the focus of the learner's attention, and the information/knowledge should continue to be paramount. Compressed video and other new technologies should or will become as commonplace as any other previous technology - with the exception of contributing more enhanced interactive delivery capabilities. Any additional emphasis on the technology and design must come from within the discipline of instructional technology.

In addition to the rapidly changing technology and the expanded theory building, the final part of the triangular shift in the development of instructional technology is the emphasis on research, and particularly empirical research. Wittrock (1979) and Gehlbach (1979) who emphasize research on attention, cognitive learning, memory, aptitude, and other psychological constructs are representative of the "new" research emphasis in instructional technology. As with so many other emerging disciplines, these researchers and others have used resources from many other related areas to support their hypotheses and theories. This practice is necessary because there has been a lack of theoretical and applied research in the instructional technology discipline, thus, a void of specific research findings in the actual field of study. The unparalleled inclusion of the new technologies with cognitive learning, aptitude, instructional psychology, and learner interaction provides an extensive store of unique research potential.

The previous limitations of using research from other disciplines to support instructional technology follows Gagne's observation that research from the field of audio-visual communication contributed greatly to "the body of knowledge called instructional technology;" (consequently), "the continuation of research efforts in this field did, however, contribute critically to another development: the definition and central focus of the field of instructional technology." (Gagne', 1987, pp. 2-3) Just because the focus on instructional technology was very recent does not mean it was not emerging several years earlier; albeit, more by trial and error than by design. It was not until the early to mid-70s that research began to show student learning was controlled partially by particular "types of instruction," and by "motivational procedures within the school." (Wittrock, 1979, p. 7) Unquestionably, learning-at-a-distance was incorporated in education (specifically in adult education), it was better suited for some students in particular situations than it was for others. Unfortunately, there was very little research and theory building within the discipline to find out why.

Again, when Gagne' referred to instructional technology as a field of the nontraditional sort because it was not old enough to be counted as a traditional discipline, and while influences of certain trends could be identified and observed as they converged and other influences remained indirect and less clearly perceivable (Gagne', 1983, p.1); it is possible he did not give enough credit to the past technological advances and how they applied to the multiple of instructional situations throughout history. The deficiency he speaks of, however, was inherent in the lack of theory building and research for which the possibility was always there.

There is one other more subtle reason this discipline went unnoticed. Specifically, the field of instructional technology has few, if any, historians to record their progress and contributions. As mentioned before, most of the professionals in the past concentrated on the technology. This does not mean there has not been any confluence which would define a field of instructional technology. Even in the contemporary setting there is a concentration on the design of instruction and the technological aspects of the field, with an increasing emphasis on research, but a continued noticeable lack of any historicism. It is possible Gagne' is correct, when he states the "influences remain indirect and less clearly perceivable," simply because of this void.

As is apparent in this cursory overview, scholars in the field of instructional technology have a multiple and varied selection of options to pursue in this emergent discipline. The point is that how these options are viewed and balanced is vital and will effect the developmental trends of this academic endeavor. In the final analysis, a discipline is no better than the composite of all its interacting elements. The best theory and the finest research must also have superior dissemination. The lack of superlative quality in any area will result in an assessment of mediocrity for the remaining areas. Thus, in instructional technology an effort on all fronts must be pursued and developed. The interactiveness and importance of theory building, technology, research, and application must be advanced and recorded that it may be developed into a "traditional discipline," in the field of education. With this type of cooperative effort, the discipline can advance much more quickly and, by so doing, appropriately utilize the advanced technology it has at its disposal.

Distance Education Concepts

The technology explosion of the eighties has promoted "distance education" to be at the forefront of educational innovativeness throughout the 90's and beyond. In 1989, it was reported that the "interest in telecommunicated distance is growing so rapidly that it is impossible to accurately document the many projects presently underway or being considered in the United States" (Barker, Frisbie & Patrick, 1989, p.24). That trend has not changed with the increased capabilities of telecommunications and the several other computer based delivery systems for distance education which have become available. "A long list of communications technologies includes, among others, compressed video, cable television, audiographic radio, bulletin board systems and integrated systems which link videodisks and microcomputers via telecommunications to provide access to large amounts of material and interactive communication" (Cochenour, 1992, p.150). Although distance education has a known history of over 100 years, it was in the mid-80s that education at a distance made a bid for legitimacy, specifically due to the before mentioned technological explosion, and a demand for lifelong learning among the adult population. Moore reported "the end of the eighties sees us on a threshold of a new phase of evolution for the application of communications media and education. These include the already long and established but still underutilized medium of audio conferencing, a relatively new medium of computer conferencing, and most importantly the application of video conferencing..." (Moore, 1988, p.7).

Cochenour asserts that the advanced "technologies have given a dynamic character to the field of distance education. Techniques, definitions, capabilities, and decisions are all affected by the continued development and dissemination of new technologies" (Cochenour, 1992, p.150). Indeed, during the latter part of the 80s the "dynamic character" of distance education created considerable discussion and conflict among authorities in the discipline of distance education. The controversy primarily centers around the issue of defining "What is actually meant by *distance education*?"

One book which has comprehensively explored this conflict is *Foundations of Distance Education* by Desmond Keegan. In that work Keegan has thoroughly covered the historical roots of the problem and continued the debate right up to 1990 (Keegan, 1990). Likewise, the diversity of opinions are very apparent throughout the scholarly journals dedicated to distance education. Shale states that "distance education is beset with a remarkable paradox - it has asserted its existence, but cannot define itself. Anyone working in distance education would be likely to claim to 'know it when I see it'" (Shale, 1988, p.25). Barker, Frisbie and Patrick (1989) report that "whole interest in distance education continues to grow, efforts to define the concept remain inconsistent, and in many cases dated and incomplete" (p.20).

Rumble (1989) affirms that "the definition of distance education is currently the subject of a lively debate in the literature, largely initiated by Keegan....His seminal work set the tone for subsequent debate, which has included contributions from Baath, Wille'n, Holmberg, Thompson, Garrison and Shale, himself, Tight, Shale, Ljosa, and Barker et al" (p.8). Rumble, in turn, provides his version of a working definition, to which Diana Carl has this response.

> The debate over what constitutes an adequate definition of distance education continues with Rumble's article. His encapsulation of the term leaves doubts about how well his definition serves the development of the discipline. My opinion is that the definition presents many difficulties and does not represent distance education as it exists in other forms (Carl, 1989, p.65).

All of these authors dwell on a defense of their position and reject those who are not in agreement with them. The supporting research and writings of these experts depend wholly on their specific definitions and limitations of distance education, and consequently, this results in some distinctly conflicting perspectives and conclusions to which students in this area are exposed . This exposure is not necessarily negative since it does create a necessity for contemporary scholars to deal with these differences and inconsistencies; and in turn, they must arrive at their own definitions and hypothetical constructs. The difficulty created by the bickering over definitions and lack of consensus among the authorities is a weakening of the discipline at large, and the tendency to create at least the illusion that there is no common body of knowledge that can be agreed upon by the leading authorities in the field. In the long range the discussion of these differences may result in a stronger foundation on which distance education theories can be built; but for the moment they seriously thwart any effort to deal with the development of the field of instructional technology generally and the area of distance education specifically (Silvey, 1992, pp. 28-29).

There are many people in various factions that believe distance learning can transform higher education, but the field is still struggling at the terminology level. For example, there are several terms that are used to refer to instructional techniques for dealing with students apart from the main campus area. Some of these terms mean the same things, some do not. Regardless, the field is still in the throes of outlining the appropriate theory base and defining operational concepts. There is not room to deal with this subject in detail, but some concepts need to be addressed to provide some context for the discipline. Keegan (1990) has provided a definition of distance education that has become the standard against which others are compared. Not everyone agrees, but he provides a starting point. Keegan's definition addresses the five key characteristics by which distance education has generally been identified. These include: (1) the separation of teacher and learner throughout the length of the learning process; (2) the influence of an educational organization in the planning, preparation, and provision of learning services; (3) the use of technical media to unite teacher and learner and carry the course content; (4) the provision of two-way communication between teacher and learner; and (5) the general absence of the learning group during the learning process so that the learner is dealt with as an individual and not in groups.

Each of these points or characteristics has been debated in the literature, generally leaving one with the feeling that distance education is a difficult concept to define (Cochenour, 1992). It would be counterproductive to repeat and attempt to resolve all of the issues and characteristics discussed within the various definitions; however, students with an interest are encouraged to refer to the works previously cited by these authors to more fully comprehend the debated differences involving definitions. Certainly scholars of this area of study should take issue with authorities who make such claims as the following: "In this study an attempt at further precision is made from time to time with the use of the term 'conventional, oral, group-based' education in place of 'face-to-face'" (Keegan, 1990, p.20). With very little analysis one readily knows that distance education utilizing telecommunications would certainly be "oral" and would quite likely be "group-based;" which in turn would render the following statement by Keegan to be both illogical and unacceptable. He asserts that "in contrast with conventional education which is oral and group-based, distance education shatters the interpersonal communication of the face-to-face provision and disperses the learning group throughout the nation" (Keegan, 1990, p.3).

After reviewing the many conflicting definitions, there is no question that "a broadening of the definition of 'distance education' is needed in order to clarify the inherent strengths that new technologies bring to the field, to recruit new audiences to the benefits of distance learning, and to guide further study and research in this aspect of outreach education" (Barker, Frisbie & Patrick, 1989, p.21). Responding to that advice, these authors would add the admonition, "and at the same time not restrict the taxonomy to eliminate the older methodologies and technologies of distance education." Within this framework it now becomes feasible to divide the field into two major categories: (1) distance education which is correspondence-based, and (2) distance education which is telecommunications-based (Barker, Frisbie & Patrick, 1989).

The following definition by the authors of this chapter attempts to, (1) encompass the two major categories of the field; (2) resolve some of the conflicts posed by other definitions; (3) address the key characteristics by which distance education has generally been identified; and (4) not define the concept of distance education so broadly that it renders it an academic discipline with no boundaries or delimitations. Certainly this definition will not be acceptable to all persons; however, it will be the operational definition assigned to the substance of this text - with the pious hope it does not add to the current controversy. Perhaps Malcolm Knowles identified the resolution to this seeming problem of total acceptance when he stated, "...the only realistic answer is that a theory (or philosophy or definition) is what a given author says it is: if you want to understand his thinking you have to go along with his definitions" (Knowles, 1990, p.5).

We define "distance education" as an academic discipline dedicated to an organized system of transferring (delivering) purposive educational information and materials to a receiving individual(s) and/or group(s), for a planned educational experience or result; through a medium (technical, mechanical, electronic, or any other) other than the conventional face-to-face (interpersonal) classroom relationship. There may or may not be immediate two-way communication, and the recipient(s) will not be under the continuous immediate direction of the sender (facilitator or teacher), nor in the same classroom. Progress of the learning individual(s) (receivers) may or may not be monitored and/or evaluated, depending on the existence of any contractual arrangements.

This definition strives for the flexibility necessary in the vast variety of situations which exist in distance education and the complications posed by the combinations of the multimedia available through the recent technological explosion. The professional divisiveness of continuing to spend an inordinate amount of time and energy arguing over definitions and their characteristics have been addressed in a recent publication (Silvey, 1992). The following discussion is an adaptation of that "Forum" to the specific area of distance education. Keep in mind throughout this discussion that we must address the dynamic character of the field of distance education brought on by technological development, which has affected the techniques, definitions, capabilities, and decisions regarding distance education.

A trend within the academic community is the resistance to distance education course work and degrees because of credibility concerns. Within the education discipline a syndrome of needless legitimizing and unwarranted restrictions for the existence of certain beliefs and standards can be detected. Knapper points out the painful truth that "in universities with both traditional on-campus courses and distance programs, the latter often have to struggle for legitimacy, and recognition that standards are equivalent to those of regular offerings" (Knapper, 1988, p.63). The consequences of this syndrome is retardation of desirable growth and development of instructional technology and distance education. Scholars of any discipline must respect divergent points-of-view and take positive steps to reconcile the various differences (real or imagined), and present some compatibility within the discipline - even if this compatibility only manifests itself in the acceptance of divergent points-of-view. Just because someone does not relate to a discipline as someone else thinks they should, does not mean either party is wrong. It often seems that self-interest is the basic reason we still engage in the defensive syndrome of legitimizing and justification of a personal position rather than viewing the situation in a universal perspective.

With the rapid development of technology, we must use every means of distance education to enhance the adult learning process. Michael G. Moore asserts the "...desirability to provide educational access for students who would not have the opportunity to undertake education through residential programs. These 'distant' learners include those whose job demands, family responsibilities, and other time constraints make traditional educational access unavailable" (Moore, 1988, p.7). We have long since moved from considerations that limit such components as education by letter; printed learning materials; audio-visual teaching; educational radio and television; programmed learning; computer-based instruction; independent study; private study; and learning from teaching materials as not being methods to be identified as distance education (Keegan, 1990, p.76). The scope of distance education must be expanded to include all means of delivery systems, not just those of a personal preference. Distance education needs to utilize all the resources available, in order to reach as many people as possible to satisfy the educational needs that exist (or will exist) in our society.

Recognized authorities and professional leaders cannot be content to continue doing what has been done without seeking new and very different (creative) horizons. The security of the institutionalized educational process is no longer sufficient. The barriers must come down and every technology, methodology, and theory available must be implemented and tested. This process must start by permitting any definition (however broad or restrictive), any parameter, any methodology, and all technology to be promoted and tried. We must view an eclectic approach which satisfies the efforts of each educator, researcher, learner, or theorist to at least be given a chance to succeed - until or unless proven unacceptable or undesirable.

Distance education must be initiated, promoted and implemented in all its various forms. Traditional limitations of what distance education/ learning entails or means is not acceptable in these times. To extend this notion a bit farther, a survey of professionals suggest this type of effort should not be undertaken in isolation. They recommend we should form alliances between adult educators, distance educators, communications specialists, and education oriented professionals already experienced on our campuses (Delbecq & Scates, 1989, p.20). We simply must address the "dynamic character" of the field of distance education brought on by technological development. There is little doubt the techniques, definitions, capabilities, and decisions have all been affected by the continued develop- ment and dissemination of new technologies (Cochenour, 1992).

Telecommunications Concepts

Of the two categories of distance education (correspondence- based and telecommunications -based), telecommunications is of most importance for creating a continued growth and interest in improving interactivity in distance learning. The term telecommunications is a broad one that encompasses both voice communications and machine-readable signals or digital communications. Another, related term that is being widely used in distance education is teletraining. Chute, Balthazar, and Poston (1988) refer to the category of instruction that is telecommunications-based as teletraining. They define teletraining as "a complete system that integrates the planning, delivery, and management of training by using a combination of information technology and teleconferencing services." (p.55) Telecommunications then can be seen as a concept of electronic communication and networking, while teletraining is the use of telecommu- nications to accomplish distance education or training.

Perhaps the best way to examine these terms or concepts is to compare them with related terms along a continuum. Open learning is used to describe a wide variety of learning situations and is considered to be a broader term than either instructional technology or distance education. It would, in fact, consider distance education to be a subset. The two primary characteristics of open learning are the removal of traditional barriers to participation in the learning environment and the provision of greater responsibility to the student regarding learning decisions. Viewed in a continuum, open learning would be the broadest concept and teletraining (with each specific delivery system) would be the narrowest (Cochenour, 1992). Figure 2.1 is one possible way to compare these concepts.

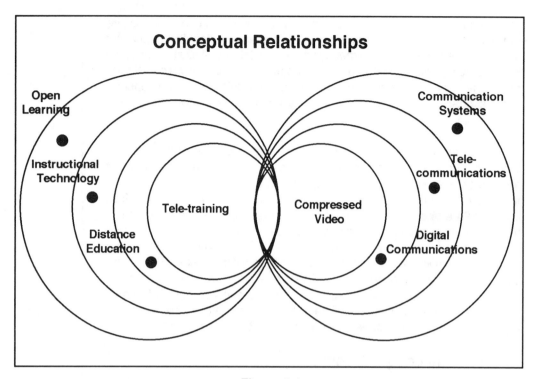

Figure 2.1
Relationship of distance education terms

The schema of telecommunications-based distance education by Barker, Frisbie & Patrick (1989) provides a general outline of the possible links in this category. They include: (1) Two-way voice link, two-way video (full motion) link; (2) Two-way voice link, two-way video (freeze frame) link; (3) Two-way voice link, one-way video (full-motion) link; (4) Two-way voice link, one-way video (freeze-frame) link; and (5) Two-way voice link only. (p.22) The first link provides the greatest possibility of interactivity, and the last link provides the least amount of interaction.

The primary difference in these various telelearning links is the amount and level of interactivity that is permitted between the facilitator and the learners, and the learners with other learners. Compressed video has a very high level of interactivity if properly used. In comparison, audio teleconferencing employs voice links that permits audio interactivity only. This is a lower level of interactivity than a system where two-way audio links are combined with video links. The video link may be real-life freeze frame images transmitted via slow scan television, computer-generated, freeze-frame graphics relayed via microcomputer, or a full-motion television image over microwave, ITES, cable, fiber optics, or satellite delivery. The ideal, and typically the most expensive configuration, is two-way voice with two-way full-motion video which makes the technology and distance as transparent as possible. Compressed video is a technology that allows such a high level of interactivity, but is more cost effective since it requires less space for transmission. One goal of teletraining is to provide an optimum setting for the delivery of information and learning, and compressed video systems are one of the single best choices for such a delivery setting.

A review of the literature reveals a semantic maze of terminology to describe the technological configurations used in delivering the various types of telelearning in distance education. A brief discussion of the technological configurations applicable for distance courses will give the student some notion about labeling various electronic delivery systems. The list is by no means all inclusive. The many terms found in the literature include "telecommunications," "audio-conferencing," "video-conferencing," "pretaped telecourse," "teleconferencing," and "audio teleconferencing." The purpose for introducing here the variety of labels listed above is to highlight the premise that presently there is no universal acceptance of labeling for any specific type of teletraining technology. If distance education is to be widely used in several disciplines (outside instructional technology), and by a diverse instructional staff, it would be desirable to have a taxonomy which is a little more clearly delineated.

Kinney describes teleconferencing as "the operator-assisted connecting of more than three persons...into one 'bridge' that allows all persons to hear and to speak" (Kinney, 1991, p.21). The University of Missouri-St. Louis offered a "telecourse with pretaped videos followed by audio teleconferences. Henschke chose to call that process "Telecommunications" (Henschke, 1991, p.9). The Graduate School of Education of the University of Toronto has distance education classes of a comparatively low level technology which they call "audio-conferencing" which involves only audio bridging via telephone. Gunawardena tells us the "term 'videoconferencing' is used to refer to live, interactive, one-way video with two-way audio programming" (Gunawardena, 1990, p.38). The brochure issued by the University of Wyoming School of Extended Studies and Public Service states: "Audio teleconferencing is voice communication among three or more individuals or groups simultaneously over the telephone lines....In most instances, the audio portion of the class is supplemented with prerecorded videotapes."

Essentially, the confusion exists because of the vast variety of technology that is available and can be combined as best fits the situation. Because of these combinations of technology, the distinction of any system using them becomes blurred; however, the learners whom are assessing a program via distance education should be properly oriented to the technology being used so they will be neither disenchanted or have false expectations. When an instructor is preparing for any distance education class, they also must have enough familiarity with the capabilities and limitations of the technology to deal with unusual situations as they arise and to motivate the students in this nontraditional situation. So too must they be able to assess what technology is available and what combination of resources will produce the best results.

As with "distance education," some of these definitions create misunderstanding. For example, the definition currently in the brochure used by the University of Wyoming School of Extended Studies and Public Services, warrants modification for the following three reasons: (1) it is not necessary to have "three or more...groups" to effect a distance education class over the phone lines via teleconferencing; (2) it is undesirable (if not virtually impossible) to have "voice communication among three or more individuals or groups simultaneously over the telephone lines;" and (3) the term "audio" is misleading because the audio portion of the delivery system is supplemented with prerecorded videotapes.

As was earlier stated, "there are several terms that are used to refer to instructional techniques for dealing with students apart from the main campus area. Some of these terms mean the same things, some do not. Regardless, the field is still in the throes of outlining the appropriate theory base and defining operational concepts." This struggle with the terminology, however, should not consume an exceptional amount of time and energy. This would only thwart development of the field in the areas of theory building and research.

An essay, written by Prokasy, outlines the implications of using the new instructional technologies and moving towards the concept of a virtual open learning university. He identifies several areas of likely change within the university environment including faculty-student interaction, instructional policies, enrollment and scheduling, curriculum development and assessment, allocation of resources, research, and library services. Others have discussed in varying detail similar points for the focus of possible change (Blumestyk 1991; Strain 1987; Rhoades 1990). There is general agreement that acceptance of the telecommunications technologies for the delivery of instruction means that change will be necessary if the technologies are used in meaningful and effective manners. Below is a brief introduction to some of those specific changes that have been suggested.

Distance education in general and teletraining specifically will most likely alter the teaching role of many faculty members. These technologies may force faculty into acting more as resource managers and less as conveyors of course material. More time and effort will be spent in the planning and designing of instruction and less in the delivery. Faculty will most likely need to do more joint problem solving and consulting with students and less assessment and reviewing. Electronic mail will make faculty more available and collaboration will occur more frequently in this medium reducing the need for face to face meetings. Students can be more proactive, responsible, and flexible (Prokasy 1991; Strain 1987).

Policies, procedures, regulatory control, and other administrative controls both local and external will certainly need modification. Scheduling of lines and equipment, transferability of credits, traditional territories and infringement of service areas, budgeting and ownership, continuous rather than lock-step enrollments are all issues of control and responsibility and all will be affected. Prokasy states that pedagogical technology "cannot play a major role in any level of education without significant institutional change" (Prokasy, 1991, p.109). So, if teletraining has a chance to fulfill its potential, change must occur. It is, however, precisely the factors mentioned above that are the most resistant to change. The largest hurdles for change will not be technological but sociological (Reiser 1987; Kirkpatrick 1987).

Many issues and obstacles are associated with broader university access, distance education, and the electronic technologies; however, it appears continued developments in these areas are inevitable. Regardless of one's individual position and willingness to accept teletraining, training and education will continue to expand through the delivery systems available with telecommunications technology. Procedures must be developed to work with such systems and meet those challenges that come with new techniques in order to take full advantage of telecommunications developments (Cochenour, 1992).

Conclusion

In conclusion, anyone interested in instructional technology, distance education, or a particular type of teletraining, has a responsibility that goes far beyond learning a specific type of delivery system. They must understand the effects of the technology on the total educational process; the conceptual relationships of the technology to the areas of distance education and instructional technology; the interaction of student/facilitator/instructional design and their effects on the learning process; and the integration of theory and research into the development of instructional programs. Efforts must be made to define such concepts as instructional technology, distance education, telecommunications, and open learning; to incorporate the external factors regarding finances, administration, evaluation, and networking; and to be accountable for the political, ethical, legal and moral issues.

Technology is only the tip of the iceberg, with other more relevant and related areas of knowledge to be assimilated before the application of any teletraining can be effective. In the final analysis, the students are more important than the technology - how effectively they learned as opposed to how great the technology was. Hopefully, this chapter has given some insight to an overall perspective of the field of study including instructional technology, distance education, telecommunications, and the complex relationships therein. This overview may promote a better understanding of the general framework of these areas of academic endeavor and the broad scope of intellectual possibilities they pose for the students' study, application and research.

References

Barker, B.O., A.G. Frisbie & K.R. Patrick. (1989). Broadening the definition of distance education in the light of new telecommunications technologies. *The American Journal of Distance Education, 3*(1), 20-29.

Blemenstyk, G. (1991). Many attempts at distance learning are impeded by unforeseen political and financial problems. *Chronicle of Higher Education, 38*(9), A23-A25.

Carl, D.R. (1989). A response to Greville Ramble's 'on defining distance education. *The American Journal of Distance Education, 3*(3), 65-67.

Chute, A.G., L.B. Balthazar & Poston C.O.. (1988). Learning from teletraining. *The American Journal of Distance Education, 2*(3), 55-63.

Cochenour, J. (1992) Academic issues: The virtual university. In L. Saunders (Ed.), *The Virtual Library: Visions and Realities* (pp. 145-159). Westport, CT: Meckler.

Delbecq, A.L. & D.C. Scates. (1989). [A summary of issues surrounding the use of television for distance education]. Unpublished photocopy of data.

Gagne', R.M. & Dick, W. (1983). Instructional psychology. *Annual Review of Psychology, 34*, 261-289.

Gagne', R.M. (Ed.). (1987). Introduction. In R.M. Gagne', (Ed.). *Instructional technology: Foundations* (pp. 1-9). Hillsdale, New Jersey: Lawrence Erlbaum.

Gehlbach, R.D. (1979). Individual differences: Implications for instructional theory, research, and innovation. *Educational Researcher, 8*(4), 8-14.

Gunawardena, C.N. (1990). Integrating telecommunication systems to reach distance learners. *The American Journal of Distance Education, 4*(3), 38-46.

Henschke, J.A. (1991). Innovating with telecommunications. *Adult Learning, 2*(4), 9-10.

Keegan, D. (1990). *The foundations of distance education* (2nd Ed.). London: Routledge.

Kinney, M.B. (1991). Teleconferencing - a powerful management tool. *Adult Learning, 2*(8), 21-23.

Kirkpatrick. D.L. (1987). *How to manage change effectively.* San Francisco: Jossey-Bass Publishers.

Knapper, C. (1988). Lifelong learning and distance education. *The American Journal of Distance Education, 2*(1), 63-72.

Knowles, M. (1990). *The adult learner: a neglected species.* (4th Ed.). Houston, TX: Gulf.

Moore, M.G. (1988). Editorial - telecommunications, internationalism, and distance education. *The American Journal of Distance Education, 2*(1), 1-7.

Prokasy, W.F. (1991). The new pedagogy: an essay on policy and procedural implications. *Innovative Higher Education, 15*(2), 109-115.

Reiser, R.A. 1987). Instructional technology: a history. In R.M. Gagne', (Ed.). *Instructional technology: Foundations* (pp. 11-48). Hillsdale, New Jersey: Lawrence Erlbaum.

Rhoades, G. (1990). Change in an unanchored enterprise: Colleges of education. *The Review of Higher Education, 13*(2), 187-214.

Rumble,G. (1989). On defining distance education. *The American Journal of Distance Education, 3*(2), 8-21.

Shale, D. (1988) Toward a reconceptualization of distance education. *The American Journal of Distance Education, 2*(3), 25-35.

Silvey, L. (1992). Forum: the adult education explosion. *MPAEA Journal, 20*(2), 27-34.

Strain, J. (1987). The role of the faculty member in distance education. *The American Journal of Distance Education, 1*(2), 61-65.

Wittrock, M.C. (1979). The cognitive movement in instruction. *Educational Researcher, 8*(2), 5-11

3

Considering Compressed Video Use

Steven G. Sachs

Introduction

The decision to use compressed video should not be taken lightly. It is not technology that lends itself to a quick and inexpensive trial. There are a number of factors to take into account before proceeding to purchase and install a compressed video system. As many organizations have found, compressed video can be an effective tool when there is a match between these factors and the organization's plans. Similarly, there are a number of factors that must be considered in deciding how the system will be operated. These factors can influence the type of system to be installed and the on-going costs of the system.

Selecting Compressed Video

Why Use Compressed Video

The most basic question any organization should ask before proceeding with a compressed video system is why the system is needed in the first place. Here are some of the most common reasons for wanting a two-way video system:

1) provide access to instruction/training for students at a remote site;
2) eliminate or reduce travel time and cost;
3) eliminate isolation by giving those at remote sites a feeling of direct involvement;
4) expand or share resources and expertise among sites;
5) generate revenue by expanding programs to new audiences;
6) eliminate or reduce time away from jobs and families by reducing need to travel;
7) eliminate the need to bus students to special classes by taking the instruction directly to the students;
8) provide a physical presence at remote sites; and
9) improve the speed and accuracy of responses to questions or problems at remote sites.

While any organization can probably identify one or more of the reasons from the preceding list that would be beneficial to its operation, it is important that the specific reasons for proceeding be clear *and be agreed upon by the key participants and decision makers in the organization.* If the primary reason for installing a compressed video system is to reduce travel cost, the system needs to be designed to do that, and the cost savings should cover the cost of the compressed video system. If the reason for the compressed video system is to have a physical presence at the remote site, there needs to be prior agreement that a <u>video presence</u> will meet that need. Knowing these things in advance and having broad agreement about the reason(s) for implementing the system will make everything that follows easier.

Two-way Video

Even after identifying one or more reasons for a video system, it is still possible that compressed video is the wrong system for the organization. Compressed video is a *two-way* video system. The questions to ask are, "Is two-way video needed?" Would one-way video with two-way audio (via telephone) do as well? What does the return video accomplish? Is it worth the cost?

Another consideration is whether the system would really be interactive, even with its two-way video capability. For example, if there are going to be large numbers of participants at the remote sites or a large number of remote sites, will many of the participants really get to interact? Of course, this has to be balanced against the political reality that two-way video appears more like a traditional class or meeting and may be more acceptable that one-way video with two-way audio.

See Part II Section I

Virginia, for example, operates an extensive program of video courses for its K-12 schools. These courses are delivered by satellite with one-way video and two-way audio. They originate from several electronic classrooms in different regions of the state. The goal is to reach as many schools as possible, with enrollments for each class in the hundreds of students. This is a cost-effective strategy and one where two-way video would not be practical given the number of sites and audience size.

By contrast, Northern Virginia Community College installed compressed video to link its five campuses. Since the college already offered a large selection of traditional distance education courses using one-way video, the compressed video system was designed to offer an interactive alternative for students at remote sites where enrollments were too small for regular face-to-face classes. Without the compressed video course, the only alternative for students at these sites was the non-interactive one-way video course. The small number of sites and audience size made two-way video a good choice.

Sometimes there are other reasons for two-way video, as in the case of United American Reporting Services. As they describe in their User Profile in Part Two of this book, their function as a court reporting service demands that their clients be able to see both the person at the remote site and in all parts of the room at that remote site. Otherwise, there would not be confidence in the legal proceedings being conducted over the compressed video system.

Live vs. Taped

Another consideration is whether live video is even necessary, or whether a taped presentation(s) would meet the organization's goals. While a live video presentation can be more flexible, more timely, and can often adapt quickly to participant needs or other unanticipated situations, it does have limitations. Even the best planned live video is spontaneous and can have errors where something is misstated and not corrected, something is omitted, or transmission problems interrupt the program altogether. Weather problems at either the sending or receiving sites can play havoc with schedules, preventing the participants from attending.

Live video can take longer than a taped presentation to communicate its basic message since non-essential communication often takes place. While social chit-chat can be desirable to bond sending and receiving sites, there is a price to be paid in terms of time. For example, at one institution it was possible for an instructor to cover all the content in a course through lectures and demonstrations with 15 hours of video taped lectures. In a live two-way video class, it took over twice as long to cover the same material. Neither approach is necessarily wrong, they are just different. If time is a factor, this is worth considering.

Another aspect of the live vs. taped issue deserves mention. Taped presentations allow time-shifting by participants. All the participants do not necessarily have to be in the same room at the same time. Furthermore, if needed, participants can replay the tape as often as necessary to master the content or to understand the message. In addition, taped presentations can be transmitted in a variety of ways and at almost any time. Tapes can even be sent through the mail. Transmission of live presentations, on the other hand, is much more limited in terms of when an audience can be expected to attend. Using two-way *audio* conferencing along with video tapes can be an effective strategy that incorporates advantages of both approaches when two-way video is not essential for other reasons.

Fixed Sites

One of the major considerations in deciding to use compressed video centers are the sites to be included. Unlike some other forms of video, compressed video generally requires fixed sites due to the equipment involved in transmitting and receiving the signals. While the codecs, monitors, cameras and microphones can be moved from room to room, it is not really practical to move them from site to site on a regular basis. The equipment is somewhat bulky and sensitive. It can easily suffer from the jostling of any move—especially if it has to go outdoors in bad weather. It also can be time consuming to set-up and adjust for each new physical setting.

Each compressed video site must also be equipped with connections to the transmission medium, most of which are point to point as compared to traditional video that goes out into the air for everyone to receive. The typical compressed video signal travels via T-1 or 56 Kbps telephone lines leased from the telephone company in advance; microwave which requires transmitters, receivers, and towers at each site; VSAT (very small aperture terminal) satellite transmissions that require uplinks and downlinks at each site; or fiber optic lines between sites. All of these can be arranged, but may be technically difficult, politically impossible, or very expensive. Many cannot be arranged or routinely changed overnight, though this is changing as new services from phone companies are making compressed video connections between sites almost as easy as regular long distance phone calls. It is still necessary to have the right equipment in place at each site and to have established the procedures for accessing the phone lines. Therefore, the cost for each site, the number of sites, and the availability of each site are important considerations. If fixed sites are not practical, compressed video may not be a good choice.

The University of Wyoming arranged for different network connections in separate locations, allowing them to move their equipment from one location to another as needed. Ascend Communications of Alameda, California, makers of inverse multiplexing equipment that allows compressed video calls to be made just like regular long distance calls, described in a recent seminar a similar arrangement at their headquarters that allows individual offices to move the compressed video equipment from office to office as needed. This encourages its use by placing it in a familiar environment just like a traditional phone.

Cost

While compressed video systems are expensive, cost should be balanced against the alternatives to determine whether they are excessive. Costs need to be compared to the potential audience size and the cost of alternatives such as bringing the audience to a central site or sending a person to the remote site(s). Costs need to be examined in two categories: start-up costs and on-going costs. Frequently, compressed video can be a very cost-effective technology. In the case of St. Vrain, as described in their User Profile in Part II of this book, compressed video was the least expensive alternative. For Northern Virginia, the same was true since any other strategy would have required towers that were both too expensive and politically impossible to construct.

Start-up Costs

One frequent mistake made by those who decide to install compressed video systems is that they initially base their start-up cost estimates primarily on the cost of the codecs, room monitors, cameras and video switching equipment. While these are certainly major costs in the project, there are many more that need to be included. For example, there may be a cost if a room is dedicated for compressed video use. If that room could have been used for a "live" class of 30 students, but instead is used as a compressed video site for 10 students, this is a cost. Some potential sites may not be willing to endure the lost revenue involved. Another "room" cost is furniture and fixtures. It may be necessary to refurnish each of the compressed video sites with tables and chairs, carpeting, wall treatment, electrical outlets, etc. If there are many sites this can be a significant expenditure. On the other hand, a number of institutions have simply used existing classrooms without investing in any particular acoustic or lighting enhancements. The important point is to consider these factors in advance.

Another, often overlooked, cost is space. The compressed video equipment and related switching and transmission equipment takes up more than an insignificant amount of space. If space is already in short supply, this can be a major problem.

Transmission systems also come with a variety of hidden costs. There is the basic cost of the transmission equipment such as transmitters, receivers, multiplexers, down converters and lots of other technical items. There may also be "connection and installation" charges for phone company lines. Legal fees and licensing costs for microwave and satellite transmission can be significant. There may even be on-going lease fees of thousands of dollars a year for use of tower space and roof space for antennas where these facilities are not owned by the organization itself.

There is cost involved in getting the compressed video signal from the point where it enters the building to the room(s) where it will be used. Depending on the distance and type of cable required, this can cost several dollars per foot plus several thousand dollars at each end for line drivers or similar equipment that converts the signal to the necessary form for that cable. Newer compressed video equipment is designed to operate on easier to use cable, like the twisted pair commonly used for standard telephones. There are some distance limitations, though, so each site must be considered separately.

Compressed video, regardless of the claims of some vendors, is rarely a *plug-and-play* system. You do not just unpack the components, plug them in and start operations. Therefore, it usually takes experts to install and "tweak" the system to get all the components communicating correctly with each other, all the interfaces synchronized and to get the system operating in the intended manner. Installation cost is rarely included in the list prices from vendors.

One other aspect of the actual start-up costs of a compressed video system that is usually overlooked is the cost of a back-up system. If the compressed video system fails, what will the organization do? The cheapest option is to simply cancel the class or meeting until the system is operational again. If this is not possible or practical, then there has to be a back-up system. This may involve having spare codecs and cameras or having audio conferencing equipment available that can be used while the video system is down. Figure 3.1 lists some of the key considerations in deciding how to use compressed video.

<u>Considerations in Deciding to Use Compressed Video</u>

- Is there agreement on the need for a video system?
- Is two-way video needed?
- Is a live presentation needed?
- Are semi-permanent receive sites available?
- Are rooms available at each site?
- Is a transmission system available between sites?
- Is there space for the compressed video equipment at each site?
- Will technical support be needed at each site, and can it be provided?
- Is there enough money for equipment and installation?
- Will use of compressed video save money over alternatives?

Figure 3.1

On-going Costs

Typically, organizations arrange special funding for the start-up costs associated with a compressed video system since they involve large sums. On-going operating costs, though, frequently get much less attention in the planning process. This may be due to wishful thinking on the part of the organization, the result of inadequate planning, surprises from vendors who change their maintenance policies, or the lack of solid experience from other users since compressed video is still a relatively new technology.

The easiest on-going cost to estimate is the cost of transmission. Most transmission services or technologies are reliable and there is a solid user base that can provide information on reliability, maintenance cost and life expectancy of the equipment involved. There are established rates for telephone company services as well.

The overlooked on-going costs center on three areas: personnel, maintenance, and equipment replacement. A compressed video system is going to require personnel to operate and maintain it. Even the simplest system is going to take someone to tackle problems, train users, and make the connections among sites. While the operation of the systems has gotten easier so that existing staff can often assume the operation of the compressed video system as part of their regular duties, this may not always be the case. Each new combination of sites will take at least a little time to connect and insure that the signals among sites are clear. Time may be required for someone to travel to remote sites for installation, maintenance, troubleshooting, etc. Some organizations may do on-site training, as well, but training is being done over the compressed video system itself in many organizations, which makes it easier for existing staff to handle. Staff are also going to be sick some days and want to take a vacation. This means that more than one person must be able to operate the system. If new staff are necessary, they will need office or work space in addition to the space occupied by the compressed video equipment itself. Personnel considerations, though, do not need to pose an overwhelming burden. It appears that most systems can operate well with a combination of one or two key people who are well trained and a variety of part-time people to assist at remote sites on an as-needed basis.

Northern Virginia Community College's system uses somewhat older and more temperamental technology to link classrooms at each of five sites. Initially, technicians were constantly kept busy balancing audio for each new class or meeting to eliminate echoes between sites. However, switching to push-to-talk microphones eliminated almost all of these problems, making the system much easier for faculty and students to operate on their own. A technician at a central location can monitor system operation and is able to handle problems by phone from the other compressed video sites.

At the University of Wyoming they use graduate students to start compressed video sessions. These graduate students are then available across the hall if further help is needed. For the first few sessions the graduate students operate the compressed video equipment. Then they identify a class facilitator whom they train. Class facilitators are usually rewarded with extra credit or are offered some credit tuition free, depending on what they do. Many instructors are also quite willing to operate their own equipment.

One of the biggest surprises facing compressed video users is maintenance and repair. Unlike traditional audiovisual and video equipment, compressed video equipment has proven to be somewhat less reliable and more expensive to repair. It is not uncommon to have to repair compressed video codecs every several years. In a large network, that means repairing several codecs every year. While the organization may plan to have all the equipment covered by maintenance agreements so that these costs are predictable, the annual investment may be substantial. For example, if the maintenance agreement cost for a $30,000 codec is five percent of the list price, the annual cost per codec is $1,500.

The cost of repairing codecs not covered by maintenance agreements can also be substantial. Within a single year, one vendor went from charging for time and materials, typically $500 per repair, to a flat fee. The flat fee started at $1,500 per repair and jumped to $3,000 per repair. This was to encourage users to purchase maintenance agreements which cost approximately $2,000 per year per codec. Since most, if not all, repairs to codecs and switching equipment must be done by the manufacturer, it is no wonder that maintenance cost can be hard to accurately budget.

One other on-going cost that needs to be considered is the cost of replacement equipment. Not only will some equipment such as microphones and cameras be broken or perhaps even stolen, the expensive codecs and switching equipment will not last forever. In some cases, ongoing maintenance agreements, though expensive, will provide some security. However, with the rapid changes going on throughout the compressed video industry, organizations are likely to want to upgrade or replace their systems after a few years. It would not be surprising if the industry itself helped organizations make this decision by ending technical support of older equipment as new generations of equipment come along. Where possible, planning for this replacement as an annual on-going cost will make the process easier than having to obtain the large amount of money necessary to replace or upgrade an entire system at one-time. Opponents of compressed video can have a field day pointing out that the organization already paid a lot for the existing system. Figure 3.2 summarizes some of the major on-going costs associated with a compressed video system.

On-going Costs of a Compressed Video System
Transmission between sites:

- Technical personnel
- Site facilitators
- Maintenance and repair
- Replacement equipment
- System upgrades

Figure 3.2

Operating a Compressed Video System

There are many considerations involved in successfully operating a compressed video system. While it would be nice if there was a single prescription for success, such is not the case. Structuring the operation of a compressed video system must take into account the unique nature of each organization and the limitations or opportunities it presents. The key to success, though, is that all the issues are considered and addressed so they do not present critical problems at a later time. Organizations can tailor the operation of a compressed video system to meet their specific needs. Among the issues that must be dealt with are lead-time, access to support services, audience sophistication, leadership, ownership, expectations and scheduling.

Lead Time

Perhaps the most frustrating aspect of selecting and installing a compressed video system is time. After all the time involved in researching systems, preparing specifications, purchasing and finally installing the system, most organizations cannot wait to actually use the new technology. Therein lies the danger. For some reason, high technology projects always seem to take longer than planned to reach full implementation. Either the design or purchasing takes longer than expected; installation runs into trouble, or some other factor causes unforeseen delay. Meanwhile, the organization is anxious to see some tangible return on its large investment and is pushing for implementation. Implementing the system too soon, before all the bugs are worked out, can lead to system failures and bad reputation for compressed video that will be hard to live down.

The worst example of this often takes place in the academic setting where class schedules are set well in advance of the start of classes. There may be tremendous pressure to schedule classes to be held using the compressed video system before the installation is complete on the assumption that the system will be operational before classes start. If there has been inadequate planning and testing, the first semester or two may be very rough experiences for everyone involved.

By contrast, a company installing a compressed video system to reduce travel costs for meetings can show almost immediate results as soon as the system is operational by simply scheduling a meeting. Consider how impressive it must have been when Apple Computer first linked its California site with its site in France for a meeting. Not only were costs saved, but there was no lost time for overseas travel!

The solution is to build in adequate testing time where users can actually try-out the system without making a commitment to its full-time use. This also has the benefit of communicating to everyone that the system is still in the development stage and will get better. If outside events force a particular starting date, it is important to work backwards from that date to insure adequate testing and experimentation time. Research, design and procurement phases may have to be shortened. All too often, these early phases are left intact and the testing time is cut.

Support Services

When the compressed video system is used primarily for meetings or short training events, support services at the remote sites may be very simple to provide. For example, the only support services needed may be a telephone, a way to mail materials to and from participants, and perhaps a FAX machine for last minute items. A room facilitator might not even be needed. The bigger the group and the more complex the set-up, though, the more support that may be needed. Similarly, if the compressed video system is being used for academic classes, provision must be made for registration, submitting and returning homework in a timely fashion, taking tests, getting access to library and computer resources, and counseling or advising services.

Audience Sophistication

The sophistication of the prospective audience also has a lot to do with operational decisions for a compressed video system. The more sophisticated and motivated the audience, the more responsibility they will take, and they will take charge of the technology so that it does not interfere with their participation. The less sophisticated the audience, the more technical support that may be needed. There may even be need for at least a part-time on-site facilitator for leadership and on-going group support. Even in public school applications, the students themselves may be more technologically sophisticated than their teachers, and will assume responsibility for making their time on the system productive.

Leadership

Unlike some innovations, e.g. personal computers, it is hard for individual innovators to provide all the necessary energy and decision-making the system will require. A successful compressed video system must have a centralized support system that can coordinate planning, financial details and technical support instead of leaving it up to each of the sites themselves. In addition, it is the central support system that must serve as the cheerleader and facilitator that encourages users and promotes new uses of the system.

Ownership

Among the on-going operational considerations that is often totally overlooked is that of ownership. Support and use of a compressed video system is usually enhanced if the remote sites feel they are integral parts of the compressed video network as compared to servants of the network hub. These remote sites must have a feeling of ownership of the system. They should be active, interested partners rather than reluctant participants who are waiting for some other solution they really want—like a live presence instead of two-way video. The remote sites need to make some commitment to making the system work. To accomplish this feeling of ownership the remote sites must feel they have some control over schedules and operation of the system.

Another way of gaining commitment is to make sure that there is something for everyone offered on the compressed video system. For example, California State University at Bakersfield is linked to Tehachapi High School, 50 rugged miles away. Not only can high school students take courses using the system, teachers can take courses to fulfill continuing education requirements and local residents can take life-long learning courses. Murray State in Kentucky and the North Dakota Interactive Video Network are other examples of this type of multi-use system.

Among the alternatives for gaining commitment and instilling the feeling of ownership are such things as giving remote sites a role in the planning process, making them active participants in scheduling, having the remote sites share in the financial costs and rewards of the system, and sharing in the origination of programs over the system. One of the best strategies is to operate on the basis of signed agreements among the sites that detail the responsibilities and commitments of all parties. It is less the agreement itself than the process of arriving at it that provides the benefit.

Expectations

Successful operation of a compressed video system is often determined by expectations that precede installation of the system. The definition of the job to be done may make it impossible for the system to be successful, even if technical operation goes perfectly. For example, if the expectation is that the system will generate large enrollments, but the remote sites only choose to receive very specialized classes that attract small enrollments, the system may be viewed as a failure. Similarly, if the expectation is that the system will save money by reducing the need for travel, but the organization continues to hold meetings at a central site while having extra meetings over the compressed video system, it is not likely that money will be saved. Again, the system may be viewed as a failure because expectations were not met rather than because of technical or other operational problems. If the goal of the remote sites is really a building or a more frequent physical presence from the central site, a dedicated compressed video classroom may never satisfy the remote site and leaders at that site may continue to work aggressively for the solution they really wanted even if it is at the expense of the compressed video system.

To deal effectively with expectations, it is important to have a clear explanation from the beginning of what the system is, what sites it reaches, what it can do, and for what it will be used. This explanation should find its way into agreements with the participating sites and to the decision-makers within the organization. The expectations of the remote sites must be taken into account early in the planning process so they can be dealt with realistically. Accurate and realistic cost and revenue projections should be made and distributed to all those involved. Ideally, at least some criteria for success should be discussed and agreed upon during the planning phase of the project.

Scheduling

Given the large investment an organization will make in the compressed video system, it is desirable to see it used frequently. Frequent use, though, can pose scheduling conflicts—especially if the equipment can be rolled from room to room for almost spontaneous use. Therefore, some kind of centralized scheduling system is needed, even if the system is open for anyone to use it. Someone needs to assume responsibility for avoiding scheduling problems. As use increases, there are a number of scheduling issues that will need to be addressed. Rather than trying to deal with these issues each time they come up, it is a good idea to have general rules and procedures in place.

Among the issues that might be covered by a set of rules and procedures are such things as the following: Who can have access to the system? Is the system only available to selected departments, managers, and faculty, or can employees and students have access to the system for their own uses? Is the system available to groups outside the organization? If so, what is the cost to them? What types of uses are appropriate for the system, and what uses or which individuals have priority and can bump others on the schedule? When can cancellations of scheduled uses be made and who can do the canceling? Can a remote site arbitrarily cancel use of the room dedicated to compressed video at the last minute to accommodate some other use of the room? How will scheduling disputes be resolved? Even with the best of planning, scheduling problems are bound to occur. Figure 3.3 lists the decisions that can affect the design and operation of a compressed video system.

Operational Considerations for a Compressed Video System:

- Is there enough time allowed for testing the new system?
- Have support services been established at each site?
- If the system will be used for instruction, have arrangements been made at all sites for registration, testing, library resources, handouts, homework, computers, labs and other academic services?
- Will room facilitators be needed to operate equipment at remote sites?
- Is there a back-up plan for times when the compressed video system fails to operate correctly?
- Is there a central system manager to coordinate planning, operations and use?
- Is there support of compressed video at the remote sites?
- Is there agreement on what the system is expected to do for the organization?
- Is there a process for scheduling the system and resolving schedule conflicts?

Figure 3.3

Summary

It seems like there is an endless array of considerations that must be taken into account when dealing with compressed video. In fact, there are so many considerations that it may seem like success with compressed video would be nearly impossible given that there are so many things technically and operationally that could go wrong. However, as the User Profiles show, there are quite a few successful compressed video systems in operation. The reason they are successful is that they have found ways to deal with the issues raised in this chapter. In all honesty, they did not always deal with these issues up front or deal with them well when the issues first came up. Nevertheless, the more that these considerations are dealt with early in the process of selecting and implementing a compressed video system, the smoother that installation will go and the quicker the system will be able to achieve successful operation.

4

Compressed Video Facilities

Steven G. Sachs

Introduction

While many compressed video systems are housed in special wheeled cabinets with names like "roll-about," and are designed to be portable, special facilities may be required depending on the size of the potential audience and additional equipment added to the basic system. For example, audience size will determine the size of video monitors or screens needed, audio requirements, and seating. Similarly, if the facility requires a fax machine, computers, extra cameras, and extra monitors, portability can be affected.

The Typical System

The typical compressed video system requires a variety of wires, connectors, cameras, monitors, microphones, carts, and related equipment. Sometimes, this equipment can be stored out of the way in a closet or cabinet or mounted unobtrusively on a wall. Nonetheless, it has to be somewhere. Here is a brief description of the typical compressed video facility system.

- Electrical connections for all the cameras and monitors.

- At least two or three cameras: one would be aimed at the participants plus a copy stand or overhead camera for showing visuals (much like an overhead projector). If the system is designed for classroom use, there may be at least three cameras with one or more aimed at the students, one at the instructor, and the overhead camera.

- One or more television monitors: depending on the equipment selected, there has to be at least one television monitor to show the remote site. Some systems use two monitors. One shows the remote site and one shows the images on the cameras in the room itself. If the system is in a classroom, there will need to be separate monitors for the instructor and the students. The student monitors will need to be in the front of the room; the instructor's monitor(s) may be at the back of the room, mounted in a console on the instructor's desk, or hung from the ceiling in front of the instructor.

- One or more microphones for the participants and the instructor, if there is one.

- A switching panel, remote control or computer keyboard for selecting cameras and operating special effects.

- A codec to process the video and audio signals for transmission.

- A telephone to call remote sites or for getting technical assistance.

- Connections to the transmission

- Electrical connections for all the cameras and monitors.

There are a variety of other pieces of equipment that are found in some systems. There may be one or two VCRs, an audio mixer to control the microphones, a computer and printer, a graphics tablet for hand drawing and controlling special effects, a fax machine, a separate speaker system to supplement the small speakers in the television monitors, or even audio tape recorders and phonographs, and uninterrupted power supply units to keep the equipment operating during power failures.

Like it or not, most of the equipment listed above has to be connected by wires and cables. If the system is self-contained in a custom designed cart and designed for small group use, there may be a minimum of wires and cables outside the cabinet. There will be one cable to the overhead camera, perhaps one to the microphone(s), one to an electric outlet, and one to the transmission line. However, the bigger the audience, the more wires and cables there will be that need to be concealed. For example, with a larger audience more microphones may be needed, and they will be farther from the audio connections on the codec or audio mixer. There also will probably need to be more television monitors and cameras, each of which requires cables and connection to electricity.

Wires and cables can be concealed, but this requires planning and may influence the type of furniture to be used in the facility.

Room Set up

See Part II

Modern compressed video equipment is designed for use in almost any office or room setting. No special lighting or acoustic treatment is needed, especially for use with small groups. The compressed video equipment can be rolled from office to office or from meeting room to a lab, depending on where it is needed. One, or at most two, microphones with minimal sensitivity and a single camera aimed at the participants are usually adequate. Manufacturers claimed that these packaged systems eliminated the need for fancy, custom designed video rooms. For uses with only a few participants at each site, the manufacturers' claims are correct.

Many organizations, though, have begun looking at compressed video for delivering instruction or holding meetings for larger groups. These new uses require additional cameras and microphones to cover the whole group. Seating patterns are also different. While two or three people can easily sit in front of the television screen and face each other as well as the remote site, difficult choices have to be made to accommodate larger groups. For instructional uses, students are used to facing their instructor, so seats can be arranged in rows to face the television monitors. For meetings involving more than four or five people, though, it is often difficult to arrange the seats so everyone can comfortably see each other and the television monitors at the same time. This may affect group dynamics, making it harder for participants to talk with each other in the same room than for them to talk with participants at the remote sites. Furthermore, the technical limitations of the cameras and microphones also limit the options for seating medium to large size groups.

It is somewhat a question of which comes first, the selection of equipment or the selection of a room seating arrangement. Ideally, the equipment should be matched to the intended use, but sometimes that is not possible. For example, if desk-top microphones are used, traditional student armchair desks arranged in rows or theater style seating can be a problem. Not only will it be harder for students to share microphones, it will be harder to conceal the microphone cables. An alternative is to mount the microphones from the ceiling or on the walls. Once mounted, though, it is hard to change the seating arrangement without running the risk of seriously disrupting the microphone sound pick-up patterns. On the other hand, using tables and chairs in the room, while good from the perspective of the microphones, may seriously limit the number of participants who can be accommodated in the space available. Other creative solutions are possible.

Both the University of Wyoming and Northern Virginia Community College have their instructors wear lavaliere microphones, but make other arrangements for students. Students at the University of Wyoming pass around a microphone in larger group settings, while students at Northern Virginia have push-to-talk microphones on the student tables. Originally, Northern Virginia had a microphone on a stand for a French class. Students would walk up to the microphone in pairs or in small groups to interact with each other or with the other site. Even though students like this approach and it worked well, putting microphones on the tables solved a number of other logistical problems.

Cameras can also limit the options available for room setup for larger groups. Most cameras have a limited field of view. That is, they can only show a certain number of seats at any given time. This is a factor of both the camera lens and the distance of the camera from the audience. To show the largest number of people, the image size of each person must be smaller, and the entire image may be distorted. In its extreme, the distortion may give a fish-eye look to the remote site like that associated with security cameras and mirrors. One way around this problem is to add remote control devices to the cameras that allow them to be moved and zoomed in or out from a distant location. It is also possible to use extra cameras to show different parts of each room. However, these extra devices add cost to the system, and add additional tasks for the meeting leader or instructor to perform.

Room arrangement is also influenced by the size of television monitors that are used with the system. Small monitors are very good when the system is used for meetings with two or three participants at each site. With larger groups, larger monitors are needed. Larger monitors, though, can be harder to move around. Furthermore, larger monitors can be uncomfortable for people sitting close to them. Unless the monitors are mounted on tall stands, people's views can easily be blocked by those sitting in front of them; but larger monitors cannot always be put on tall stands. To get around this, some organizations have mounted monitors from the ceiling. Some participants, though, do not like the feeling of looking up and may complain that the monitors block their view of the front of the room. It can be hard to please everyone, so it may take some experimentation to find the best compromise.

Monitor size is also affected by the types of images that will be shown and how the particular compressed video system handles those images. For example, if the system displays images from several remote sites on a single television with a split screen, each image will be relatively small. This may require a larger monitor to make the images clearly visible to all participants than would be needed for a system that only shows a single site at a time with a correspondingly larger image size. The same consideration affects the display of text. If a great deal of computer generated text or other computer screens will be shown, monitor size must be increased or more monitors will be needed so participants can sit closer to the image.

Most audiovisual textbooks provide guidelines for monitor size based on seating arrangements and expected audience size. These texts also describe microphone options to help in selecting the right pick-up patterns. Some vendors have also started preparing guidelines to help organizations select the right mix of components for intended use(s) of compressed video that go beyond the standard small meeting format.

Environmental Concerns

Modern compressed video systems no longer require fancy, custom-designed rooms. As described earlier, the equipment can generally be rolled from room to room with minimal trouble for use with small groups. However, attention should be paid to the physical environment of the room used with the compressed video equipment. Such factors as electric power, heating/cooling, and lighting can all affect system success. In most modern facilities, there is plenty of electric power with outlets on every wall; plenty of power, that is, for traditional uses. Things have changed dramatically over the past few years. Not only might there be many pieces of equipment requiring electricity in the room with the compressed video system; there may be dozens of computers, printers, fax machines, lamps, radios and other items on the same circuit but in different rooms. At some point there may not be enough electricity to go around.

At three of the University of Wyoming's sites, so many things were plugged into the uninterrupted power supply units that capacity was overloaded and the system shut down. At Northern Virginia Community College, so many computers and related equipment were on the same circuit as the multiplexer connecting the codec with the T-1 line that the multiplexer partially shut down and would not pass the signals through. So, while everything appeared to be operating correctly on the T-1 line, the compressed video system did not work. This was an easy problem to solve once it was finally tracked down, but tracking it down was very difficult.

Another common problem with the proliferation of technology is that interference or noise that affects system operation can be created on the electric circuit. In one case, a refrigerator in one room was on the same circuit as computers in another room. Every time the refrigerator compressor came on, computer errors started appearing. The best advice is to attempt to provide separate circuits that are isolated from other equipment for the compressed video system.

Heating and cooling considerations can have a real impact on the compressed video system. Unlike early electronics that generated large amounts of heat, most modern equipment does not affect the room temperature greatly. Instead, people do things in the name of security that make the compressed video facilities very unpleasant. For example, if there is a dedicated room for compressed video, it may be kept closed when not in use. This results in the room either being excessively hot or freezing cold—depending on how the building ventilation system works. To solve the problem, fans are brought in. Fans generate noise that drives the audio system crazy. If the room is uncomfortable, people will blame it on the system.

Similarly, just because a system is portable does not mean it will be moved to an appropriate room. Rather than moving the system to a larger room, too many people may try to crowd into a small office to participate in a meeting. Not only might seating be uncomfortable, the room may become extremely stuffy after only a short time.

Many people think that extra lights must be added to a room in order to use it for compressed video. This is not necessarily the case. The typical overhead florescent lights in most rooms are adequate for modern low light cameras. Where the lighting is poor, it is usually possible to use brighter bulbs or add light fixtures. The exception is in auditorium or theater settings.

Special lighting may be required for these facilities.

While the lighting may not be a problem for the cameras, it can be a problem for the participants trying to view the television monitors. If the room is too bright or too dark, it may be uncomfortable to view the monitors. Many rooms only have two options for lighting—on or off. With all the lights off, the room is too dark for taking notes or too dark for the cameras. Dimmer switches or lights that can be turned on or off in sections may be helpful.

One other aspect of lighting causes trouble in some rooms. This is glare from windows. Glare can show up on television screens or make it impossible to use cameras. It can severely limit the options for arranging the room to its maximum advantage. Window blinds become an important fixture in such rooms, but most users do not want to sit for a long time in a room where the blinds must always be closed. They might even prefer a room without windows! It is not that different from the early days of audiovisual aids when rooms could not routinely be made dark enough for teachers to show films.

Space Needs

It is easy to underestimate the space required for a compressed video system. The problem is not with the basic equipment since most rooms can accommodate a codec, monitor and cameras. Space problems come from trying to accommodate switching equipment, line equipment to connect the compressed video signal to the transmission system, monitoring equipment, and housing any technicians who will operate the equipment. In many cases, space is already a problem because facilities were not designed to accommodate the new computer technologies already in place before the introduction of compressed video to the organization. Equipment rooms and telephone closets are small and poorly ventilated. Audiovisual departments and media centers are already full. Central computer centers are overstocked with equipment, network connections, and staff.

Where the compressed video system is based around a central hub with remote sites connected like the spokes of a wheel, there are special space considerations. Ideally, the hub of the compressed video system will provide a way for a technician to set-up the necessary connections, monitor the on-going video conferences and connect the video signals to other systems. Technicians should have the capacity to record tapes, connect the compressed video network to either cable or satellite systems, or redirect the signals to another facility for viewing the on-going conference. This requires working room, patch panels, room for a VCR, as well as a monitor, phone, and perhaps even a codec. This approach is more likely to be found in large, centralized systems like Nebraska's NEB*SAT, Northern Virginia and some of the other statewide systems. Other networks, though, have organized more at the individual site level and take care of such functions as video taping right at the local site and put less emphasis on connecting to other transmission systems or other networks.

One very neat approach to making space available is to provide a small room for the equipment and technician adjoining the rear of a dedicated compressed video room. This space needs access to both the compressed video room and to the hall or another office area. Not unlike a projection room, this allows the technician to be close at hand yet remain unobtrusive. Of course, this will not work for organizations where the equipment is rolled from room to room.

Fixed vs. Portable Systems

A number of organizations have made their compressed video systems portable so they could move the equipment to an appropriately sized room or specialized lab depending on the need. Operationally, portability is much harder for large group applications of compressed video equipment if they involve much equipment beyond that contained in the portable cabinet.

While most of the equipment and connections necessary for a small meeting can easily be housed in the cabinet provided by the compressed video manufacturer or system integrator, the system must still be connected to phone lines, transmission lines, and electricity. The number of connections and adjustments that must be made increases dramatically as the potential audience size increases. There are extra cameras, microphones and television monitors to connect. The audio system may have to be readjusted to the new microphone arrangement. Furthermore, if the system does not operate correctly, it can be time consuming to identify which of the added components is at fault. Making the system with many components portable also limits the availability of the system since moving and resetting the system can be a time consuming process. Moving from one small room to another small room to accommodate different groups' territorial needs is possible, even if it is only being done to satisfy internal politics. Moving between a small room and a larger room to accommodate different size audiences is more complicated, but it can be done with some careful planning.

For example, a system can be set up as a learning carrel in a high school for specialized classes not usually available due to low enrollments at that particular school. The equipment can be shifted to a regular classroom for special presentations of interest to an entire class. While the entire class may not be visible on the single camera included with the system, that is not necessarily a problem for this particular application. If it is, an additional camera can usually be plugged into the system quickly. When the class is finished, the equipment can be moved back to its original location. There is an even bigger advantage for applications involving younger students since the interactive characteristics of compressed video are highly motivating.

One successful approach that can maintain portability and provide for the extra equipment needed for a larger group is to pick a medium-sized or larger room as a compressed video facility. Equip it with cameras so it can be used as a classroom with one camera set to show an instructor in the front of the room and one or more to show the participants. When the equipment is moved to the larger room, only the cart with the codec and monitor(s) has to be moved; everything else is already in place and only needs to be connected to the equipment on the cart.

Another approach is to create a small compressed video work station in a larger room. This area might even be separated from the rest of the room with moveable partitions. The rest of the room can be equipped with extra cameras, and the audio system can similarly be made slightly redundant to accommodate different size groups in a single room. Through very simple controls the appropriate cameras and microphones can be activated.

Another, though less desirable approach, is to fully equip two rooms with cameras, microphones, VCR's etc. Portability is achieved by moving the codec alone. The value of this approach is determined by how much time there is to make the change between rooms, the staff time available to make the change and re-adjust the system, and the number of devices that must be connected to the codec (e.g. camera cables, audio cables, monitors, and related control devices). There can easily be ten or more cables to connect.

A variation of the two-room approach is to have adjoining rooms equipped with the codec positioned between the rooms so it can serve each room from one location. The appropriate cameras, microphones and television monitors are selected through the use of a patch panel, switcher or similar device. If there is enough space, a small room for equipment and for a technician to operate and monitor the system can be provided between the two compressed video rooms.

The key to portability, especially where larger groups are involved, is advanced planning in the selection of equipment and the design of the facilities. Just because the compressed video equipment is housed in a cabinet with wheels, there is no guarantee that it will fit though an organization's doorways, or even fit into cramped space in a lab or small office. It may not even fit on the raised stage of a meeting room or large lecture room if there are steps to negotiate. Someone has to take a look at the locations where the equipment will actually be used to determine how portable the system can really be.

Security

With all of the expensive equipment involved in a compressed video system, security can be a major concern. At a central site, there may be enough traffic or normal security that theft or vandalism is not a factor. At remote sites the equipment may prove to be a tempting target—especially since cameras, VCR's and monitors are portable and easily used elsewhere. Some equipment can be locked up in a cabinet, and carts can be rolled to a secure location; however, much of the equipment, such as extra cameras and microphones, may be left in place in the room. Many security cables that rely on adhesives can be pried off, so components either need to be bolted down, the facility locked up, or some allowance made for potential theft losses.

The biggest danger, though, is not always theft. Frequently, equipment gets <u>borrowed</u> and gets reinstalled incorrectly, or is not returned on-time. Similarly, equipment may be adjusted for one use and not reset for the next user. For example, at Northern Virginia Community College, equipment at one site was frequently out of adjustment. It appeared that someone was periodically coming in overnight and tampering with the controls. After considerable detective work it was discovered that the security staff would come around at night and *turn off* every piece of electrical equipment in every room. They even found switches no one ever thought would be turned off. In another case, the overnight cleaning crew would switch the television monitors to regular TV so they could watch commercial television programs while cleaning. Frequently they would forget to switch the system back to compressed video use before leaving. When the participants arrived for their compressed video meeting, they thought the system was broken since they could not get a picture from the remote site.

Future Facilities

Enhancements to compressed video technology are taking place at an amazing pace throughout the industry. These enhancements will have an impact on compressed video facilities as well. Systems designed for true desktop use or personal computers will make portability decisions easier. These desktop units will have simple hook ups and be very useful for meetings. It is even likely that academic institutions can set up compressed video labs in the same way that they now have computer labs. Students can join different conferences from individual work stations. Connections will be made through public carriers rather than dedicated end-to-end networks. The larger "roll-about" units will be reserved for larger group meetings and will be left in place rather than moved from location to location.

The movement to less expensive PC-based systems will have tremendous impact on public schools—especially in rural areas where the students do not typically have access to the range of advanced placement courses available in urban areas. Compressed video systems will be more affordable and more prevalent. Similarly, community colleges will be able to become *windows on the world* for their communities by providing links for business, industry, the medical profession and even government officials to resources outside their communities. Since many academic institutions are already having trouble accommodating space for computer labs, the spread of compressed video systems will further tax existing facilities.   International standards will allow compressed video systems from different manufacturers to communicate with each other, so organizations can join conferences without having to *match* brands of equipment. Furthermore, the long distance telephone companies will do more of the matching and bridging of signals, reducing the reliance on private dedicated networks to connect sites. Transmission of compressed video at reasonable cost will become easier and more routine over the regular telephone system, just like making long-distance phone calls, reducing the need for some organizations to invest in expensive video bridging equipment in order to connect multiple sites.

The future also suggests that networks will make increasing use of mixed models for transmission. Compressed video may be transmitted over phone lines for some remote sites at the same time microwave transmissions of regular video are connecting other sites. In some organizations, compressed or regular video will be sent out by satellite with return signals from the remote sites by telephone or even the new picture phones being promoted by AT&T and soon by MCI. These mixed models may simplify some networks, but will increase the need for well-trained technicians at the hub of each network.

Summary

Compressed video systems place a variety of demands on an organization. Not only must decisions be made about room size and seating arrangements that will affect the type and placement of equipment in a room, space must be provided for network equipment and technicians. Electric power and lighting must be taken into account. Security, especially at remote sites, is also a factor in planning. While there are a great many options available to an organization planning a compressed video system, it is important to minimize the focus on one or two options and set up the system to function well in that environment.

5

Financial Planning

Steven G. Sachs

Introduction

Compressed video systems are expensive. They cost a lot to install and a fair amount to operate. It is not uncommon for organizations to pay from $500,000 to over $1.5 million for multisite networks. Individual sites can cost anywhere from $40,000-$100,000 to install. Even with these costs, compressed video systems can be cost effective if adequate planning is done and the system is carefully managed. Unfortunately, most organizations focus all their attention on the initial costs of installing the system and give little thought to the ongoing financial decisions that need to be made.

Financial Planning Phases

For financial planning purposes, it is useful to think of the life of a compressed video system in terms of seven phases: initial planning, system design, procurement, installation, startup, operations, and upgrade/replacement. Each phase has different funding needs and requires different management strategies.

Initial Planning

The first step in any organized effort to implement a compressed video system is the initial planning and investigation phase. This is where the basic questions of needs and alternatives are dealt with. It is a time of surveys, discussions, long distance phone calls to organizations that already have different kinds of systems, and even travel to visit those more experienced sites. Sometimes organizations provide a special budget for this phase. More often, though, these costs are not excessive and can be absorbed within existing administrative budgets.

System Design

Once the decision to proceed with a compressed video system has been made, serious planning efforts must begin. Usually there are special purchasing procedures for investments of this size, and prudence dictates making careful choices among alternative vendors, hardware, options, and even technologies. Typically there is a committee in charge of this process, and the cost of their time may have to be accounted for. In addition, if there was not much travel in the initial planning phase, the committee will want to visit actual compressed video installations during this phase.

The role of consultants in the design phase varies greatly. In some cases, consultants have been hired to help design the system and select the most appropriate options. This is a cost. However, in other cases, the vendors have provided design assistance at no cost. In fact, a number of vendors now represent several compressed video manufacturers and help the organization select the most appropriate technology and options for the planned use and available budget. Decisions on whether consultants will be used and how many people will travel to see compressed video systems in operation will determine whether a special budget is needed for the system design phase.

Two developments over the past several years have helped organizations make better decisions during the design phase. First, there is more competition among compressed video manufacturers and resellers. Second, it is easier to test compressed video equipment between actual sites that will be part of the planned network. Early compressed video often had to be demonstrated between two rooms in the same building since transmission was an expensive and difficult thing to arrange for an equip-ment trial, and vendors were not anxious to tie up their equipment for any length of time for such trials. The only other option was to visit existing compressed video sites. Northern Virginia Community College frequently hosted groups wanting to see a system in operation. Unfortunately, the groups from each organization tended to be small and often had plans to configure and use their proposed system differently than Northern Virginia. The visitors often lamented the fact that they were never really able to see what they most wanted to see. The best they could say was that they saw compressed video work and talked to people who were happy with it.

Several organizations have used the new competitive nature of the compressed video market to good advantage. The University of Wyoming ran a pilot project over three months during which they tested the products of four vendors. The University of Utah and the Maricopa Community College District in Arizona are among the many others that have also arranged demonstration projects prior to purchase. These projects have helped to build support and identify important features desired in the new system. More people from the organization can be involved in the review process than would ever be possible through field trips to other facilities.

Testing the equipment prior to purchase, though, adds some costs to this phase of the project. The vendors may not provide the necessary transmission system, the transmission costs, or the costs for making any necessary room modifications such as adding electrical outlets or the cables necessary for the new equipment.

While other chapters go into much greater detail on the equipment, facilities, and other cost items that need to be considered in the system design, Figure 5.1 lists some of the major equipment categories that must be accounted for in the financial planning that takes place during the design phase.

Major Compressed Video Equipment Categories

- Compressed video equipment (codecs, network switches, cameras, microphones, etc.)
- Room alteration
- Cabling and connectors
- Furniture
- Transmission equipment
- Connection to transmission system
- Legal fees, permits and licenses
- Equipment installation
- Consultants

Figure 5.1

Procurement

The procurement phase is a logical extension of the design phase. It is not uncommon to have continued involvement of consultants to help in evaluating bids or in negotiating price and installation details. Depending on the nature of the procurement process, the biggest cost during this phase may be time. The writing of even the simplest of bid packages is time consuming. There are meetings among all the relevant parties within the organization, each having a unique perspective on how the materials should be written. Even after the first draft is written, there is negotiation among those planning to use or run the system and those in charge of the procurement process to reach a final bid package. Some individuals may focus on performance guarantees and penalties for failure to comply with the bid specifications. Others may focus on the training aspects of the new system. Some may want more detail on the technical details involved with transmission. The list could go on and on.

When the package is presented to prospective bidders, they will have a variety of questions about the meaning of certain parts of the bid package which may take time to research and answer. For example, if it is not clearly stated, they will want to know which rooms will actually have cable installed for the new system, or how many remote control devices must be provided, or how many spares must be included. In short, any place that there could be multiple interpretations will result in a question. There will also be meetings and tours designed to clarify the exact nature of the work to be done and the specific physical setting involved in installing the system. There will, of course, be meetings to review bids received in order to select a final vendor. All of this takes time. Even if a formal bid process is not required, compressed video is not something that can be purchased by going out to an electronics store and picking it up one afternoon.

Installation

The biggest costs are incurred during the installation phase. This is when equipment is delivered, rooms are modified, wiring is put in place and technicians are trained. Hopefully, there will be no surprises and the system can be installed within the bid price. The more detailed the planning and the more carefully the specifications are written, the more likely this will happen.

Some organizations plan to save money by doing all or part of the installation on their own. However, they often take many things for granted, assuming that the costs will be absorbed or not amount to more than pocket change. At Northern Virginia Community College, the college put in its own cables between the telephone rooms where the T-1 line entered each building and the classrooms where compressed video would be used. When the vendor went to install the equipment it was discovered that no one had arranged to have the special computer connectors put on the end of the cables. This oversight added $75 per cable end to the cost of installation. With well over 20 connectors involved, this amounted to a $1,500 surprise!

At the University of Wyoming there were no standards for much of the smaller equipment at each site. Some sites used uninterrupted power supplies, some did not. Some used push-to-talk microphones, while others used low-profile tabletop microphones. The sites used whatever they had available. This made trouble shooting by phone or over the compressed video system extremely difficult since it was often unclear exactly how the equipment was configured. This is a drawback of trying to save money. The solution is to have detailed diagrams of each site or to standardize the equipment and installation even if the organization is going to do the installation itself. Northern Virginia took the standardization approach and found it very successful. The lesson to be learned is not that cost saving is bad. It is that even if the organization plans to do some of the installation itself, the work needs to be planned as carefully as if it was going to be put out for bid.

Startup

Even in the best designed systems, things are going to happen during the first few months of operation that do not happen as planned. Some equipment may have been omitted from the original order, some equipment may work but may not do the required job, extra equipment may be needed to cope with unexpected circumstances in day-to-day operations. For example, at Northern Virginia Community College extra microphones may be required to capture the audio from all the participants. The extra microphones made it difficult to adjust the audio to eliminate echoes. Finally, it was decided to use push-to-talk microphones in place of the original tabletop directional microphones originally ordered as part of the system. This decision was reached after testing several hundred dollars' worth of other solutions. The conversion to the new microphones ended up costing over $600 per site for microphones, cables and an audio mixer during the startup phase.

Even when the equipment is just right, other things can go wrong. If careful attention was not paid to electrical circuits beforehand, it may be necessary to run new, isolated circuits to avoid interference from other equipment. Even seemingly trivial things can come up during the startup phase. It may be necessary to add window blinds to reduce glare or to add a speaker system to overcome ambient noise that no one noticed when the room dedicated to compressed video was originally being considered. All of these additions to the system cost money. If no money is reserved for this phase, serious problems can result.

Operations

The installation and startup phases for most compressed video systems should not last more that a year. This is important since most warranties on the major system components expire after one year. By that time, surprise expenditures should be over and it should be possible to predict a fairly stable budget for ongoing operations. One of the major costs during this phase is equipment maintenance and repair. Maintenance agreements can run as high as $2,000 per unit or more per year. Repairs for major components not under a maintenance agreement can run as much as $3,000. In a large network, these costs can easily run $10-20,000 per year! This amount might be hard to absorb without new funding.

Another ongoing operational cost involves personnel. Even if no new technicians were hired during the installation and startup phases, it may be necessary to add technicians or other facilitators as the compressed video system gets more use. It depends on the organization and the complexity of the system. At the University of Wyoming, new technicians were not hired. A number of existing staff were able to solve problems at the various sites over the phone. Graduate students and room facilitators drawn from the compressed video classes help keep the system running. While these students are not expensive, they do represent some cost such as the provision of one hour of free tuition as compensation. At Northern Virginia Community College, one technician was added and one faculty member received a slightly reduced workload to help facilitate use of the system. Each organization needs to make its own determination about additional staff. For the most part, though, it is not necessary to add full time staff for every site. One technician or one coordinator can deal with many sites. This is especially important for public school applications where small schools typically have very little media support as it is, and have no prospects of adding additional staff.

The key to success in the personnel area is to be sure that there are several people familiar enough with the system to turn it on and talk through the most common problems. The chapter on Supporting Compressed Video goes into a little more detail on trouble shooting problems when there is not a technician at every site.

There are always lots of little costs in operating a compressed video system. While every organization has its own category system, Figure 5.2 lists some of the most common cost areas.

Useful On-going Cost Categories

- Major equipment
- Office suuplies
- Audiovisual supplies
- Repair/maintenance
- Personnel
- Travel
- Transmission

Figure 5.2

There are also a number of hidden costs that can be overlooked in any category system. For example, organizations with maintenance agreements on the major equipment may forget to budget for repair and replacement of small items. In compressed video systems that include fax machines, someone has to budget for the fax paper. Similarly, if videotapes are going to be made of classes or meetings conducted over the compressed video, someone has to pay for videotape. Figure 5.3 lists some of the *hidden costs* in operating a compressed video system.

Upgrade/Replacement

The final phase in the financial planning process deals with equipment upgrade and replacement. All systems age and may become outdated. If maintenance agreements have been purchased for all the equipment, it may age slowly and even be upgraded at no additional cost. On the other hand, after 58 years (or less), it should come as no surprise that the equipment needs to be replaced. Replacement may be necessary for the equipment to be compatible with other organizations which have newer equipment, or because the old equipment has become too unreliable to use for important events. Organizations that can budget every year for the ultimate replacement of the equipment are lucky. Those that must operate on an annual basis with no carry over funds must plan ahead for replacement and build their case early. Waiting until the equipment begins failing on a regular basis may undermine the necessary support for equipment upgrade.

Hidden Costs in Compressed Video Operation

- Maintenance agreements
- Small equipment repair
- Spare equipment
- Supplies for mofifying compressed video rooms after installation (cable, connectors, wire molding, sould conditioning, etd.
- Travel to remote sites for planning, training and repairs
- Site facilitators/technicians
- Duplication of manuals and instructions
- Fax paper
- Video tape
- Phones and lines charges for regular phone service between sites.

Figure 5.3

Funding Options

No discussion of financial planning would be complete without some mention of alternative funding options to pay for the purchase and installation of the compressed video system. Some organizations will be large enough to allocate the necessary funds as part of their regular budget process. This may be possible because of the potential savings or through use of discretionary funds. Others will have to seek special funding.

Grants and Special Appropriations

One of the most obvious strategies is to obtain a grant from a foundation or corporate sponsor, or to obtain a special appropriation from a government body for the installation and startup costs. Among the arguments that can be made to justify special funding are cost savings from reduced travel, reduced cost for providing new or expanded service at the remote sites, ending isolation of rural locations, stimulating or supporting economic development at the remote sites, or as part of a long range plan to expand markets and services.

While some organizations seem to get grants on the flimsiest of proposals, most grants require a great deal of research and writing. The research should be designed to obtain solid figures on the needs and benefits of the proposed system. It should include information on the potential audience size, costs savings as compared to travel, new services that can be provided and how often they are likely to be used, how much the system will cost to operate and how that will be provided. If possible, the grant should include funds for some personnel, especially a grant manager to oversee the installation and startup of the system.

Whatever the funding approach, there should be written agreements from all participants assuring access to the facilities needed and insuring their participation in the programs offered over the compressed video system. To result in a successful project, the funding must realistically cover all the costs of the installation and startup phases, and make sure all the key parties have agreed to participate. It should capture the imagination of decision makers within the organization and of those providing the funds, and must have a high-energy devoted manager to bring all the pieces together.

Fundraising Campaigns

Grants and special appropriations are not the only funding option. Organizations can run special fund raising campaigns to seek donations from both the main site and at remote sites. Involving the remote sites in raising the necessary funds through fund raising campaigns or through cost sharing has the advantage of giving remote sites some ownership of the system and encourages them to take an active part in insuring the system's ongoing success.

Cost Sharing

There can be cost sharing among sites to help raise the necessary funds. A variation of this strategy involves splitting the costs across fiscal years to reduce the cost taken from any single budget. Within an organization, it may also be possible to draw funds from several different departmental budgets, when each of those departments are expected to share in the use of the system. Installation and startup funds do not always have to be drawn exclusively from the budget of the department that will ultimately operate the system.

Leasing

Leasing is another strategy that sometimes can be used to make a compressed video system affordable. Leasing arrangements spread the cost of the system over a number of years. While it may cost more in the long run than an outright purchase, the lease terms may bring the annual cost of the system within reach of the organization. Even if the manufacturer or vendor does not offer leases as a routine practice, there are firms that specialize in equipment leasing. Leasing is useful if the organization cannot borrow the money directly from a lending institution. The leasing company plays the role of middleman to make the entire transaction possible.

Sources of Ongoing Revenue

Paying for the ongoing operation of the compressed video system does not always have to be at the expense of a single departmental budget. There are several ways that costs can be shared, but there are also several cautions that must be considered before trying to pass on costs for use of innovative technology. Potential users may be reluctant to pay to try a new system. If a service is free, there is much less risk for the user. Therefore, the decision to raise revenue by passing costs on to users should not be made lightly and may need to be phased in over time.

One simple source of revenue is to charge a modest fee to users of the system. Potential users may already be used to paying fees for such things as satellite downlinks or meeting rooms at remote sites, or use of video services to prepare video taped presentations that will be replaced by the live two-way video system. Outside groups may want to use the system for their own meetings. Groups may want to substitute the compressed video system for use of a satellite delivery system. Others may want to be trained in the use of new technologies. All of these groups may be charged a fee.

There are several ways to make these user fees more acceptable. Certain classes of users can be subsidized by offering them lower fees or no fees at all. For example, those that helped raise the initial funds that paid for the system may get a certain number of free uses or may never have any cost to use the system. Some users may pay a lower fee based on their relationship to the owners of the system. There can even be different levels of service depending on how much support the users need. It is always a good idea to establish the rates and categories of users in advance so that fair and accurate prices can be quoted quickly. Even with published rates, fees can be discounted or waived as a political gesture or to encourage repeated (volume) use of the system.

At Northern Virginia Community College, for example, there is a graduated rate structure for all telecommunications services. Rates are based on the prorated cost of the equipment involved over its expected life plus the personnel costs involved in providing the service. At one end of the graduated scale there are no charges made for most services provided to faculty and staff of the college for college projects. The rates are used to keep track of the relative cost of services provided to the college. Other colleges and state agencies are charged a subsidized rate based only on the prorated equipment costs. Personnel costs are generally not charged. Other outside groups, though, are not subsidized are charged the full costs and may even be charged a surcharge. This means that campus committees and classes cost nothing for the users while another state agency might pay $82 per hour per site to use the system. An outside business group might pay $106 per hour per site. By comparison, the college charges outside groups $44 per hour as a satellite teleconference receive site. The North Dakota Interactive Video Network charges similar rates. Non-university use costs $125 per hour plus $10 per hour for onsite technical support. These rates are relative and are presented only as an example.

Another type of user fee is to charge individual participants. Depending on the nature of the organization and of the events being held over the system, it may be appropriate to charge a participation fee, a special tuition fee or a subscription fee. Just as participants may pay to attend a special lecture or a satellite teleconference, they may pay to attend a compressed video event.

Recent advances in compressed video technology that make it possible to use the telephone companies' regular switched networks on a dial up basis have greatly enhanced the ability of compressed video systems to raise revenue from outside groups. Instead of being limited to predetermined locations on a private, dedicated network, compressed video connections can be handled much like a regular long distance telephone call. Users can select their own sites (as long as they all have compressed video equipment) and let the telephone company make the necessary temporary connections. The user only pays transmission costs for the time used, not for 24 hour dedicated lines.

General Budget Rules

Every organization has its own particular rules and procedures for budget management, and it is impossible to review all the different options here. There are some useful general strategies for managing the compressed video budget that are worth considering. These are applicable no matter what specific procedures are required.

The three most useful budget rules for anyone working with a compressed video system are *consistency, planning* and *record keeping.* There is no question that people are going to ask questions about the costs and benefits of the system. It is very difficult to go back and reconstruct usage and cost figures a year later. Planning for the eventual reports that will have to be written is essential. Planning ahead allows the data to be collected in an organized way. People will want to know how many uses, how many participants, who used the system and for what purposes it was used, how many travel dollars were saved, how many personnel hours were saved, and even how many events were held that might not have been if people had to travel to a central site instead of using the system.

The ease with which meetings can be set up between two locations in different parts of a state or even the country that are part of a network makes it possible for physicians to consult with experts, or engineers to consult with manufacturers, almost instantly. These are often situations where face- to-face meetings would otherwise never have been held or would have taken days to arrange. Being able to look at an X-ray or diagram over a compressed video system offers a tremendous advantage over sending it by fax or overnight mail and then consulting by long-distance telephone call. Keeping track of these uses is extremely important as a way of justifying the costs involved in operating the system

Consistency is another aspect of the same process. Classifying and recording costs in a consistent way along with counting usage in common terms is much easier than going back later and relying on individual's memories about "what did we do about…?", or "why did we…?"

Good cash and spending plans are critical in the early phases of a compressed video project. During the installation and startup phases there will be many unplanned expenditures. Being able to tell exactly how much money is left in the budget is critical to avoid catastrophe. The link between the spending plan and the available budget centers on encumbering funds. Not only is it important to keep track of what bills have been paid, it is also necessary to know what bills are going to come due. Some accounting systems are very complete and track this data quickly and accurately. Other systems focus more heavily on the cash side of transactions and have a considerable lag time between the time of purchase and when the cost data shows up on the accounting system. The compressed video manager can get into trouble if too much reliance is placed on this latter type of system.

In organizations that are going to charge users as a way of funding the compressed video system operation, there is an even heavier demand for accurate record keeping and follow up. Not only must users be billed in a timely manner, it is important to follow up and make sure payment is received. While this may seem obvious, within many organizations internal billings are treated very informally and it can be very difficult to track the transfer of payments between departments.

Though not usually considered part of the financial system, it is important to keep good utilization records on the major compressed video system components. These records should include significant repair histories and costs for each piece of equipment. While system costs will probably be reported in summary fashion rather than component by component, the individual records become very useful in considering whether maintenance agreements would be cost effective and in determining whether a component should be repaired or replaced. This is another area where it is very difficult, if not impossible, to reconstruct the data after several years have passed. Relying on individual staff memories is a very poor substitute for good record keeping.

Maintenance Options and Considerations

One of the largest ongoing operational expenses will be in the area of equipment maintenance. As described earlier and in other chapters, maintenance costs can easily run in the thousands of dollars per unit. There are a number of factors that need to be considered before choosing the appropriate maintenance strategy. Each has its own operational and financial impact.

Maintenance Agreements.

Maintenance agreements provide fixed annual costs for equipment maintenance and repair. The organization pays a set fee up front, and simply calls on the vendor anytime service is required. This straight forward approach offers several advantages. First, it gives the organization a stable maintenance and repair budget since costs are known (at least for major system components). Second, it identifies who is responsible for trouble shooting and repairs. If it were not for the fact that maintenance agreements can be very expensive on compressed video equipment, the decision to purchase them might be very simple.

The pricing of maintenance agreements varies from manufacturer to manufacturer and from vendor to vendor. Typically, maintenance agreement cost is based on a percentage of the equipment's list price. However, there may be discounts, markups or other factors that make this a less than precise rule of thumb. Needless to say, the cost of a maintenance agreement on a compressed video codec can run $2,000 or more, and $5,000 or more per year on a piece of switching equipment. Many organizations are not willing to make this large an investment. These organizations prefer to pay for repairs as they are needed.

Manufacturers and vendors often employ a variety of tactics to encourage the purchase of maintenance agreements. For example, they may include free hardware and software upgrades as part of the maintenance agreement. They may give priority service or provide free loaner equipment to those with maintenance agreements. They may also charge extremely high prices for repairs to equipment not covered by a maintenance agreement.

The alternative to maintenance agreements, paying for repairs as they are needed, is not as simple a procedure as it sounds. Repair charges may be based on *time and materials* or on a flat fee. While a flat fee may seem preferable, since it provides a predictable amount for financial planning purposes, it can mean paying $3,000 for a $100 repair. It may also be necessary to pay both for the time a technician is on site repairing the equipment *and* for the technician's travel time. Even with a flat fee repair charge, the technician's travel time may be an added charge. Compressed video technicians usually have large service areas, so travel time can be significant. The cost of shipping the equipment to the manufacturer may be an added cost if on-site repair is not possible. Some compressed video equipment manufacturers do very little, if any, on-site repair so that all units have to be shipped out if repairs are needed. For complicated or unusual problems, it may be necessary to bring in a technician, at extra cost, to help with trouble shooting the system. Furthermore, upgrades have to be purchased and the organization may even have to pay an additional fee to have them installed. Another consideration is that since equipment not under a maintenance agreement may not get priority service, spare equipment may be needed to replace broken units in order to keep the compressed video system operational. Figure 5.4 provides a list of comparisons between paying for individual repairs or purchasing a maintenance agreement.

Comparing Maintenance Agreements with Paying for Repairs	Maintenance Agreement	Paying for Repairs
Cost per item or per repair	$	$
Priority service	yes no	yes no
Loaner equipment	yes no	yes no
Delivery time for loaner equipment	days	days
Technician response time	hours	hours
Typical repair time	days	days
Shipping costs included	yes no	yes no
Estimated shipping costs	$	$
System upgrades included	yes no	yes no
On-site trouble shooting	yes no	yes no
On-site trouble shooting cost	$	$
Repair warranty length	months	months

Figure 5.4

If an organization has the funds and chooses to purchase maintenance agreements, a number of things should be clearly stated in the maintenance agreement, and the organization should make sure that it takes advantage of these provisions. First and foremost, there must be a written agreement and not just an invoice for the maintenance agreement. The agreement should detail what is covered and what is not covered. For example, will the agreement cover repairs to a codec that has been dropped or one that has a cup of coffee spilled on it?

The agreement should include specifications for the maximum response time it takes to have a technician respond to the site of the broken equipment. If the equipment is not to be repaired on-site, the agreement needs to clearly spell out who is to package the broken equipment, as well as who is to arrange for shipping it and who pays for the shipping. If the vendor or manufacturer is to handle the shipping, the response time to start the process moving should be specified.

If replacement equipment will be provided for equipment being repaired under the terms of a maintenance agreement, the nature of the replacement should be clearly detailed. For example, will the replacement be a loaner with the original piece of equipment to be returned after repairs, or does the customer get to keep the replacement? Will the replacement equipment have to be shipped from some central point, or will a technician bring it *and install it*? If the equipment must be shipped, will it be shipped overnight or by standard transit? Is there an extra cost for overnight service? What happens if there is not a replacement piece of equipment to bring or ship?

The maintenance agreement should specify the expected repair time and provide a process for resolving problems if repairs take longer than the specified time. This is usually referred to as an escalation procedure. Escalation procedures usually provide a chain of command that is either automatically notified or that the customer can notify in the event of repair problems or undue delays. Figure 5.5 lists items that are useful to include in a maintenance agreement.

<u>Useful Maintenance Agreement Items</u>

*   Detailed descriptment of coverages
*   Duration of agreement
*   Maximum technician response time
*   Site responsibilities for shipping broken units to manufacturer
*   Availability of loaner equipment
*   Cost of loaner equipment (including return shipping)
*   Time for delivery and installation of loaner equipment
*   Expected repair time
*   Free upgrades
*   Conditions for item replacement vs. item repair
*   Escalation procedures
*   Problem resolution
*   Renewal procedures
*   Reinstatement or inspection fee for lapsed agreements

Figure 5.5

If an organization changes its mind about a maintenance agreement after the warranty term has expired, manufacturers may require a reinstatement or inspection fee. This fee may be as much as $1,000. The purpose of the fee is to insure that the equipment is in working order before putting the piece of equipment back under a maintenance agreement.

One Final Caution

One way that some organizations attempt to insure a successful installation and start-up of a compressed video system is through the procurement process itself. The bid specifications are written so tightly and with so many mandatory provisions that the procurement process sometimes ends up backfiring on the organization. Instead of ending up with a turn-key installation that provides a smoothly functioning system, the organization is left with nothing or with giant headaches and lots of unanticipated extra costs. Bid specifications must be carefully written and should result from thorough planning. It is the *mandatory* conditions that are the potential culprit.

Mandatories are the provisions that each vendor *must* accept, provide in the system, and quote pricing for. Purchasing agents like mandatory provisions because they supposedly create a level playing field against which competing vendors can be compared. It reduces the amount of judgment that must be employed in evaluating each bid, and makes it easier to defend the selected bid against challenges. These are good things! Program staff like to use mandatories because they insure that the important characteristics of the system are included in the bid price and do not come as surprise extra costs later. The problem comes when an organization gets too cute or too restrictive with the mandatories.

Here are three examples of how mandatory provisions fouled up projects involving new technologies. In one case, all vendors had to provide a price for a four-hour response time for service calls. One vendor did not provide a price since it did not offer that service guarantee. Instead, this vendor felt that its system's redundancy, reliability, and its remote help staff and system diagnostics would be sufficient. This vendor had dozens of satisfied customers with successful installations who could vouch for the accuracy of the company's claims that the lack of a four-hour response time was not a problem. The organization that was evaluating the bids could not even consider this information. Even in light of this new information, they could not decide whether the lack of a four-hour response time was critical. They could not, for example, simply deduct points from that vendor for that particular aspect of the bid and let the other factors fall where they may. The vendor was thrown out of consideration as *non-responsive* because it did not provide all the *mandatory* information. The vendor could have quoted a ridiculous and unrealistic price and remained in the competition.

In another case, a technical error dealing with mandatories was not discovered until after the bids had been opened and the bid price quotes made public. Since all the vendors failed to meet the mandatory condition, even though it was actually an error in the bid package, all bids had to be thrown out. The bidding process had to be started over. The difference this time was that everyone knew the low price, which meant that everyone wanting to bid in the second round had to cut their profit margin significantly. When the new bids were opened and a final award made, the new low bid was significantly below the original low bid. Was this good for the organization putting in the system? The successful bidder had to cut costs somewhere, which is not necessarily a good way to start a relationship.

The final example involves a detailed bid package for a comprehensive voice-data-video system. The bid package was long and complex and asked the vendors for suggested strategies to meet the organization's operational needs. Unfortunately, the specifications were written in such a way that there were dozens of statements that said "should" and others that said "must." It was not always clear which statements were mandatories and which were not. None of the bidders responded to all the mandatories in their initial responses. Unlike the earlier example, in this case they were given a second chance to provide the missing information. Ultimately, though, it became almost impossible to compare and contrast the competing proposals. Instead of creating a level playing field, the mandatories created a impossible maze of confusing responses and potentially fatal challenges. Finally, all the bids were thrown out. In this particular case, though, the time for action had passed and the project had to be scaled down and re-bid to include video only.

The issue is not whether to have mandatory provisions. It is that they should only cover really important legal and operational issues. They must be clearly spelled out, and perhaps even listed separately in such a way that prospective bidders know that they will be thrown out of the competition if they do not accept or answer those provisions. The organization should not be put in the position of having to select a vendor based on a technicality.

Summary

Financial planning is an important part of successful compressed video operation. From the initial planning phase, through procurement, installation and the ultimate upgrade and replacement of the system, there are different financial and management decisions to be made. Even with the best of planning, though, flexibility needs to be maintained in order to cope with the unexpected expenses that come with actual experience using the system. Good planning does not end with a successful installation, either. On-going maintenance and repair issues, along with decisions on whether or not to charge system users fees as a source of revenue, require careful consideration. Haphazard financial planning and sporadic record keeping on system use can have extremely detrimental effects on the ultimate success of the compressed video system.

6

System Management: Evolutions and Patterens

Barbara T. Hakes
Steven G. Sachs

Introduction

A review of emerging utilization of compressed video in various sectors of society reveals developing patterns of system management. Chapter 7 discusses network management structures while this chapter focuses on inter-institutional or agency management. Here we have summarized the trends in administration and management across higher education, K-12, and the private sector based on the user profiles contained in Part II of this book. We received some user profiles too late to summarize them in this chapter so we urge you to refer to Part II, (latest user profiles unclude the University of Oklahoma School of Library and Information Studies and Florida State University).

See Chapter 7

The nation is searching for ways to think, learn and work more efficiently and effectively. Compressed video technology and its next generations offer new ways for us to accomplish these goals. As Guthrie-Morse and Julian (1989) state," doing more with fewer people will be at the heart of institutional survival in the coming decade". In the same article the authors also point out that as institutions begin to carefully examine how they are using human resources they will find strategies for downsizing while simultaneously increasing efficiency. An example from this article,on page 3, cites "A primary reason for change in the traditional mode of instruction might involve the inordinate amount of time spent by faculty traveling to remote sites to teach. For example, West Virginia Northern Community College found that the equivalent of one FTE (full time equivalent) faculty position was spent annually in travel alone."

While many organizations are in the process of learning which new administrative and management schema are most effective for meeting their needs, others cling to administrative structures that were in existence for the management and support of other services. In developing management plans for compressed video, the user profiles reviewed for this chapter show a clear trend away from infrastructure we previously thought we needed up until about 1986.

For example, in higher education we often see compressed video services being placed under the administrative umbrella of instructional

Figure 6.1
This is a typical studio-type classroom. Generally, the instructors/users must give cues to the technicians when they desire close-ups of graphic material or different camera shots. It is a relatively formal setting where students use push-to-talk microphones.

television which usually supports fixed television production studios and the employment of technicians that are necessary to operate such a facility. In institutions which already have studio facilities it may be a smart move to take advantage of existing facilities and infrastructure (see Figures 6.1 and 6.2).

In other institutions we find structures which do not provide production personnel or a large staff of technical support personnel. These organizations are usually groups which entered the compressed video world during the last two years. Such organizations place an emphasis on instructional design and an informal interaction which takes place between originating and remote sites. In the case of the latter, the conference or course facilitator, or instructor, serves also as the "production person" and "system operator" and the emphasis is placed on communication rather than polished studio production. The facilities used for compressed video sites are generally ordinary classrooms as opposed to expensive studio classrooms (see Figures 6.3A and 6.3B). In the January 1991, issue of *Applied Networks*, Caroline Michel states "Early use of video conferencing required the design of a room dedicated to the purpose which could cost upwards of a million dollars for each site. Few organizations could justify such a large investment.   The primary trends driving compressed video technology forward are technological developments, falling transmission prices and standards development and compliance," (P. 1).

The capabilities of various vendors' compressed video products affect the types of facilities necessary and the management structures

Figure 6.2
This is the control room located adjacent to the classroom pictured in Figure 6.1. Facilities such as these can cost $200,000 or more and require a staff of production personnel and technicians.

required to support them. Depending on the needs of an organization there are certain advantages and disadvantages to the administrative and management patterns reviewed in this chapter.

Management - The Infrastructure

The infrastructure necessary to support a compressed video network varies depending upon 1) the users needs and goals, 2) the size of the network, 3) the network configuration, and 4) the types of facilities being used. The infrastructure is a critical element in the success of the compressed video network. Attention to such details as having a telephone in each conference room, a site coordinator (who makes sure the room is reserved, open and ready for the session), a session facilitator and other support system elements are fundamental to the smooth operation of any network.

Figure 6.3A
This is an ordinary classroom equipped with a typical compressed video system which is operated primarily by the user. It is an informal setting in which seating, microphones and cameras can be arranged differently to accommodate the needs of various users.

There is little need for any organization which is just getting started with compressed video and distance learning to start from scratch in finding out how to develop the necessary infrastructure to support the system. Many detailed manuals have already been developed by other users for this purpose. We have included two such guides in Appendices A and B of this book.

See Appendices A and B

Appendix A contains a guide to instructional design for compressed video by Barbara Orde. Appendix B contains a portion of the guide titled the North Dakota Interactive Video Network: A Practical Guide to Teleconferencing and Distance Learning. Another excellent guide has been produced by the Center for Educational Development in the College of Community and Human Services at New Mexico State University, Las Cruces, New Mexico 88003. The guide is written by Tomas E. Cyrs and Frank A. Smith, and is entitled "Teleclass Teaching: A Resource Guide." This guide contains an excellent section on maximizing interactions during a telelecture.

Figure 6.3b
On the few occasions when technical support is required   solutions to problems are often found through a telephone discussion with a technician located elsewhere.

Overview of User Profiles

Colleges and Universities

In some states there is a coordinating group consisting of representatives from institutions of higher education, the public schools and state agencies that develop the policies for use of the compressed video network. For example, Wyoming has a Compressed Video Governance Committee which meets regularly to deal with issues of scheduling, policies and priorities. This summary reveals a number of different management patterns ranging from cooperatives between state agencies, educational institutions and the private sector to independently managed networks for educational institutions. It also reveals differences in management patterns which are directly tied to the types of facilities and equipment being used. Vendor selection also appears to influence the types of facilities and technical support required. Some management and support models are more labor intensive than others. At this point in time, compressed video networks are too pigeon-holed to be convenient for people to hook up nationally. Additionally, development of the new H.261 CCITT standard and compliance with that standard are still in their infancy making it difficult for dissimilar codecs to talk to each other.

North Dakota University

North Dakota had two projects for distance learning that received funding at the same time, the USDA Rural Health Project and a legislative appropriation made to The North Dakota University System. The two groups receiving this funding joined forces to develop and create the existing North Dakota Interactive Video Network (ND IVN). Higher education credit classes comprise 60-80 percent of the usage. Meetings are the next largest usage group. The teacher education department is not presently using the system although their students do take classes over the network.

North Dakota has a state committee which does the scheduling through a network of site coordinators. There is a state director for this committee. According to the user profile (contained in Part II of this book) submitted by Dr. Ron Stammen, from the Educational Administration program at North Dakota State University, the State Board for Higher Education recently delegated the Outreach Services at the University of North Dakota to take the state directorship starting the 1992-1993 school year. Russell Poulin serves as director of the ND IVN. The compressed video schedule is on an accessable file on the Higher Education Computer Network. The University of North Dakota's Outreach Services provides technical support for the compressed video systems and an infrastructure to assist with course development, administration and management. A technician is required to be in or near every room for every event.

The Rural Health Association was given top priority on the network. Level two priority was given to the MBA programs at the University of North Dakota and North Dakota State University/Tri-College University as a cohort program. Additionally, the educational administration program at these institutions was granted level two priority in February 1992. Third priority was granted to credit classes which were not part of an organized degree program; fourth priority to extension programs, non-credit classes and professional development seminars. Fifth priority was given to all other uses. The Higher Education Telecommunications Advisory Committee developed these network priorities.

According to Stammen (user profile, Part II of this book), as of October 1992, rates charged for state government, the private sector and any non-University System entity for using the T-1 based compressed video network are as follows: $125 per hour for scheduling the network and $10 per hour, per site, for technical assistance. There are no transmission costs for educational applications. Continuing Education continues to pay $10 per hour, per site, for technical support for courses they sponsor. The network consists of fourteen interconnected classrooms located in universities or colleges in eleven sites. The network was constructed during the 1989-1990 school year and uses leased telephone lines. Compression Labs Inc. (CLI) codecs are being used. The studio-type classrooms are supported by technicians. ND IVN has initiated a pilot project to explore the use of very small aperture terminals (VSATs) as a potential transmission medium for compressed video.

Wyoming

Planning for the Wyoming compressed video effort began in the fall of 1989, with pilots conducted during the spring of 1991, vendor selection in the fall of 1991 and network activation in the spring of 1992. The University of Wyoming purchased compressed video equipment to be located on each of the state's seven community college campuses. The School of Extended Studies and the College of Education at the University each conduct educational outreach programs. These programs are administered within the University by the respective heads of each of these units; the Director of Extended Studies and for the College of Education, the Associate Dean for Graduate and Continuing Professional Education. These two administrators in turn report to the Associate Provost for Academic Affairs. Together these units plan which courses/programs will be offered each semester over the compressed video network. This schedule is then given to the State Telecommunications Network which schedules the appropriate times from the total time allotted to the University.

In Wyoming, a unique partnership between the University and the public schools, called the Wyoming School-University Partnership (WSUP) uses the compressed video network to cooperatively design professional development programs. Teams of public school professionals and University faculty are funded under a grant from U S WEST to engage in the development efforts. Each team is designing a learning experience which can be offered via compressed video for credit. While the management of these teams and their program development falls under the U S WEST grant, their use of the compressed video network is managed through the University's College of Education. The WSUP is exploring ways to develop a compressed video network that will be compatible with the present network and plans to bring at least three school districts onto the network during 1993. Some of the goals being targeted by the development of this school district network are the offering of preservice and inservice programs; provison of a teacher support system; coaching and mentoring of teacher interns; support of exemplary schools in each district called for by the Centers for Teaching and Learning in each and creation of more equitable curricular offerings across districts. The WSUP has representation on the State's Video Governance Committee.

The University has been given priority on the network because it purchased the equipment for the remote sites at the community colleges. However, the community colleges do provide space on their campuses for this equipment and often provide a site facilitator or coordinator. In other cases, the University pays a site facilitator for each session at the rate of $10.00 per hour. In some instances, students are hired on the Work Study program to serve as site facilitators and other students serve on credit-based internships as distance learning facilitators. Still other students receive one credit hour's worth of free tuition to serve as the facilitator in a course in which they are enrolled. The State's Telecommunications Office provides network operators and scheduling services and space on its leased

AA - Any Agency

CC - First Priority to Community Colleges

SGT - First Priority to State Government Training

UW - First Priority to University of Wyoming

Time	Mon	Tu	Wed	Th	Fri	Sat	Su
7 am	SGT	SGT	SGT	SGT	SGT	AA	AA
8 am	SGT	SGT	SGT	SGT	SGT	UW	AA
9 am	CC	CC	CC	CC	CC	UW	AA
10 am	CC	CC	CC	CC	CC	UW	AA
11 am	UW	UW	UW	UW	UW	UW	AA
noon	UW	UW	UW	UW	UW	UW	UW
1 pm	UW	UW	UW	UW	UW	UW	UW
2 pm	UW	UW	UW	UW	UW	UW	UW
3 pm	UW	UW	UW	UW	UW	UW	UW
4 pm	UW	UW	UW	UW	UW	UW	UW
5 pm	UW	UW	UW	UW	UW	UW	AA
6 pm	UW	UW	UW	UW	UW	AA	AA
7 pm	UW	UW	UW	UW	UW	AA	AA
8 pm	UW	UW	UW	UW	UW	AA	AA
9 pm	UW	UW	UW	UW	UW	AA	AA
10 pm	UW	UW	UW	UW	UW	AA	AA
11 pm - 7 am	AA	AA	AA	AA	AA	AA	AA

Figure 6.4
Priority Time

land-line network (a combination of fiber optic and T-1) at the rate of $40.00 per hour for educational uses (regardless of the number of sites, up to fourteen) and $50.00 per hour for all other users with an additional charge of $10.00 per site, per hour, for each site included beyond one.

A State bid process selected VideoTelecom which provides the H.261 CCITT standard video compression algorithm and its proprietary algorithm. Transmission rates are presently at 384 kbps or 1/3 of a T-1 facility.

Like North Dakota, there is a governance committee. The State's Compressed Video Governance Committee is chaired by a representative from the University, in this case the Assistant to the President for Information Technology. The Committee began meeting in June of 1992, to establish the guidelines, policies, procedures and priorities for scheduling and using the network. Figure 6.4 contains a diagram of how time is presently blocked on a priority basis for use of the network. Each potential user signs a contract with the State Telecommunications office agreeing to book their priority times at least 60 days in advance. A copy of that contract is contained in Appendix D. Any user may schedule the network in any other users' unscheduled time with the understanding that they may be bumped from that schedule by the priority user for that time. Ultimately there may be a fee added for the use of the sites to defray equipment maintenance and depreciation costs. Maintenance is presently provided by University of Wyoming Technicians and the State Telecommunications Office in cooperation with the U S WEST/VideoTelecom technician.

See Appendix D

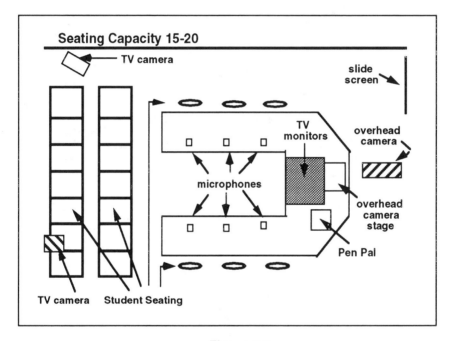

Figure 6.5
A studio-type videoconferencing classroom

Three compressed video facilities are presently managed by the University on its own campus. Two of these facilities are fixed-station video facilities (one for conferences and one for large classes) which were constructed for video production prior to the University's acquisition of compressed video technology (see Figures 6.5 and 6.6). The compressed video equipment, located in the College of Education, has been moved from one location to another. CV classes, can originate anywhere in a building where lines are available to connect the CV system to the network being used. Thus the third facility at the University is a standard classroom which contains a movable unit (see Figure 6.7).

In August of 1992 this unit was moved to another ordinary classroom for a one week long class which enrolled 82 students at nine sites including the University site in the College of Education. The University is able to generate two compressed video sessions at the same time as long as no two sessions require the same sites to receive. When more equipment is installed at the remote sites, program scheduling will be expanded.

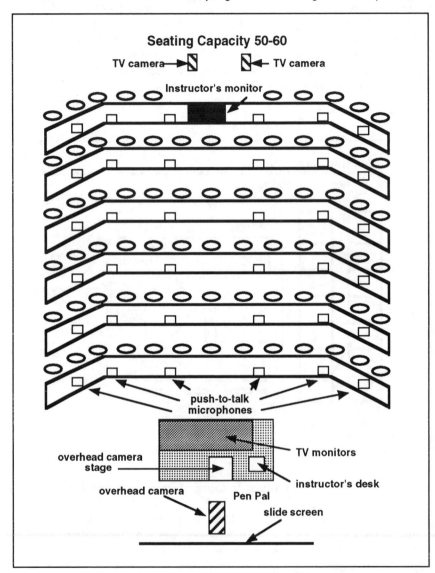

Figure 6.6
A standard studio-type video classroom

Northern Virginia Community College

Unlike Wyoming and North Dakota whose networks were developed through state-wide partnerships, Northern Virginia Community College's (NVCC) successful Interconnect project exemplifies the linkage of five campuses located in different political jurisdictions. Compressed video was the only option available at the time for linking the campuses. No ITFS licenses were available, and open air transmission would have required extremely high towers, which were too expensive and politically unrealistic. NVCC first began using compressed video and a T-1 network for courses in the fall semester of 1990, though it was installed in 1989. The Associate Dean for Instructional Technologies and Extended Learning at NVCC, Dr. Steven Sachs, directs the Interconnect project. The system is operated by NVCC's television center staff. A technician sets up the conference/class

Seating Capacity 15-20; flexibly arranged

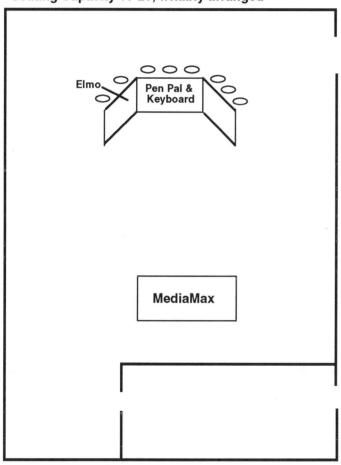

Figure 6.7
A rollabout in a standard classroom

and provides help by phone or directly over the system. In each location a campus audio-visual technician is supposed to turn on the equipment. The students or the instructor operate the system which uses VideoTelecom equipment, and often turn it on and adjust it without waiting for an AV technician. The technician at the NVCC television center, who has other responsibilities, starts each session, but does not monitor the entire session as long as the system appears to be operating well. NVCC has installed simple ABCD switches at some of its sites in order to be able to move the system to different rooms, but found the movement to be too time consuming to be practical. Three campuses have equipment in classrooms that seat 20-25 students each. The two other campuses have the equipment in rooms that seat 12-15 students.

The College leases T-1 lines which are used for compressed video transmission and its own computer data network. The video runs at 768 kbps. All Interconnect switching and scheduling is done from the hub campus at Annandale, Virginia. `The college mainframe computer center provides the multiplexing of data and video signals onto the T-1 line. A 14 port VideoTelecom DVBX is housed in the Television Center, one floor above the computer center. The compressed video classroom of the Annandale campus is also part of the Televion Center complex. In addition to that classroom, one of the VideoTelecom CS-300 codecs is installed in the Television Center control room with the DVBX. This allows the technician to monitor sessions. An additional codec is installed in another room at the Center. This second room is primarily used to receive saellite teleconferences and video tape lectures and is rarely used for classes. Instead, it is used for training and demonstrating compressed video use when not used for other events.

Scheduling of the compressed video system is handled by the Associate Dean's office. He owrks with administrators and faculty at the five campuses to select the courses to be offered on the system each semester. Typically, courses are offred on either a two-day per week schedule for day and afternoon classes, or a one-evening per week schedule. Most classes involve only 2-3 sites plus the control room, though it is technically possible to connect all five campuses. Time is available on the system most afternoons to acommodate campus-to-campus meetings. For the most part, faculty volunteers suggest courses to be offered. Enrollments from students at distant sites are credited back to the instructor's campus. Instructor training and coordination is also managed out of the Associate Dean's office rather than by Television Center staff. One faculty member is released from one class each semester to help with this aspect of system operation.

Since the hub of compressed video network is at the Television Center, it is a relatively simple process to transfer the compressed video signals onto the state's microwave network which connects the public television stations, with the local cable-tv systems and with satellite uplinks. The same connections also work in reverse giving the campuses access to these electronic resources as well.

The ultimate decision on which courses will be received on a campus rests with that campus' Provost and the appropriate academic division. Generally, the courses offered over the compressed video system are ones not available at that campus or not available in that time slot, e.g., day vs. evening. There is no charge for the use of the system by college faculty and staff.

Murray State University

Located in Murray Kentucky, Murray State University began using compressed video for outreach in June of 1990. Like Northern Virginia Community College, the Murray State Network known as the West Kentucky Interactive Telecommunications Network (WKITN) now links a total of eight sites which include community colleges, public schools and the University of Kentucky. The WKITN coordinator, located at Murray State University, is responsible for insuring the successful operation of all parts of the system, the technical infrastructure of the network, all liaison with the telephone company and maintenance of the equipment and software. The network is scheduled through an assistant to the coordinator. The assistant coordinator also manages student assistants and provides instructor training.

Instructional delivery has the highest priority and other applications are scheduled on an equal basis with secondary priority. The Continuing Education office provides instructional support services such as graphic production and pays each network instructor a stipend to develop his/her first course. The WKITN Coordinator is located in the Center for Continuing Education and Academic Outreach at Murray State. The VideoTelecom based network transmits over T-1 facilities at a rate of 384 kbps. The classrooms are ordinary classrooms where instructors or students turn on and operate the equipment. Plans are being made to expand the network to nine more sites.

The California State University

The California State University (CSU) uses a compressed video network between its twenty individual universities to share courses. CSU began use of compressed video in 1989 from the Bakersfield campus studio classroom to a similarly equipped facility located at Tehachapi High School. Some of the codecs being used in the system are early generation CLI and GPT models which require nearly a full T-1 bandwidth for acceptable teaching quality. The user profile we received did not provide a great deal of information about system management. However, CSU is interested in expanding its network and is conducting a three month pilot to explore the potential of compressed video for administrative uses between the Southern California Office of the Chancellor and CSU Sacramento.

Nebraska Educational Telecommunications Commission

Like Wyoming and North Dakota, Nebraska supports a multi-agency network. According to William Ramsay, Director of Engineering and

Technical Services for the Nebraska Educational Telecommunications Commission (NETC), spectrum was available in the NEB*SAT satellite transponder to support a number of digital channels capable of compressed video transmission but these channels could not support full-motion video (see user profile in Part II of this book). Compressed video is used primarily for instruction and involves both two-way and one-way applications. The largest user is the University of Nebraska Medical Center College of Nursing. The state's community colleges also use the system. Most compressed video utilization presently comes from higher education. Technical coordination and scheduling of the network are handled by NETC. The NEB*SAT Coordinating Council establishes network policies. The Governor of Nebraska appoints representatives from the various educational institutions within the state to the Council. The Council makes recommendations to the Nebraska Educational Telecommunications Commission. Since the transponder and equipment are owned by the State of Nebraska there are no time charges for transmission. However, some institutions make a charge to defray personnel costs for providing classroom space. Each institution establishes its own priorities for scheduling and provides its own technical support for the facilities. The State of Nebraska issued a Request For Proposal (RFP) in the fall of 1990 for compressed video equipment. All classrooms utilize VideoTelecom's MediaMax 386 and have multiple monitors and two or three cameras. The level of technical and other support for compressed video varies from institution to institution.

Columbia University

Columbia University began using compressed video in 1986 because users wanted two-way interactive video and it was the only practical alternative at the time. Their CLI system uses AT&T T-1 facilities and is used for higher education course delivery and graduate level engineering courses. Little information was provided about the management of their system.

University of Maryland

Through the coordination of the University of Maryland System Administration Office, a 1991-1992 compressed video pilot project was conducted between three campuses using the University's telecommunications infrastructure. The Maryland Consortium for Distance Education developed a Strategic Plan which serves as a guideline and resource for development and expansion of the Maryland network to eventually interface with national and international compressed video networks. The Maryland Interactive Video Network (IVN) is coordinated and managed through the University of Maryland System Administration (UMSA) office. UMSA invited several interested parties together to see if a partnership could be developed between other remote campuses. The result of that meeting was a large number of requests for class scheduling and equipment purchases. Based on those requests, USMA coordinated a system-wide video network purchase which began in May of 1992 and will continue for two years.

USMA purchased an extra video codec to be used for the Chancellor and staff to participate in state-wide conferences. This codec serves as a backup system in the event of hardware failures in the network. VideoTelecom equipment was selected for the state purchase. The network utilizes T-1 for transmission.

The University of Alabama

According to Phillip Turner, Assistant Vice Chancellor for Academic Affairs, at the University of Alabama, the Intercampus Interactive Telecommunications System (IITS) became operational in September of 1991(see user profiles Part II of this book). VideoTelecom equipment was selected and it uses T-1 lines for transmission. The University pays about $4,000 per month for lines connecting four sites. The lines have been leased for a three year period. The video conferencing equipment is housed in regular classrooms in which very little modification has been done. The equipment is operated by faculty and by students who are either work-study or graduate assistants. There is one half-time technician on call at each site.

Maricopa Community Colleges

Compressed video became operational in the spring of 1990. A demonstration project was held during the spring of 1989, in which NEC VisualLink 3000 units were used to connect two colleges. Maricopa Community Colleges own the equipment and the network so they do not incur additional costs for operation. The maintenance and operating costs are part of the overhead of their network operations. The network uses seven NEC VisualLink 5000 codecs and a "home grown" multi-point control unit. The Maricopa Video Conferencing Network (VCN) is an institutional network. The network has a coordinating committee which meets monthly to discuss scheduling and governance issues.

Most instructors choose to switch between remote sites themselves rather than to direct technical personnel to do the switching. Faculty have expressed a desire to maintain the flow of the instructional process by their own means. When a portable system is put in place in a new room, a technician assists with the set-up. Although some sites have now developed a video conference cart which includes all of the needed components. According to Janet Whitaker, Director of Instructional Technology at Maricopa Community College, Deans and other executives are more likely to use this type of hardware configuration. Technicians are on call, but for the most part during a session the system is operated by the group using the network.

Network scheduling is done centrally and support is provided from the VCN. Requesters for network time are referred to their origination sites for assistance on the use of the rooms. VCN also requests that non-educational users arrange for one of their group to be remote "leaders and greeters." The VCN Coordinating committee helps develop instructional schedules. Scheduling is one of the main concerns and takes place one year in advance of the class offering.

West Virginia Northern Community College

At West Virginia Northern Community College (WVNCC) compressed video was first used in 1988. T-1 lines were used for transmission and CLI codecs were purchased. Support is provided by the Audio Visual Services department and from the Learning Resources Center staff. The facilities are largely instructor driven. The WVNCC campus is linked with the New Martinsville campus. Specially equipped rooms are located at each site.

Oregon Ed-Net

At the writing of this book, the authors/editors had not received-up-to-date information on Oregon's Ed-Net. The state-wide network provides educational telecommunications devices for state agencies, higher education, community colleges, medical centers, business and K-12 schools. In 1991, Hezel Associates was hired at the request of the state legislature, to monitor management, marketing, programming funding, technology implementation and system design, performance, and reliability. Based on Hezel Associates' evaluation report, the legislature approved additional funding. According to StrataGems (February 1991) Oregon Ed-Net "provides three networks: a one-way video, two-way audio satellite network that will be used primarily K-12 schools and state agencies; a two-way video via VSAT Network that uses compressed video on 15 channels; and a terrestrial network for voice and data." Oregon Ed-Net offices are located at 7140 SW Macadam Avenue, Portland, Oregon 97219-3013.

K-12 SCHOOLS

We received only one K-12 user profile. The following are some of the ways in which school districts might benefit from the use of a compressed video network. It can be used for:

1. Staff development.
2. Inservice programs.
3. Exchanging expert teachers beween districts.
4. Collaborative curriculum planning.
5. Receiving credit courses.
6. Bringing in expert scientists or other content persons from college and university campuses to the district.
7. Engaging students in collaborative learning programs among the districts.
8. Conferencing between sites about a variety of issues and topics.
9. Student confrences or meetings.
10. Student contests in various areas.

11. Career counseling for students with professors at a university or community college talking about different programs.
12. Advising about college problems.
13. Modeling outstanding programs for each other.
14. Providing more opportunities for teachers to meet wth each other to improve education in their own programs.
15. Providing equity in curricular offerings across all districts.

These are only a few of the examples of how a compressed video network can be used by districts. Other uses might include sharing of programming for gifted and talented students and administrative applications.

St. Vrain Valley School District

St. Vrain Valley School District, located in Longmont, Colorado, began using compressed video in 1991 between two sites to deliver classes. The sites were St. Vrains' smallest 7-12 school and one of the district's two largest 9-12 schools. The district uses VideoTelecom systems and transmits over dedicated T-1 leased lines. The district plans to incorporate the use of the T-1 facility support its telephone and data system, and to expand its network to all six of its high schools. St. Vrain foresees crossing school district lines in order to connect their schools with other high schools, a community college and a nearby university. The district employs an audiovisual technician who responds instantly to any system failures. The technician has a toll free telephone number provided by U S WEST.

Someone at each school needs to be trained to provide "first alert" assistance for teachers. In one school both the principal and the media specialist have teamed up to provide this support. The district has been working with its Board of Cooperative Educational Services (BOCES) over the past two years to develop other connections in the state.

The Private Sector and
Governmental Agencies

United American Services, Inc.

United American Services, Inc. (UAS), located in Texas, is a court reporting firm which thinks it is very important for attorneys to have the ability to see the person they are interviewing or deposing. A vendor competition was held and VideoTelecom was the system of choice. Their network uses Sprint's fiber T-1 Meeting Channel for its connectivity. UAS pays a monthly access charge of $503. They began using compressed video in 1989. Their system is currently being used mostly by corporations in a conference room environment. UAS provides a conference room much like any attorney's office. Three employees are trained to operate the system on an as-available basis. Sprint's Meeting Channel schedules most of their conferences. They follow the operating policies established by Sprint. Transmission speeds vary according to their customers' desires.

Joint Warfare Center, Hurlburt, Florida

In an article titled "Joint Warfare Center Uses Mediaconferencing To Enhance War Games," the editor of Communication News (October 1991) describes the following application. The U. S. Military has long-standing experience with the use of wargame software and state-of-the-art computers for training. The Joint Warfare Center recently (1990) blended compressed video conferencing with its computer simulation training. It purchased six PC-based, VideoTelecom compressed video systems and a multiway switching system. To meet the Center's requirements for portability and durability, custom-made rugged carrying cases were constructed for all of the units. The "mediaconferencing" system allowed the Central Command to utilize a wargame exercise through the Joint Warfare Center immediately prior to their deployment to Operation Desert Shield. The exercise was called Internal Look '90. It involved a number of high-level staff officers participating from locations scattered throughout the nation. By using the mediaconferencing system the Joint Warefare Center was essentially able to "transport" exercise staffs located in geographically dispersed locations and put them in the same room. While this article describes more of an application than a management structure it does have implications for management in the sense that it is possible to assemble a somewhat mobile videoconferencing system. As compressed video technology decreases in size and weight and increases in functionality true portability is becoming a reality.

References

Guthrie-Morse, B. & Julian, C. The Small College's Tool For Effectiveness: Telecommunications. *AACIC Journal.* October 1989. pp.42- 45.

Joint Warfare Center Used Media Conferencing to Enhance War Games. *Communications News,* October 1991. P.23

Michel, Caroline J. Videoconferencing: Out of the boardroom and into the workgroup. *Applied Networks.* January 1991. Volume 4 Number 1 p. 1.

"Oregon Legislature Authorizes Ed-Net Spending" StrataGems. Hezel Associates. Sycracuse, New York. Vol., 1 No. 3, February 1991. P. 1.

7

Patterns of Electronic Networking

Barbara T. Hakes
Richard T. Hezel

Introduction

This chapter provides an overview of network governance patterns and carriers for compressed video being employed across higher education, K-12, and the private sector. This overview is based on the user profiles contained in Part II of this book and on an annual telecommunications survey conducted by Hezel and Associates for Annenberg/Center for Public Broadcasting (CPB). As compressed video applications emerge, new models will develop. Network governance patterns include public broadcasting groups, state telecommunications administration divisions, higher education institutions, state departments of education, private corporations/business, and federal government as coordinators of training or educational telecommunications. Based on the user profiles contained in Part II of this book, we discuss selected network designs and governance patterns and their relative advantages and disadvantages along with the advantages and disadvantages of the carriers being employed, such as T-1, fiber optic land lines, satellite, and very small aperture terminals. Since these terms may be foreign to some readers we have attempted to discuss them in ways which the non-technical reader can make use of the information. Additionally, we have provided a glossary at the end of this book which is partially based on Harry Newton's *Telecom Dictionary*. Another extremely useful resource is the International Video Teleconferencing Source Book published by AT&T in 1992. The source book contains a section on video conferencing tips as well as alphabetized listings of videoconferencing facilitated by country, state and city. Additionally, international demonstration facilities are included. Each listing provides the video telephone number (if available), the contact person, contact phone number, transmission rates, the brand and model of codec, encryption type, carrier provider and whether or not it is a public or private facility. Copies of this source book are priced at $4.99 per copy (for shipping and handling) and can be ordered through the following address: International Video Teleconferencing Source Book, P. O. Box 9005, Paterson, NJ 07509-9936.

A user profile for U S WEST Communications was received from Laura Simmons-Lewis just prior to submitting the book for publication. It is

See
Glossary

contained in Part II and provides an excellent over view of a very large corporate videoconferencing network.

Patterns of Network Governance

Based on the user profiles which we were able to compile (Part II) we identified six patterns of network governance or coordination. Richard Hezel, (1990) in his publication *Statewide Planning for Telecommunications in Education* 1990, identified four of the same patterns of governance we identified from user profiles, which are: public broadcasting groups, state telecommunications administration divisions, higher education institutions, and state departments of education serving as telecommunications coordinators. While Hezel's survey addressed educational telecommunications of all forms in the public sector, we have included training and development in the private sector and governmental agencies and have focused on compressed video. In fact corporations and governmental agencies were among some of the first users of compressed video.

Hezel (1990) poses the following questions and provides this overview of governance structures in educational telecommunications.

1) Is there an ideal structure for governing educational telecommunications?

2) Should telecommunications systems be planned through existing agencies or a consortium of agencies?

A variety of telecommunications planning and coordinating structures are used across the states, and the states continue to use idiosyncratic systems for governing and coordinating the operations of educational telecommunications. There is evidence, however, of a growing desire to adopt planning models from states that have exhibited the greatest success in their distance learning systems.

Public Broadcasting Organizations as Coordinators

Thirty-one states have statewide educational broadcasting authorities, usually as public station licensees. The authorities or commission are typically independent agencies (e.g., Iowa, Kentucky, Maine, Oregon), but many have formal or informal associations with the State Department of Education or the major state university system (e.g., Nebraska).

Coordination of Educational telecommunications public broadcasting licensees has advantages and disadvantages. On the one hand, public broadcasting licensees have an educational orientation and the technical facilities and expertise to make programming broadly available. Many broadcasters are also keeping current on alternative educational technologies so they can help educators in technology selection and utilization.

On the other hand, the programming and technical priorities of public broadcasting licensees sometimes run counter to the priorities of other agencies within the state. Community licensees, for example, often place greater importance on adult and cultural programming than on formal instructional programming, whereas stations licensed to state departments of education can be expected to provide more instructional and in-service programming for K-12 schools than for colleges.

Educational institutions have a natural affinity with public broadcasting systems. Educational institutions have curriculum and programmatic expertise to complement broadcasters' technical expertise. Coordination by public broadcasting authorities needs to be facilitated where a state public broadcasting system exists and the state commission holds licenses for all or most of the stations. In those cases, the public broadcasting authority is typically closer to the state government and its agencies and their mission. Consequently, the ability to coordinate telecommunications facilities for education is greater.

In many instances, however, public broadcasting organizations have restructured their commitments to broadcast instruction. Many licensees, especially community licensees, have development a great interest in "public" and cultural programming than in traditional educational or instructional programs. Some public broadcast stations are attempting to help agencies find new avenues of delivery of K-12 programming (e.g., through video cassettes and overnight feeds to release the daytime broadcast schedule for branch audiences programs.

State Telecommunication Administration Division as Coordinators

Some states have assigned the coordination of all state telecommunications procurement to an office or division with a department of administration, budget, or planning. Such divisions are often given responsibility for procurement of telephone systems and provision of telecommunications networks for state agencies and, in some cases, for public elementary, secondary, and post-secondary educational institutions. Degree of control and coordination varies considerable. In some states telecommunications divisions assert specific control by assessing institutional needs and making final decisions to purchase equipment and services on the basis of judged efficiencies. In other states, the divisions serve a coordinating function, assisting schools, educational departments, and higher education in their own needs assessments while attempting to obtain cost-effective service for institutions. In still other states, educational institutions, independent of the divisions, develop their own telecommunications systems.

One of the major advantages of coordination by telecommunications divisions is that the division can cut across artificial boundaries, turf issues, and territoriality that prevent educational institutions from planning together. Many educators have a distaste for forced cooperation, but the distaste can be reduced by offering special incentives, such as cost-savings on telecommunications. Generally, telecommunications division coordination is most satisfying to all parties where each agency has an appreciation and an understanding of the others' needs, and especially where the telecommunications administrator takes educational programmatic needs as the first priority in establishing a system.

Higher Education Institutions as Coordinators

There are very few cases where higher education institutions provide statewide planning coordination. In many cases, the higher education institution develops telecommunications plans, then invites other institutions to cooperate on the planning. In numerous states, colleges and universities are absorbed in developing new educational markets, and telecommunications systems provide the means for delivering higher education to advanced placement high school students and home bound adults. As a result, telecommunications planning by higher education institutions is often fragmented. In few states do many or all post-secondary institutions participate in the planning, so statewide consensus is difficult to achieve. Furthermore, colleges and universities are notoriously independent in adopting technology. As in 1987, many universities appear to be installing satellite uplinks with no clear pragmatic need. Some respondents felt that there has been a sense of competition among colleges on the acquisition of technology. Such competition is exacerbated by the granting of special status with concomitant privileges to some state universities. Such favored status sometimes results in inequitable distribution of telecommunications resources to particular colleges. Even coordinating boards, which often have a mandate to equalize programs relative to resources, cannot completely check universities' development of telecommunication resources, and private colleges and universities that receive little or no state funding are often beyond the control of coordinating boards.

Some educators defend individualistic technology development in higher education in the name of a free marketplace in educational telecommunication. Initiates are most likely to originate at individual schools, not from coordinated activities, it is felt.

State Departments of Education as Coordinators

State Education Departments are usually bound by principles of equity in education, so that, on the face of it, they tend to treat their constituents in a fairly uniform way. Since there is, hypothetically, an equal relationship between the department and each school district, the department is usually a good focus of telecommunications planning. Furthermore, most education departments have the personnel to develop and implement technology initiatives. In states like Kentucky and Virginia the departments of education are providing broad funding to all school districts for the installation of satellite reception equipment.

In education departments where technology personnel are not available, uses of technology tend to be more restricted and traditional, and the department cannot be expected to provide technology leadership. In such cases, individual school districts emerge as innovators, after which schools cluster together to form ad hoc constortia.

Many school districts have individual arrangements with colleges or universities to receive advanced placement and enrichment courses via telecommunications systems. Those individual arrangements tend to frustrate planning for a single educational telecommunications system, but it appears to satisfy the immediate needs of the school districts. States such as New York, as noted above, offer technology initiatives to encourage ad hoc connections, especially where several school districts or educational service units have formed consortia to promote telecommunications efficiencies.

Nationwide Growth in Compressed Video

The potential for the use of compressed video systems is being reviewed by educational institutions, business, governmental agencies and others at an ever increasing rate. As the communications industry moves

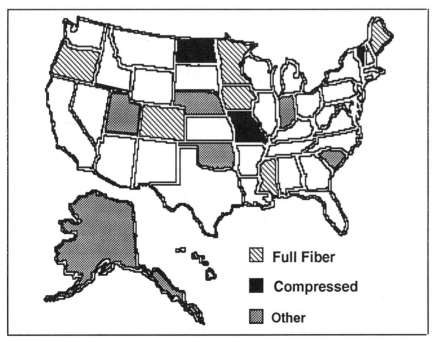

Figure 7.1
State Video Backbones Implemented or Planned 1990

away from analog to digital video, the relative costs of being able to support two-way video networks are decreasing rapidly. The University of North Dakota Interactive Video network published the following figures (7.1 and 7.2) which illustrate the growth in compressed video utilization and the networks that are supported by a state backbone.

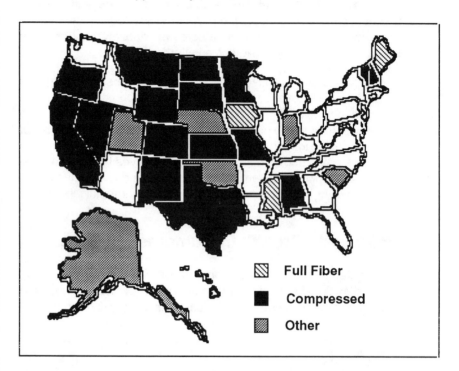

Figure 7.2
State Video Backbones Implemented or Planned 1992

Based on the user profiles contained in Part II we have the following observations to make. The majority of compressed video users are transmitting via T-1 facilities which may be a combination of fiber optics and regular T-1 land lines. Most are transmitting at a rate of 384 kbps which uses one quarter of the capacity of a T-1 with the remainder of the space being available for multiple video conferences or other uses. Where dedicated T-1 service is being leased by organizations, these groups often transmit compressed video at higher bandwidths and/or additionally support their own telephone and data transmission networks. Many users of dedicated T-1 service express their frustration at not being able to get fractional billing for the 1/4 T-1 space they utilize. If carriers would consider providing fractional billing, demand for compressed video service would increase dramatically.

The new inverse multi-plexers now make fractional billing possible by accessing 56K lines. The latest model codecs also support this capability.

Another force making the 56K network available is that organizations are turning to it to handle peak-load data transmission instead of leasing excess capacity on T-1s that is not used.

Some groups are exploring the potential of very small aperture terminals (VSAT) which can send and receive data for the transmission of compressed video. One state among our user profiles owns its own satellite transponder and equipment and makes no charge for transmission of compressed video. For readers who may be interested in a detailed discussion of T-1, we recommend *The Guide to T-1 Networking: How To Buy, Install and Use T-1, from Desktop to DS-3*. The guide was written by William A. Flanagan in 1990 and is published by Telecom Library Inc.

Depending upon how networks are configured, the costs of transmission vary. Dedicated T-1 networks for compressed video often are forced to charge a relatively high per hour rates in order to cover their monthly billing for the service from the telephone companies. If networks can be shared by state agencies, educational institutions and the private sector more economical per hour rates may be available for users. Daly (1992) provides an excellent discussion of compressed digital video networks. Network types include private, public, public switched, and integrated services digital networks (ISDN). The majority of the networks represented through the user profiles are primarily leased T-1 services which are used by the lease holder to meet a specific need and in turn are subleased to other users or employed to support other data communications needs of the organization.

Several institutions already have or are planning layered networks. "Layer networks" or "bundling" are terms used to describe networks which handle a range of voice, video and data networks for the network users. Other network designs may be dedicated to a single use. Examples include a network which bundles audio conferencing (via telephone), compressed video conferencing (via T-1, digital microwave or VSAT), computer conferencing (via digital microwave ,T-1), and multimedia conferencing (via T-1, digital microwave or VSAT). Such layering provides a redundancy of connections which can continue if one system should fail. Planning layered networks is highly complex and requires careful thought regarding the proximity of physical facilities and scheduling. Some institutions conduct simultaneous audio and video conferences. Those who have access to the course/conference at a compressed video site receive video while other sites are added to the course/conference by audio conference only. Public schools and other organizations are working out arrangements with local cable companies to use their facilities for the transmission of educational compressed video courses or programs. The use of two video switches is providing some networks with a lot of flexibility and results in several advantages including reduced T-1 costs, needed redundancy, multiple simultaneous interactive video sessions, extra connections to outside agencies, and a direct interface to future reservation systems using switched 56 service on demand.

Overview of Selected Compressed Video Networks

North Dakota

In North Dakota, two projects were simultaneously funded; one was the North Dakota School of Medicine and the North Dakota State University Extension Service for delivery of health majors to rural areas. The other was a legislative appropriation which was made to the North Dakota University System Office. The two projects joined forces and formed a Joint Technical Subcommittee to explore how the two groups could support the same network. An analysis was conducted of alternative delivery technologies including phone conferencing, one-way satellite video, and analog two-way video. We quote the following observations from Russell Poulin's user profile. Russ Poulin directs the ND Interactive Video Network

Phone Conferencing

North Dakota used (and still uses) phone conferencing. Continuing medical education and meetings have been the primary user of these services. While many applications work very well through audio-only delivery, others are enhanced by including a video element. Addressing rural health needs was a main goal of the grant funding received. The ability to see and demonstrate concepts was considered an important addition to that which could only be done through phone conferencing .

One-way Satellite

Satellite has the advantage of covering a wide geographic area with relatively little equipment investment at receiving sites. However, there were several disadvantages for the applications we envisioned :

Inappropriate Technology for Goals — One of the major goals is to teach credit classes to specific sites with limited to small enrollments. A satellite's footprint would cover not only all of North Dakota, but also most of the rest of North America. This is technology overkill for a class of twenty students. The temptations of wide delivery areas and cost factors drive usage to courses that enroll hundreds of people. Using one-way satellite for meetings, non-credit seminars or other low volume uses is cost prohibitive.

Multiple Origination Sites — Each of our campuses has something of value to offer to the others. The expense of an uplink would allow only one origination site. With a compressed video network each campus has an equal ability to originate programming.

Production Costs — To be effective, one-way video requires a higher level of production than two-way video. Since interaction is limited, the presentations need greater attention to television techniques and instruction style. Instruction becomes more of a performance than with other technologies.

Transmission Costs and Availability — Transmission costs have remained high. Scheduling transponder time is another factor. Often the transponder time is not available at the same time that the room or the instructor is available. Demand for satellite time is increasing and there have been considerable writings, of late, on the looming supply problem.

Analog Two-way Video

During the decision-making process a group of rural phone cooperatives was very adamant about bidding a fiber optic, analog, two-way video network. This option was rejected for the following reasons:

Cost — The phone cooperatives provided a bid for their proposed solution. To reach the proposed sites, the transmission costs were six times greater than the lowest bid for compressed video. When including the higher start-up costs for compressed video along with the transmission costs, the ratio was 4.5 times greater than the compressed (video) bid. Additional campus cabling costs for fiber optic lines would also have been incurred, and are not figured into the above ratio.

Availability — Due to fiber optic unavailability in some parts of the state, the cooperative also proposed delaying installation for one year while it buried cable.

Flexibility — The analog model was based on a model that allows a maximum of four sites to connect simultaneously. With compressed video, up to 14 sites can be included in a single conference.

The Future — The communications industry is abandoning analog solutions for digital ones. The promise of combining voice, data, and video transmission signal through the use of digital technologies is tremendous.

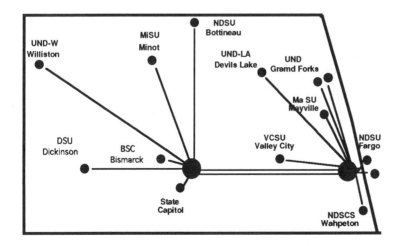

Figure 7.3
The North Dakota Compressed Video Network

It is better to struggle with the infancy of an emerging technology than the death pangs of an old one.

Transmission of North Dakota's compressed digital video occurs over a T-1 network which in some places is fiber optic line, but in most places is normal T-1. Costs for using the network are $125 per hour plus $10 per site, per hour for technical support. Figure 7.3 depicts the North Dakota compressed video network. North Dakota is also exploring the potential for VSAT satellite transmission.

Virginia

Virginia provides a good example of the pigeon-holed phenomenon indicative of compressed video systems nation-wide. Virginia already operates several electronic networks for distance education. There is a microwave network connecting the public television stations and satellite uplinks across the state. A number of the larger colleges and universities are also connected through this network, which provides one-way video and two-way audio for a variety of graduate-level engineering and upper division courses, along with numerous special courses for K-12 instruction. The community colleges have not made much use of this network.

A second network is located in the southeastern part of the state and makes use of ITFS, public television and cable television to link educational institutions as well as student homes. The community colleges in that region offer traditional one-way video, teleconferences on this network.

A third network is located in the northern part of the state. Northern Virginia Community College and George Mason University are linked by microwave, ITFS and direct connection to that region's cable-TV systems. They use this network to offer traditional one-way video telecourses.

Finally, there are the compressed video networks. One is located in northern Virginia. Another is located in southwest Virginia. A third may be located in the western part of the state. None are connected to each other! In fact, there is presently no way to directly connect all 23 of Virginia's 23 community colleges with each other.

Statewide emphasis has not been placed on two-way video networks. Historically, the emphasis has been on public broadcasting, satellite uplinking, ITFS, microwave, and statewide voice and data systems. For a long time, the state was very reluctant to even consider compressed video outside of the project at Northern Virginia.

Recognizing this problem, the Virginia Community College system has undertaken a planning effort to develop a network design for voice, data, and video by December 1993. Without such a plan, it is feared that additional hundreds of thousands of dollars will be spent building systems that can never be effectively interconnected, even though interconnection will be essential to delivering work force training and a full range of courses to every region of the state. Given the mountainous topography in the western part of the state, it is likely that compressed video will be a significant component of this network.

Northern Virginia Community College, does not pay any transmission costs. These T-1 costs are paid by the Computer Center since it must maintain the T-1 lines to interconnect the campuses with the mainframe.

Wyoming

The Wyoming State Network (an open architecture system) currently provides a major telecommunications highway using digital T-1 facilities leased from the telephone company and connected to various strategically installed multi-plexors and video codec units for the rapid transmission of data and compressed video (see Figure 7.4). The Wyoming State Network is currently used to connect the cities of Cheyenne, Laramie,

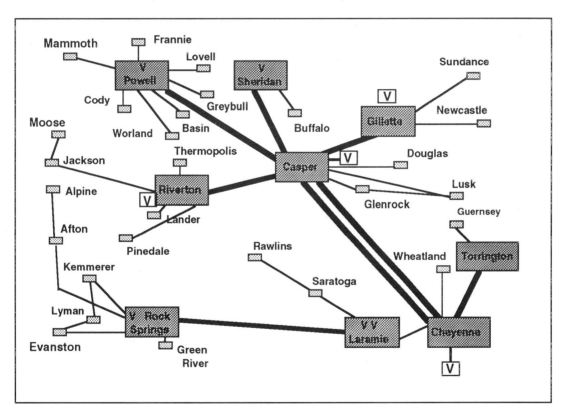

Figure 7.4
The Wyoming State Network

Rock Springs, Casper, Riverton, Powell, Sheridan, and Gillette through a multi-point interactive compressed video bridge using 384 kbps.

See Part II
Section 1

In Wyoming, the impetus for creating a compressed video network came from the state's only four year institution of higher education, the University of Wyoming, the public schools and the state's eight community college campuses. The State's Division of Telecommunications Office agreed to provide space on its existing data network for compressed video transmission. At this time only land lines are being used for transmission. In an effort to assure compatibility of compressed video technology at all potential sites, a statewide committee, consisting of representatives from the aforementioned groups, issued a request for bid to compressed video vendors. In November, 1991, a state contract was offered to VideoTelecom. Because all educational institutions in the state worked collaboratively with state government to build the compressed video network, costs have been minimized. The cost of using the network is $40 per hour for educational applications (point to point or up to 14 locations) regardless of the number of sites. For governmental agencies and other users, the cost is $50 per hour for the first site with an additional $10 charge per hour for each site included beyond the first location. Clearly, Wyoming through this collaborative effort has developed a cost-effective system. As of January, 1992, all of the State's community colleges were linked with the University. Several public school districts are planning to develop their own networks which in turn will be connected to the state backbone (see Figure 7.4). In Wyoming, fractional billing for T-1 service is not yet a reality, so reaching small rural communities is still a problem. The state is, however, working on a variety of options with the major telephone company and the independent carriers to address this

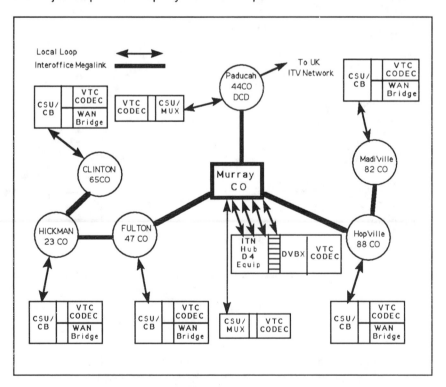

Figure 7.5
The West Kentucky Interactive Network

problem. A statewide governance committee consisting of representatives from state government, the University, the community colleges, the public schools and the private sector is over seeing the operation of the network which is managed by the State Telecommunications Office.

West Kentucky Interactive Telecommunications Network

Murray State University decided to use compressed video over other available options to avoid having to develop and support the entire delivery infrastructure, and to insure that geographic location would not restrict institutions from becoming part of the network. Murray State decided to use the public switched telephone. Other options to compressed video were studied such as analog delivery over fiber optic lines, microwave, ITFS, and satellite delivery. Approximately $80,000 is budgeted annually to cover line charges, maintenance, and to support two full time employees and numerous part time student workers. Figure 7.5 diagrams the West Kentucky Interactive Telecommunications Network.

See Part II

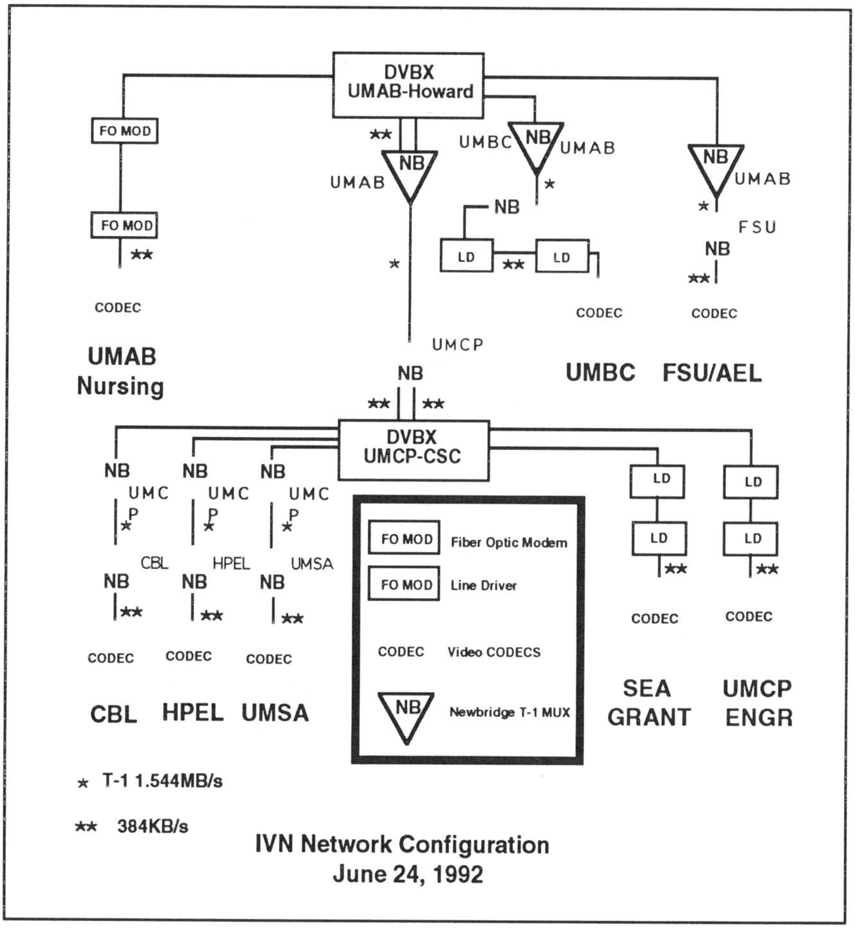

Figure 7.6
IVN Network Configuration

University of Maryland

The interactive Video Network (IVN) will be expanded to include the western and eastern geographic regions of the state. Figure 7.6 and 7.7 depict the current University of Maryland Network. The University intends to expand its video conferencing network to include computer applications, remote printing, facsimile, and eventually packet switched networks connected to LANS and interfacing with multimedia applications.

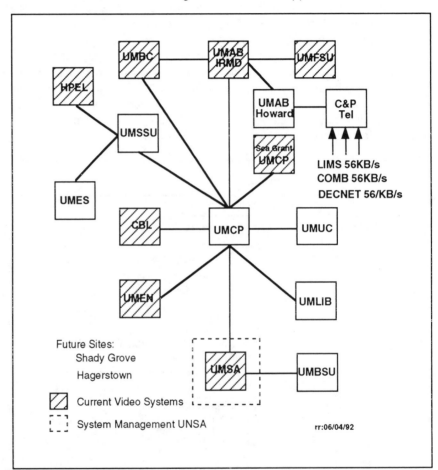

Figure 7.7
University of Maryland Intercampus Telecommunications System

References

Daly, E. *We've Got To Start Meeting This Way.* KJH Communications 2nd Edition. 1992

Hezel, R. *Statewide Planning for Telecommunications, 1990.* Annenberg/ CPB 1990

Newton, H. *Newton's Telecom Dictionary.* Telecom Library Inc. 4th edition. 1991

8

Vendor Selection: Judging the Alternatives

The Multiple Vendor Shoot Out Versus the Lone Vendor Take Over

Barbara T. Hakes

Introduction

At the heart of making any decisions about the selection of a compressed video vendor is needs assessment. This chapter discusses needs assessment and provides a generic needs assessment format which can be adapted to any user's interests. Additionally, the chapter provides an overview of vendor selection for compressed digital video being employed across higher education, public schools and the private sector. As compressed video applications emerge new models will develop.

All too commonly, there is no systematic process involved for selecting compressed video equipment. In other cases, there have been carefully planned "shoot outs" involving all of the major vendors of compressed video technology and tightly designed bench marks which each must meet.

Needs Assessment

In this section we discuss needs assessment. Appendix E, contains a generic needs assessment tool which can be adapted to meet most users' interests. It is designed to obtain a community profile for systems which will be supported by a large number of users from different sectors of society. Needs assessment is usually the first step in acquiring any new technology, however, if organizations simply examine their travel budgets, which support various activities, and analyze how many dollars and how much human productivity can be saved through the elimination of certain travel, this analysis itself will often justify the installation and use of a compressed video network. Daly (1992) provides an excellent model for conducting a cost/benefit analysis in business, industry and governmental agencies.

See Appendix E

**See
Chapter 10**

**See
Appendix H**

We thought it would be helpful to provide you with some lessons we learned at the University of Wyoming which are useful in developing and conducting a needs assessment. The issues of how and by whom your compressed video equipment will be used are critical to vendor selection. Yet, needs assessment is difficult when potential users have had no previous experience with compressed video equipment and a truly interactive video and audio link. As we point out in Chapter 10: Issues in Course Design; when asked "How would you like to use compressed video?" the unfamiliar, future user will reply, "Well, what can it do?" To help us show potential users what it could do, we conducted a pilot in the spring of 1991. Appendix H contains guidelines for conducting a pilot. During that pilot, at the University of Wyoming, in the College of Education , we discovered several issues which can assist in conducting a needs assessment. By providing potential users with an opportunity to gain first hand experience with a two-way interactive video network a much more accurate needs assessment can be obtained. Over a three month period four vendors loaned their equipment to the College for a live point to point link with a high school located 250 miles from the University. The vendors supplied their "roll around" models for a "test drive" at no charge. All vendors' equipment was operated at 386 kbps, although we also did a test at 112 kbps. The State Telecommunications office provided the T-1 link for the pilot. The facilities at each site were ordinary classrooms which were made available to any and all potential users. Community college faculty and administrators, public school teachers, students and administrators, university faculty and students, private corporations, service groups and agencies, legislators and others participated in the pilot for a wide range of purposes. Our observations throughout the pilot revealed the following:

1) When using the system for the first time people didn't actually realize it was interactive until they themselves interacted with someone at the remote site. Prior to that interaction they sat passively in the room as if they were watching their television set at home.

2) Persons who used the system more than once began to suggest all kinds of potential applications for the technology.

3) People who used the system on a frequent basis regularly brought new people with them to share the experience.

4) After about 20 minutes of interaction, most users said they no longer noticed the slight image blur with rapid movements. As compression algorithms are improved this blurriness is becoming less and less detectable.

5) Those who actually controlled the system (i.e. moved and focused cameras, displayed visuals, or used interactive graphics) became very animated and excited about the technology.

6) When the pilot was over, people were actually upset that the compressed video link was no longer available.

In short, the pilot helped us obtain a far more accurate picture of what capabilities we needed and what kind of support and training would be required to successfully use the system. Any group considering the purchase of compressed video technology would be well advised to spend some time with various vendors products and test a wide range of applications.

As Wayne Vickers, Director of Instructional Television and Computer Services at Florida State University, said in the user profile contributed to Part II of this book, "If there is one thing we could recommend for anyone considering video teleconferencing in the classroom, it would be to become familiar with all of the options available. Costs are coming down and features are going up, which is always a good situation for resource constrained institutions."

See Part II, Section 1

Prior to, and during the pilot (in the spring of 1991), we also talked to people with other institutions around the country who were already using compressed video. When we compared the information gleaned from those interviews with our experiences with the pilot, we discovered that in higher education there were some frequently held assumptions regarding how and by whom the compressed video technology should be used. These assumptions include:

● the system will be used only for course delivery;

• all faculty will lecture;

• television studio type classrooms with special lighting, fixed seating and push to talk microphones are needed;

● the instructor will need to prepare a shooting script;

• technicians are required to operate the system;

• faculty don't want to operate the equipment—it's too complicated;

● we must train remote site facilitators;

• the equipment must stay in one location;

• public school students will be turned off by the technology because it offers a less than broadcast quality picture;

• elementary school children can't operate the equipment;

• some face-to-face meetings are necessary.

While we admit there are exceptions, our experiences during and since the pilot have proven all of these assumptions to be largely incorrect.

Here is what we have discovered.

The system will be used only for course delivery.

To date our compressed video network has been used for conferences, curriculum meetings, state-wide planning committees, governmental agencies, advising, masters thesis and doctoral dissertation defenses, coaching and mentoring distant student teachers, professional development, provision of remote site public school experience for teacher education students, cooperative learning with students at different sites working on a problem together (public schools and college), team teaching sharing an expert and conducting laboratory experiences. Other potential applications on the horizon are career counseling, health care training for rural communities, OSHA and firefighters training to name a few.

All faculty will lecture.

Some faculty may try to lecture. Training is critical for an interactive system. If faculty lecture, they will be dead in the water in five minutes. If certain faculty only want to lecture they should be encouraged to develop mail out video tapes which can later be discussed by audio teleconference. Our experience has involved many faculty who conduct small group activities over the compressed video network and others who conscientiously work on techniques to stimulate the interactivity which justifies the use of the compressed video network.

Television studio type classrooms with special lighting, fixed seating and push-to-talk microphones are needed.

The University of Wyoming has studio classroom facilities and we do have one codec connected to those facilities. However, such facilities are far from being necessary to use the compressed video system we purchased. We have a second codec in a roll about unit in the College of Education. We have moved that unit from the room it is in to a larger room in our Laboratory School which has no special lighting or acoustic treatment. The remote sites, of which there are presently eight, are all configured differently and are of varying suitability in terms of lighting, acoustics and size (see Figure 8.1). In those facilities we can arrange the room to meet the needs of the group using it - for whatever purpose. We find the push-to-talk microphones located in some of those facilities to be a problem because users forget to turn off their mics and too many open mics can cause audio feedback on the network. Pancake or flat type microphones, while always open, can be muted at each site by one command from the instructor/ operator, alleviating the need for each user to remember to turn off her/his microphone. We've discovered there is no need to invest large amounts of money in studio-like facilities. The less formal arrangement of these sites as opposed to the studio setting appears to be more conducive to interaction. If mobility is a consideration, the user will need to make certain that the location to which the CV unit will be moved contains the necessary

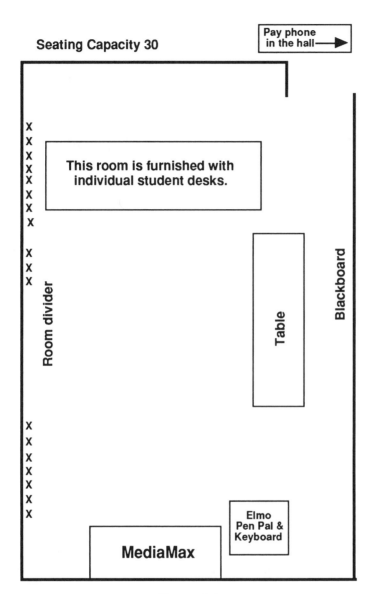

Figure 8.1
A diagram of a facility in which seating and other elements of
the room can be arranged to meet the needs of the users.

connections to the network being employed. For example, if landlines are being used check to see that there is a T-1 drop in the room. Will there be a second telephone available for trouble-shooting and other communications?

The instructor will need to prepare a shooting script.

Where video production is the goal this is a necessity. With compressed video classes the focus should be placed on instructional design and the training of session facilitators to induce interactivity. Since the facilitator, or a volunteer, can switch to graphics or printed material and operate the camera(s) with out the aid of a technician sessions are far more candid and relaxed than in the formal television studio setting where cues must be given to camera people to use graphics and change camera shots. In the compressed video environment the instructor can focus more on teaching and less on production.

Technicians are required to operate the system.

Depending upon how a given user intends to install their system, system operators may or may not be necessary. In our television classroom technicians are necessary to operate the cameras from a central control room. In our facility located in the College of Education, and at our remote sites, the session facilitator or instructor, volunteer students, or paid site coordinators operate the system. Some students have objected to operating the system because they feel they miss part of the class by concentrating on the operation of the equipment. We have, however, found that if instructors distribute class notes and other handouts ahead of time, and they aren't lecturing where students must take notes, this is far less of a problem. The degree of user friendliness varies from vendor to vendor. We have a turnkey system which is very user friendly.

Faculty don't want to operate the equipment—it's too complicated.

Some do and some don't—but most do like to operate the system after they have become familiar with it because it places them in control of their materials and their session.

We must train remote site facilitators.

We make a distinction between site coordinators and site facilitators. Coordinators are responsible for scheduling the CV room and making certain it is open and ready for use by the scheduling group. Facilitators actually help conduct the session itself. Facilitators perform such responsibilities as powering up the system, operating cameras and peripheral devices, collecting and distributing materials, and sending and receiving faxes (see figure 8.2). Sometimes, the site coordinator also serves as a facilitator.

While it is extremely useful to have trained facilitators available on call for the remote sites, it is not always necessary. We have found we can train someone who has not previously seen the equipment to perform basic functions quite easily in about 10 minutes. What is important is that each remote site should have a telephone installed in the room with the compressed video equipment. This allows the originating site to talk with any remote site that for some reason may not have their compressed video system operating. It also allows the remote site to call the originating site if for some reason it is not receiving the video conference/class.

Figure 8.2
Here the facilitator is seated next to the overhead presenter and the PenPal™ graphics pad so she can move the cameras and control the graphics capabilities

Facilitators can be volunteers from each group. They can also be paid or, if taking a class, be given one credit of free tuition in exchange for their assistance. One of our remote sites has trained a cadre of students, paid through the Work Study program. These students are on call to facilitate sessions.

The equipment must stay in one location.

Yes, if your codec is serving a television studio type of facility. No, if it is housed in a roll around cabinet along with the multiplexer and there is a T-1 drop or connection to the network in the location to which you are taking it. While you don't just pick it up and carry it down the hall, you can roll it to facilities such as laboratories or other specialized settings.

Public school students will be turned off by the technology because it offers a less than broadcast quality picture.

As compression algorithms improve compressed video comes closer and closer the the quality of broadcast video. We have found no problem at all with students using the technology- in fact they appear to be more highly motivated when using this technology than they are in a standard classroom.

Elementary school children can't operate the equipment.

We have seen third and fourth grade level students operating the equipment in cooperative learning sessions. They did a better job than many adults. One class has met regularly over the system with another class. They have been taking turns teaching each other about writing (see Figure 8.3).

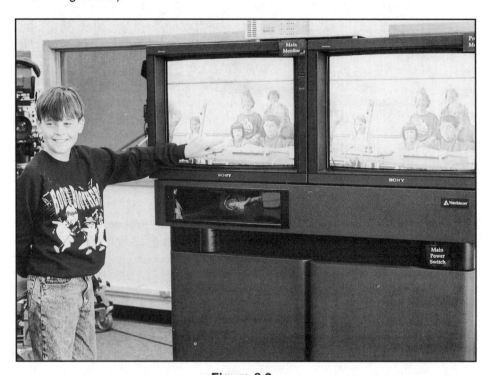

Figure 8.3
Here a student teaches other children how to operate the compressed video equipment in a local loop back mode (there is no remote site connected). This mode provides an excellent environment in which to train new users.

Some face-to-face meetings are necessary

This is a mind set that is hard to change. We have had several groups who have never met face-to-face and they have developed very strong bonds.

Other Factors To Consider In Preparing For A Needs Assessment

Steven G. Sachs, Associate Dean, Instructional Technology and Extended Learning has shared what he learned from their experiences with vendor selection at Northern Virginia Community College. Upon completion of the first year of operation of a compressed video network connecting Northern Virginia Community College's five campuses, we received the inevitable flurry of requests for information. Potential buyers are eager to know if the equipment works, why we chose the equipment we did, and what we would do differently. In addition, there are lots of others who are looking for solutions to their communication problems and want to know if compressed video conferencing might work for them.

Not surprisingly, the questions we were asked became repetitive. People wanted to know such things as:
- How is the picture quality — or how does the picture quality compare with brand X?
- What transmission speed are we operating at?
- What are we using to carry our signal — T-1, fiber, microwave, satellite?
- Is the system hardware or software based?
- Are we going point-to-point or point to multi-point?
- What "bells and whistles" are we using—split screen, data screens, remotely controlled cameras, and interactive graphics?
- What courses are we offering and how did we select them?
- How are we supervising the classes, instructors and the system?
- What are the on-going costs and have we done a cost-benefit study?
- How did we select instructors to use the system and what training did we give them?
- How do we handle student testing and handouts?

All of these are very good questions and need to be addressed. What is surprising, though, is how many of those who asked these questions are genuinely surprised when told that these are not the most important questions. When the really important questions were shared with them, they usually admitted to never having given the questions much thought. In fact, most of them admitted that they really never thought of video conferencing as anything more than just fancy technology. They never really realized that they were still primarily going to be working in the people business.

Many potential users seem to think of a video teleconferencing system as a single monolithic device. In fact, there are a lot of choices and variations in how the system is configured. It is how the desired variations and choices are assembled that determines whether the system will make it possible for the people who use it to be successful.

Here is a list of the questions that are really important to consider in choosing a compressed video system along with a very brief observation of the significance of the question. These questions have been derived from the belief that we are in the people business and that our primary focus should be on making the hardware meet the people's needs instead of making the people adapt to the hardware. They are also derived from our experience with those factors that have proven to really make a difference.

- Will there be technicians at each site and will they have to be present during each class or meeting?

If the system is complex or requires operation from anywhere other than the instructor's teaching position, costs go up significantly.

- Who will participate and what is their skill level and motivation? What kind of picture and instructional techniques will they need in order to feel comfortable?

Will they want to see a traditional classroom setting and see other students with whom they interact? Will they be satisfied with primarily seeing only the instructor, or will they need to see all of the sites?

Figure 8.4
Some settings require the presence of a technician to keep the system functioning

- How many monitors and of what size will fit in the designated room? How many viewers will they accommodate?

It is possible to use only a small monitor for the originating site's view of its own location. This minimizes the self consciousness some people exhibit when they are able to see themselves on the monitor.

- What kind of microphones will be comfortable for students and instructors — push-to-talk, or unobtrusive pancake microphones?

Having to walk up and turn on a microphone can spoil the flow of spontaneous discussion. Similarly, push-to-talk microphones, if students forget to turn them off, can cause problems with audio feed back on the network. Open pancake or flat microphones are the least obtrusive and can be muted site by site.

- What will the rooms be like at each site? Will there be desks or tables? Will sound conditioning be possible? Will the room be long and narrow, or square?

Sometimes it is not possible to make the room accommodate the equipment needs (especially audio and the camera's horizontal field of view).

- Where will the audio come from — monitor speakers in the front, overhead speakers, or monitors in the back?

Matching the studio speakers to the group is critical. If the studio is too loud it can cause echo or be garbled. If the sound comes from an unnatural location it can be very distracting.

- What size groups are likely to use the system?

Can the cameras, monitors, microphones, image size accommodate them?

- Will the teaching position be fixed behind a control panel or can the instructor move around?

If the instructor can roam around, what kind of microphone will be used? Will a white board or overhead camera be used? How wide a camera shot will be needed?

- Can the room seating be arranged in different patterns?

Some video conferences can very successfully accommodate small groups seated in clusters if the room is flexibly furnished.

Compressed video technology is emerging at such a rapid rate that what may have been your vendor of choice six months ago would no longer be the vendor you would choose. The development of the new H.261 CCITT standard for codec compatibility and other evolving standards for compressed video are important elements to monitor. Up until 1989, there were

See Chapter 1

only a few big name vendors operating in the compressed video market-place. Chapter 1, contains a list of vendors. Since 1989, new vendors have entered the market with highly competitive products. The "Cadillacs" of earlier codec vendors are racing to upgrade their products' capabilities to match or exceed the systems of the relative newcomers. Prior to 1989, most purchases of compressed video equipment were made without any vendor selection process. Selection was based on the word of a single vendor and that vendor's referral to other groups who had installed its equipment. Since that time compression algorithms have been improved to transmit increasingly higher quality video and audio over lower and lower bandwidths. Additionally, some vendors are moving toward PC based systems that offer a range of multimedia options. Increasingly, new users of compressed video systems are staging vendor shoot outs.

Setting The Stage for Vendor Shoot-Outs

See Part II

See Appendix G

As Randall Donahoo, Director of Information Technology for St. Vrain Valley School District reminds us in his user profile, contained in Part II, many third party teleconferencing vendors are still learning their own systems, and they do not understand classroom needs. At St. Vrain, Randall says, "We've had to make many adjustments in our equipment arrangements, but we knew that would be the case. Generally speaking, the system works well." At Wyoming, we reviewed the products of four vendors. In every case we found that the vendors themselves really didn't understand educational needs. This is changing too as more and more vendors are selling systems to educational institutions. What is a shoot out? It is a systematically planned competition which requires all participants to demonstrate their abilities to meet the same set of criteria. These criteria include such things as playing a pre-produced high quality video tape through their codecs at varying transmission rates; demonstration of all peripheral capabilities such as interactive graphics and overhead camera devices; the user friendliness of the system; the number and types of human interfaces such as hand held remote controllers; maintenance and technical support; and other criteria of importance to the potential purchaser. A spreadsheet similar to the template provided in Appendix G may be useful for recording comparisons between vendors on the various baseline criteria.

Of equal importance to baseline criteria is the setting from which the shoot-out is to be conducted. All vendors' equipment should be tested in the same environment. Also of importance is the amount of time and the level of technical support required to set up each vendor's product.

An extremely important element to include in the shoot-out is evaluation input from people "in the trenches" who may be using the equipment on a regular basis, such as technicians, instructional designers, conference leaders and classroom instructors.

What does it take to stage a shoot out? We have examples from networks who have recently held shoot outs. We cite their user profiles for a description of the process they followed.

Montana

According to Janice Bruwelheide Associate Professor of Instructional Technology in the Department of Education at Montana State University, the selection team was identified and work begun on specifications and proposal bid requirements in November of 1991, so that timelines for a July equipment installation could be met. The call for compressed video vendor proposals was sent in January, 1992. The bid specification document was approximately sixty pages and it was developed by a representative of the Telecommunications Bureau of the Department of Administration with substantial input from the selection team. The six member team was comprised of representatives from the following areas: Office of the Commissioner of Higher Education (Bruwelheide); two technical representatives from the University of Montana and Montana State University; an educational technology expert from the Office of Public Instruction; and two representatives from the Department of Administration. The selection team developed the evaluation documents and point matrix, reviewed all proposals, rated the vendor demonstrations, and summarized rankings of each vendor. Selectors were advised to keep accurate records and maintain confidentiality throughout the entire process. All equipment demonstrations were held during March and April, 1992. Demonstrations were held in Helena in order to equalize physical conditions. Final selection was made in May 1992, and requisite contractual procedures instituted. The compressed video system (CLI Rembrandt II VP Gallery units) is operating through inverse multiplexing in a dial-up environment.

North Dakota

North Dakota was one of the first states to develop a compressed digital video network that allowed multiple sites to connect to each other. The network was designed during 1989-1990. Studio classrooms were developed at each site. The joint Technical Subcommittee, established to develop the network, set the requirements and technical specifications for equipment through consultations with experts in different audio/video technologies and instructional design from different campuses. North Dakota University was chosen as the bid agent. Three equipment bids were advertised:

1) For the compression equipment (codec's and switches)

2) For the remaining classroom equipment (cameras, microphones, cables, wires, etc.)

3) For construction of the teaching console and cabinets.

The North Dakota Information Services Division, the state telecommunications agency, advertised a bid for the communications lines. All of the bids were due in late May 1990. Bidders had about 60 days to answer the bids. Results were compiled and final decisions made at a meeting on June 14,1990.

The Joint Technical Subcommittee reviewed the submitted bids, considered the alternatives (especially resulting from substitutions or additions to the bids by vendors), and made a recommendation on each bid. The recommendation was presented on June 14, 1992. A major change to the recommendation was made at the meeting (two switches instead of one) and the plan was adopted.

The following is a list of reasons for making the selections for each bid:

1) Compression Equipment — The Joint Technical Subcommittee created a video tape that each vendor had to run through their compression equipment at 1/4 T-1, 1/2 T-1, and full T-1 transmission speeds. Both sound and video had to be on tape. The tape was a very important step in the selection process and was especially helpful to the participants at the June 14 meeting. Bid price was also a major factor. Compression Labs, inc. was selected as the codec vendor because it:

    a) had the best audio handling protocols;

    b) had the second-best picture quality;

    c) had the best multipoint control unit;

    d) had the lowest bid price.

2) Classroom equipment - Todd Communications, because of best bid price

3) Console construction - March and Brother, because of best bid price

4) Communications lines — US WEST was chosen for intra-LATA communications on the basis of bid price and US Sprint was chosen for inter-LATA communications on the basis of bid price.

Utah

Ed Ridges, Associate Director of the Utah Education network indicated that Utah in presently in the process of identifying a vendor. They began the process by hosting a nationwide shoot out. They invited all eight codec vendors to participate in the event and configured the equipment in such a fashion that the evaluators were unable to determine whose codec was being demonstrated. They developed their own tape which included more action than the standard video conference would include. Over the course of two days they saw presentations from 7 of the 8 participants. They required the demonstrations to be   H.261 compatible and to meet all iterations of the CCITT standards. This effort resulted in a short list of four vendors, each of whose products appear to meet their needs.

Wyoming

In March, April and May of 1991, four vendors provided their compressed video roll-about units for a pilot project which used the units for a wide range of applications. Since all groups interested in compressed video had agreed to share the State's already existing network, a state-wide bid committee was formed in June of 1992, to draw up specifications for a request for bid from compressed video vendors. The committee consisted of representatives from state government, the community colleges, the University of Wyoming and the public schools. A representative from the State Telecommunications Office chaired the ten member committee. The Committee complied with the process and procedures of the State Purchasing Office throughout the bid process. Appendix F contains a copy of the rating sheet the committee used to evaluate the various vendor's proposals. The Bids were due in October of 1991. The six proposals received were evaluated by the Committee using the rating sheet. The two top vendors were invited in for a side-by-side shoot out. Each vendor made a formal presentation to the committee of the same duration. The committee then put each vendor's systems through side-by-side tests with video tape, running at 112 kbps, 384 kbps and 756 Kbps. The committee then once again used the rating sheets to evaluate each vendor. Results of that process identified VideoTelecom as the vendor of choice based on 1) features, 2) upgraded through software, 3) user friendliness, 4) PC base, 5) it came with the H.261 CCITT standard and a proprietary algorithm, 6) picture and audio quality, 7 multipoint capabilities, and 7) price.

Other States/Organizations Who Have Sponsored ShootOuts

Other organizations that have sponsored shootouts or have conducted different types of vendor selection processes are listed here. Their contact persons' names, addresses, and phone numbers are listed in the user profiles contained in Part II. These include, among others, Murray State University, United American Reporting Services, West Virginia Northern Community College, Nebraska Educational Telecommunications Commission, The University of Alabama System, and the University of Wyoming.

Selection criteria and bench marks

During the Wyoming pilot and our bid process we learned very early on that when asking vendors if they offered certain features or capabilities they would usually say "we can do that." The issue is not whether or not they can do it, but how easily and at what cost? The criteria provided below may or may not be features every organization is interested in. We were concerned about finding a system that was a turnkey (one button on) unit that provided as many instructional tools (multimedia) as users might potentially need. Additionally, we wanted to find an open architecture system, if possible, that could be upgraded by software as opposed to swapping out boards or firmware. We soon learned that while all vendors could supply most of them, some vendors did not have certain features fully integrated into their system and others used non-standard jacks for connecting peripherals. We also were interested in finding a system that was very user friendly and would not require a technician to operate each unit. During the pilot we were very careful to be present throughout the setup of each system from the uncrating to the power up stage. There were significant differences in vendors' products in the degree of integration of the components, or rather the lack of integration. Some vendors' products required the extensive connecting of components and long hours on the telephone with other support technicians (two days in one case). Other vendors' products were uncrated and operational within a half a day. Some vendors have plainly marked the connections for peripherals (e.g. Mic 1 in, Video 1 in, Video 2 in, etc.) while the backs of other vendors units were a maize of unlabeled jacks, plugs and ports. The bottom line is that if you want a certain capability make certain all vendors demonstrate that capability.

Video tape bench mark or side-by-side comparisons

Either a video tape bench mark or a side by side comparison is useful. Following the North Dakota model, provide a video tape which contains a wide range of motion and audio handling segments which each vendor must send through its codec and tape the codec output for your review. It is, however, difficult to top a side-by-side, live test in the same room, under the same lighting and acoustical conditions. In this situation you can also easily compare parallel capabilities, ease of use and other features. With the video tape you have only a comparison of the video and audio quality and no comparison of all of the other capabilities and features.

Multipoint capabilities

Can you cascade (hook together) multipoint control units, MCU's to handle larger conferences? If so, how many sites will cascading accommodate? Some networks described in the User Profiles (Part II) decided to purchase two MCU's or switches because it provided them with greater flexibility in the sense that where there were sufficient numbers of codecs and transmission space they were able to conduct multiple conferences. When going through an MCU is the system still capable of remote site camera control, interactive graphics and the sending of facsimiles or are those features disabled? Does the system have lecturer or director control (the ability for the session facilitator to select the site s/he wishes at any given time)? Is polling available (an option to program the system to automatically poll different sites at preselected time intervals, e.g. every three minutes, five minutes or other interval of one's choosing)? Does the MCU operate by voice activation (when someone at a remote site speaks the video switches to that site)? Can you set up the MCU or system to automatically display the site name when a given site comes on the monitor?

Upgrades

Compressed video technology and compression algorithms are changing at a very rapid rate. Are a certain number of upgrades guaranteed, or will you have to purchase them? Are they software, firmware or hardware upgrades? Will you have to pay an installation fee? If not already available on the system, can it be upgraded to include the new CCITT H.261 standard?

Peripherals

Does the system allow for the attachment of a facsimile machine? Can you bridge in an audio conference to the videoconference? Does the system have the capability of presenting 35mm slides, photos and other graphics? Can you digitize and store these slides on computer disk ahead of a conference / presentation / class? Does the system allow for the use of an overhead presenter as a writing, graphic, or three dimensional object presentation pad? Does the system support interactive graphics where each site can interactively label or work on a slide, graphic or diagram? Does the graphics capability allow for different pen colors and sizes of type? Can you interface a computer with the system to interactively work on software or conduct software training? Can you interface videodisc, CDROM, a VCR and multiple cameras? Can you use a lavilere microphone?

Human interfaces, numbers and types

As Steven Sachs discussed earlier in this chapter, regardless of the technology employed we are still in the people business. Can users operate

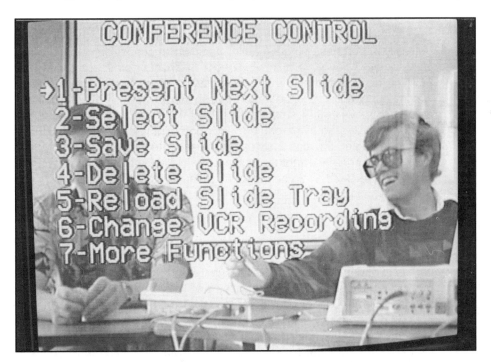

Figure 8.5
Two system users prepare to digitize slides for use in an up-coming compressed video session by using a PC-based pull-down menu to select options

the system in more than one way? A hand held remote control is a very useful feature. A graphics tablet or touch pad with icons and layered menus is another useful feature. Yet a third means of controlling the system can be through a computer keyboard. Different users have varying levels of comfort with each of these interfaces. The more options that are available, the more likely it is that each person is going to be able to find one with which s/he is comfortable. Regardless of the device being used to control the unit, are the options and directions easily accessed and clear to users? (See Figure 8.5.)

Flexibility

Whether or not you choose to purchase all of the options described in this section (and some come standard with certain vendors' products) can options be easily added at a later date should you choose to expand the capabilities of the system?

User friendliness

The more user friendly the system is, the sooner it will become almost transparent to its users. The more transparent a system is, the more likely it is to be used. The cost of training is another issue related to user friendliness. User friendly systems cut down on training time dramatically.

Moveability

None of the systems on the market are moved quickly or easily unless you purchase single monitor units which almost all vendors offer. Nonetheless, people are moving them to specialized laboratories and facilities or to larger rooms to accommodate bigger audiences. System weight, construction and the wheel base should be carefully examined if you do plan to move your systems around. Another issue related to transportability is the degree of integration. The more highly integrated a system's components are, the less likely one is to encounter something that doesn't work when it arrives at another location. We did actually load ours into a van and haul it to Casper, Wyoming for a conference demonstration and it still worked when it arrived there and when it returned.

Audio

Audio is perhaps the most critical element of the system. The various vendors' products provide significantly different levels of audio quality, echo cancellation capabilities and audio room adjustment algorithms. Some vendors' products provide good echo cancellation and support diagnostics which may be activated each time the system is moved to a new location. These diagnostics can be used to adjust the acoustics to the room. Are the audio levels easily adjusted, or does it require a technician to adjust audio levels? If the audio level is too high in a given location it can cause an annoying echo on the network. One vendor provides a pull down menu with directional arrows to adjust the audio up or down. Is there an easy way to adjust audio transmission rate so it is in synchronization with lips?

Video

Video becomes less of an issue each quarter as compressed video vendors are rapidly improving the motion handling capabilities of their compression algorithms for transmission at lower and lower bandwidth. Vendors are now touting picture quality which rivals the 30 frames per second of regular television. As new developments occur with inverse multiplexing we will see even greater improvements in video and lower transmission rates.

Turnkey system

A system that will turn on with one button is often desired. We have found our turnkey system to be extremely easy for people to use.

Lease purchase

At the present time the costs for a full blown compressed video system is still quite high if you purchase a fully equipped unit; between $55,000 and $80,000 per site. Because the technology is changing so rapidly, some organizations are leasing their equipment. Others have entered into lease purchase agreements.

Require a Technician to operate

As Steve Sachs mentioned earlier, if the system has to be operated by someone remote from the location of the instructor or for the instructor because of its complexity, costs go up dramatically. The new compressed video systems on the market will work in most normal classrooms and can be operated by the session facilitator, a student, the instructor or work-study students. If studio-type classrooms are constructed, the more likely increased technical support will be needed.

User Support

Different vendors provide very different levels of support for users of their products. Be certain to have this carefully defined.

Maintenance

Vendors are changing the terms of their maintenance programs regularly. Some institutions/networks purchase an extra codec which is available should a system go down. Again be certain to have the maintenance options carefully detailed.

Training

Training can be a hidden cost or it can be provided at no charge as part of the contract negotiations. Sometimes training is provided at no charge but the purchasing group pays travel for those who attend the training which is often at a headquarters site. Training by most vendors is at three levels:

1) technical support,

2) end user applications, and

3) MCU operations and technical training.

Some vendors provide training over compressed video to your remote sites at no charge. The quality of training provided by some vendors needs substantial improvement and should be revised to include educational institutions as the target audience.

See Appendix C

We found that we needed to develop our own customized training at the University of Wyoming. The School of Extended Studies produced a short training tape and set of printed instructions. The graduate students in adult education and instructional technology in the College of Education developed the task analysis for system operation contained in Appendix C. This document is also used for training.

Installation

Installation charges vary from vendor to vendor, but need to be included as part of the cost of the system.

CCITT Standards and demonstration of talking to dissimilar codecs

As we rapidly approach the day when we videoconference outside of our own networks this becomes an important issue. Ask for a demonstration.

While we have learned a great deal in our dialogues with other institutions and from the user profiles, our experience only represents one institution and synthesis of what we have been able to compile from other users. The above is not an exhaustive list of criteria, yet, we hope it will be helpful to organizations that are contemplating the purchase of compressed video systems.

References

Daly, E. *We've Got To Start Meeting This Way*. KJH Communications 2nd Edition. 1992

9

Non-traditional Applications of Compressed Video

Barbara T. Hakes

Introduction

In this chapter we will examine the range of applications being made with compressed video in colleges/universities, K-12, and the private sector. The University of Wyoming's College of Education has been exploring some unique applications for teacher preparation and K-12 institutions which will also be discussed in this chapter. We use the term "traditional" applications to refer to those applications we found most frequently employed through the user profiles contained in Part II of this book.

In the United States live, two-way interactive video is being used in our educational institutions for distance learning in a variety of ways. The most common applications are the delivery of courses to remote sites and the sharing of instructors between institutions (Daley, 1991), (Descy, 1991). Some institutions are exploring more non-traditional applications of interactive video such as mentoring and coaching student teachers, team teaching, cooperative learning between different school districts, faculty development and simultaneous preservice and inservice (Hakes 1991), (Rezabek, Hakes 1990). Configuration of the interactive video systems used by various institutions ranges from systems which provide full motion video and utilize electronic classrooms or television classrooms which require the support of technicians to turnkey systems which are menu driven, operate at compressed motion rates, and can be easily operated by the students or the instructor in the program. These systems require little technical support, are very user friendly and can be "wheeled around" from room to room provided the necessary cable, fiber optic, or T-1 drops are available in the rooms being utilized.

As the use of compressed digital video expands new areas of application will emerge and are emerging as we write this book. The configuration of compressed video sites often affects the applications being made. In some cases applications are constrained by the design of the site.

How is compressed video being used?

At the University of Alabama, CV is being used for the traditional applications of delivery of graduate and some undergraduate courses. But the University is also using its network for thesis and dissertation proposal meetings, colloquiums and all types of meetings.

Over the NEB*SAT system in Nebraska, compressed video is used primarily for instruction and involves both one- and two-way applications in one to one and one to multiple sites configurations. The first and largest user is the University of Nebraska Medical Center College of Nursing. Other users are the state and community colleges. Teleconferencing by state agencies and other educational users is a secondary priority.

California State University makes use of its network to provide courses within its own service area and share courses among its campuses. Interest in videoconferencing for administrative uses is growing, particularly in light of recent fiscal crises and limited travel budgets. The Sacramento campus has had a connection to the Sprint Meeting Channel for over a year. Recently, the local operating company has loaned two codecs and software to CSU for a three month pilot. One has been installed at the Southern Office of the Chancellor, the other at the Sacramento campus. The intent of the pilot is to test the feasibility of administrative teleconferencing.

The Maricopa Community College Video Conference Network (VCN) supports activities as varied as the people in the system. The original intended use was for shared instruction, either as distributed classes to linked colleges by one originating site, or as team teaching projects where classes are separated by distance but with faculty participating from both sites. Committees and councils frequently meet on the network for planning activities. Distinguished visiting lecturers are often scheduled on the network to be shared with remote colleges. The coordinating committee of the network meets monthly to discuss its operation and to develop the inter-college instructional program. Additional requests have come from the college community to provide staff development and training. An unex-pected use of the network has been for technical backup of satellite programs coming in by Ku-band or C-band satellite. If the downlink fails at one location it is picked up by another and transmitted over the compressed video network to the location where the failure occurred. The most recent request from a new group has been student government. Each college operates its own student government association. Now the student asso-ciations meet over the network to plan and coordinate activities. West Virginia Northern Community College, in addition to traditional applications, uses its network for meetings, workshops and training and development activities.

Murray State University plans to use its network for advanced placement courses between sites and the public schools as it is currently providing selected undergraduate courses. It also uses its network for student counseling, meetings and demonstrations. Additionally, time is provided for research and development of new applications and technolo-gies. From the outset, efforts were made to make the classroom atmo-sphere as user friendly as possible. Network classrooms look very much like regular classrooms with extra televisions instead of television studios with desks. Multiple microphones are switched through an intelligent audio mixer which provides natural sounding audio without the interference of push-to-talk switches. The instructor controls the camera selection with a simple remote control while a student worker takes care of fax transmissions, monitors and the operation of the system. This user friendly environment is able to support a wide range of applications as compared to studio-like environments.

The University of Maryland's system is used for interactive video conferences and group seminars in addition to offering postgraduate curriculums. In North Dakota, higher education classes comprise about 60-80 percent of the compressed video network usage each month. The next highest use of the system comes from meetings from higher education, faculty, presidents, extension service, system-wide councils and others. Northern Virginia Community College presently uses its network for delivery of courses but the network is also heavily scheduled for meetings.

United American Reporting Service, a court reporting firm, offers services to attorneys who are interviewing or deposing a person. The firm's system is currently being used mostly by corporations in a public room environment.

In addition to using its network for course delivery, the University of Wyoming has been exploring other applications which may be useful for education users in other states. In the fall of 1989, the College of Education at the University of Wyoming (the only four year institution of higher education in the state) became interested in finding ways to do interactive video with the state's K-12 schools for the purposes of providing professional development for teachers and more classroom observations for its teacher education students. Wyoming has a population density of 4.7 people per square mile. Our exploration of transmission alternatives found two-way satellite cost prohibitive and we needed a solution that was interactive. The transmission of analog video required too much space on the carrier, whether it was satellite, microwave, or land lines, to make it cost effective. We knew that some businesses were using compressed digital video because it required less carrier space and was thus, less costly. We began to explore the compressed video alternative. We wanted to make certain that the system we chose would meet our needs. Chapter 8, Needs Assessment, discusses how we went about identifying those needs. From that assessment we learned that the system we should purchase ought to have the following characteristics:

See Chapter 8

- high resolution interactive graphics capability;

- the ability to digitize and store visual information;

- a fax capability;

- the ability to be moved;

- a variety of user interfaces so that most users could find one with which they felt comfortable;

- remote site camera control;

- a video tape play and record capability;

- remote diagnostics;

- software upgradeable (computer based).

Why did we want all of these features? Largely because K-12 schools and teacher education programs are dynamic environments where a variety of media are used for teaching and learning. Students no longer sit in rows with teachers at the front of the classroom lecturing. We knew that to accommodate a range of teaching and learning styles we needed a multimedia system that was flexible, somewhat movable and very, very, very user friendly. We were looking for a system that would be as transparent to the user as possible. Such a system we knew would not limit the possible applications we wished to make in the way that other systems would. For example, while we have a wonderful television studio classroom and a video conference room at the University it would have been an unnatural environment for students in K-12 settings. As a result we were looking for a system that would function well in an average classroom without major investments in special lighting, acoustics or technical support staff. We conducted a three month pilot program in the Spring of 1991, held a state-wide bid process in the fall and installed a network. During the Fall of 1992, the University purchased compressed video systems for each of the state's seven community colleges and the network became operational in January of 1992. Our next phase is to develop the network with the public schools. We have described here, some of the applications we tested during our pilot project where we were linked directly with a high school in Gillette, Wyoming.

Background

In 1985, the John Goodlad School/University Partnership (the Partnership) began in the State of Wyoming. The Partnership continued to expand until in 1992 it included fifteen school districts, the laboratory school at the University of Wyoming, and the private sector (see Figure 9.1). In keeping with its goals to institute changes in education, the simultaneous renewal of schools and the education of educators, the Partnership has been increasingly involved in collaborative efforts. These efforts have resulted in many changes to improve education at all levels; from the mutual development of a new teacher education program at the University of Wyoming to joint ventures between the state's public schools, the university, the State Department of Education and the state's businesses. In November of 1990, through these efforts, the Partnership was announced as one of two national pilot demonstration sites for educational reform. The announcement was made at an invitational forum sponsored by the Exxon Foundation in Washington, D.C. This national acclaim was the result of site visits conducted by the Education Commission of the States, the American

Association of Colleges of Teacher Education, and the National Center for
Educational Renewal.

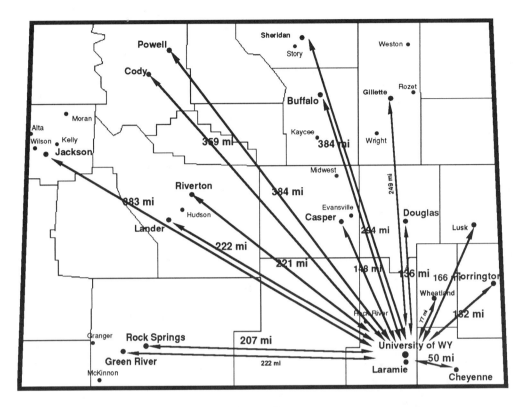

Figure 9.1
The Wyoming School-University Partnership: Sharing best practices
in education.

A Compressed Video Network

A significant factor which contributed to the selection of Wyoming
for the national pilot demonstration was the Wyoming Centers for Teaching
and Learning Network (the WCTLN). The WCTLN is comprised of the fifteen
school/university partnership schools, which includes the university laboratory schoo (see figure 9.1). While there are 49 districts in the state, the
Partnership districts enroll over 70% of the state's students. Ultimately, the
Partnership schools will become hubs for the expansion of the WCTLN to
other districts in their region.   Until last year, the Partnership program
networked itself largely through face-to-face meetings and audio teleconferences. The newly adopted teacher education program (jointly designed by
the Partnership schools and the University) called for earlier and more in-
depth clinical experiences for preservice teachers, inservice programs for
practicing professionals, faculty development for college faculty, improved
ways for mentoring student teachers, as well as providing a teacher support

system. The new teacher education program will warrant its graduates. As a result, it needs a system to support beginning teachers through their warranty period. In order to meet all of these needs, the Partnership felt it was necessary to explore new ways of bridging the vast distances between the University and the Partnership schools.

Wyoming is a rugged, rural state with a small population scattered over a wide geographic area. Our state has been aptly described as a medium–sized American town with very long streets. It is a town inhabited by a people who possess a true pioneering spirit, and an appetite for quality and progressive goals. Forty–nine school districts employ 8,000 certified educators. There is only one University and seven community colleges. Currently 48% of all Wyoming residents live in "frontier" counties. In fact, the entire State could be classified as "frontier" because the population per square mile of 4.69 falls below the established limit of six persons per square mile. According to the 1990 census, 71% of the population of Wyoming is classified as "rural population".

As the state's only four–year institution of higher education, the University of Wyoming has a mandate to serve all of the residents of Wyoming, but the College of Education only has reasonable access to fewer than one–fourth of the state's public schools. The College of Education, with

UW Photo

Figure 9.2
Multiple groups representing higher education, the public schools, state agencies, and the private sector tested compressed video's ability to meet their needs during the 1991 Wyoming Pilot Project.

its laboratory school, the Wyoming Center for Teaching and Learning at Laramie (WCTL-L), and the state's only teacher preparation program, has substantial need to network with the public schools around Wyoming to increase clinical experiences, provide faculty development opportunities, and collaboratively develop instructional resources, projects, programs and curricula. By the same token, geographically isolated schools need to network with other schools and the university in order to provide equal educational opportunities for the state's students and professional development programs for teachers.

These needs, along with others, prompted the WCTLN to explore the feasibility of developing a compressed video (live, two-way interactive audio and video) network. In March of 1991, the WCTLN initiated a pilot project to serve as a demonstration for the evaluation of compressed video systems and to test and develop various models and applications in teacher education and faculty development, (see figure 9.2). Compressed video networks have been used in higher education for several years, primarily for the delivery of college credit courses and training programs. The public schools, and teacher education, have not used this technology in non-traditional ways (other than standard course or program delivery) to improve teaching and learning in their respective environments

The compressed video pilot was set up between two sites 250 miles apart (Gillette and Laramie) and was conducted over a three month period. During this period, the WCTLN designed numerous applications for preservice/inservice education and faculty development to test the feasibility of using compressed video technology in those areas. These tested applications are being implemented as a regular part of the Partnership agenda to improve preservice/inservice teacher education during the fall of 1992 and the spring of 1993.

During the fall of 1991, the College of Education was awarded a grant of $304,000 from US WEST for the Video Education Interactive Network (VEIN) project over a three year period. One of the goals of VEIN is to develop a coaching and mentoring model for teacher interns and to develop a support system for first and second year teachers. Additionally, VEIN is developing five other programs which can be used for simultaneous preservice and inservice programs. The compressed video network allows us to simultaneously provide professional development opportunities for teachers in the state while at the same time providing them to our on campus preservice teachers. This means that when teacher interns move into the schools they will work with teachers who have gone through the same programs. Beginning in March of 1992, teams of public school and university faculty have been meeting on a regular basis over compressed video to develop the VEIN programs. The first of the five programs was offered for credit over the compressed video network in the fall of 1992. This first program is for coaching and mentoring over distance using compressed video. The other programs will be offered beginning in the spring of 1993.

Thus, our applications are exploring ways in which compressed video can be used to develop curriculum and courses in collaboration with public school teachers and the University. They are also developing models for cooperative learning, team teaching, coaching and mentoring, and teaching critical thinking skills and problem solving (see figure 9.3). We will share here some of the reactions of people who used the compressed video system during our pilot and initial program development.

"Some of the latest technology on the campus at the University of Wyoming is the compressed video capability. I have been impressed with

Figure 9.3
Here, members of the critical thinking skills team meet to develop a course.

the potential of this medium after only one experience," says Dr. Cary Lester, Professor of Educational Administration. Mary Pendleton, a student teacher in Gillette, Wyoming, had this to say: "Compressed video is an excellent teaching tool, it helped me receive immediate feedback from others to help my professional growth." "Imagine twenty-eight language arts methods students gathered to observe a sixth grade writing lesson and talking face-to-face with the teacher, the student teacher, and the sixth graders after a lesson is finished. No big deal, you say? Yes it is, if the college students are in Laramie, Wyoming, and the sixth grade class is 250 miles away in Gillette," exclaims Professor Leslie Johnson. The College of Education at the University of Wyoming and its fifteen partner school districts are exploring new ways to provide preservice, inservice and faculty/ staff development opportunities.

Networks of varying technologies and designs are being developed at an increasing rate to support and improve our educational system at all levels. Many networks are targeting real-time two-way interaction that make possible the types of dialogue quoted in the previous paragraph. Some networks use broadband, fiber optic, delivery (Daley,1991), (Schiller & Noll, 1991), (Descy 1991) to exchange a wide range of information (audio, video and data) between multiple sites simultaneously. These networks can provide full motion video in real-time interactions between sites. Some networks utilize "electronic" or "television" classrooms in which a heavy financial investment has been made and which require technical support personnel. Many networks utilize their systems to dispense instruction in the same way as we do in traditional classrooms — lecture, and reading assignments with the only practice coming in the form of worksheets or tests. While interactive networks (two-way voice and video) allow the sharing of expert teachers to provide a richer array of offerings in the curriculum one wonders how they will really affect student learning if traditional instructional methods are still being used. At the College of Education, University of Wyoming, we have two primary goals: 1) the development of a network which utilizes as little space as possible for live two-way audio and video on a T-1 carrier, and 2) how such a network can be used to provide a) more clinical experiences for preservice teachers, b) faculty development opportunities, c) a teacher support system, d) opportunities to share and exchange resources and, e) increased inservice programs. We assume the system will also be used for more traditional course delivery - but we intend to design those courses in ways which stimulate interaction and provide a great deal of practice in highly realistic environments.

At the end of the three month pilot, during which four vendors demonstrated their capabilities, we concluded that we could achieve goal number one as listed in the previous paragraph. Further, we had an opportunity to do some formative evaluation of the applications listed in objective two. The pilot project also demonstrated that if we had a fiber optic or T-1 network in a given building, the compressed video systems that were demonstrated could be moved from room to room in the building and hooked to various drops. As a result we could avoid the necessity for supporting a variety of technicians and large financial investments in a fixed electronic classroom. Also we could commit more time and resources for teacher and student training and instructional design. Here we specifically discuss the applications we tried during the pilot program.

What Is It Like To Be in a Compressed Video Session?

"It's so exciting, I can hardly believe we can get regular, personal support from our mentor teachers at the University," exclaims a student teacher in Gillette, Wyoming, as she talks with a professor in the College of Education. People involved in a compressed video session have the ability to simultaneously see and hear each other, while they share printed material via fax, or use computer graphics to simultaneously label a diagram or solve a problem. Additionally, each site has the ability to select and control multiple devices at the other site (point to point) or their own, via remote infrared control. During the pilot, children in the laboratory school at the university and children in the Gillette public schools, along with students, teachers, and faculty, had access to several cameras at each site, as well as videodisc players, fax machines, and computers that were connected to the compressed video system. Two teacher interns in Gillette said, "It gave us a chance to share our experiences with soon-to-be student teachers." Another teacher intern said, "It surely is nice to see some familiar faces in a 'strange land'." Two third grade students said, "It was like being in two places at once. You can meet someone new without even going anywhere!"

During the pilot project, we also tried several different models for simultaneous preservice/inservice education and faculty development. Faculty development presents an interesting dilemma. According to Goodlad (1990),

> "Professors in colleges and universities who engage seriously in preparing educators for the nation's schools straddle two cultures: that of higher education and that of the K-12 educational system. A quarter-century ago - a period of time transcended by the career span of many teacher educators still teaching - the culture of the school entered significantly into their mission. They not only taught the campus curriculum for prospective teachers but followed their students into the schools to supervise the student-teaching experience. Publication was expected on some university campuses but on others it was appreciated."

This quarter-century-old model could be used to move us much further toward solving today's faculty development dilemma, because it suggests opportunities for simultaneous preservice/inservice education and numerous faculty development opportunities. "Today the culture of the college or university, far more than the culture of the schools, is the compelling context for teacher educators. Higher education has evolved substantially within the career span of many professors, profoundly changing the expectations and circumstances under which they work. The impact of this evolution on those who prepare teachers and, indeed, on teacher education programs has been substantial." (Goodlad, 1990). At the University of Wyoming, with the state's only four-year teacher training institution, this impact is deepened by the geographic distances separating the College of Education from the state's public schools. The professors who do engage themselves with public schools jeopardize their promotion through the ranks to full professor because of shear lack of time for research and publication due to heavy travel commitments. As a result, today's expectations actually discourage professors from becoming actively involved in the public schools. The use of compressed video is helping the College of Education find solutions to the dilemma outlined here by Goodlad.

During the pilot project, we were also determined to learn as much as we could about how we might design simultaneous preservice, inservice and faculty development experiences. Employing all we could from our quarter-century-old model, these experiences were designed around the following assumptions:

1) the public schools can model innovative applications for preservice students;

2) the public schools can provide rich faculty development and classroom based research opportunities;

3) the College of Education and its laboratory school can provide a petri dish for nurturing experiments in educational reform;

4) the public schools can implement the successful experiments tested by the university.

5) the public schools provide an excellent source of formative evaluation regarding the quality of teachers being developed by the university;

6) the university can be a source of inservice opportunities for the public schools;

7) the public schools can provide an abundance of clinical experiences for preservice teachers;

8) time for the human resources involved in this list of assumptions is not available to achieve all of the above;

9) the ideal situation would be for all human resources to be part of each other's culture in some overlapping set;

10) In order to achieve preservice, inservice and faculty development simultaneously, we would need to design experiences which are very different from the approaches typically used for such programs.

These ten assumptions are not all inclusive, but they did guide our thought processes as we recruited volunteers for the applications we conducted during the pilot program. In order to accommodate these assumptions, it was clear we would have to create an environment in which preservice teachers, professional teachers and college professors could interact in clinical settings; both with, and without children. The key word in the last sentence was "interact." Interaction, involving a knowledge base and its immediate application or use, fosters the greatest opportunity for the highest level of outcomes for all people involved. Clearly, the passive lecture format could not be used to satisfy the aforementioned ten assumptions. Here are descriptions of some of the sessions we designed and others that just happened because we had the right combinations of people working together in the right environments. The scenario and the quotations are real but the actual names of the participants have not been used.

Scenario 1 - Simultaneous Preservice, Inservice and Faculty Development

Beth Johnson, an elementary school teacher in Gillette, her class, and student teacher, Victoria Wilson, met over the compressed video network with a language arts methods class taught by Dr. Ellen Jones at the University in Laramie. Mrs. Johnson and Victoria taught a lesson to the class in Gillette, using a specific instructional strategy, while the methods class observed. Following the lesson, preservice teachers in Laramie asked questions of Mrs. Johnson, Victoria, and the children in her class. On several occasions, the preservice teachers asked questions which utilized concepts from recent classroom research and new instructional strategies. If Mrs. Johnson was not familiar with the concept or terminology contained in the question, she in turn asked the methods class to explain. The result was an informal inservice education event. Clearly, the preservice teachers in Laramie were able to be involved in a clinical experience with a model classroom teacher, and the methods professor, Dr. Jones, had an opportunity to renew her involvement in the public schools which evolved into a faculty development opportunity for Dr. Jones.

Dr. Jones further describes the experience: "An electronic classroom furnished with interactive video provides the magic. In a recent observation like the one described above, the classroom teacher taught a writing lesson, the student teacher contributed a part, and all the methods students watched. Simultaneously, the students in Laramie listened to periodic comments by the methods teacher about what was going on and what to pay special attention to. In subsequent discussion, the college students were very enthusiastic about this chance to 'visit' a classroom. They felt very close to what was occurring 250 miles away."

"But all the value didn't go one way. The sixth graders got a chance to reflect on their learning experience and to explain aspects to the college student questioners. The classroom teacher gained new insight into some sixth grade responses to writing that caused her to reconsider some of the teaching tactics she had been using. We all learned as a result." Dr. Jones continued by saying, "The compressed video link between public schools and the College of Education opens all sorts of new doors. Other recent uses that I have enjoyed include a chance to serve as a writing consultant in an inservice activity and the opportunity to schedule a guest speaker for my graduate class in curriculum development. The opportunities seem endless. I can hardly wait!"

While the use of compressed video cannot replace actual experience in classrooms, it does provide the opportunity to increase the exposure of preservice teachers to clinical experiences. It also increases the opportunities for professional teachers to engage in inservice experiences and for teacher education professors to become involved in faculty development. In the scenario just described, Dr. Jones could also have planned some simultaneous classroom based research, allowing her to fulfill part of her research obligations for the university while she was actually teaching her class. If Dr. Jones had taken her class to Gillette for the same purpose, they would have spent eight hours driving and probably stayed overnight. During the four sessions the class spent with the Gillette site, they would have lost 32 hours in driving time, alone and, as a result, probably would not have engaged in this experience because of the lost time and the expense involved.

Scenario 2 - Mentoring and Coaching of Student Teachers

During the pilot program, Dr. Judy Milton, in Laramie, met on a biweekly basis with eight student teachers in the Gillette school district. The student teachers were able to talk with Judy about their experiences and to seek her council on various matters ranging from housing to curriculum. Based on what we saw during the pilot, it is clear to us that the compressed video network can provide an excellent support system for not only student teachers, but also for teachers who may have limited peer groups in their own districts. Judy had this to say about the experience: "Working with compressed video systems has been a wonderful window of opportunity (literally and figuratively) for me as a faculty member in the college. I was able to have a conference with a group of student teachers in Gillette. We discussed how their student teaching matched up with expectations previously held and could talk about their futures as educators now that they have crossed over from one side of the desk to the other. It was delightful for me to keep track of their progress via face-to-face contact on the video system." Jim Fulton, the field coordinator in the Gillette area said, "The opportunities presented by compressed video, which could help student teachers in outreach areas of the state, are almost without limit. The intimacy of this technology between the university and the students is probably the most positive factor."

During the fall of 1992, (through a cooperatively developed course on coaching and mentoring under funding from US WEST) we expanded this model to allow supervising teachers to meet with their student teachers on a scheduled basis for observation using the network. Because of the vast geographic distances between the university and many of the schools in which our teacher interns are placed, it is difficult for their supervising professors to visit them in their classrooms on a regular basis. The compressed video network allows us to increase the number of these planned observations.

Scenario 3 - Cooperative Learning and Team Teaching

Joan Rand, an instructor in the College of Education's laboratory school met with Ted Newton, a fifth grade teacher in Gillette, to plan how they might use the compressed video network with their classes. The results of that planning, were team taught experiences and sessions taught by their students on the subject of writing. Students in the classes in Gillette and

Laramie took turns operating the compressed video network at each site. Each week, the Gillette students would teach the Laramie students something about writing or vice versa. Joan states, "We hope to be able to continue next fall, and I venture to speculate that all areas of the curriculum could be taught through the video. We hope to introduce the students to real live children's authors - Ellen Jones and Semanthia Green from this end. Also, most teaching strategies, such as cooperative learning, learning cycle and classroom management could be used and demonstrated. Using the interactive video for inservice is limited by only one's imagination. Small groups of college students could join together at each site and interact with the elementary/secondary students or watch and interact from one site while a class is being conducted at another."

"One would like to speculate that perhaps some long distance practicums could take place. It's not the same as actually being in the classroom, but I believe there are some ways this could be accomplished." These compressed video practicums would not replace the "real in classroom" experiences but would provide additional experience. The students in Mrs. Rand's classroom added:

1) "It was like being in two places at once."

2) "You can meet someone new without even going anywhere."

3) "You can teach a lesson like you were on the phone except you can gesture and see each other."

4) "It's convenient - you don't have to drive to another place."

5) "I liked learning and using the technology."

Scenario 4 - Formal Inservice Programs

Dr. Vance Sterling met four times with Ed Jefferson and a number of teachers in Gillette to conduct a math workshop. The workshop focused on the use of manipulatives to teach math. Vance sent a kit of materials to Gillette High School before the workshop, and the teachers in Gillette used the kit during the workshop sessions that followed. The teachers were actually able to see close up demonstrations much better (using an overhead camera) on the compressed video system than they would have been able to see them in a regular classroom.

Conclusions

These are descriptions of only a few of the applications made during the pilot project and applications now in use or being developed for use over compressed video. Based on the results of the pilot, we believe that we have only scratched the surface in examining the potential usefulness of the compressed video network. The Partnership does not view the network as a replacement for anything, but rather as a powerful tool which facilitates the exchange and sharing of a vast range of resources. This exchange and sharing has the potential to significantly improve the education of educators and the renewal of schools. We have gained incredibly valuable experience with the use of compressed video in some very non-traditional applications. We continue to learn each day as new ideas for applications come from our partnership schools, faculty at the university, preservice students, and, perhaps one of our most important sources for ideas, the children in the partnership schools.

References

Daley, A. (1991). Broadband Networks: Bringing the Information Age Into Schools. *Tech Trends, 36*(2), 13-17.

Descy, D. E. (1991). The KIDS Network: Two-Way Interactive Television n Minnesota. *Tech Trends, 36*(1), 44-48.

Goodlad, J. I. (1990). *Teachers for our Nation's Schools.* San Francisco: Jossey-Bass.

Hakes, B.T. (1991) Removing the Walls of Schools and Teacher Preparation Institutions. In D.Carey, R. Carey, D.A. Willis, J. Willis (Eds.), *Technology and Teacher Education Annual - 1991* (pp. 152-154). Greenville, N.C.: Society for Technology and Teacher Education.

Hudspeth, D. R., & Brey, R.G. (1986). *Instructional telecommunications: Principles and applications.* New York: Praeger.

Moore, M.G., & Clark, G. C. (Eds.). (1989). *Readings in principles of distance education* (Readings in Distance Education No. 1). University Park, PA: The Pennsylvania State University.

Moore, M.G., & Clark, G. C. (Eds.). (1989). *Readings in distance learning and instruction.* (Readings in Distance Education No. 2). University Park, PA: The Pennsylvania State University.

Rezabek, L. L., & Hakes, B. T. (1990). Teaching Telecommunications: Promoting practice and potential. In D. W. Dalton (Ed.), *Proceedings of the 32nd annual international conference of the Association for the Development of Computer-Based Instructional Systems* (pp. 413-418). Columbus, OH: Association for the Development of Computer-Based Instructional Systems.

Schiller, S. S. & Noll B. J. (1991). Utilizing Distance Learning in a Large Urban School System: The Prince George's County Public School's Interactive Television Program. *Tech Trends 36*(1), 23-27.

United States Congress, Office of Technology Assessment. (1989). *Linking for learning: A new course of education* (OTA-SET-430). Washington, DC: U.S. Government Printing Office.

10

Compressed Video: Instructional Design Issues for Education and Training

Cecelia Box

Introduction

Compressed Video, by its unique nature, holds intriguing challenges and opportunities for instructional designers. This chapter is not intended as a how-to manual on designing instruction. Rather, we will create both a broad and narrow context for the discussion. We begin with a broad critique of the current state of instructional design and its ability to adapt to new technologies such as compressed video. In the second part of the chapter, we will discuss various aspects of compressed video within a generic instructional design framework. These aspects include both theoretical ideas for the future and very practical advice based on our current experience.

In order to discuss applications of instructional systems design (ISD) for new technologies such as compressed video, we need to first establish a context for talking about instructional design in general. The growth of ISD has in many ways neatly paralleled the growth of new technologies, particularly computer-based instructional systems. The logic of instructional design and the logic of computer systems seemed to be rooted in similar languages and philosophies. However, new technologies like compressed video (CV), while building on the foundations of computer-based systems of the past, are providing capabilities for the display and delivery of information which do not much resemble the traditional branching programs of early CAI. If anything, compressed video creates a more organic and spontaneous exchange of information. The technological elements of the system become transparent, with the emphasis instead on the people and materials involved in the exchange.

What does this mean for instructional designers and for the instructional design process? We think it indicates a need for new ways of thinking on the part of designers. Compressed video pushes at the envelope of the possible. As of the publication of this book, the design process is not only a question of designing to the media's capabilities, but discovering what those capabilities are; in many cases it seems to involve inventing those capabilities. The designer not only must provide answers, but must invent the questions.

The Current State of Instructional Design

In recent years, many people in the field of Instructional Technology have begun to question the applicability of traditional instructional design models and approaches to new technologies and learning environments. Despite the fact that ISD has enjoyed considerable growth in the last few decades, the field has drawn fire on several fronts. The criticisms can be roughly grouped under three categories: theoretical/psychological, cultural, and technological. Theoretical/psychological criticisms focus on the behaviorist roots of instructional design, and assert the field's failure to adjust to more current psychological theory, especially cognitive processing or information processing theory. Early concepts of instructional design grew out of assumptions, based on several centuries of scientific thought, that knowledge was objective, quantifiable and predictable. However, just as science is redefining the universe in much more relative terms, human knowledge is also being re-examined and re-expressed in terms of a similar relativity. Some writers feel that instructional design as a field has not kept pace with new developments in other fields. Hannafin (1992) states, "Developments in cognitive psychology... have implications beyond our predominating externally centered designs" (p.49). Along the same lines, Tennyson (1990) proposed a cognitive paradigm of learning for use by instructional technologists. Jonassen (1990) has argued for a constructivist approach to designing instruction. Because of the relatively subjective view of learning contained in cognitive processing theory and particularly in constructivism, such calls have far-reaching implications for instructional design models, which were conceived as a means of prescribing and controlling the learning situation.

A number of writers have contributed critical analyses of the ISD field in a broader social context. Nichols (1990) reiterates calls for an acknowledgment of the personal construction of knowledge by learners; but also notes that knowledge construction takes place in a broader cultural-social context, of which designers should be more actively aware. This point is particularly relevant to instruction delivered via compressed video, and will be addressed on a more practical level later in this chapter. Nichols also points out that "the content and methods of our teaching inherently portray an ethic of some kind or another, that 'technical progress is good' for example" (p. 25). The medium of compressed video sends a powerful message about the ability of technology to create a very human form of communication. However, the designer must also be aware of the wide range of possible attitudes among users, particularly in the event of technical difficulties. Anticipating and addressing users' attitudes, and fostering positive attitudes toward - and interactions with - the system can be a critical factor in the success of an instructional unit on CV.

Some commentators have focused on issues of control. Damarin (1991) cites the tendency of ISD approaches to portray the learner as a passive entity to be manipulated. "The generic learner does not behave but exhibits behaviors, is not able but has capabilities, does not look at things but is presented with stimulus material, does not perform but meets criteria and so on; in short, 'the learner' is positioned as non-autonomous and passive by the language, attitude and rigors of educational technology" (p. 116). Hawkridge (1991) identifies larger issues concerning technology's impact on humans in general and moral justifications for the kinds of planning and control implicit in educational technology. While CV is a uniquely intimate medium, instructional designers should be aware that new or different design approaches may be needed to enhance and facilitate the human interactions without excessive control.

Another criticism of ISD concerns the relationship of ISD to emerging technologies. Merrill, Li, and Jones have proposed what they have labelled ID_2. Their new model incorporates technology both as the object of instructional design efforts (though ID_2 is applicable to less technical delivery media as well) and specifically as an instructional design tool (1990b). Merrill, et al., outlined a number of limitations of traditional instructional design, including its offer parts rather than integrated wholes, its limited prescriptions for both knowledge acquisition and course organization, a failure to integrate the phases of development, and its tendency to design learning which is passive rather than interactive. Another criticism is that traditional design procedures are exceptionally labor intensive (1990a).

Focusing more specifically, instructional designers have been trying to develop modifications or improvements to the traditional steps of instructional design. Some of those efforts focus on efficiencies within specific steps, such as Gagne's and Merrill's (1990) clarification and elaboration of the process of identifying instructional goals. Noting that most meaningful instructional goals are fairly complex, Gagne and Merrill propose the concept of an enterprise, which they define as "a purposive activity that may depend for its execution on some combination of verbal information, intellectual skills, and cognitive strategies, all related by their involvement in the common goal" (p. 25). Thus, instructional goals, in order to prescribe the most meaningful forms of learning, may integrate three types of enterprise schemas: denoting (labeling name, class, function of an entity), manifesting (demonstrating a process), and discovering (revealing a previous unknown entity or process). The idea of using integrative goals provides flexibility while addressing higher level learning.

Others have focused their efforts on modifying the total design process. These modifications are usually based on the experience of professional designers in the field, and are a response to general criticisms of the applicability of a formal design process in the "real world". According to Tripp and Bichelmeyer (1990), "It is rarely argued that the systems approach is efficient. Indeed it is sometimes admitted that ISD is costly" (p. 31). A number of alternative design approaches have been proposed, among them Tessmer and Wedman's (1990) "Layers-of-Necessity" model and Tripp and Bichelmeyer's' (1990) rapid prototyping design strategy. Both of these approaches will be discussed in more detail in subsequent sections of this chapter.

A Generic Instructional Design Model

In order to facilitate our discussion, we will talk in terms of a generic model of instructional design process, synthesized from a number of sources, including Dick & Carey (1990), Gagne & Briggs (1979) and Briggs & Wager (1981). According to Tessmer and Wedman (1990), most ID models are "more alike than different" (p. 78). In constructing a synthesized model, with four main phases, we do not intend to imply that other steps not explicitly labeled here, are unimportant. Instead we have subsumed many of those other steps within our four phases and will address specifics as we proceed. Our concept of four phases is not unique, and is not proposed as implying any new constructs. We are simply building a framework for our discussion.

Our use of a generic model may also be considered a reflection of the attempts by a number of writers who have suggested ways to streamline instructional design processes. Tessmer and Wedman (1990) offered an alternative to traditional design models which imply a rigid sequential progression through all design steps for every project. They refer to their alternative as a layers-of-necessity design model. Though the model Tessmer and Wedman propose does not differ from basic instructional design phases in the recommended design activities, it does just that: recommends rather than prescribes. They believe that designers should be guided by principles rather than procedures, and that design approaches should be tailored to and reflective of the specific needs and constraints of the specific learning situation and its surrounding organization.

A slightly different alternative approach was proposed by Tripp and Bichelmeyer (1990). They draw from a software design methodology called *rapid prototyping*, although they are careful to point out differences between software design and instructional design which are also quite relevant for compressed video. "Software designers deal with systems that are based on mathematical logic. Instructional designers deal in part with computer software, but primarily with systems based on human cognition, which entail more uncertainty and accept more ambiguity" (p. 34). Rapid prototyping is defined by the authors: "...after a succinct statement of needs and objectives, research and development are conducted as parallel processes that create prototypes, which are then tested and which may or may not evolve into a final product" (p. 35).

Within the context of four general phases, we will follow the same philosophy as Tessmer and Wedman (1990) and Tripp and Bichelmeyer (1990). That is, we will discuss what is effective in traditional instructional design and how to maintain the integrity of good design while accommodating to the challenges and constraints of real world situations. Our discussion will center around the following phases of design: Phase 1: Defining the learning goals, the learning situation and the learner; Phase 2: Determining

Objectives and Assessment approaches; Phase 3: Developing materials and media; and Phase 4: Formative and Summative evaluation. We will discuss what has traditionally been performed or implied in each phase and what differences arise when working with new technologies. This generic design model is illustrated in Figure 10.1.

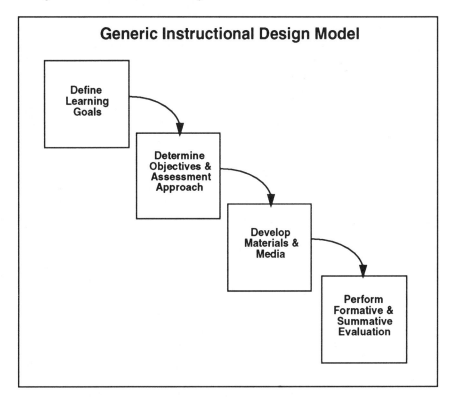

Figure 10.1
Generic Instructional Design Model

Since CV is a new technology, we will not talk much about empirical data. We will, however, share some informal observations based particularly on our experiences in Wyoming. While we have now begun to integrate compressed video into our regular schedule of courses, we have also done some informal exploration of the potential of this medium. Specifically, during the summer of 1992, we held a week-long course on evaluation methods for in-service teachers. Eighty students attended the course at eight sites throughout the state, with the primary instructors based on campus in Laramie, and site facilitators at each remote location. The course served several instructional and promotional purposes and was highly successful. It also provided us, as instructional designers, a very concentrated and rich environment in which to study the applications and effects of compressed video. We will refer to this course throughout this chapter. For the reader who would like a more detailed procedural guide for designing

Compressed Video instruction, we suggest you refer to Appendix A of this book titled "A Guide to Instructional Design for the Compressed Video."

Phase 1: Defining the Learning Situation

Where do you start the process? In the ideal world, we start with either an identified need or a needs analysis in an identified area and follow through until the need has been met, assuming it can be met through instruction. When working with new technologies, one problem with traditional instructional design models quickly becomes evident. Rather than emerging as part of the solution for given needs, the technology itself often drives the need or creates the need. For example, in Wyoming, distance education has always been an issue. Communities are small, and distances are long. There is only one university, the University of Wyoming, and it is located in Laramie, at the far southeast corner of the state. Distance education in the past often meant the University airplane delivering instructors to isolated locations, where they delivered their class and then were flown back to Laramie. While courses were delivered to students at a distance, obvious constraints limited those services.

With our acquisition of a compressed video system, which included a compressed video unit placed in each of the seven community colleges around the state, suddenly those learners at a distance were much closer. Constraints such as distance, costs, and faculty resources abruptly faced redefinition. For the College of Education, a new group of constituents emerged. Teachers seeking continuing professional education, who had until now been limited to the occasional field course or a summer of relocating to Laramie, now were a year-round group of available and eager learners. Not by accident, the installation of the compressed video system in the College of Education coincided with an increased emphasis on school reform which partnered public schools in the state and the University in a number of on-going projects.

See Chapter 2

In many ways, the use of a compressed video system is likely to involve the designer in larger issues than instruction alone. Distance education in general creates a broader field of action for the designer than, say, the design of a traditional CAI module (for a more detailed discussion of distance education and how it relates to CV, see Chapter 2). Designing a CAI lesson, no matter the complexity, basically involves the building of a product, which can then be disseminated to a large number of sites, where it can be used repeatedly, functioning as a self-contained and predictable unit. Contrast that with the components of a unit of instruction delivered via compressed video. The attributes of compressed video are such that effective instruction (instruction which uses those attributes for maximum instructional effect) will involve significant amounts of live interaction between sites, whether primarily conversational, auditory, visual, or computer based. Large numbers of students at multiple sites may be interacting with the material and with each other. As in a traditional classroom, these interactions will color and sometimes change the content of the course.

Later in this chapter we will propose a model for designing for the ambiguous nature of the interactive electronic classroom.

Needs Assessment

While our situation is somewhat unique, our experiences with compressed video in Wyoming have provided us opportunities for framing some generalizable observations about designing for this new technology. A major impact on the design process lies in the area of needs assessment. Eventually, we can foresee that compressed video will become a well-understood delivery option. Today, compressed video is still more or less in its infancy, and we find that assessing needs often leads us into a chicken-or-egg dilemma. If instructional designers are still experimenting with the capabilities of compressed video, users from other fields, while often enthusiastic, are even less clear about the potential applications. This can lead to circular conversations that sound like this:

Designer: What do you *want* to do in your course?

Instructor: What *can* we do (with the technology) ?

While our instinct is to always lead people back to their instructional goals as the driving factor, we have to acknowledge that such free-form approaches to instruction can conceivably lead to new discoveries about the potential of the medium. The concept of needs assessment changes from a traditional assessment of instructional or even organizational needs; it becomes instead a pragmatic balance between insuring effective instruction and allowing for experimentation within the medium.

The availability of a compressed video system impacts curricular decisions as well. In the past, curricular offerings in the College of Education were driven mainly by degree requirements. Occasionally courses have been offered to meet specific or short term needs, but the constraints of minimum enrollment requirements limited the number of such classes, either on campus or at any one field site in the state. Now, every course offered has a large pool of potential registrants with no geographic barriers. It seems an easy prediction that in the future many more courses will be designed and delivered to meet specific in-service needs for teachers throughout the state, as well as entire degree programs. Rather than attempting to simply transfer content and course structure from the traditional classroom, courses which are designed specifically for delivery via compressed video will require new approaches.

Media Selection Process

Another distinct component of the instructional design process in more traditional models such as Dick and Carey's (1991), is selection of the delivery medium. Other chapters of this handbook address that selection process in detail. What is important to instructional design is that this decision, rather than being driven by the instructional goals, is often predetermined. CV requires a large commitment from the organization. The commitment must then be justified by its use. While this is obviously a political rather than an instructional fact, it is important for designers to remember. In matching the medium to instructional uses, the designer may in a sense be "retrofitting", looking for applications of the selected medium which maximize instructors' goals, or working with instructors to modify their instructional goals to take advantage of the new medium in ways that will strengthen the instruction overall.

Analyzing Learners

It often seems that we analyze the learner primarily or solely in relation to the content to be taught. While this may be the most appropriate approach when finite skills or knowledge are being taught, other learning situations may call for a more detailed look at the nature and needs of students. We might informally describe this as the difference between instructional and educational settings. Instructional situations could be considered as those in which narrow and specific content is being covered with limited expected outcomes, as instruction is commonly viewed in business and industrial settings. Educational situations would encompass more of the activities of traditional educational institutions, at whatever level. In these situations we are not only working toward the accomplishment of specific educational objectives, but are also guided by a sometimes vague but pervasive idea... that of shaping an "educated" person. Particularly in the field of education, the traits, skills and needs that the individual brings to the learning environment are highly important, whether we address those traits in assisting that person as a learner, or develop those traits to shape a more effective teacher.

As we plan instruction for CV, we try to anticipate not only the instructional needs of students, but also their attitudes toward the medium as well. We have observed some patterns in these attitudes. First, people are drawn to the almost magical ability to communicate with someone at a distance. Our attitudes about CV are strongly shaped by our experience with television. Maybe that's why, when watching someone at a remote site, it comes as a mild surprise when that person addresses us and our questions directly. After all, this looks just like TV, and TV doesn't talk back (at least not yet). It fits our schema about TV that we can watch others. The knowledge that we are also being watched is a little more novel.

The other side of this issue is people's reactions to seeing themselves "on TV". Children who have worked with the system are much less self-conscious than adults. They are fascinated with the system and adapt quickly. Adults are slower to adapt, though they too learn to become comfortable quickly as the technology recedes and the content and interactions draw their attention.

That some people feel a little traumatic on first seeing themselves on video is nothing new. Instructors who use videotaping to help students work on presentation skills have developed protocols that allow those students to view their taped presentations in private. Many of us still cringe at hearing the sound of our own voices on audiotape as well. Still, the impact can be greater on some people than others, as evidenced by the site facilitator in an early CV meeting who sat under the table for the entire session rather than be seen on camera!

Much of this natural reaction can be alleviated by providing students opportunity at the start of the course to experiment hands-on with the equipment. One of the great assets of CV is its ease of operation. When students feel free to move the camera from person to person or to switch from camera views of the class to the graphics pad, anyone who is uncomfortable is empowered to move the camera elsewhere.

Students' attitudes about being on "television" have implications for both instructional designers and course facilitators or instructors. These implications have to do with the types of instructional activities used and with classroom management. As in any group, some people will do more talking than others. Those students who tend to be quiet anyway may well be even quieter when intimidated by the idea of having their image and words projected to relatively unknown people elsewhere. Instructional activities should be designed to provide all students opportunities (or sometimes requirements) to practice, to reflect, to voice their thoughts. If intersite communications are an integral or beneficial means of accomplishing the course goals, some structure should be provided so that the talkers do not always dominate. The quiet students should be given enough structure to reduce their anxiety about participating.

We would add a note here, since we are discussing human interaction factors, about presentations via CV, whether delivered by students or instructors. In our experience, everyone has had a good time, but the most valuable learning seemed to be what went on in on-site groups. Presentations over CV to all sites were not always completely successful. The instructor's image and personality become a central focus point for the entire group. As in any learning situation, instructors who are warm, friendly, and outgoing will have more successful interactions. These same factors hold true for other presenters whether students or guest lecturers. We must also remember that straight lecture is a fairly ineffective instructional method no matter what the medium. Based on our observations, we can suggest several factors which may affect the success of spoken presentations.

- <u>Speakers who are not dynamic.</u> We live in a visually and audially stimulating media world, and people tend not to pay attention to dull speakers. Dull speakers on TV are even easier to ignore.

- <u>Factors of interference</u>. Private or group conversations often go on at a given site during presentations. These conversations may actually be valuable and relevant to the subject, but they make the formal CV presentations harder to hear. The site facilitator may sometimes have to pull the group back to attention.

- <u>"Viewability" of materials.</u> Instructor materials can (at least theoretically) be thoughtfully designed and produced ahead of time. Materials for student presentations or discussions created ad hoc may not be as easy to see or understand. While the video quality of CV is generally quite high, good graphic design is still necessary.

- <u>Interruptions from multiple sites</u>. Spontaneity is good, but when there are multiple sites, a given presenter or presentation may be interrupted frequently by relevant questions. Too many questions can disrupt the flow of information and listeners tend to loose the point. We eventually had to limit questions, or defer them until after the presentation. One way of controlling this through CV channels was to have listeners print questions and display them via the graphics pad. If the home site, or instructor site, can scan to other sites periodically, questions can be read silently by the instructor and responded to without interruption to other sites. Responses to site-specific questions, such as administrative issues can also be transmitted via graphics pad and sent only to that site.

A final related issue arises especially for the instructor who is addressing students at other sites. Protocols need to be developed for insuring that students do not use the ability to control the camera to keep themselves off-camera and out of participation throughout the course. Techniques for keeping attention in a regular classroom, such as physical movement and eye contact are not usable in a CV classroom. New techniques must be developed to create positive person-to-person interactions. Future software developments are promised which will address this issue by allowing remote control of site cameras by the instructor.

Phase 2:   Objectives and Assessment

The capabilities of compressed video systems are described elsewhere in this handbook in greater technical detail, but it is useful to discuss these capabilities briefly in terms of their implications for determining instructional outcomes. We have already described the chicken-or-egg problem of designing for new technologies. While as we have said, theoretically one determines objectives according to instructional goals, in reality no one piece of the puzzle can be viewed in isolation. The attributes of compressed video systems will undoubtedly suggest many different possibilities to the creative instructional designer.

The compressed video system with which we have worked consists of a moveable wheeled cabinet which contains two monitors, the computer processor and a VCR. Connected to this is a control panel by which participants can move the camera or switches from the main camera to a second camera connected to a graphics pad. The graphics pad functions something like an overhead projector. Paper-based materials can be viewed on screen, slides can be projected and viewed, even three dimensional objects. In our experimental week-long course, one site took pride each day in displaying the refreshments they brought in.

An additional feature utilizes the computer which drives the system. Any still visual can be stored by creating a computer file. Visuals can also be altered by using a light pen to mark or label them. Motion video can be received from another site and recorded or can be transmitted to other sites.

These characteristics fire the imagination with creative possibilities, but the challenge remains the same as always: how do we make use of this combination of media in ways that make for the most effective instruction, not just the biggest flash?

As we think about new approaches to instructional design with new technologies, it is useful to remember the unique nature of compressed video compared with other technologies of interest to instructional designers. It is interesting to note that Hannafin (1992), in his critique of ISD related to emerging technologies, focuses mainly on computer-based instruction, particularly hypermedia. Merrill, Li, and Jones (1990a, 1990b), in proposing a new ISD model, talk about expert systems and artificial intelligence. These authors do not address instructional design implications in the realm of new telecommunications technologies.

While we have little empirical data, we can make several observations about the nature of compressed video based on our experience. First, compressed video is primarily an instrument for the delivery of group rather than individualized instruction. Contrasted with hypermedia or artificial intelligence systems this is not a limitation, but rather a solution to a different instructional issue.

Second, while CV provides the capability for even direct interactions with computers (and all the possibilities that capability implies), we believe the unique potential of CV lies in its human-to-human interaction. The positive response of learners to CV instruction seems related at least in part with a feeling that their constituency, that of distance learners, is being acknowledged and addressed. One purpose of all distance education is to include widespread audiences in a larger educational community.

Our successful use of compressed video, and the great enthusiasm with which it has been met here in Wyoming, leads us back to the understanding that much of the educational process (as opposed to a narrower definition of "instruction") is social, and the desire for social interaction is a basic need among humans. While some needs may be more efficiently met through individual computer-based learning, a more holistic view of the educational process acknowledges the need for learning with and from others, even if it sometimes appears to be an inefficient use of time.

The content and materials for an instructional unit in CV may be painstakingly prepared in advance, with the appropriate care given to cultural and other audience factors. However, the live and spontaneous nature of the medium requires a heightened awareness of the kinds of messages which may be communicated, intentionally or unintentionally. While we strongly urge the avoidance of the "talking heads" model of delivery that marked early instructional video programs, we must still acknowledge the importance of the human communication elements that are both a characteristic of CV and one of its strongest benefits. Objectives which can integrate human communication characteristics of CV with clearly defined student performance expectations will lead to the most successful instruction.

Objectives and assessment approaches are logically discussed together. The nature of the objectives will dictate the nature of the assessment. In what ways might the medium of compressed video affect the kinds of learning outcomes we expect? We can compare CV in this respect to both classroom instruction and other forms of distance education.

One factor which influences CV instruction is time. CV provides real time interactions between instructor and students and among students themselves. However, the nature of these interactions is specific: the interactions relate to what is said and done while on the system. Written communications, other than graphics, must be either mailed or fax'd. This poses not only a logistical problem, but an issue about objectives as well. Does the nature of the course content require a large writing component? If so, the objectives need to be carefully devised, so that criteria required are those that can be realistically assessed, with the necessary practice and feedback along the way. If you know that it will be impossible to provide quick enough turn-around in grading assignments to provide adequate learning opportunities to students, then you may need to modify the objectives

One way to address assessment (and the underlying objectives) is to involve learners in the assessment process. We are primarily talking about adult learners here, although some of these approaches will work with young learners as well. Rather than designing objectives which hold the student to a standard determined and controlled by the instructor, guidelines may be provided, and peer evaluations used, with the instructor facilitating the process. Another approach is to use a contract structure. That is, assignments and criteria are provided, and students contract for their grades accordingly.

The above discussion assumes that you are working in a situation where grading is required. But even if you are free from the requirement to assign grades, is it still necessary to assess the attainment of objectives if you are to provide meaningful learning experiences.

As always, instruction, should be as meaningful as possible, as "real world" as possible. One approach to the challenge of making instruction meaningful is the use of integrative goals. Gagne and Merrill (1990) describe this method in which cognitive schema are created into which subsequent information can be integrated throughout the instruction. This not only creates a more meaningful context for the learning but may also build outcomes which lead learners to synthesize the learning rather than approaching it as a number of discrete units of information.

Figure 10.2.
Alternative Assessment Activities.

This approach of creating a cognitive context for the instruction may be particularly appropriate for compressed video. If maximum use is to be made of all the various channels of communication and interaction available with CV, the instructional designer needs to work at integrating objectives, presentation mode, required student behaviors, and the channels through which those behaviors will be expressed and evaluated.

Objectives which are expressed in integrated final products are useful when teaching with CV, partly because so many different ways are open for students both to create and to share those products. Although research papers and tests may be appropriate for some types of learning, such paper-based objectives and assessments make little use of alternative kinds of knowledge demonstration and sharing, such as using graphics to represent and synthesize issues, linking to computer programs to share projects based in other technologies, or creating videotape presentations. The structuring of objectives into more meaningful collective outcomes is also congruent with adult learning principles, which direct us to involve the learner as an active participant in the earning process, drawing heavily from prior experience and addressing individual learning needs.

Considerations in Selecting Outcomes

In practice, if not in theory, the determination of the kinds and number of objectives to be addressed will be affected by a variety of factors, not all of them instructional. Among the factors which may have a bearing on selecting objectives for compressed video instruction are:

* The nature of the course (e.g., for credit in a degree program or for continuing education?).

* Class size. Very large or very small groups can affect interaction dynamics as well as logistics.

* Constraints of distance on handing in and sending back papers or other assignments.

* Importance of group vs. individual efforts in processing the content.

* Requirements for assessment. Traditional testing may not be appropriate for logistical reasons, such as the inability to monitor each site, or simply because testing is often not the most appropriate assessment for graduate level courses or for adult learners.

* Projects or activities that can be used to encourage interactions at and between sites.

* Need for clear guidelines or checklists. Distance increases the potential for confusion about assignments.

* Potential for use of self-assessment tools or contracts, so students can evaluate their own work.

* Research components. The instructor must provide readings or make certain students have access to libraries, which may be unlikely, particularly at rural remote sites. Access of libraries through computer-based databases may provide additional resources.

PHASE 3: Developing Activities/Media/Materials

In discussing the development of instructional media and materials, we will not consider here all steps in development, which have been well covered elsewhere. Instead, we will point out the areas in which the demands of compressed video seem to call for additional or different approaches. Those areas include the role of the instructor; technical preparation, and training the trainer; specific skills needed by the designer; the interactivity factor; and a model for developing instructional strategies for compressed video instruction.

The Role of the Instructor

Compressed video instruction could theoretically be delivered with no instructor at all, simply by presenting various instructional materials in some appropriate sequence. However, it has been our experience that one of the primary benefits of CV is the face-to-face contact of real people across distances. The natural emphasis on human interaction leads logically to a discussion about the role of the instructor in compressed video instruction. As we said earlier, the instructor who falls back on the "talking head" model will be no more successful in compressed video than in any other medium, and perhaps less so. If the aim is merely to impart information in a one-way channel, it would be more cost efficient to mail out videotaped lectures.

If the instructor is to play an integral role, if only to facilitate the flow of CV-mediated activities, then specific thought must be given to the nature of that role during design and development of the instruction. Concentrating on the role of the instructor is not a usual ISD value. Kerr (1989) has criticized the tendency of instructional designers to ignore or downplay the importance of the teacher, especially in educational institutions. According to Kerr, "... schools as a social institution collectively have other (and many would argue, more important) purposes than the transmission of information to their charges. Teachers, too, are more than classroom-based implementors of instructional strategies" (p. 6).

The instructor in a compressed video course will play a variety of roles, instructional, social, and technological. He or she is responsible for designing instructional goals and activities that will be meaningful to a variety of students at a variety of distance sites (there may or may not be a distinction between the designer and the instructor). He or she is responsible for coordinating all the parts of that instruction, and all media involved. In class, he or she is responsible for creating and monitoring student interactions, an effort more demanding in CV than when all participants are in the same room. Particularly if students are participating at multiple sites, the instructor must be aware of the group dynamics of the whole group and each of the distance sites. CV provides the ability to switch immediately between sites, but the instructor must think to do so, and must draw on each site (and each individual) as much as possible without being perceived as favoring a particular site. In our experience, where there was a group on campus with the instructors, as well as numerous groups at distance sites, there were some (albeit joking) comments about the on-campus students being more of an "in-group".

A few general notes on communications for the benefit of the instructor may be useful at this point. CV provides many of the channels of regular communication: speech, facial expressions, gestures; but these channels are not as completely usable as they would be if you were taking to someone in front of you. Humor works well, and seems to facilitate the forging of bonds between students and instructor at distant sites. Hesitation seems to be somewhat magnified (those awkward moments when, as an instructor, you start to respond to someone and then just kind of fade away....). Those moments are perceived more closely at remote sites. Learners seem to look at the instructor at a distance a little more closely, perhaps because they're aware that their time and access is limited, or because the instructor takes on a slightly more iconic role than he or she would if actually present for others to take other sensory cues from.

Training the Trainer

In addition to managing the instructional process, the instructor must manage the delivery system. What this entails will vary with the type of system your organization selects. Some compressed video systems are geared to formal classroom set-ups and may require technicians to operate. Because we were interested in educational applications and in exploring all the potential creative uses for CV, we selected a system that is movable, easy to start, operate, and shut down. We have been able to use graduate students as interns who provide technical support for faculty in the College of Education.

CV is extremely easy to operate, and even troubleshooting and diagnostics are relatively simple. However, anyone who has worked with any kind of media understands Murphy's Law. If anything can go wrong it will. CV constitutes a complex interaction between sites and over communication lines, whether telephone lines or satellite. Occasionally connections may go down through no fault of your own. This is nothing more than an inconvenience, but one which a little forethought and planning can help make less inconvenient.

We can offer several suggestions for anticipating down time. First, designate a site facilitator. This person can be one of the class members or someone else familiar with the content who perhaps would like some experience with the material or the media. The site facilitator can assist by facilitating group discussions, or by being the contact person if you need to call the site, either during class or between class sessions. This person can also help administratively by distributing, collecting, or mailing papers or other materials.

A site facilitator can also help with our second strategy suggestion. Be prepared with an alternative activity. Sometimes keeping group discussion going at each site will provide students with meaningful learning even when off-line. Additional readings are another meaningful alternative activity. It is not necessary to make complete alternative lesson plans for each session, but it may be helpful to provide general guidelines for facilitators at the beginning of the course so that some kind of contingency plan is in place. As students get familiar with CV courses, their anxiety with the technology seems to diminish. But glitches at the beginning can create anxiety and leave students with a sense that they have not gotten full benefit from the instructional situation.

Another suggestion is to build in time at the beginning of a course for some games or other informal activities to get students used to the system, and to let them have some hands-on experience. We have found this approach very helpful. Students start off with a positive experience, removed from the formal structure of the course. An atmosphere of free communication and humor add much to CV courses, and help make the most of the spontaneous nature of the medium.

Checking Out System Components

The advantage of compressed video lies in its capacity to integrate many different media. This also means the instructor and the site facilitator need to be aware of these media at each site. We include here a sample list of components to check out before class starts.

See Chapter 11 for more on technical training for instructors

- <u>Telephone</u>. There may be phone lines to the CV console, but not always another line available. If there are problems with the connections, phone contact may be needed. We've also used an audiobridge connection as a back-up option.

- <u>Fax machine</u>. A facsimile machine is particularly useful for spontaneous sharing of print materials between sites. While the instructor should plan well ahead in distributing course materials, students may bring things to class or create materials which are too complex or unreadable to rely on transmission via the graphics pad. A fax machine and a copier make sharing between sites possible immediately.

- <u>A contact person at the facility</u>. Who is in charge of unlocking the room, finding additional chairs, adjusting the heating or cooling or supplying access to a copier or facsimile machine?

- <u>Peripheral equipment available at each site</u>. A well-planned system will address this question during installation. However, it is best not to take for granted that all equipment will be available when needed. In our situation, the instructors planned to show videotapes produced by participants at each site and assumed each site was equipped with a VCR wired into the compressed video console. When it was found that not all sites had the expected equipment the activity had to be altered.

Design Skills for Compressed Video

Creating instruction to be delivered via compressed video poses interesting challenges and opportunities for the instructional designer. One the useful skill for a designer is a strong sense for matching appropriate activities to the outcomes, the media being used, and the level and types of interactions. This is similar to the tasks of designing for multimedia, but adds the human, real-time interest and potential unpredictability of live interactions.

A related issue in understanding the total design is the economic factor in using on-line time. While CV may be an inexpensive alternative medium when compared to instructors traveling to distant sites, there is still an on-line cost, generally charged by the hour. The designer should develop a realistic sense of cost vs. benefits. Time on the CV system should be used wisely, with an eye for which content and activities lend themselves to the medium and what supporting activities can be used outside of "on-line" time.

The designer (or instructor) for CV instruction should also have a solid understanding of visual design, specifically as it relates to video-based graphics. Some understanding of audio production can also be useful, since the audio channel is a primary source of information. The number and quality of microphones can affect the effectiveness of instructional communications. It can be difficult to retain attention as students focus on the video over long periods of time. If audio from other sites is poor, attention will flag.

Designing for Interactivity

CV makes use of interactivity in two ways. First there is the interaction of students and instructors, and the interaction between sites. This interaction is an integral part of the instructional process and should be planned for in designing the course or other instructional unit. Some suggestions for incorporating interactivity into the instructional design will be offered in the following section on instructional strategy.

The second type of interaction is that of participants with the technology. As stated earlier, the compressed video system that we use is simple, and we provide students on-going opportunity to manipulate the different components. In fact, we have found that it is beneficial for the instructor to assume a hands-off role when there are students present. The control panel uses a light pen and a system of icons which are intuitively obvious to use. Encouraging interactions like this has helped us move students quickly from nervousness about the system to treating the technology as just one more tool for communication. Interacting with the controls also encourages students to be active participants in the learning process.

An Analogy for Designing Instructional Strategies for Compressed Video

Throughout our discussion we have stressed the exciting nature of CV that lies in its ability to facilitate human interactions. We can perhaps foresee a time when this technology will become so commonplace that it is viewed as just another classroom experience. However, at this point, we can profit from the factors of novelty and enthusiasm in the same way computer based instruction has done.

Instructional design for compressed video thus becomes a balancing act, trying to make the most of the spontaneous communication possible while also trying to ensure the efficient and effective achievement of objectives that ISD was developed to address. Because ISD models are relatively prescriptive, and also because they tend to focus on controlling all aspects of the learning situation, they may not be perfect models for designing interactive learning via CV. In trying to describe more fluid instructional strategies, we offer one suggestion to designers for visualizing the components of CV based instruction.

Figure 10.3 shows the flow of instruction during a CV class or course. The main flow, top to bottom, can be thought of as a river. The main channel represents the planned objectives and corresponding activities. This might also be described in terms of critical path. How critical the path is depends on the nature of the instruction itself. Points placed along the main flow represent the critical information and activities necessary to maintain the logic and integrity of the overall instructional goal. There may be implied or explicit temporal sequences which can be shown in the direction of the flow.

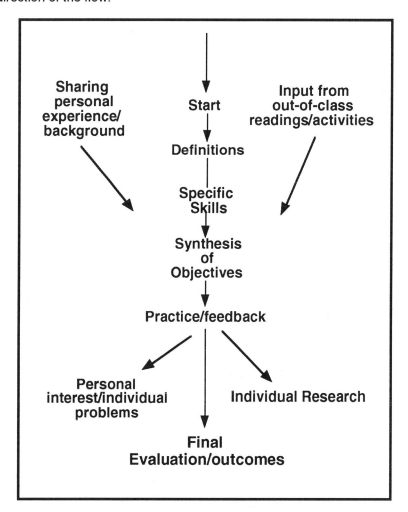

Figure 10.3
Flow of Instruction in a CV Course

Branches are of two different types, and represent the kinds of decisions instructors make on a continuing basis. These decisions are related to the flow of discussion and information in class. Instructors must constantly make decisions on how closely to monitor discussion, while continually analyzing the flow of topics to determine their relationship to the main topic and their relative value to either the achievement of course goals or the general benefit of students in some larger context. In-flowing branches indicate potential areas in which students may contribute individual experiences, insights and suggestions which add to the main flow of instruction. In the planning stages the designer may use such in-flowing paths as a visual means of anticipating the learners' prior knowledge and interests. For example, in the telecourse to which we have been referring, the students were in-service teachers from a number of school districts. Therefore, the designer could logically predict that instructors and facilitators could draw on ideas, examples and issues from a variety of content areas and grade levels. A similar prediction could be made that students would express a need to know how the content of the course, alternative evaluation methods, would affect their overall requirements for accountability in their own classrooms. Making these inferences about what the learners would bring to the learning situation allows the designer to plan ways to make the content and activities more relevant.

The second type of branching is that of out-flowing streams. These out-flowing branches represent issues that may arise in the classroom. These issues are unintended as outcomes and may represent either individual or group interests. Where the in-flowing streams represent decisions of the instructor during the course to integrate interests into the main body of instruction, out-flowing streams represent decisions either *not* to include issues which arise or to modify previously designated outcomes. Such decisions may be made because the new issues are irrelevant to the main objectives, because they are of interest only to a few, because they are too complex or time consuming to deal with in the time limits of the course, or for other reasons. The decision to treat issues as out-flowing branches must be made by the instructor, weighing the factors in the context of the class. Out-flowing branches can be addressed in several ways. One is to simply direct interested participants to pursue new interests on their own. Possibly the instructor can provide direction or references in support. The second option is to adapt the set objectives and outcomes of the course by individualizing requirements for a person or a group. This provides another way of tailoring instruction to individual needs, and should be reserved as an option of the instructor.

Clearly this model is not intended to provide step by step procedures, although it builds on the foundation of regular ISD procedures. Rather, we are presenting one method of visualizing an approach to what is a common dilemma in this type of interactive design.

Phase 4: Formative and Summative Evaluation

In any instructional design project, evaluation should be given serious consideration. When working with new technologies it is particularly important to collect evaluative information precisely because, as instructional designers, our assumptions and enthusiasms may tend to color our perceptions. While many of the benefits of compressed video are clear, the costs of the system alone make it imperative for us not only to design for the most effective use but also to hold our efforts up to rigorous standards in assessing that effectiveness. It is in the evaluation of our products that we can continue to improve and refine what we do.

This includes, as stated in all instructional design models, both formative and summative evaluation. Chapter 11 discusses participant evaluation of compressed video courses. The processes of formative evaluation are addressed in detail in Chapter 12. For that reason, we will concentrate this discussion on summative evaluation.

See Chapters 11 and 12

Issues of summative evaluation for compressed video are similar to those in evaluating learning via any delivery system. Perhaps the main difference lies in the choices of media for both delivery and assessment of the learning. A number of studies support the idea that methods of assessment should parallel the methods of delivery. Tulving and Thomson (1973), for example, describe memory processing in terms of encoding. "Specific encoding operations performed on what is perceived determine what is stored, and what is stored determines what retrieval cues are effective in providing access to what is stored" (p. 369).

The practical implications for this view of learning are clear. CV instruction tends to rely heavily on visual stimuli. The designer therefore needs to give serious consideration to forms of assessment which will be congruent with the visual form in which the information was presented. This may pose some challenges, as the standard verbal, paper-based methods of assessment are much easier to use.

In a broader context, the nature and purpose of evaluation in educational settings is coming under fire from many sources currently. According to Herman (1992), "Educational assessment is in a process of invention. Old models are being seriously questioned: new models are in development. Open-ended questions, exhibits, demonstrations, hands-on experiments, computer simulations and portfolios are a few examples" (p. 74). Throughout this chapter we have referred to the potential of CV for incorporating diverse media channels into the instructional experience. Those options hold true for assessment activities as well.

Herman also summarizes other research findings about effective assessments which seem well-suited for CV instruction. She notes that "meaningful learning utilizes self-regulation and reflection and that affective and metacognitive skills are important in motivation." Specifically applicable to CV, "...groups may facilitate learning by modeling effective thinking strategies, scaffolding complicated performances, providing mutual constructive feedback, and valuing the elements of critical thought" (p. 75).

Regardless of the level of instruction presented over CV, whether for public schools, higher education or other training situations, the call for more authentic forms of assessment is valid. Designers can play a critical role in reshaping how we think about evaluation, including influencing those with whom we work. In our experience, both in education and industry, evaluation has suffered from a lack of understanding by client groups of both goals and techniques. The idea of building in assessment procedures and

approaches before designing the instruction, one of the great strengths of
ISD, is particularly foreign to many people. Yet, especially in working with
new technologies, the information that we can gain from strong evaluation
efforts maybe invaluable in helping to improve our instructional efforts.

Summary

In this chapter we have offered a blend of theory and practical
experience which we hope will be helpful to people beginning to work with
compressed video-based instruction. The uncertainty in working with a new
technology is, we think, clearly out weighed by the exciting challenges that
compressed video presents.

As instructional designers continue working with compressed video,
and with other "cutting edge" technologies, it will remain important to our field
to continue collecting information, both anecdotal and empirical. As with
other technologies, the tendency with compressed video has so far been to
get out and try things, and that enthusiastic approach has, for us in Wyoming
and elsewhere, already resulted in a number of exciting instructional efforts.
No doubt many readers can already, or soon will be able to, contribute their
own suggestions and improvements. Thus, we have offered not a definitive
view of CV instruction but rather the opening dialog in what we anticipate will
be a long and exciting exploration.

References

Briggs, L. J. and Wager, W. (1981). *Handbook of procedures for the design
of instruction*, second edition. Englewood Cliffs, New Jersey:
Educational Technology Publications.

Damarin, S. K. (1991). Feminist unthinking and educational technology.
Educational Training and Technology International, 28 (2). 111-
119.

Dick, W. and Carey, L. (1990). T*he Systematic design of instruction*, third
edition. Glenview, Illinois: Scott Foresman.

Gagne, R. and Briggs, L. (1979). *Principles of Instructional Design*, 2nd.
ed. New York: Holt, Rinehart, Winston.

Gagne, R. and Merrill, P. (1990). Integrative goals for instructional design.
Educational Technology Research and Development, 38 (1). 23-
30.

Hannafin, M. J. (1992). Emerging technologies, ISD, and learning environments: critical perspectives. *Educational Technology Research
and Development*, 40(1). 49-63.

Hawkridge, D. (1991). Challenging educational technology. *Educational
Training and Technology International*, 28 (2). 102-110.

Herman, J. (1992).   What research tells us about good assessment. *Educational Leadership*, 49 (8). 74-78.

Jonassen, D.H. (1990). Thinking technology: toward a constructivist view of instructional design. *Educational Technology*, September. 32-34.

Kerr, S. (1989). Technology, teachers, and the search for school reform. *Educational Technology Research and Development,* 37 (4). 5-17.

Merrill, M. D., Li, Z., and Jones, M. K. (1990a). Limitations of first generation instructional design. *Educational Technology*, January.

Merrill, M. D., Li, Z., and Jones, M. K. (1990b).   The second generation instructional design research program. *Educational Technology*, March.

Nichols, R. G. (1990).   A challenge to current beliefs about educational technology. *Educational Technology*, November. 24-27.

Tennyson, R. D. (1990).   A proposed cognitive paradigm of learning for educational technology. *Educational Technology*, June. 16-19.

Tessmer, M. and Wedman, J. F. (1990).   A layers-of-necessity instructional development model. *Educational Technology Research and Development*, 38 (2). 77-85.

Tripp, S. and Bichelmeyer, B. (1990).   Rapid prototyping: an alternative instructional design strategy. *Educational Technology Research and Development*, 38 (1). 31-44.

Tulving, E. & Thomson, D. (1973).   Encoding specificity and retrieval processes in episodic memory. *Psychological Review, 80* (5), 352-373.

11

Supporting Compressed Video

Steven G. Sachs

Introduction

Successful use of compressed video requires an array of support services to take care of logistical needs. It takes more than just scheduling the system and turning it on to make it an effective resource for the organization. There are technical considerations, site coordination, user training, and policy issues that have to be accommodated. If they are dealt with ahead of time, they are less likely to develop into crises in the critical early stages of compressed video use. This chapter will deal primarily with educational settings. However, most of the points offered here apply to any type of organization using compressed video.

On-Site Support

At its most basic level, there is certain support compressed video users will initially expect at every site. These include such things as: technicians, test proctors, room facilitators at remote sites, registration services, mail service between sites, telephone, fax, copy machine, equip-ment spares (in case an item fails), plus security for equipment and personnel. It is worth noting that just because these support services are expected does not mean that all have to be provided. It is often sufficient to make sure that users understand what services will be provided and how they need to address issues such as handouts and mail. Specific examples of how these services are dealt with by organizations using compressed video can be found in the User Profiles or from the contacts in Part II of this book.

Initially, the most basic concern of users always seems to center on technical support. The user wants to know what kind of help will be available on site if something goes wrong or does not work correctly. Some organizations already have a technician or other technologically oriented individual at each site who can absorb compressed video support as part of the regular duties. Some provide a room facilitator at remote sites while others rely on participants to handle most of the technical operations. These individuals are linked to technical support by phone. These are not trivial decisions. They have budget and equipment selection considerations.

Both the University of Wyoming and Northern Virginia Community College have found that faculty and participants using compressed video are quite capable of operating their systems and dealing with most common problems. At Wyoming, selected students are trained to become facilitators and receive extra credit or partial tuition support.

In the corporate world, the flexibility of compressed video systems that can be wheeled from office to office has minimized the role for full-time technicians devoted to compressed video. Instead, users increasingly are turning to each other for technical support when the system develops a problem.

Since it is often too expensive or impractical to provide a technician, or even a room facilitator, at each site, the system needs to be simple to operate. In addition, there needs to be independent access to technical support that is not dependent on the compressed video system working (e.g., a separate telephone line). After all, if the video system is not working it cannot be used to get technical help! It also is a good idea to have some kind of back-up system the user can implement if the compressed video system does not work as planned and technical support by phone does not solve the problem. Examples of good back-up systems are speaker phones for small groups, or relatively inexpensive audio conferencing units such as those from Darome, NEC and Polycom which have microphones and a speaker built into a single unit. Even if the video does not work, the audio portion of the meeting or class can go on uninterrupted. Some compressed video systems even allow audio-only sites to be routinely added to a conference where the other sites are using both audio *and* video.

One of the most important things that needs to be done in the area of on-site support is to develop complete and accurate documentation of the compressed video system and support services *at each site*. Without this documentation it is very hard to provide help to users over the telephone. The documentation needs to indicate what types of equipment are in use at each site, how it is connected, initial equipment settings, what support services are available, how they are obtained (e.g. where the fax machine is located and who installs new paper), contact people at the site, etc.

Another approach to on-site support is to standardize the equipment and the configuration at each site. This allows individuals to accurately describe each component at any site by looking at their own site. It is also very helpful to label unfamiliar equipment at each site and to post the initial settings in a convenient location. This can save many panic phone calls when things are slightly out of adjustment. Each of these strategies helps the users take control of their site instead of leaving them at the mercy of the equipment.

Technical Support Services

Technical support of compressed video systems requires much more attention than many vendors would have people believe. Few, if any, systems are suitable for simple "plug-in and play" operation. This becomes even more true as additional components are added such as extra microphones, VCRs, computers, fax machines, etc. Technical support services fall into five categories: remote-site set-up, trouble shooting, help access, technician training, supplemental equipment.

Remote-site Set-up

In the ideal system, participants at the remote sites could walk into the room with compressed video equipment, throw a single switch and begin their video conference. Many systems come very close to this level of operation; though it can take a year of trial and error to get there. With the variety of components that must work together, few systems stay in perfect adjustment all the time. Most adjustment problems can usually be traced to human error. Audio levels can be set too high, receiving volumes can be too loud, microphones can be left in the wrong place so they pick up too much audio from the speakers, push-to-talk microphones can be left open, etc. In other cases, components may be turned off incorrectly, cables can come loose or switches can be in the wrong position. Sometimes the problem may be that the system is confused and just needs to be turned off and back on again. All of these are relatively simple problems that can be easily remedied *if* a person knows how the system operates, what clues to look for and what steps to follow. Remote sites need support through a room facilitator, on-site technician, phone line to an experienced technician at another site, or at least a set-up checklist to assist them in starting up the equipment and dealing with any initial problems. Otherwise, if a problem develops, no matter how minor, the participants may become frustrated, give up and leave.

Trouble Shooting

One of the most important areas of technical support is in the area of trouble shooting to identify system problems. Getting the system quickly back into working condition starts with identifying the problem. Most systems will have at least one person, either a technician or system manager, who is extremely familiar with the system and knows the root cause of most problems almost immediately. However, if the problem is at a remote site, this person may have to depend on other individuals' eyes and ears to describe the problem and help remedy it. Furthermore, problems may not always develop when this *expert* person is available. Problems may develop when the system expert is on vacation or out sick. Worse yet, the expert may leave for another job. For these reasons, trouble shooting deserves some advance planning.

As noted above, there needs to be easily accessed documentation showing the type and arrangement of equipment at each site. There needs to be a list of phone numbers, fax numbers and contact people for each site. Without this information, the system expert may be "blind" trying to help another site.

There should be a list of steps anyone can follow when trouble shooting a problem. This list should be clearly labeled and attached in some way to the compressed video equipment so it is always handy even if the equipment is moved from room to room. This list may take the form of a checklist describing the questions to ask, the system settings to verify, and a set of actions to take that would *usually* bring the system back to working order. For example, the list might start with a problem description such as, "We can see people at the other site, but we can't hear them." This can be followed by a list of settings to verify or things to try, followed by the name and phone number of whom to call if these things do not work. Other typical problems that might be listed include: "We see ourselves in both the local and remote-site monitors;" "There are loud echoes in the audio;" "We are getting a message on the screen that the other site is not on;" "The other site can't see the video tape we are showing;" "The other site can't see the graphic from the overhead camera." The system expert, along with others who have helped resolve system problems, are the best resources for creating this list. When it is finished, it should be tested on real problems-even by the system expert.

At the same time a trouble shooting procedure is being established, system back-up procedures need to be developed. If there is a back-up system, who decides if it should be used? Who sets it up? How are delays to be handled? Is there replacement equipment that can be installed and is there time? Who needs to be notified when there is a problem, and how soon should they be notified? All of these are questions that are better addressed before a problem develops than after a small problem turns into a crisis unnecessarily.

Help Access

Users of a compressed video system need to know how to get help if a question or problem develops. It does not matter whether the participants are at a main site with technicians nearby or at a remote site by themselves. They not only need to know whom to contact and how, they need to know that it is okay to ask for help and to make suggestions for improving the system so it better meets their needs. Help can be provided in many ways depending on the audience, the sites, and the nature of the compressed video system itself. One strategy is to have technicians at every site. However, this can be very expensive, and is probably not necessary. A variation is to have a room facilitator or a designated contact at each site who is not a technician but is familiar enough with the system to work with a technician by phone to remedy most problems. With some groups who use the system on a regular basis, one or two participants at each site can be trained to operate the system and to work with the technicians. In some cases, it is enough to provide the participants themselves with phone access to the technician or to have a technician monitor all activity over the compressed video system and interact with participants as necessary.

It is also a very good idea to prominently post phone numbers on the compressed video equipment for people who can provide help with problems. If all else fails, users can call for help even if the trouble shooting checklist is missing or the room facilitator is absent. It is important that several numbers be listed or that the number be one that is always answered. Nothing is worse than calling for help in a panic when there is only one phone number and getting no answer or getting an answering machine. In a similar way, a help number should not be tied up on long calls unrelated to the system. There have been reports of evening technicians who are working alone using the *help line* to make personal calls to pass the time. When a problem developed, the remote site could not get a call through to that technician. Murray State University came up with a clever way to prevent this problem. They use a pager to alert their technician that help is needed! In another case, the evening classes began at 7:00, so the technician's shift ended at 8:00 on the assumption that everything would go smoothly after the sites were connected. Everything did go smoothly until 9:00, an hour before the class was due to end. Luckily, there was a back-up system in place, or the class would have had to be dismissed early.

In business environments where the staff rely on each other for technical support there is always the danger that all the knowledgeable users will be out of the office at the same time. This can leave an new user in a bad spot if a problem develops. It only has to happen once to discourage new users from trying the system.

Technician Training

Even if the vendor provides initial training as part of the system installation, there will need to be on-going technician training. Technicians leave for other jobs, take vacations, get sick, or may just need help as use of the system grows. The amount of training and who will provide it depends on a number of factors. First, it is important to define the limits of what the technician is to do and what will be left to an outside vendor. In some systems, the technician will do the major trouble shooting and even replace major components that fail. In other systems, the technician may try to isolate the problem, but will primarily be limited to making adjustments. In this case, the amount of training needed may be minimal with a good trouble-shooting checklist being of more help.

Where technician support is limited or it is difficult to train additional technicians, there are several strategies that help keep the compressed video system operating. The most obvious one is to purchase a maintenance agreement that includes on-site service for the major system components. If a problem develops that the available staff cannot readily solve, they call the vendor for service. Another strategy is to have spare equipment that can be substituted for equipment which is suspected of being the cause of the problem. It must be decided who will determine if equipment should be replaced, who will do it, and where will the spares be kept. The technician only needs to know how to connect the new equipment, not how to fix the old unit or even how to be sure the old unit was the problem. Finally, where possible, redundancy can be built into the system. While it may not be feasible to have two codecs in every room, the system can have extra microphones and cameras ready to install, or an audio conferencing unit can always be hooked up so it is ready for instant back-up and can serve as redundancy for the audio channel.

Supplemental Equipment

Equipment other than the components of the compressed video system itself will need consideration and may also need technical support. There may be a fax machine that periodically needs new paper and may require service. Lights in the room with compressed video equipment may burn out and need replacement. Someone needs to be sure there is blank paper and appropriate pens for the overhead camera or the white board, if one is used. The room needs regular cleaning, and the furniture may even need special set-up for some occasions. If a speaker phone is part of the room equipment, it may need to have the batteries changed from time to time. All of these issues need to be thought through and plans made for who will be responsible for taking care of them. Things can be left up to the users, but they need to know this in advance so they can be prepared!

User Training

Compressed video users do a much better job with a little training. The most obvious training topic is basic operation of the system. Meeting leaders, trainers and faculty need to know enough about the system to feel comfortable and in control. At Northern Virginia Community College and the University of Wyoming, user training starts with such things as turning on the system, changing cameras, adjusting audio levels, etc. Then the most common problems, which are almost always related to audio, are dealt with. Northern Virginia does not go into advanced topics since its system does not support many of them. Instead it puts the rest of its attention on helping the faculty develop better lesson plans for use with compressed video. Wyoming does provide advanced training after users have mastered the basic operation. This allows users to take advantage of all their system's capabilities without becoming totally overwhelmed at the beginning. Ideally, individual users will have an opportunity to practice using the system before the real meeting or class takes place. Among the most effective user training strategies is to work with users in groups. The groups should have both new and experienced users so they can benefit from each other's ideas and experience. They should develop and share meeting or lesson plans, and practice using the system with each other so that they get the feel from both the leader and participant perspectives. They can learn procedures or protocols for working at a distance, such as how to ask participants at a remote site to speak up, or to be sure to let the remote site know it is okay to interrupt since it might be hard to see someone whose hand is raised. Faculty may teach part of one of their regular lessons to other users. Those users can give the faculty member feedback and suggestions for improving the presentation, pacing and involvement of the learners. Meeting leaders can *meet* as a group to discuss meeting strategies. This gives them a first-hand look at how a meeting would run on the system. These sessions also develop support groups that relieve the system manager and technician(s) of having to personally solve all the user's problems and helps come up with ideas for improving the system and its use.

One of the hardest lessons users need to learn is the necessity for advance planning. It is much more difficult to walk into the room at the last minute and *wing it* when dealing with remote sites. Handouts and other materials usually must be sent in advance. Activities need to be planned more carefully to accommodate special needs of the participants at the remote sites. Strategies are needed that make participants at the remote sites feel involved. It is even a good idea to have a back-up plan in case there is a system failure that delays the start of the meeting or class.

One other very important topic that user training must cover is how to take advantage of compressed video's two-way capability. Compressed video is interactive. If that interactivity is not going to be used, it would be cheaper to just send a video tape to the other sites and have a phone conference at a later time. There are a number of strategies for encouraging interaction among sites. Here are just a few:

• Participants at each site can have responsibility for teaching each other about different topics.

• Sites can compete against each other.

• Each site can critique another site's performance, ideas, or presentation.

• Sites can alternate giving summaries after each topic is presented or they can quiz other sites on the topic.

• Sites can work as teams to present examples or role play aspects of the topic being presented.

• Participants at each site can caucus and report back to the whole group on how they *feel* about a topic, how they would solve a problem, or how the topic would affect them and their site.

There are several common factors in all of these strategies. First, they all require participants to actively think about the content or topic being presented and deal with it in some way. Second, responsibility is shared between the group leader or instructor and the participants for presenting information. Third, they do not allow for simple "yes/no" or "true/false" answers. Fourth, they use friendly competition to motivate participants. Finally, they let participants work together collaboratively rather than putting individuals on the spot. One of the worst ways of encouraging interaction is to simply ask the remote site, "Are there any questions?" As a rule of thumb, some kind of interaction activity, even a simple polling of how participants feel, should occur every 5-10 minutes. A good user training program should include a chance for participants to sit through a 10-15 minute lecture so they can experience how boring it is.

In some organizations it may be difficult to train top administrators, or even to get new users to attend training before they attempt to conduct a meeting or class on the system. Rather than denying access to these individuals, or letting them have a bad experience, it may be necessary to provide meeting support services. These support services may be as simple as providing a room facilitator who acts as a security blanket for participants uneasy about the technology to actively doing the camera switching and handling other operational tasks during the meeting. At the very least, some kind of printed directions or tips should be provided to occasional users of the system.

Documentation also deserves mention under the heading of user training. The North Dakota Interactive Video Network has produced an extremely detailed user's guide to their system. It covers everything from the system configuration to suggestions for effective use of the system. It has illustrations and diagrams as well. This type of resource material is useful from several standpoints. It is helpful for the new user because it gives both nuts and bolts information as well as an excellent overview of the whole system and its many components. It is also a useful record of how the system is configured, why it is configured that way, and even gives some insight into the direction the designers of the system would like things to move. All too often, people working with compressed video systems are too busy building their systems and working side-by-side with users to document what they have done and why they have done it.

Policies and Procedures

There will be a temptation during the start-up phase of a compressed video system to have a minimum of policies and procedures. The goal probably will be to encourage as much use as possible and learn what works best before carving anything in stone. Nonetheless, the sooner some of the obvious issues are dealt with, the smoother the start-up will be. The mere fact that the issues are considered may identify important things that have been overlooked, even if the specific policies and procedures cannot yet be specified. There is no one right way to handle these issues. Each must fit within the organization's culture and climate.

Remote site logistics require special consideration. How will materials for the remote site get mailed or delivered, and by whom? Who will receive them at the remote site and who will distribute them to participants? Will participants have access to a copier and fax machine? If so, how will costs be handled? Will copies be provided free to participants or will they have to pay? If tests have to be given, who will administer them? How will test security be dealt with? How will the tests get back to the instructor? If equipment breaks down at the remote site, who calls for repair and who pays for it? What are the responsibilities of the remote sites and of the network hub? Who is responsible for making sure those responsibilities are met? Who is responsible for scheduling at each of the sites? Who can cancel sessions which are scheduled on the compressed video system?

The unique nature of compressed video results in some other special problems that need consideration. Since it is possible to observe a meeting or class in process without the participants or instructor being aware, policies and procedures may be needed to prevent abuses. For example, can supervisors or visitors or even other students observe a session without permission? Whose permission is needed? Can a vendor bring prospective customers for a tour to view the system in operation? Are there limits on showing off the system? If a vendor wants to use the organization as a reference, who provides that reference?

The ability to tape meetings and classes also raises the issue of intellectual property rights and copyright. Who decides whether a tape will be made of a meeting or class? Who *owns* the tape? Who can view it or distribute it? Is there a cost for taping? Who owns the copyright?

It is even worthwhile to consider how print materials are to be sent between sites. While this may seem to be obvious, there are some significant cost considerations. For example, Columbia University uses overnight mail to send assignments back and forth between sites. They assume the cost for this service. If this approach is used by other organizations, they need to be aware of the cost and decide who will pay for it. Many users, given the chance, will wait until the last minute to prepare materials for meetings. Then, they will need to fax them to the remote sites. If the materials are lengthy, this can be an extremely time consuming and expensive process. Without some guidelines, fax costs *and tying up of the organization's fax machine(s)* can become a significant issue. Even room clean-up can become an issue if there are not agreed upon procedures in advance.

Typically, organizations turn to other more experienced compressed video users for advice on how to handle these types of policy and procedure issues. The User Profiles in Part Two of this book are good starting places.

Graphics and Computer Support

Users of a compressed video system are going to want to use graphics and computers for their presentations. Some will already be experienced enough with overhead projectors and computers to figure out how to make the system do what they want. Others will need a great deal more help. There are several basic approaches for helping users. One approach is to provide direct support to users either for a fee or for free. The user decides what is needed and the support service does the final design and production. Another approach is to set up a do-it-yourself facility complete with the appropriate hardware and software for making legible materials and putting it in a form that can be used with the compressed video system. In either case, it is a good idea to give users a variety of samples and guidelines that show formats and styles that work well. Users should also be encouraged to make some test materials that they can try out on the system before they go to the trouble of making the materials they will actually need for their meeting or class.

To deal with concerns for quality of the materials used on the compressed video system, users need guidelines that help them select or make materials that will be legible on a television screen. This is quite different than the overhead projector they may be used to using. First, the image size may be smaller than the screen they are used to. this can affect letter size. Second, they may be used to using paper oriented the long direction or portrait style. For television, they need to use paper oriented horizontally or landscape style. Any good audiovisual materials textbook can give guidelines for matching visuals to the audience and television screen size.

See Chapter 15

Users, especially teaching faculty, also need guidance on how to deal with copyrighted materials. While it may be permissible to show a page from a book on the overhead camera, it is probably not permissible to play a copyrighted video tape to remote sites over the compressed video system without first obtaining permission.

Some compressed video systems allow the images from computer screens to be sent between sites. This is a nice feature for meetings where there are only a few participants at each site and they can get close to the television screen. In classroom situations, though, the image size from the computer may be too small for all students to see. If this is the case, there are several ways to overcome the size problem. With advance preparation, students can get handouts that show the same detail that will appear on the screen. The instructor can highlight parts of the visual, and students can look at the paper copy for detail. The instructor might also make paper copies of the computer screens and show them on the overhead camera which can be zoomed down to enlarge a particular part of the page, then zoomed back out to give the bigger perspective of the page as a whole. An alternative is to distribute copies of the computer disk for students to run at the remote site on an LCD panel that projects a larger image. To do this, it may be necessary to have software and licenses for each site, as well as extra audiovisual equipment.

It may also be possible to make a video tape of the computer images that participants can view in small groups later. There are a variety of units in varying price ranges that convert VGA output from a computer to a video format. The general overview can be given to the large group, with participants being expected to review the tape on their own or in small groups where they can get close enough to the screen to see the necessary detail.

Participant Evaluation

One of the best indicators of how the compressed video system is working comes from participant evaluations. Participants should provide feedback about the system at least once for each course and periodically for meetings. The logistics for collecting, analyzing and reporting this feedback needs to be established in advance, so the opinions of participants at remote sites is sure to be included.

Participants should be asked questions about the course or program, the presentation, and the support services. Just as with any class or meeting, it is useful to know if the topic was valuable, the length was right, and how participants felt about the experience. The presentation, though, is different than in a traditional face-to-face meeting. Participants should provide information on how well they could see the television monitors, if they could see the visuals clearly, if the audio was clear, and if they had enough opportunity to participate. Finally, participants should comment on the support services available at their site. Were these services easy to access, were they easy to use, did they help?

Two of the most valuable parts of any evaluation are the written responses from participants and the responses to the global questions such as, "Overall, how would you rate this class/meeting?" or "Would you recommend this class to a friend?" or "Was this an effective way to have a meeting?" Great care needs to be taken in writing these global questions so that it is clear as to what the participant is responding—the content presentation or the compressed video system. For example, when the participant answers the question, "Would you recommend this class to a friend?" does that mean subject matter and this instructor, or does it mean this class *using compressed video?* When in doubt, ask both questions. It will help in interpretation of the data.

Summary

A successful compressed video system requires more than just working equipment. There needs to be a carefully planned set of support services that take into account how the system will be used and what assistance users may need. This support includes provision for helping users when the compressed video system is not working properly as well as such simple things as replacing fax paper or remote control batteries so they do not malfunction during a meeting or class. Providing support services does not always mean adding personnel. In most cases, compressed video users can solve problems with a minimum of help over the phone.

12

EVALUATION TECHNIQUES

Wilhelmina Savenye
Cecelia Box

Introduction

Compressed Video Instruction (CVI) is one of the new interactive technologies which is changing the ways we teach and learn. As with any systematically-designed instruction, CVI courses should be pilot-tested and refined prior to full-scale implementation. Developers can use the tried-and-true techniques of formative evaluation, and this chapter will present several ways to apply those techniques to CVI. However, new technologies for distance learning and communications, such as CVI, stretch how we deliver instruction in complex ways. Alternative evaluation methods emerging in the field of instructional design for interactive technologies offer us the chance to enhance learning from CVI. This chapter will cover how to plan evaluations, how to determine the major evaluation questions, how to collect evaluation data, and how to report results and make recommendations for improving CVI course development and evaluation. While the primary focus of this chapter will be on compressed video used for instruction, also discussed will be evaluating compressed video for teleconferences.

The focus of this chapter will also be on more structured formal formative evaluation efforts. However, the authors recognize that, given the newness of compressed video, much instruction may be designed, developed, and delivered on a more spontaneous or ad hoc basis.

It is strongly recommended that all compressed video networks consider a systematic formative evaluation plan, for reasons which will be elaborated in this chapter. The lack of an overall formative evaluation plan should not, however, preclude individual efforts. Many of the guidelines in this chapter can be adapted for use by any instructor designing for compressed video course delivery.

Formative evaluation is conducted in order to improve instructional programs through revision (Dick & Carey, 1990; Gagne, Briggs, & Wager, 1988; Morris & Fitzgibbon, 1978). The value of formative evaluation was recently illustrated in a meta-analysis study by Fuchs and Fuchs (1986). In the 21 studies reviewed by these authors, it was found that when formative evaluation was done during development of instructional materials, students subsequently learned significantly more from the revised materials.

What is of concern during evaluation of CVI may vary somewhat depending upon the setting in which it occurs. Compressed video and other distance learning systems are usually considered expensive, and the decision to develop these systems and courses is not made lightly. In most settings, whether in education or in business, CVI offers education and training opportunities and certain economies which could be offered no other way. For example, cost restrictions may dictate that advanced courses for a very small number of learners each at scattered worksites or campuses not be taught at all, unless they can be taught by one instructor using distance learning. In most settings, the overall purpose for conducting evaluations is to ensure that learners' needs are being met in a cost-effective manner using CVI. System funders and developers will be concerned that the right courses are reaching the right students or trainees, that these individuals are mastering what must be learned, that faculty and students are satisfied with the ways CVI allows them to teach and learn, and that the system is operating well on a technical and logistical level.

While "summative evaluation" (Dick & Carey, 1990) may be conducted several years after a CVI system has been operating, usually in order to describe final impact of the courses or to determine the worth of the entire system, typically developers and managers are more concerned with conducting formative evaluations to improve the system in its early stages. The focus of this chapter will primarily be on conducting formative evaluations of CVI, because of the potential impact of formative evaluations on improving instructional effectiveness.

Plan the Evaluation

Most instructional design models recommend that formative evaluation be carried out toward the final stages of development of the first version of an instructional system. Most authors, however, indicate that formative evaluation is an on-going process and should be carried out at many stages during development. Dick and Carey (1990), for example, recommend that formative evaluation include reviews of draft materials, and several one-to-one tryouts with individual learners using very rough drafts of materials, small-group tryouts, and finally larger-scale field trials.

As Savenye (1990) recommends for interactive video instruction, and since CVI systems are expensive and complex, developers would do well to consider performing formative evaluation activities during all phases of design and development. For example, perhaps instructors could be enlisted to teach sample lessons at other local institutions which have CVI or other types of interactive video/distance-learning systems even during the planning stages of the project to develop an in-house expertise and understanding of the unique characteristics and requirements of compressed video. It may be possible to test equipment from numerous vendors, as well as to try out various classroom or training center setups in the local region to assist in writing specifications for the new system. More specific advice on the selection process is discussed in Chapter 8: Vendor Selection. After the system is in place, or if even some components are in place, one or two pilot courses or short courses may be offered to work out the bugs in the system, prior to full-scale implementation.

Regardless of how formative evaluation will be conducted, it is always beneficial to bring evaluators on board early in development. They may assist in getting the word out to field-test instructors and managers at other network sites about what types of data will need to be collected, for example. Evaluators are often helpful, as well, in determining what courses should be offered, on what schedules, and at which sites by conducting needs assessments early on, as the technical systems are being completed. Finally, evaluators can conduct surveys or interviews with prospective faculty and managers to determine any concerns or needs they have before courses begin. This may "head off at the pass" potentially serious problems, such as an inadequate system for delivering course materials on time, or faculty who need some release time (albeit perhaps difficult to achieve with tight budgets) in order to adapt their courses to CVI delivery during the semester prior to their teaching their first CVI course. Planning the evaluation early thus ensures that it will be effective in meeting the project's requirements and goals.

Determine the Primary Goal of the Formative Evaluation

Although CVI developers may need answers to many questions regarding how to improve their systems, it is usually best to decide upon one clear goal for the evaluation. Usually this goal is some version of, "How effective is the system in enabling students or trainees to learn?" Especially when working with a restrictive budget, having one major goal in mind will help drive the process efficiently by fostering more productive evaluation efforts among team members.

Determine the Major Questions to be Answered by the Formative Evaluation

The major questions to be answered in most CVI evaluations lead to the primary goal - how effective is the system in aiding student learning? From this goal, three major evaluation questions can be derived:

1)   How well do the CVI courses help the learners learn (an achievement question)?
2)   How well do the learners, instructors, and managers or administrators like the CVI courses (an attitude question)?

3)   How well is the CVI system working (an "implementation" ques-
        tion)?
(Higgins & Sullivan, 1982; Morris & Fitzgibbon, 1978; Sullivan & Higgins,
1983).

From these three major evaluation questions issues related to the
specific CVI system and courses can be developed. While many questions
may be related, these questions may be classified into the general categories listed below.

Instructional Design and Effectiveness:
    Overall System Impact
    Course Design
    Learning Achievement
    Instructor Effectiveness
Attitudes:
    Satisfaction of Students with the CVI System
    Satisfaction of Instructors with the CVI System
    Concerns of Managers or Administrators (on campus or at
        remote sites, if applicable)
Implementation:
    Quality of the Technical and Logistical Aspects of the System,
    including:
        Video and audio quality
        Interactivity among students and instructor during class ses-
            sions
        Delivery of other course materials, such as syllabi, handouts,
            practice and reference materials, assignments back to the
            instructor, and test materials, as relevant
        Availability of other resources, such as books or computer
            access, as necessary
        If the CVI system is also used for teleconferencing, additional
            evaluation questions related to effectiveness for telecon-
            ference leaders and participants may be generated.

Figure 12.1 at the end of this chapter presents a sample list of
questions, which may be incorporated into questionnaires or interview
protocols to ask learners, instructors, course managers or administrators,
and possibly employers of students. To answer each question, CVI
evaluators will want to decide what data should be collected, and what
methods to use to collect those data. Next evaluators will develop the data
collection instruments and procedures, and then determine how data will be
analyzed. One way to plan the evaluations to both keep the focus clear and
make procedures most efficient is to develop a matrix to guide the evaluation. Under each major evaluation question can be listed the related sub-
questions. Beside each question, as headings across the matrix can be
placed "data sources" (instructors, students, course managers or administrators, reviewers, etc.), "data collection methods" (measures of learning
achievement such as pretests, post-tests, or grade comparisons; measures

of attitudes such as questionnaires, structured interviews, observations; and measures of success of implementation, which can also include questionnaires, interviews and observations, but may include reviews by experts, and reviews of institutional data), and methods of analyzing the data (Savenye, Maher, & Colombo, 1983). An example of such a matrix is presented in Figure 12.2.

See Chapter 10

As introduced in Figure 12.2, the sample matrix for planning an evaluation, many methods may be used for collecting data to answer the evaluation questions. In fact, most designers recommend using multiple methods to ensure that vital questions are answered, that nothing is overlooked, and to yield a valid picture of how an instructional system such as CVI is meeting the needs of learners, instructors, supervisors and administrators (cf. Dick & Carey, 1990; Popham, 1975).

In the most powerful approach to conducting an evaluation to improve a CVI system, both "traditional" and alternate methods for collecting

Evaluation Questions	Data Sources	Possible Instruments & Procedures	How Data Will be Analyzed
1. How well did students learn?	Students	- Pretests (if any) - Posttests	Frequency Tables
	Instructors	Comparison of grades of students in CVI courses with those in traditional courses	Possible ANOVA
		Questionnaires or interviews with former students managers/administrators	Summaries
		Documentary Data	Summaries
		Observations of performances on-the-job or in simulations	Coding & Summaries
		Product evaluation	Checklists & Summaries
2. How do CVI students feel about learning via CVI?	Students (CVI & those in reg. courses)	-Questionnaires - forced-choice items - open-ended - Interviews Observations	Possibly ANOVA Summaries Summaries

...Complete evaluation plan by continuing to determine data sources, instruments, procedures, and analysis methods for all evaluation questions.

Figure 12.2
Example Matrix of an Evaluation Plan for CVI (with sample questions)

data will be considered in order to yield a true picture of "what is really happening." Traditional methods include design reviews, tests, questionnaires and interviews; less-commonly used alternate methods include on-the-job observations, learning product evaluations, participant observations and case studies (Savenye, 1992). As recommended by Jacob (1987) in her review of qualitative, or naturalistic, research traditions, methods should be chosen by deciding which are most appropriate for answering the particular question. Newman (1989) reminds us that a learning environment can be altered by a new instructional technology. We are therefore working in dynamic environments in which any changes made affect other components of the CVI system, so keeping an open mind and using a diverse toolkit of methods gives an evaluation breadth and power.

Additionally, as CVI is a relatively new development in video-based distance learning, we can encourage CVI developers and evaluators to contribute to the efforts of newcomers to CVI by publishing the results of their evaluations. Describing system design, instructional and evaluation procedures, results, recommendations and any other words of wisdom, may save others from making costly mistakes and will improve developments in CVI. This book represents such an effort.

The following section of this chapter will introduce the multiple methods which may be used to conduct formative evaluations of CVI. While evaluators are free to use almost any method to answer any question, the methods in this section are organized by typical types of questions answered using each method.

Collecting Evaluation Data on Instructional Design and Effectiveness

Overall System Impact

Enrollments. In any evaluation, administrators and funders will often be most interested in the effects of the overall CVI system. Evaluators commonly address this issue first by describing the entire CVI system. For example, Manning and Sachs (1992) in their report of the evaluation of the Northern Virginia Community College Campus Video Interconnect, reported on the number of classes offered using the system, along with the numbers of students enrolled in each course by educational site. They also described the types and numbers of teleconference meetings held using the system, and the numbers of participants in the meetings. Constituents can thus easily see the numbers of students who are able to take courses using the CVI system, along with the departments and colleges which are able to expand their offerings and enrollments geographically.

Cost benefits. When possible, evaluators may determine cost savings engendered by the CVI system. For example, it is likely to be less expensive to offer courses from one main campus via CVI than to send instructors to many different sites. In training settings, it is usually less expensive to deliver courses via CVI than to fund the travel and lodging costs of trainees from many regions. Similarly, costs of offering teleconferences can be compared with costs for bringing participants to the same meeting site.

New offerings and opportunities. In many cases, the CVI system will offer educational and communication opportunities that the institution was unable to offer using traditional means. Therefore, evaluators may be able to describe these enhancements to the learning or broader organizational environment. For example, some companies or educational sites may use the system to bring in guest speakers for weekly informal seminars that were not offered at all previously, or might use the system to conduct instruction or business in new ways. Brainstorming meetings or focus groups might be held. If possible, evaluators may be able to determine cost benefits in terms of improved performance, productivity or processes and can report these. For specific guidelines on conducting a cost benefit model, especially in business settings, see Daly's (1992) *We've Got to Start Meeting Like This: A Primer on Videoconferencing.*

Instructional Design Reviews of CVI Courses

One of the most critical issues in evaluating all instruction is that of curriculum alignment (Higgins & Savenye, 1983). The concern is whether course objectives, instructional activities and content, and tests match. Curriculum alignment is usually evaluated by collecting from instructors examples of their objectives, instructional materials and tests. Many instructors may not write course objectives, but these can be inferred from purpose, outcome or goal statements in syllabi, readings, etc. At times, evaluators may choose to observe samples of the course lectures and activities, in person or using videotapes, to review the instruction, practice and feedback given by the instructor for various objectives. In large CVI systems it is likely that only a sample of courses or of course materials can be reviewed. Asking instructors for their original course materials can at times be touchy, so here, as always, the rapport, sensitivity and professionalism of the evaluators comes into play. Geis (1987) in his recommendations for reviewing interactive instruction, states that reviewers might be content experts, instructional designers, instructors, people who have might special knowledge of the students, educational leaders, managers, supervisors, administrators, and former students.

Learning Achievement

Of primary concern in CVI instruction is whether the system and courses are effective in fostering student learning. In collecting and reporting achievement data, evaluators must follow institutional and ethical guidelines regarding confidentiality of grades, scores and job performance. Ethical issues are discussed in detail in Chapter 15.

See chapter 15

Tests. There are various methods of measuring learning, the most common being tests. As discussed earlier, tests are only useful if they match the course goals and objectives. Evaluators will usually look at student performance on instructor-developed tests, such as the midterm and final exams. Occasionally, especially for newly-developed courses or special workshops, both pretests and post-tests will be administered to more clearly determine learning gains from the CVI course, as separate from learning through other possible factors.

Grade comparisons. If instructors teach different sections of the same course via the CVI system and in the traditional manner on campus, average grades for students in the two groups can be compared. One would not expect grades to be higher in the CVI section, of course. What evaluators may seek to determine is that participating in the CVI courses is as effective in helping students learn as is participating in the traditional campus-based courses. For example, members of Arizona State University's Instructional Design Services (1984) in an evaluation of an interactive television program compared the mean final grades of over 1000 students enrolled in 33 courses offered on campus as well as via ITFS to nine remote sites. They found that grades were virtually identical. Manning and Sachs (1992) reported similar equivalencies, but noted that there may be differences related to site, day or evening classes, and different student populations.

Self-evaluation by students using questionnaires or interviews. In some cases, it may not be possible to collect achievement data using grades or tests and, particularly in informal learning settings or business information settings, it may be sufficient to ask learners to themselves rate how much they learned from a CVI course or workshop. Self-report data is of course limited in that it is often biased; learners may answer what they think the evaluator wants to hear, or learners may not be able to determine how much they have learned, especially when learning virtually-new content. However, there are times when evaluators must be concerned with learner perceptions of the value of a course in terms of how much they believe they have learned. On a questionnaire, students could simply be asked, "How do you rate your skill in _____ now?" or "How much do you feel you learned in this course?" or "Describe what you knew about this subject and compare it to what you know now."

Ratings of student learning by other constituents. It may be desirable for evaluators to question the supervisors, managers, or administrators of students or trainees to determine their perceptions of how much students learned. These individuals can also be asked, again using questionnaires or interviews, how well the learners are now performing on subsequent measures in an advanced course, or how well they are now performing their job duties. As with grades and test scores, evaluators should be sensitive to confidentiality issues, especially when discussing employees' on-the-job performance.

Documentary records. Evaluators may require access to institutional or organizational data, such as the grades or test scores mentioned above. Additional data may provide creative insights regarding the effectiveness of the CVI system. Benefits of learning via CVI may show up in lower absentee rates, or in decreased reports of losses, errors, complaints or violations. Benefits may also be reflected in increased activities, sales, efficiency, or reduced learning or training time, and these also may appear in organizational data.

Such documentary evidence is necessarily more inferential or correlational than directly causal, due to the many external factors which may influence an organization and thus must be interpreted cautiously. Still, using organizational data to study long term effects of training represents a potentially valuable evaluation tool, and a more sophisticated systemic look at training than merely analyzing the attainment of course objectives.

Observations of performance on-the-job or in classroom simulations. Transfer of skills and knowledge gained via CVI to real-world situations may be the most critical learning issue in some cases. With some careful planning, diplomacy, and observance of organizational rules and norms observations of student performance on job tasks or in classroom simulations can be accomplished using methods adapted from ethnographic research (For further information about conducting ethnographic or qualitative research, see, for example, Bogdan & Biklen, 1982; Strauss, 1987).

If observations are planned, it will need to be determined who will conduct them, how records will be kept and of what performances, how inter-observer reliability will be established, and how the data will be coded, analyzed and reported. Observers will need to be trained, and typically some instruments must be developed, such as checklists of behaviors, or forms for coding categories of qualities of performances. Many times it is not practical to follow learners into their job settings or advanced courses. It still may be possible to observe actual skills by helping instructors set up classroom simulations or role-plays, for example, of negotiation, sales, interviewing, or goal-setting techniques.

Learning products. In some courses, the best way to determine how well students have learned may be to evaluate the products they develop or processes they follow. In fact, Linn, Baker and Dunbar (1991) have noted that educators are increasingly concerned that traditional testing may not adequately assess complex performances. For example, the final product in an art course may be a painting which demonstrates the techniques taught in the course. In other courses, the products might be models, research papers, screenplays, portfolios of writing, etc. Evaluators may collaborate with instructors to evaluate the success of the CVI courses or workshops in helping students develop products that are equal in quality to those produced by students in on-campus courses, or products which could not result from on-campus courses due to the types of assignments and projects

CVI students at distant sites might be able to complete. Again, as recommended by Dick and Carey (1990), Sullivan and Higgins (1983), and most other instructional developers, a checklist should be used to evaluate the quality of the students' products. One reminder in evaluating these processes and products is that learners cannot be expected to master complex skills without adequate practice during the instruction.

Concerns about the adequacy of traditional testing are particularly strong in public schools, where there is a growing movement away from such testing, and toward what is being called authentic assessment (Kleinsasser & Horsch, 1992). Such a concern is not new to the field of instructional design, as we have commented elsewhere in this chapter about the related issue of curriculum alignment. The capabilities of CVI bring new perspective to what is possible in evaluating distance learning. Some of the alternatives suggested by Herman (1992) as valid tools for authentic assessment, such as portfolios, demonstrations, and exhibits, may be particularly well suited for the interactive environment of CVI.

Instructor Effectiveness

As in any type of instruction, one critical factor in the success of CVI courses is the students' perceptions of the effectiveness of the instructors. No matter what technology is used, or none, to deliver instruction, there are many instructor factors that cut across all courses. Questions about these factors which may be included on student questionnaires or in interviews with samples of students are shown under the heading "Instructor Effectiveness" in Figure 12.1, sample items for questionnaires and structured interviews in CVI Evaluations. Figure 12.1 is located at the end of this chapter. For example, evaluators could ask students their perceptions of: how fair the tests were in measuring what was taught, how organized were the lectures, how clearly the instructor spoke, how well the pace of the course fit their needs, how useful were the course assignments and activities, how well the instructor emphasized key points, how available was the instructor (in person, or by phone or possibly even by electronic-mail) in providing consultation to students, how effective was the instructor in making students at CVI distant sites feel part of the course, how knowledge-able and up-to-date was the instructor about course content, and how well did the instructor motivate students.

Other questions students may answer about the instructor are specific to CVI. These questions are also woven into various other sections of Figure 12.1, particularly "Interactivity among Students and Instructor" and "Quality of the Technical and Logistical Aspects." Such questions include how clear and legible were the instructor's visuals when using a graphics pad or chalkboard, whether the instructor looked at the camera, how easy it was for students at remote sites to get feedback from the instructor on assignments, and how well the instructor used the interactive audio system to conduct discussions among students at all sites and to answer students' questions during class sessions.

Determining Attitudes and Perceptions

An important goal of any CVI evaluation is to determine how satisfied students, instructors and other collaborating individuals, such as managers or administrators, are with the CVI system. The most common methods for collecting data about attitudes and perceptions are questionnaires and structured interviews, administered either to all members of a target group, or a representative sample. Before discussing the types of questions asked in CVI evaluation, this chapter will present some general issues related to developing and administering questionnaires, interviews and alternate methods for collecting attitudinal data.

Methods Used in Determining Attitudes

Questionnaires. Evaluators may want to compare the attitudes toward a course or topic of students who participated in CVI with those students who participated in a traditional version of the same or a similar course. A similar approach was used by Savenye and Strand (1989) who found that students who participated in a full-year videodisc-based high school physical science curriculum generally held more positive attitudes toward science and how they learned science than students who took the course via traditional instruction. In a somewhat different approach, if the primary goal of the CVI course or workshop is to improve attitudes, evaluators may decide to measure attitudes of learners before starting the course and after its completion.

Questionnaire items and directions should be written clearly, and the entire questionnaire or survey should be as brief as possible. Only questions directly related to the major goals of the CVI evaluation should be included. It is always worthwhile to try out a draft version of the questionnaire with several representative learners, or instructors or managers, as the case may be. It could be found for example, that directions are not clear, or that some items ask two questions at once, thus making the items unanswerable. Participants may also mention issues or concerns that the evaluators had not known to include in the questionnaire. For ease of summarizing and analyzing, most questions should be forced-choice, such as Likert-scale items. At the end of Figure 12.1 is a note that includes examples of some possible response scales which may be used with questions. It is useful, however, to also include some open-ended questions, such as those which ask participants for what they liked best and least, or for their recommendations for improvements in the CVI system. Answers to these questions can be classified into general categories and summarized in the evaluation report.

Structured Interviews. Interviews may also be conducted with representative samples of participants. Evaluators may supplement questionnaires with interviews with individuals or small groups of participants to ensure that no major issues were left undiscovered in surveys. With limited budgets, or when participants are unlikely to complete and return question-naires, it may be that interviews are the sole means of determining attitudes of learners, instructors, and others, such as managers or administrators. If this is the case, care should be taken that representative subgroups of participants, such as those at different sites, or young and older students, or those at educational institutions as well as companies, are interviewed. Interviewing is labor intensive, so questions making up the interview protocols should be determined in advance. Some of the questions presented in Figure 12.1 may again be used for this purpose.

A notable side-benefit of conducting interviews at CVI sites is that participants may realize that system developers and administrators care enough about their satisfaction with the system to make the effort to visit sites. Some students in evaluations have reported a better attitude toward the system and their courses after such interviews and site visits, which may include observations.

Some Alternate Methods for Determining Attitudes. Attitudes toward the CVI system may additionally be determined by conducting observations of instructors and learners using the system. Observers may note that due to technical problems, such as those discussed in the following section of this chapter, students are unhappy with their classes, as indicated by coming late to class, talking through the instructor's video lectures, making frequent negative comments, or not participating in the class discussions.

Satisfaction of Students and Instructors and Concerns of Managers or Administrators Regarding the CVI System

Questions which may be used to determine the attitudes and concerns of all participants who use the CVI system are presented in three sections in Figure 12.1. For example, students may be asked questions about the CVI course offerings and schedule, their feelings about being an active member of the class, their recommendations for the course, and whether they would take a CVI course again.

Instructors are critical to the success of CVI, and their perceptions of how well the system works for them in teaching are important. They can be asked, for example, whether the audio system easily allows them to answer students' questions and conduct class discussions; how well the delivery system for tests, assignments and other course materials is working; how successful the visual graphic system is; comments they may have regarding any support or training they feel is necessary; and their recommendations for improving the system.

On-campus or remote site course managers, institutional adminis-trators, and trainees' supervisors and employers are also important partici-pants in a successful CVI system. These individuals may be asked whether there is any support they need for improving the system, their recommendations, and their perceptions of how well the students are learning and valuing the CVI courses.

Evaluating Implementation of the CVI System

As in the previous discussions, questions regarding how well the CVI system as a whole is operating to meet learner and instructor needs are typically answered using questionnaires and interviews. Figure 12.1 presents questions that may be asked regarding the quality of the technical and logistical aspects of the system. For example students may be asked their perceptions of the quality of the video and audio signals and whether visual aids, such as instructor drawn equations and overhead transparencies are shown on the screen long enough for students to take notes. A critical concern in CVI courses is that students at remote sites can participate interactively in class discussions, can easily ask the instructor questions and in general feel like active members of the class. Questions related to these factors should be asked. Both students and instructors need to be asked their perceptions of how well materials such as syllabi, handouts, tests and readings are being delivered to students, and how effectively the system is working in getting tests and assignments to the instructor for grading and getting instructor feedback returned to students.

An additional system implementation question is how effectively the system is providing students access to any required resources, such as library materials, computers and other instructional equipment. It is in the area of implementation that observations may be particularly useful for evaluators. Observers may note improvements in the system that are necessary, but which students, or instructors, who tend to accept the limitations of their existing classrooms, might not mention. For example, observers might find that remote classrooms have a significant proportion of inoperative equipment, or equipment configurations may be changed and not put back in place when the rooms are used for other purposes. Observers might find that learners do not know how to participate most effectively, for example, if microphones are placed between several students or are suspended from the ceiling, some students may not speak loudly enough to be heard. An exemplary research study which used observations of classroom teachers to determine how they assess their students and their perceptions of testing was conducted by Higgins and Rice (1991), and may be a valuable reference for evaluators interested in conducting structured observations. As noted in earlier, observations must be planned, observers trained, and it must be decided what will be recorded and how these observations will be summarized.

Another alternate technique for evaluation of how well the CVI system is working is called "participant observation," derived from ethnographic studies in anthropology. In this technique interviews and observations are conducted by participants. For example, the aid of instructors, managers and administrators might be solicited. These individuals could be given samples of the types of evaluation questions to be answered, and they might make notes to be shared with evaluators, perhaps at regular intervals in meetings, by mail, electronic-mail or even by telephone. Similarly, representative students could be asked to answer questions periodically, or more loosely to keep notes or a journal about their attitudes toward and concerns about learning via the CVI system. Occasionally for short courses, CVI developers or evaluators may choose to become students in a CVI course to experience and describe the CVI system from an insider's point of view.

If observations cannot be made in person, videotapes of sample representative classes may be made, and the evaluators may later review these tapes. In a small evaluation, observations may be made and recorded informally. In a larger evaluation, evaluators usually would view a few tapes and from them derive a coding scheme or checklist to be used in reviewing all the tapes, to make data analysis and reporting more efficient.

Reporting Evaluation Results and Recommendations

CVI evaluators will combine and describe their results in a concise report. It should also be remembered that evaluation reports which are too long may not be read. The exact form of the report will depend on who the target reader is. In a small, informal evaluation conducted primarily for system developers, the report might simply present a table of the achievement results, description of major findings regarding participants' attitudes and a summary of the implementation issues, followed by a brief list of recommendations for improvements to be made in any component of the system.

In longer reports to be read by administrators, funders and members of the professional community, the following format may be used. A one-page executive summary is usually prepared. The full report may begin with a summary of the background of the CVI project or system and its major goals and purposes. A section describing the major evaluation purpose and questions follows. Next, the methods used in conducting the evaluation are described, including the numbers and types of courses, students, instructors and others who participated in the evaluation. In a section entitled, "Results", the major findings of the evaluation are reported. It is often most convenient for readers if results are presented under headings for each major evaluation question or sometimes sub-question. In the text of the report only major findings or those of most important should be reported. Summaries of all results can be presented in tables or figures, and, if necessary, more complete descriptions of data may be included in appendices.

In instructional CVI, learning achievement is usually most important and so results illustrating how well students learned are presented first. Average scores are provided, categorized by whatever types of questions were answered. For example, test scores or grades of CVI students may be compared with those in campus-based traditional sections of courses. If any statistical comparisons were made, those results are presented as well. Results regarding any other learning data are summarized. For example, descriptions of self-reports, observations, or products will be included. Typically, attitudes and perception results are reported next. Once again, only major findings are discussed in the report, with references to supporting tables or appendices. Evaluators might choose to ensure that a clear picture of general participant satisfaction appears first, followed by attitudes toward specific aspects of the CVI system or courses.

Reporting the results of implementation or use questions is often a bit more complex. The most effective way to report these results is once again by major question, perhaps classified by technical concerns, delivery system issues, and interactivity, for example. Results of observations are usually coded and summarized briefly by category of what was observed. Occasionally, evaluators may choose to create a brief case study including results of evaluator observations, participant observations or even interview and questionnaire responses to create a picture of what it is like to participate in a CVI course. Sometimes, quotes from participants are included to add to the realistic flavor of the report, as long as respondent anonymity is preserved.

Recommendations for improving the CVI system and courses are usually included in a final section of the report, where they can easily be found. Some evaluators choose to report all recommendations, even those for which they know there is currently no budget. Other evaluators may mention such recommendations only briefly, and choose to focus on improvements that are more readily possible. Examples of recommendations often take the form of suggestions for additional support personnel; replacing some classroom equipment with other equipment, such as replacing ceiling microphones with microphones spaced across students' tables; and developing standardized training for instructors and teleconference participants in using the CVI system. Other recommendations might be to expand use of the system to provide new activities, like guest speakers; improve students' access to resources; or institute on-going needs assessments and evaluations to meet the changing needs of the institutions and their members. The evaluation may conclude with an overall description of the system's success and how it is meeting its overall goals, along with general recommendations for the future of the system, or for other professionals who use CVI.

Conclusion

While CVI is a relatively new technology its use is rapidly expanding in many settings. It is hoped that CVI users and developers will find this chapter useful and will adapt the questions, methods and recommendations presented here to suit their own needs. It is also hoped that those who are leading the development of CVI will continue to share the results of their evaluation efforts with all who use CVI.

Figure 12.1

Sample Items for Questionnaires and Structured Interviews in CVI Evaluations.

Sample evaluation questions which may be asked of CVI students, instructors, and administrators using either questionnaires, structured interviews or combinations (NOTE: Examples of response formats are included at the end of this figure.)

Instructional Design and Course Effectiveness

Overall System Impact
Overall system impact is likely to be measured using descriptions of numbers of courses, enrollments, cost benefits, etc.

Course Instructional Design
1. This course was well-organized.
2. The information I learned in this course is relevant to my current or desired areer.
3. The CVI course objectives, content, methods and tests matched.

Learning Achievement
Learning achievement is usually measured using pretests, post-tests, grade comparisons, observations of performances, evaluations of products, etc., but may also be determined by asking students and supervisors or administrators to report on their perceptions of what they have learned.

Instructor Effectiveness
1. Lectures in this course were well-organized.
2. The course goals and objectives were clearly stated.
3. Tests in this course were related to course content.
4. Lab assignments were related to course content.
5. Homework in this course was related to course content.
6. The speed at which the instructor spoke was too fast, too slow, or just right.
7. The instructor's writing on the graphics pad or chalkboard was legible.
8. The instructor emphasized key points during lectures.
9. The instructor used examples effectively to illustrate course content.
10. The instructor spoke clearly.
11. Overall, the rate at which this class was taught was: (too fast, about right, too slow).

12. The instructor was available for consultation during office hours.

Attitudes

Satisfaction of Students with the CVI System
1.   The schedule of CVI course offerings suited my need   (Comments)
2.   I was able to enroll in the CVI courses I wanted. (Comments.)
3.   My course administrator/manager helped make things run smoothly.
4.   Even though I viewed this course through remote delivery, I still felt like I was part of the class.
5.   I feel the production quality of this course was:
6.   I was generally satisfied with taking a course using CVI.
7.   I would take another course through CVI.
8.   I would take another course via CVI even if I was able to take it on campus.
9.   I would recommend to other students that they take a course via CVI.
10. What did you like best/least about this course?
11. What recommendations do you have for improving CVI courses or this course?

Satisfaction of Instructors with the CVI System
1.   The system for delivering course materials to sites was reliable, and materials were delivered on time.
2.   Assignments, tests, etc. from students at off-campus CVI sites were usually available to me the day after (or any desired time) students turned them in.
3.   Communication with CVI system personnel was satisfactory. (Please characterize any problems.)
4.   The system for allowing students at CVI sites to participate in class worked well.
5.   There was adequate participation from students in the studio/ classroom.
6.   There was adequate participation from students at CVI sites.
7.   The amount of time spent out of class helping CVI-site students was reasonable.
8.   My course was appropriate for delivery via CVI. (What elements of your course were not appropriate for CVI?)
9.   I received adequate training in teaching via the CVI system.(What part of the training was particularly helpful?)
10. I enjoyed teaching via the CVI system.
11. What did you like the most about teaching via CVI?
12. What did you like the least?
13. List the advantages for you in teaching via the CVI system.
14. List the disadvantages for you in teaching via the CVI system.
15. The additional work load (class preparation, grading, etc.) from teaching via CVI was reasonable.

16. Describe any comments you have regarding support from your academic department for your teaching via CVI.

17. What recommendations do you have for improving any aspect of the CVI system?

Concerns of Managers or Administrators

(either on campus or at remote sites, if applicable)

1. The additional workload generated by working with CVI courses was reasonable.

2. Describe your opinions about the video and audio quality of the CVI courses.

3. Describe any comments you have regarding the instructional quality of the CVI courses in general or of specific courses.

4. Describe what you think students at your site feel about taking courses via the CVI system.

5. Describe what impact the CVI courses have had on employee development (if appropriate.)

6. Describe any suggestions for improving the CVI system or courses.

Implementation

Quality of the Technical and Logistical Aspects of the CVI System
    Video Quality
    1. The video signal was clear.
    2. The amount of time the instructor's writing pad (or other device) was shown on the TV screen was usually too long, too short, or about right.
    3. The TV pictures (views of the class, instructor, or pad, etc.) selected for viewing during classes helped me learn the content.

    Audio Quality
    1. The audio signal was clear.

Interactivity Among Students and Instructor During Class Sessions
    1. I could easily hear questions from students in the studio/ classroom and other sites.
    2. Opportunities for class participation were about the same as in a regular class.
    3. The instructor provided adequate opportunity to ask questions during class.
    4. Class discussions were valuable.

Delivery of CVI Course Materials Among Instructor, Students and Sites
    1. I received printed class materials on time.

<u>Availability of Other Resources</u>
1.   Reserve library materials were available when needed.
2.   Computers were available (if necessary) to support this class. (other resources, as appropriate)

Teleconferencing

(Versions of above questions could be asked of those who lead and participate in teleconferences. In addition, several other questions may be asked of those who lead teleconferences.)
1.   Adequate support was available for me to use the CVI system.
2.   The CVI system allowed me to conduct this teleconference well.
3.   I would use the CVI system to conduct a teleconference again in the future.
4.   Describe any comments you may have regarding the production quality of the video and audio for your CVI-delivered teleconference.
5.   How could the CVI system be improved to make for a better teleconference in the future?

Examples of response scales include:

Strongly Agree	Agree	Neither Agree nor Disagree	Disagree	Strongly Disagree
Almost Always	Usually	About 1/2 the Time	Occasionally	Never
Excellent	Good	Satisfactory	Fair	Poor
Too Fast		Too Slow		About Right
Yes	No			

(Adapted from Instructional Design Services, 1984; Manning & Sachs, 1992; Savenye, Maher, & Colombo, 1983)

References

Bogdan, R. C., & Biklen, S. K. (1982). *Qualitative research for education: an introduction to theory and methods.* Boston, MA: Allyn and Bacon.

Dick, W., & Carey, L. (1990). *The systematic design of instruction* (3rd ed.). Glenview, Illinois: Scott, Foresman.

Fuchs, L. S., & Fuchs, D. (1986). Effects of systematic formative evaluation: a meta-analysis. *Exceptional Children, 53*, (3), 199-208.

Gagne, R. M., Briggs, L. J., & Wager, W. W. (1988). *Principles of instructional design.* (3rd ed.). New York: Holt, Rinehart and Winston.

Geis, G. L. (May/June, 1987). Formative evaluation: developmental testing and expert review. *Performance & Instruction,* 1-8.

Higgins, N., & Rice, E. (1991). Teachers' perspectives on competency-based testing. *Educational Technology Research and Development, 39* (3), 59-69.

Higgins, N., & Savenye, W. (1983). *Curriculum alignment: the problem.* Paper presented at the annual meeting of the Association for Educational Communications and Technology, New Orleans, Louisiana.

Higgins, N., & Sullivan, H. (1982). Preparing special education teachers for objectives-based instruction. *Teacher Education and Special Education, 5* (4), 51-55.

Instructional Design Services, Arizona State University (1984). *Interactive Instructional Television Program Evaluation Report for Fall Semester, 1983 .*

Jacob, E. (1987). Qualitative research traditions: a review. *Review of Educational Research, 57* (1), 1-50.

Linn, R. L., Baker, E. L., & Dunbar, S. B. (1991). Complex, performance-based assessment: expectations and validation criteria. *Educational Researcher, 20* (8), 15-21.

Manning, J., & Sachs, S. (1992). *Northern Virginia Community College Campus Video Interconnect Evaluation Report.* Northern Virginia Community College.

Morris, L. L., & Fitz-Gibbon, C. T. (1978) *Evaluator's Handbook.* Beverly Hills: Sage Publications.

Newman, D. (March, 1989). *Formative experiments on technologies that change the organization of instruction.* Paper presented at the annual conference of the American Educational Research Association, San Fransisco, CA.

Popham, W. J. (1975). *Educational evaluation.* Englewood Cliffs, NJ: Prentice-Hall.

Savenye, W. C. (1992). Alternate methods for conducting formative evaluations of interactive instructional technologies. In M. R. Simonson (Ed.), *Fourteenth Annual Proceedings of Selected Research Paper Presentations at the 1989 Annual Convention of the Association for*

Educational Communications and Technology in Washington, DC. Ames, IA: Iowa State University.

Savenye, W. C. (1990). *Instructional interactive video - what works?.* Young Academic Monograph. Washington, DC: National Society for Performance and Instruction.

Savenye, W. C., & Strand, E. (1989, February). *Teaching science using interactive videodisc: results of the pilot year evaluation of the Texas Learning Technology Group Project.* In M. R. Simonson, & D. Frey (Eds.), *Eleventh Annual Proceedings of Selected Research Paper Presentations at the 1989 Annual Convention of the Association for Educational Communications and Technology in Dallas, Texas.* Ames, IA: Iowa State University.

Savenye, W., Maher, J., & Colombo, S. (1983). *Engineering telecourse delivery: evaluation of a pilot project.* Paper presented at the annual convention of the Association for Educational Communications and Technology, New Orleans, Louisiana.

Straus, A. L. (1987). *Qualitative analysis for social scientists.* Cambridge: Cambridge University Press.

Sullivan, H., & Higgins, N. (1983). *Teaching for Competence*, New York: Teacher's College Press, Columbia University.

13

A Change Strategy for Integration of Compressed Video Systems

Cecelia Box

Introduction

Anyone who works with technology understands that things change. Equipment changes, which causes tasks to change. When tasks change, the nature of people's work may also change, which causes the organization or system to change. We have only to look around us to see the constant process of change. In this chapter we will talk about the concept of change as it affects compressed video projects and how to anticipate and productively manage the change process.

Often people think of change as something unpredictable, like an unanticipated and incidental fallout from other actions or events. Such people may tend to hold the attitude that they should simply proceed as they think best, letting the chips fall where they may. The problem is that the chips can pile up rapidly, forming major barriers to our progress.

There is a better, more informed way to approach the implementation of new technologies such as compressed video. Understanding, anticipating and managing the change process within systems are vital skills in any implementation effort. This chapter will focus on defining change, understanding the various levels at which change may occur, and examining real life experiences of people who have been change agents in the implementation of compressed video within educational systems.

Why Talk about Change and Compressed Video?

It is easy to think about a new technology such as compressed video solely in terms of its technological characteristics. If the technology is promising or clearly meets an existing need, we frequently make the assumption that it will sell itself. As we write this chapter from the perspective of the instructional technologist, we acknowledge the tendency of people in our field to embrace new technologies whole heartedly. An attraction to the new technologies and their potential is probably a major reason many of us pursued a career in instructional technology in the first place.

The same cannot always be said for others whose jobs or lives feel the impact of technology. If we view the job of the instructional technologist, or the training manager, or the personnel director or other administrator, as being the successful implementation of the appropriate technology to meet the needs of the organization or system, we have to define that job as much broader than just selecting the right equipment. The job may also include other roles: politician, cheerleader, diplomat and salesperson. Our experience indicates that the successful implementation of compressed video will necessitate one or more people playing a number of those roles as they address change-related issues.

Change and the Nature of Compressed Video

Unlike many other technologies, the nature of compressed video requires the support of a widespread organization. By its nature, compressed video links far-flung constituents who have both instructional and organizational needs. In this sense, compressed video and other telecommunications systems may require change strategies that are somewhat unique and different from the needs associated with other new technologies. As a comparison, the establishment of an electronic mail system within an organization may require training of users and an immediate or gradual revisiting of intra-organizational communications channels, but such a system is also more a matter of each individual learning to operate and utilize the technology. With a compressed video system, users may deal with technical operators, or with some systems may be easily trained to operate the equipment themselves. However, interaction with the system cannot remain at merely a personal level. Many organizational factors are involved in making a compressed video system work.

A compressed video system may upgrade or replace an older system, or it may provide totally new capabilities. Technical support may come through a number of external sources, including telephone companies, state agencies and/or other consortia. Scheduling use of the system may involve resolving conflicts between different entities. Orientation for system users must be provided. There will undoubtedly be both short-term and long-term changes in organizations which adopt compressed video systems. It is vital that the process of change be managed and facilitated if the implementation is successful.

Incremental vs. "Frame-breaking" Change

Compressed video can be examined not only in terms of the broad scope of the affected organization or system but the depth of the change as well. London (1988) describes two types of change, incremental and frame-breaking change. Different applications of compressed video have thus far involved both kinds of changes. The type of change produced may be closely related to the configuration of the compressed video system which is installed. Elsewhere in this book descriptions of actual systems are provided, but these configurations may be summarized according to two basic patterns. One pattern uses CV in a standard classroom setting, which may consist of fixed seating, fixed video monitors and microphones. Such an arrangement may follow traditional production models for television production, with technicians in charge of the equipment, including control of audio and video. In this format, instructional uses will also tend to follow traditional delivery formats. The fixed nature of the components does not allow for additional forms of interaction.

A second format for compressed video systems involves the use of moveable, multimedia equipment, flexible seating patterns, and access by learners to input and control devices. In such a format, all participants can use the various components of the system to interact in a number of ways which expand on the traditional classroom model for instructional delivery.

In the case of the more traditional format, the change is likely to be only an incremental one. The compressed video system will provide additional support for delivering traditional classroom instruction at a distance. The use of CV will add a greater degree of communication between sites, but that communication will generally be similar in kind to what would occur within a regular classroom. While we acknowledge this particular use of compressed video, our discussion will focus on the more flexible systems and applications of compressed video. Such flexible classroom arrangements provide the potential for a much greater magnitude of change, the frame-breaking change to which London referred. To use flexible CV systems to their fullest potential requires us to challenge our assumptions about instructional design, instructional materials, the roles of the instructor and the learner, evaluation methods and classroom management. When we accept the challenge of recreating assumptions about instruction and communication, the implications for change increase, perhaps exponentially.

Frame-breaking change poses a particularly interesting challenge when new technologies are involved. If we can define change according to the degree of difference from the status quo, incremental change seems merely to extend our conceptions of what we know. Many new technologies however, seem to present radical departures from both the quality and quantity of what was previously known, or previously possible. In many cases, we are presented with the technological possibilities before we have had a chance to determine what the practical applications may be. Thus, the change process regarding a technology such as compressed video may require that people be educated to see the change in terms of a new way of doing the old things, but as a way of doing things we never thought of doing before.

Human Factors and Compressed Video

Exploring the potential of new technologies requires us to focus not only on the technology itself, but on the interactions between humans and the technology. The importance of human factors in the successful implementation of new technologies has been recognized by researchers in the field of interactive systems. Weber (1992) comments that "...human factors issues often have more impact on adoption and effectiveness than hardware or software concerns" (p. 29).   Weber performed a survey of experts' perceptions about human-computer factors in interactive systems, and analyzed responses to create an interactive systems model as a systematic tool for assessing those factors.   Weber's experts believed that teachers and trainers were generally favorable toward the idea of working with interactive systems. However, "Even if fully adopted, technologies and systems will be easy to use only to the extent that user input and feedback are given full consideration in the entire cycle from development to final use" (p.38). This comment again points to the importance of involvement of the user and the organization throughout the process, from design and development, wherever possible, through installation and diffusion.

The Instructional Technologist's Role in Successful Adoptions

There is another, very practical reason why change issues should be of interest to people who work with new technologies. Without appropriate change strategies, even many worthwhile advances are often doomed to a brief flash of interest followed by quick retirement to dusty storage closets. Some technologies, such as the personal computer, stand and thrive on their own merits. Other technologies. such as Beta videotape players, were technically superior to VHS, but have all but disappeared. Once a carefully-weighed decision is made to adapt a new innovation, it is part of the responsibility of the educational technologist to try to insure that the innovation will be able to serve both individuals and the organization well, not only for the short term, but the long term as well.

What is Change?

In order to understand how to successfully implement compressed video within an organization or system, we first need to understand the concept of change, including its various levels. In this section we will define terms and discuss the levels of change, with specific attention to individual change and broader group and social change. It is of particular importance for the instructional technologist to develop an awareness of our personal biases, assumptions and paradigms is we are to attempt to address these attitudes and beliefs in others.

What is change? Most people can describe experiences in their lives which involved changes in their actions, attitudes or beliefs. Specialists in the field of change, however, are specific in their use of the term "change" and other related concepts.

Havelock (1985) defines *change* as "any significant alteration in the status quo" (p. 4). This definition might fit change of any kind. One particular type of change which applies closely to new technologies is *innovation*, which Havelock defines as "any change which represents something new to the people being changed" (p. 4).

The distinction between change and innovation may be a matter of novelty and perhaps deliberation. Some changes are natural. Examples of natural change are all around us: seasons, weather, growth and decline of people, communities and environments. Innovation, or the other hand, implies a deliberate effort to introduce a concept which people perceive as new. Both natural or deliberate changes can either be planned or approached spontaneously. "How the change or innovation comes about" is Havelock's general definition for both *change process* and *innovation process* (p. 5).

An additional term is of primary importance to our discussion in this chapter, and that is the term *change agent*, defined as "... an individual who influences clients' innovation decisions in a direction deemed desirable by a change agency" (Rogers, p. 28). We will address the role of the change agent later in the chapter.

The topic of change and its successful management has been an area of interest for social scientists for most of the twentieth century, although the idea of social change and social planning goes back much further (Benne, Bennis and Chin, 1985). It seems logical that an interest in change processes arose at a time in our history when large-scale changes were occurring with increasing frequency. Many of these changes, such as the Industrial Revolution, had widespread effects on almost everyone in society, but occurred without any overall plan. Thus along with vast benefits, there were also many detrimental effects such as child labor, which required later legislation to eliminate.

Two models for planning change emerged in the 1950's. In the engineering model, planning was done by experts who interpreted needs and requirements and devised plans. Those plans were then presented to the affected entities, who were to be persuaded of the efficacy of the proposed approach. A second model, less popular at the time, but which has been more widely adopted in the last few decades, was a clinical model. In the clinical model, the experts work collaboratively with those affected to develop a plan which reflects the needs and requirements as mutually identified by both experts and affected people (Benne, et al, 1985).

The distinction between these two approaches is important, because they arise from two distinct viewpoints which can be found in many disciplines and institutions. The question is, should those who are the experts determine the needs and solutions, or should those affected be included and thus by implication seen as having valuable knowledge and/ or experience to contribute? This issue is one we also face within the field of instructional design: who should determine the learners' needs? The answer, which applies as well to the area of change, is not always clear-cut. However, what we know about motivation and empowerment and feelings of self-efficacy should serve to point in the general direction of involvement of all affected people.

The Levels of Change

Benne (1985) identifies change as targeting either individuals, groups, communities or societies. The change process related to the installation and diffusion of compressed video systems may involve addressing change of the individual, small group or community. For our purposes, we will focus mainly on change at the individual and group level. However, we acknowledge the importance of change at the community level as well. For example, one isolated community in Wyoming voluntarily undertook a rigorous needs assessment to determine the need and the funding available locally to install a CV system, based on the potential benefits of such a system to the entire community. Such systems, which require a significant investment, call for decision making processes which involve all stakeholders.

Individuals and Change

Thinking about change on the level of individuals, groups, and communities provides a framework for analyzing how change occurs at each of those levels. It is appropriate to start with a discussion of how change occurs in individuals.

Though change reflects many organizational or group factors, we know that any change eventually has to take place within the individual. Individual change looks very much like learning. Indeed, the early behavioral theorists defined learning as a change in behavior. The two-way relationship between group and individual behaviors is complex, but in the sense that at least some of the change resides in the individual, change as a learning outcome is an appropriate interest of educational technologists.

An Analogy for Learning and Change

We can draw a number of useful concepts for thinking about learning and change from the field of cognitive psychology. One way to think about learning is in the Piagetian terms of *assimilation* and *accommodation* (Mussen, Conger & Kagan, 1974). Although Piaget's theories were originally developed as a study of developmental processes in children, his ideas have been incorporated into the broader theory of constructivism. Constructivism holds that each person constructs his or her own concepts of the world, based on individual traits, experiences and beliefs (Jonnasen, 1990). While your first reaction may be that developmental psychology is a long stretch from practical applications for change, your own experience will probably confirm that it is usually individuals who make change happen, or not happen. Developing a better understanding of how each of us shapes our beliefs and attitudes is perhaps the strongest base for developing our skills as change agents.

According to Piaget, assimilation is the process of incorporating a new object or idea into an existing idea or schema. Accommodation is the tendency of humans to change internal schema in order to adjust to the new object or idea. We can think of this two step process by using a simple analogy.

Suppose you are presented with a new sweater. The circumstances by which you acquire the sweater will have a big influence on your attitude about it. Is it something about which you've been wishfully thinking? Is it something you might like except that you detest the person who gave it to you? Is it something so unique in design you don't know how to classify it: as a shirt? a jacket? a tunic? Does the uniqueness of the garment make you uncomfortable, like that Christmas tie you know you'll never wear?

Your first task is acceptance. Will you agree to accept the sweater, or will you, for whatever reason, reject it immediately? The decision to accept is the assimilation process. If something is too strange or too different from your regular patterns, chances are the concept won't get any farther than this. Compressed video, as we discussed earlier, can be seen as either an incremental change or a frame-breaking change. If it is viewed or put forward as an incremental change, it may be more acceptable to some, but may also be viewed as unnecessary; too many other similar sweaters already in the drawer. If it is seen as too different, we may overlook it, using the same process as when we walk through a store, our eyes guided only to the colors and shapes we find naturally pleasing.

If information is not assimilated learning, and the change process, can go no further. The change agent will have to try a new approach. However, if the initial decision to assimilate, to accept the sweater, is made, then the next step can be taken.

That next step involves where to put the sweater, or the new information. Where to put the sweater is an important issue, because where it is stored will affect how easy it is to find later, and therefore how often it is worn. Consider that you have a storage chest with several drawers. If the type of sweater is very familiar to you, it will be easy to decide which drawer to place it in. If it is a turtleneck sweater and you have a drawerful, clearly it belongs with the other like garments.

But what if you have accepted this sweater, something about it pleases you or seems very functional, but it is like nothing else you have? You may then handle the situation in several ways. You may decide after all that it doesn't fit your needs and give it back. You may keep it but toss it carelessly in the back of the socks drawer and forget about it.

You may decide it is indeed a sweater but it doesn't fit in your sweater drawer, which is already filled up with more traditional sweaters. Now you are forced into a decision again: do you start a new drawer to accommodate this new garment or rearrange all the sweaters you already have so this one will also fit in the same drawer? Maybe you even need a bigger drawer.

In choosing such an everyday analogy, we hope you get the idea that this process is not a comfortable one. When faced with new information or ideas, we are forced into a series of decisions. Because humans like things to be comfortable and stable, we often tend to face the new or the unknown less than enthusiastically. We also know that tolerance of ambiguity or the unknown is a trait which varies in scope from individual to individual.

The decision to accept, whether the sweater or the idea of a new technology, is a decision to also accept some necessary shifting around of your ideas. Rearranging our drawers is a lot of work. Most of us prefer to get things stored and keep it that way. To accept the need to rearrange our ideas or our classification systems takes some kind of motivation. It is fortunate for our continuing growth that humans also tend to be a curious bunch.

But how does this understanding of internal processes relate to the task of a change agent in the real world? To start with, it should guide you to build awareness about the people in your organization, individually and collectively. In the instructional design process we call this audience analysis, and we often concentrate on the learner only in terms of content to be taught. In planning for change, it becomes more important to know about the individual in terms of what constitutes his job, how he feels about his job, what effect the planned change is likely to have on the social, functional and hierarchical characteristics of his job. We may choose, or be limited to, addressing such factors through group communication channels. But understanding the real or perceived change in the individual's view can guide us in our implementation actions. Specifically, what we or other decision makers think people "should" feel has little to do with successful change projects.

Groups and the Change Process

The stage of accommodation is where we see the larger context of the change process overlapping with individual change. Drawing on our sweater analogy, the drawer doesn't just contain items the individual has put there. There are also items put there by family, culture, friends, bosses, and co-workers. Attitudes, beliefs and values tend to be reinforced by the group.

Kuhn's work, *The Structure of Scientific Revolutions* (1970), eloquently describes the process of change as it affects groups. Kuhn studied the process by which scientific paradigms are extended, challenged and gradually replaced by new paradigms over time. Once a general area of scientific research has been defined, all subsequent research tends to build on the same framework. New experiments are based on an acceptance of existing assumptions. As a result, all study tends to continue down the same road. Expectations to a great extent dictate what will be found. Gradually, such lines of research will fade, when it appears there is little more chance of finding anything new.

But sometimes scientists do find new result¬, results that don't fit the old assumptions. When that first happens, these anomalous results are usually either explained away or ignored. But when such troublesome results start turning up in a regular pattern, finally the weight of disbelief must shift and people are forced to look at things in a new way.

Our views of the universe have undergone just this type of transformation. The first evidence that the Earth was not the center of the Universe was regarded by most as heresy. Leonardo da Vinci was forced to recant such radical ideas during the inquisition. A few centuries later, everyone had come to accept the Copernican view of the universe as truth.

The relationship of groups to change obviously has some elements of timing involved. Part of the role of the change agent is to first clearly assess the state of the group, and second, determine appropriate ways to move the group forward.

This is not to say that organizations are always resistant to change, particularly when that change is expressed through new technologies. Particularly in our society, there is a tendency to accept all technological advancements as desirable, even though there are more than enough newspaper and magazine articles to suggest that some of our technological advancements have been poorly conceived or are unquestioning acceptance of technology outright detrimental to people or to our environment. Rogers (1983) refers to this as a *pro-innovation bias*, offering the definition as "... the implication... that an innovation should be diffused and adopted by all members of a social system, that it should be diffused more rapidly, and that the innovation should be neither re-invented nor rejected" (p. 92). Note the implicit message of the pro-innovation bias; not only is the innovation good but that it is good exactly as it is. This may be of particular application to compressed video, where one of the keys to successful and innovative applications may be the ability of the change agent to "reinvent" the technology to fit the organization or system' needs. It is also the job of the instructional technologist as change agent to work for the best solution, the best use of technology, the best answer to all the questions.

When we deal with change at the group level, we must go beyond the individual to look at the characteristics of the given group, their overall paradigms about themselves, their work, their communication and their collective purpose. The change agent must be able to communicate with individual group members within the framework of those paradigms. As we think of the potential of compressed video as a frame-breaking change, we must try to understand the potential perceptions within the group which might constitute a barrier to that change. Conversely, if people see the compressed video system as only an extension of traditional ways of operating, we must build motivation for expanding beyond those traditional paradigms. In such cases, personal change will be inhibited to the extent that group attitudes are resistant. Only by guiding people to think in new terms can the benefits of compressed video be fully realized.

The Change Process in Action

Previously in this chapter we have used both "change" and "innovation" to refer to processes in which people and organizations react to new ideas. Research on the change process has come mostly from the field of communications. A specific branch of the change research has focused on persuasion and the diffusion of innovations, studying how a various new programs or technologies were introduced and looking at factors affecting the success or failure of each project.

Rogers (1983) has written about the diffusion of innovations, concentrating mainly on technological innovations. He defines technology as "a design for instrumental action that reduces the uncertainty in the cause-effect relationships involved in achieving a desired outcome" (p. 12).

Rogers' work provides a number of potential links between instructional design and the diffusion process. While we will not explore such links here, we will note that his definition of technology fits quite well with our concept of instructional technology. As we have also seen, the change or diffusion process, whether on a personal level or broader, aligns closely with the processes and goals of learning addressed in instructional design models and theory.

Rogers notes that we tend to think of technology in two components, hardware and software, but he also cites examples of technologies which consist mostly of information, such as political or religious ideas, news events, or assembly-line production. In implementing a compressed video system, the change agent may well incorporate both straightforward knowledge transfer about the equipment and its capabilities, and also more general ideas about the concept and potential of the compressed video medium.

Rogers (1983) outlines five steps in what he calls the Innovation-Decision process, the process by which an organization chooses and adopts an innovation. These steps are *knowledge, persuasion, decision, implementation,* and *confirmation.* These are stages through which individuals and the system in which they operate progress more or less sequentially. The stages therefore serve as a road map for change agents as well. The successful change agent will serve as navigator for the organization. We will discuss these stages within the context of compressed video.

The *knowledge* stage occurs as individuals or groups are exposed to the new technology and gain some understanding about how it works. In the *persuasion* stage, members of the organization form favorable or unfavorable attitudes. The *decision* phase comprises activities that lead people in the organization to making a choice regarding adoption or rejection. The system is put into use during the *implementation* stage. Finally, during the *confirmation* stage individuals or the group may look for reinforcement of the choice. If there have been conflicting information or impressions, the confirmation stage may lead to a new rejection (Rogers, 1983).

Rogers' is certainly not the only model of the change process. Havelock, for example, dealing with educational change, defines six steps in the change process: building a relationship, diagnosing the problem, acquiring relevant resources, choosing the solution, gaining acceptance, and stabilizing the innovation and generating self-renewal (1982). While both descriptions share many common features, we will refer to Rogers' framework, as it seems to lend itself more to a discussion of circumstances where the technology is already at least implicitly chosen and the change process follows. This approach, at least in our experience, is more reflective of situations in which compressed video has been introduced.

Experiences with Compressed Video

In order to provide perspective on the change process as it occurs in real life, we interviewed a number of people who have been involved in efforts to implement a compressed video system. These people were able to describe their experiences within own systems through the various stages of the change effort. Because the nature of change often involves personal efforts and insights about individuals or the nature of the organization, we have kept our sources anonymous and offer a summary of a number of different experiences from across the United States. All those interviewed had a background in instructional technology. We will refer to our interviewees simply as change agents.

Earlier, we quoted Rogers' definition of a change agent as "...an individual who influences clients' innovation decisions in a direction deemed desirable by a change agency" (Rogers, p. 28). In a broad sense, a change agent might not necessarily represent a larger organization's goals or values. In the context of implementing a compressed video system, it is probable that the instructional technologist will represent the interests of the larger organization in successful implementation. However, it is possible, as we will see from our interviews, that there may be other change agents within an organization, possibly working toward other goals. The change agent must define his or her purpose not only in terms of the explicit organizational goals but also in terms of all different interests which may be held within the organization.

We should also note here that we have used Rogers' five stages as a general organizational framework for discussing a number of specific change efforts. Some of the people we interviewed pointed out that the process did not actually take place in these discrete stages. Throughout this chapter we have tried to meld theory and practice, and we do so again here. The theoretical framework is meant to structure, not to impose artificial constraints or assumptions.

The Knowledge Stage

All the change agents we talked to cited specific needs of their organizations which CV could be addressed through, although most of these needs did not emerge from a formal needs analysis. A common need was the challenge of providing instruction over geographic distances, sometimes because the distances themselves were a problem, sometimes because there was a need to maximize resources. Sometimes the change agent was given the task of originating the search for a solution. In other cases, the change agent was presented with a decision already made to adopt CV.

A strong theme among those interviewed was their reliance on a network of contacts and professional sources to gain information. These sources included peers in the field, professional conferences, and other personal contacts. The main challenge the change agents cited at this point was not the decision to adopt the technology, but the effort to find the best system and the best vendor. Because CV is still relatively new, the change agents faced several problems related to vendors: getting clear descriptions of capabilities, verifying that the capabilities described were actually and fully available, and defining the needs regarding installation and support. Several of the people interviewed stressed the benefit of their personal involvement in writing the request for proposals, saying that defining those requirements helped insure that the final product would meet their needs.

Another common theme at the knowledge stage was the importance of as much demonstration as possible, allowing people within the organization to have free, non-threatening hands-on experience with the equipment. This provided information while also alleviating many fears, as people saw for themselves the user friendly-nature of CV systems.

The Persuasion Stage

Some of the change agents we talked to found themselves in the role of the main "salesperson" for the CV implementation. Others cited an administrator within the organization as the main leader in shaping positive opinions. Whether the main opinion shaper was one of the people interviewed or their boss, that person was seen within the organization as someone with credibility, someone viewed with respect by others. All said they were personally enthusiastic about the potential of CV.

The change agents agreed on several points regarding the persuasion process. They stressed the effectiveness of providing hands-on experience with the equipment, and of presenting the options in terms of benefits to the potential users. Most users were described as mainly interested in the impact to them as individuals. In many cases, the CV system offered an alternative to long drives, thus saving time for instructors, and saving expenses for administrators as they stretched their teaching resources.

In each of the situations described by the change agents, there were different types of organizational factors. All represented an organization which functioned as part of a larger organization. In many cases, the decision involved the need to work with outside organizations as well. Public institutions had to work with state agencies or state legislatures. In some cases, the organization of the change agent was the only group within the larger organization attempting to adopt CV. In some cases there was inter-organizational competition and conflict, which tended to place the change agent in a more difficult position. As in any turf battle, different groups tended to stress different needs and positions. Where there was internal competition, the credibility of the change agent was brought into question by the competing group.

The change agents cited a number of common fears or criticisms given by members of the organization during the persuasion stage. People were concerned about poor picture quality, poor sound quality, and the need for expensive and complicated equipment which would require technicians to support the system. Some people were resistant to changing the way they taught, and were uninterested in the potential for new delivery methods which CV promised. Others were concerned that CV was just another way to deliver the kind of "talking heads" instruction which could be done less expensively via videotape. Reliability of the system was another concern.

In addition to the benefit of hands-on demonstration, some of the people interviewed stressed the importance of choosing the right kind of demonstration project or pilot project. In one case, the change agent and his organization started demonstrating the CV system using one particular course and site. It turned out that the technology was a poor match for that particular application and did not result in positive perceptions within the organization. A different situation occurred within another organization. A project was undertaken after implementation, but with the direct intent of persuading potential users of the benefits of the system. Although the project was not cost effective in the short term, it was highly effective in involving many people in a very positive experience, which resulted in a greatly increased awareness of CV and a high demand for its use.

The Decision Stage

In most of the cases described to us, decisions were made by the administration, which tended to be enthusiastic about the system. Usually, the administration looked at the benefits in terms of money saved or resources extended. They also tended to have a sense of the positive public image which could be gained from having a CV system. In some cases, the change agent was responsible for shaping the specifics of the final decision, such as changing an original intent to select a two-way analog video satellite system to the decision to adopt compressed video instead.

There was a range of approaches to the final decision to adopt a specific product. Some institutions were constrained by budget factors. They had to spend the money within a short time frame and were unable to go through a full open bid process. Others made somewhat arbitrary decisions to adopt the first product they tested, looking only for more traditional applications.

In one organization, the decision to adopt a product was made only after a long period of investigation, during which several products were tested, and communications with various vendors led to confirmation of the capabilities of the products being tested. In this approach, the change agent found the technology was so new, there was an opportunity not only to test different capabilities, but to recommend improvements to the systems. Another of the change agents tried to requested a turnkey system, but the vendor was unable to provide it.

The question of buy-in was another issue during the decision stage. When the overall decision was made to adopt the technology, equipment was provided to some sites in one network for free. Because they had no investment, problems later arose at those sites, because there was not a real sense of ownership. Those sites did not provide dedicated classrooms for the equipment and made little effort to maximize use of the CV system.

Implementation

Implementing the CV system brought awareness of a number of new factors for the change agents. One person interviewed described problems in installing the system, due to the policy of the vendor to subcontract the installation, and the difficulty of knowing just what to look out for in a new system. This person told of problems with audio which went on for months until the problems were traced to microphones which were locked into an "on" position.

Some change agents identified issues of scheduling as a primary challenge once the system was operating. Other implementation factors included approaches to handling technical staff. Some vendors' products required more technicians than others. In different organizations the responsibility for running the CV system was given to the computer services people or the audio-visual people. Each group has specific and relatively inflexible mindsets which caused implementation problems. The computer services people thought in terms of mainframe computers rather than the personal computers which drive CV systems. The audio-visual people thought in terms of traditional studio television production rather than highly interactive spontaneous systems where students operated the equipment. One agent, in fact, said that they had come to rely more on the students in the class than the technicians to operate and trouble shoot the equipment. Not only did the students have a good understanding of the CV system, but involving them tends to increase their sense of investment in the course itself.

Other organizations have found what they feel is a more successful approach to providing technical support. In several academic institutions, graduate students serve internships by acting as technicians and trainers for the equipment. Any troubleshooting can be guided from another site by talking a site facilitator or student through diagnostic routines. One change agent estimates that only one in ten people simply refuse to touch the equipment.

Another change agent said the implementation effort within his department was the easiest part. A harder part was responding to the growing use of the system, when the original department using the system had to negotiate with the larger organization for more lines and more on-line time to meet the demand. Use within the department in that situation was about 95%. Within the larger organization, use of the same system was about 25-30%. Another change agent estimated the percentage of people at his institution using the system was about 20%.

Confirmation

The change agents identified a number of on-going issues connected to the use of the CV system. One issue concerns the need for increased technical support. New technologies are often implemented without corresponding increases in staffing. Another issue is funding for future sites on the network. Many of the systems described here were funded originally through grants. There is not always additional funding available for the purchase of additional hardware.

There are also on-going costs for repair, upgrading or replacement. One change agent estimated the life expectancy of CV systems at 5 to 6 years. Another change agent commented on the issue of working with telephone companies to insure fractional billing for rural communities so they can afford installation costs. As the technology changes, it may be necessary to consider a variety of carriers, including very small aperture satellites, microwave or land line systems.

Summary

As we have seen, the word change implies a broad and complex range of ideas. One may deal with change on many levels, from the individual to the group to the community. The nature of compressed video, viewed according to its full potential, requires a different way of thinking, both in order to realize that potential, and to communicate the potential to an organization which may not be fully prepared to assimilate such new ideas.

The managing of the change process is an exciting challenge for those involved with compressed video. Through the comments of the change agents we interviewed, we can see that managing change requires technical knowledge but also considerable understanding of human nature and the nature of your specific organization.

The long-term impact of compressed video remains to be seen. If optimally integrated and utilized, the technology has the potential to affect communications on a wide basis. As you may remember, the fourth level of change was at the level of the society. Insuring that the impact of compressed video is appropriate, positive and valid will provide a significant challenge to change agents for the foreseeable future.

References

Benne, K. D. (1985). The current state of planned changing in persons, groups, communities and societies. In Bennis, W.G., Benne, K. D. and Chin, R. , *The Planning of Change*, 4th ed. Holt, Rinehart and Winston, New York. pp. 13-21.

Benne, K.D., Bennis, W.G. and Chin, R. (1985). Planned change in america. In Bennis, W.G., Benne, K. D. and Chin, R. , *The planning of change*, 4th ed. Holt, Rinehart and Winston, New York. pp. 13-21.

Bennis, W.G., Benne, K. D. and Chin, R. (1985). *The planning of change*, 4th ed. New York: Holt, Rinehart and Winston. pp. 13-21.

Havelock, R. (1982). *The Change Agent's Guide to Innovation in Education.* 6th ed. Englewood Cliffs, New Jersey: Educational Technology Publications.

Jonassen, D.H. (1990). Thinking technology: toward a constructivist view of instructional design. *Educational Technology*, September. 32-34.

Kuhn, T. (1970). *The structure of scientific revolutions*, 2nd ed. Chicago: University of Chicago Press.

London, M. (1988). *Change agents, new roles and innovation strategies for human resource professionals*. San Francisco: Jossey-Bass Publishers.

Miller, G. and Burgoon, M. (1978). Persuasion research: review and commentary. *Communication Yearbook 2*. 29-47.

Mussen, P., Conger, J., and Kagan, J. (1974). *Child development and personality*, 4th ed. New York: Harper and Row.

Rogers, E. M. (1983). *Diffusion of innovations.* London: Collier Macmillan.

Weber, W. C. (1992). An Interactive systems model derived from experts' perceptions of human-computer issues. *Educational Technology Research and Development, 40* (1). 29-39.

14

The Politics and Issues in Telecommunications

Richard T. Hezel
Paula M. Szulc

Introduction

Telecommunications acts as a new form of currency in today's society. Telecommunications networks, regardless of size, represent a significant resource developed through sizable capital investment. Such networks also offer a potential revenue stream to investors. For educational institutions, in particular, the operation and possession of networks are points of pride and can lead to new education "markets."

Perhaps most importantly, telecommunications networks can further the reach of an organization's influence. As an organization extends its human and informational resources, its decision making causes repercussions in dozens of new and unfamiliar arenas. As a result, the development and management of telecom-munications networks and the involvement of educational systems are subject to considerable political pulls.

This chapter describes the political and institutional influences surrounding telecom-munications system planning and development. The most comprehensive sense of "politics" is used here to denote pressures and accords arising from individuals and institutions working toward common or distinctive goals. A number of approaches to telecommunications planning and system building are depicted. Within the context of planning for multi-institution telecommunications, various methods of forming and working through collaborations are described. Effective governance policies, the framework for all decision-making in telecommunications collaboratives, are suggested, and administrative management systems for educational telecommunications are recommended. Finally, specific methods of treating practical political issues of network management, such as network control and scheduling are offered. The chapter takes a broad approach to politics in telecommunications: With few exceptions, the political issues arising in the development of compressed video are similar to those apparent in full motion video or data networks.

The Political Context of Planning

Telecommunications requires planning. Costs are considerable, implementation is complex, and often, by nature, more than one institution is involved in using compressed video. The planning process, therefore, entails political consideration on the part of the organizers. At issue are the governance, control, financing, and programming of the system In a consortium of two or more schools, colleges, agencies, or businesses, the struggle to assure the best interests of one's own organization sometimes leads to conflict and, hopefully, to resolution through compromise. Even where telecommunications systems are developed by a single institution, intra-institutional politics enters into the planning process. Politics is inherent to every form of telecommunications planning.

State Political Decisions

In the United States, the federal government has declined, thus far, to take the lead in establishing a comprehensive national framework for telecommunications. Although federal govern-ment activities surrounding the development of telecommunications policy and infrastructure for educa-tion reveal increasing concern at that level, the substantial educational telecommunications decision making currently occurs at the state level. The primary political influences at the state level originate in the governor's office, at the state legislature, and from state agencies which have estab-lished identities as leaders in telecommunications.

Gubernatorial Influences

While the creation of a well conceptualized statewide telecommu-nications infrastructure is subject to diverse and numerous influences, leadership and input from the governor's office is one of the main factors in determining the successful development of any telecommunications sys-tem. Based on research on statewide telecommunications coordination (Hezel Associates, 1992), where the governor takes a strong position on planning and implementing telecommunications systems, other influential state leaders will follow. If gubernatorial leadership is absent, extensive telecommunications networks are less likely to be developed. Therefore, it is imperative that planners for telecommunications enlist, entreat, or other-wise seek the governor's support in telecommunications decision making, no matter the scale of the proposed telecommunications system.

Two states, South Dakota and Michigan, can be used to illustrate gubernatorial involvement in the development of telecommunications sys-tems. In 1991, the governor of South Dakota initiated a statewide study of telecommunications for education and economic development, resulting in a solid, comprehensive plan for telecommunications growth. As the situa-tion in Michigan shows, however, such a well-conceived telecommunica-tions plan will not necessarily lead to successful implementation. Michigan's comprehensive state plan for telecommunications lies fallow. Prepared in

1990 with the support of one Governor and the considerable energies and resources of many individuals in the state, the Michigan plan has been ignored by that governor's successor, a member of the opposing party. When telecommunications planners consider gubernatorial support, therefore, the presence of future administrations should also be accommodated as much as possible.

Legislative Influences

A nod from the governor's office does not grant manifest destiny for telecommunications planning, however. While the governor's office can initiate and set the pace for statewide and institutional telecommunications planning, on-going support from the state legislature is integral to the continued development of a telecommunications system. A state legislature can make or break a telecommunications network by its funding of activities that promote diverse principles such as equity in education, by legislation empowering public utilities commissions in matters of public utility rate structures and telephone companies' rights to provide intra-LATA services, and by funding for statewide public broadcasting. Educational telecommunications advocates must be prepared to devote considerable time to communicating with state legislators and lobbying for legislation which favors telecommunications.

There is a distinction between telecommunications legislation to encourage impartially the growth and development of systems, and telecommunications legislation to favor and repay certain constituents. Unfortunately, in some states this legislative "member item" funding of education telecommunications holds sway. Such pork barrel support contributes to a grass roots development of telecommunications use, but it also contributes to disarray in statewide planning.

Agency Influences

In almost every state, an agency is assigned the role of telecommunications equipment and service procurement. The division of telecommunications or the division of information services usually offers teleconferencing services to facilitate communication with regional and local offices, conduct meetings and training, and provide information to employees and citizens. Depending on the state, the services may extend to education. In Montana, for example, the state telecommunications office helps educators plan for school and college applications. The effectiveness of the telecommunications agency to assist education often depends on (1) whether state legislation mandates telecommunications procurement through the agency, (2) whether education groups operate substantial infrastructures independently of the agency, and (3) whether the agency has a sensitivity to the particular academic telecommunications needs of schools and colleges.

Other influential agencies may include state offices of finance, boards of regents, departments of general services, and departments of education. Such agencies have vested interests in developing and maintaining solid telecommunications systems and will view any proposed telecommunications system through agency interests. Since these agencies have devoted much time and effort to establishing their domain, their members often prefer to maintain a healthy distance from levels of cooperation that might result in the loss of control to other, "outside" organizations. Telecommunications planners who wish to coordinate among several agencies need to understand the history, politics, and use of telecommunications among potential participating agencies in the state.

Inter-institutional Politics

At the state level, planning in telecommunications usually originates from either the grass-roots or from a single coordinating agency, such as a board of regents or state department of education. State university and community college systems, public broadcasting systems, and regional education consortia often develop telecommunications plans independent from any state level guidance. In addition, local institutions such as colleges, schools, and school districts may begin using telecommunications on a small scale and gradually progress to interconnection. Although the scale of the proposed telecommunications networks may be smaller, the issues to confront and resolve are identical to those of the larger statewide systems.

When more localized, "bottom up" telecommunications planning efforts take place, the development of inter-institutional policy in the initial stages of planning becomes central to the success of a telecommunications system. Local institutions must cooperate to develop solid policies which treat each partner equitably, without the luxury of having a centralized agency to provide direction and advice. Locally focused telecom-munications planners must confront and resolve complex issues related to governance, use, funding, programming, and technology options—a tall order for inexperienced planners.

There are benefits associated with localized planning which cannot be found with state sponsored telecommunications initiatives. With well conceived policy, local telecommunications planning can surpass state sponsored efforts in their ability to meet the particular needs and demands of their region. The diversity of voices which contribute to the planning process at the local level can lead to a creative synergy unmatched by more centralized planning efforts.

Telecommunications planning, then, can result from both state and local levels. Neither planning process is inherently "better" than the other. With state level planning, support from the governor's office can be frustrated by turf battles with existing telecommunications user agencies. Local telecommunications initiatives can respond to local needs, but they seldom have the established leadership to adequately handle the multitude of planning problems. Whether the telecom-munications system results from "top down" or "bottom up" approaches, politics are fundamental to the planning process.

Leadership in Telecommunications Planning

Leadership in educational telecommunications planning and implementation is as varied as the technologies, programming, and services offered over the hundreds of existing networks. There are seven broad categories of organizations and institutions which have taken the lead in educational telecommunications planning in different states: (1) departments of education, (2) boards of regents, (3) major universities, (4) other state agencies, (5) public broadcasters, (6) independent agencies, and (7) clusters. Although many coordinator-leaders from among these groups are very well respected, they often draw criticism from other institutions. Where criticism arises, it is often because of the differing goals of the institutions and individuals representing the institutions.

In states such as Texas, Michigan, and Florida, the state Department of Education (DOE) has emerged as the driving force in planning educational telecommunications. The Department of Education has accepted considerable responsibility for drawing up and submitting to the legislature a technology plan for public education which includes the statewide use of telecommunications. The DOE then implements on a statewide level the guidelines established by the technology plan. Issues such as equity of public education and access to information in rural or underserved populations are usually at the heart of telecommunications initiatives sponsored by state Departments of Education.

Often, the state board of regents or the university system in a state assume leadership roles in developing educational telecommunications. Their interest in telecommunicated instruction is quite natural: the need to share limited resources compels the use of telecommunications. Also, given the recent widespread decline in enrollments of traditional-age students throughout higher education, the use of telecommunications in higher education is easy to understand. Telecommunications can be employed to expand the market for higher education by delivering instruction to hard-to-reach adult populations and generate new enrollments and tuition from non-traditional students. Boards of regents and university systems in states such as Oklahoma and Wisconsin have established statewide systems for the distribution of telecourses, and in doing so, have quickly become veterans in educational telecommunications planning.

As noted above, in some states, a state agency has assumed a leadership role in planning for and providing educational telecommunications. Departments of administration, information services, and telecommunications have served as centralized coordinating bodies. Virginia's Department of Information Technology (DIT) offers a good example of a state agency which coordinates educational telecommunications initiatives. Frequently, however, educators view departments of administration as procurers of cost-effective telephone equipment and services, not as agencies that are prepared to design systems appropriate for instruction.

Public broadcasters have been in the forefront of educational telecommunications in many states. South Carolina, Nebraska, Iowa, and Kentucky have served the citizens of their states by offering high quality educational programming and services to public school children, higher education, and adult learners. Because of their technical and programming expertise, leaders from state licensed public broadcasters have organized and participated in telecommunications planning initiatives, usually with a focus on televised instructional delivery, but increasingly with interests in computer data services and live distance education.

A rare approach for the coordination of educational telecommunications is to establish an independent state agency to oversee all planning activities. Oregon Ed-Net and the Massachusetts Corporation for Educational Telecommunications (MCET) were both created by statute to assume responsibilities for their state's educational telecommunications needs. To date, Oregon Ed-Net has been extremely well received, which might lead to more states' following this model for their planning.

Some states remain dedicated to the independence of their local school districts. In Minnesota and Kansas, for example, in the absence of centralized guidance small clusters of schools, school districts, higher education, and private industry have banded together to form local collaboratives. In these states, the entire spectrum of telecommunications technologies is employed to deliver instruction. Differences in the technologies and equipment standards and protocols used by the independent clusters have led to difficulties in the integration of the numerous systems. If economies of scale and integration are an eventual goal of the clusters, however, standardization must coexist with the independent planning.

Decision Making In a Multi-Institution Telecommunications Initiative

The planning for and development of a telecommunications network is an enormous undertaking in terms of both capital and human resources. Rarely, if ever, is one institution or organization capable of fronting the costs and providing all the necessary expertise for a telecommunications network. The involvement of more than one organization is essential for economies of scale to come into effect and for informed decision making to occur.

Telecommunications consortia involving education, government, and private industry have been formed to provide instruction and services to a number of populations while striving for cost effectiveness. Consortia have often benefited from the wealth of ideas and talents of their participants. Many consortia have met with mixed results, however, primarily due to difficulties centering around the key issue of governance.

Two planning styles can be employed when forming consortia: lead institution planning and collaborative planning. With lead institution planning, a single institutional participant, because it has more resources or greater urgency to use telecommunications, assumes the majority of the responsibility for planning. The stronger institution may have a greater voice in planning due to a number of factors. The institution may contribute more financial and human resources than any of the other consortium members. The institution may have a historical influence in educational telecommunications and an established turf. The institution may have significant political support from the governor's office or state legislature. An advantage of lead institution planning is that decisions can quickly be reached.

Collaborative planning involves participants which have about the same voice in decision making. This planning style is commonly found in states which do not have strong central guidance from the governor's office or state agencies. With collaborative planning, the emphasis is on reaching decisions which equitably benefit all participants.

An advantage of collaborative planning is that decisions tend to reflect the needs of a greater number of populations, rather than serving the needs of a particular entity. Unfortunately, such planning strategies usually require lengthy discussions. Agreements are often difficult to reach.

Governance of Telecommunications Systems

The governance of collaborative telecommunications projects can be a very delicate topic—and one that demands considerable attention and policy development. Seldom does governance policy simply evolve— collaborative participants need to understand the terms of their membership and how telecommunications decisions are to be made for the group.

Governance structures arise from within or from outside the collaborative. Either the collaborative members themselves jointly decide on the governance, the lead institution unilaterally dictates the governance structure, or a governance mandate is issued by the governor's office or the state legislature. The first offers greatest flexibility, the last the least. Few participants are satisfied for long with lead institution governance, and eventually it is likely to lead to the dissolution of the collaborative arrangement.

Even after the decision has been made to collaborate, participants may have entirely different expectations of the system and its operations, the structure, and their responsibilities. Unless governance structures are perceived as equitable, participants representing smaller institutions may feel disenfranchised. Over time, each institution's changing needs may bring the institution into conflict with the governance structure originally established for the telecommunications system. One way to keep the governance structure and policies in synchronization with changing needs is to develop a clearly stated, jointly accepted mission statement, goals and strategies, all of which should be reviewed every two years or so. Without a strategic plan and periodic review, policies become ossified merely through historical inertia and accumulation of weight.

Closely associated with governance are user policies dealing with channel allocation and scheduling. Collaboratives can deteriorate where those policies and procedures are not balanced to provide for the best interests of all participating institutions. One state educational telecommunications system was established by a state agency to serve all of the state's educational needs. When the system was built, however, only one institution, the state university, was prepared to use the system. Strong interest from the department of education some years later brought all three institutions into conflict over the use and scheduling of limited channel capacity. The conflict required outside mediation for its resolution.

Funding

The operation of telecommunications systems requires two types of funding: initial capital costs and on-going operation costs. Federal involvement in telecommunications initiatives is usually in the form of start up grants for initiatives. Much as we prefer to believe that the government allocates grants for capital costs on a competitive basis, evidence suggests considerable political leverage is employed in decisions about funding.

To date, the most extensive use of federal funds has been the US Department of Education's Star Schools initiatives, initiated in 1988, which promote the formation of multi-state, multi-institution educational telecommunications consortia, and the National Telecommunications and Information Administration's (NTIA) Public Telecommunications Fund Program (PTFP), which supports the development of the public telecommunications infrastructure.

States also provide financing to educational telecommunications initiatives in the form of competitive grants, offered through the department of education, and member items, of "pork barrel" funding.

Recently, telecommunications providers such as telephone companies, equipment companies, and cable television companies have become involved with funding for educational telecommunications. The contribution of members of the telecommunications industry is sometimes in the form of outright gifts of equipment, cable, and receive dishes, sometimes in the form of reduced-rate services. Such gifts usually have attachments—that the educators make a longer-term commitment to the vendor's technology. Telephone companies offer fiber and switching. The cable television industry has used a portion of its profits to fund Cable in the Classroom, a service which provides free cable installation and programming to schools passed by cable lines. In many cases, individual cable companies also provide televisions and VCRs to schools. Among much controversy, Whittle Communications has provided more than 10,000 schools with satellite downlinks and classroom television, in exchange for mandatory 12-minute daily segments which include commercials.

The quest for technology funding has led many educational institutions into political alliances that might never have been considered, except for the need to share resources through, and costs of, telecommunications. Because of the need to collaborate for cost-effective instruction through telecommunications, schools, colleges, and agencies have learned to cooperate as they have not previously.

Conclusion

In any political arena, the relationships among individuals and institutions, as well as among elected and appointed officials, have tremendous impact on the shape of decision making. In this chapter we have attempted to describe the unique multi-tiered arena of telecommunications and demonstrate the complex role politics assumes in the planning and use of compressed video telecom-munications systems. It is doubtful that a single institution, organization, or agency will ever have the critical mass of human, financial, and physical resources to lobby for, develop, and implement a sound telecommunications system. The barriers to successful collaborative telecommunications planning are not technical, but are based on the willingness of participants representing many different interests to cooperate and communicate. The necessarily collaborative nature of telecommunications planning is a reality that will continue to confront, challenge, and, at times frustrate participants. Cooperative planning, however, will also lead to productive projects far beyond the capabilities of any single-institution telecommunications initiative.

15

Ethical Issues in Compressed Video

Mary Alice Bruce
Richard A. Shade
Dorothy Jean Yocom

Introduction

Ethical considerations become increasingly complex as the use of compressed video technology for teaching and learning advances. As institutions and organizations actively promote and participate in distance learning, professionals must expand their awareness and sensitivity to ethical practices (Sherry, 1991). Throughout decision-making processes, professionals must weigh possible advantages and disadvantages regarding the needs and welfare of the users of technology. Emerging ethical issues include respect and fairness to users, privacy, informed consent, confidentiality, and freedom of choice.

Core principles include "nonmaleficence (doing no harm), beneficence (benefiting others), autonomy (respecting a person's right to make choices), justice (being fair), and fidelity (being faithful and keeping promises)" (p. 241). While professional ethical codes may not address specific concerns in an ever-changing society, knowledge of ethical principles facilitates responsible action.

The cornerstone of ethical decision making is the application of general ethical principles which underlie ethical codes of the helping professions. Kitchener (1991)

To stimulate and clarify the development of responsible behaviors, the authors utilize the problem-posing model of Strom and Tennyson (1989) within the context of compressed video teaching and learning. Discussion of perspectives that seem to lead to ethically appropriate behavior encourages an interactional approach, avoiding a dichotomous view. Critical consideration of various problem solutions, guided by ethical codes and standards, may enhance the strength of professionals involved in conflicts of decision making (Kitchener, 1991). Situations in this chapter may be generalized to a variety of outreach services, thus producing challenging opportunities to value and demand ethical practices. Authors' responses and discussions are interpretations, not necessarily the correct answers. Readers must consider influencing factors of situations, institutional philosophies, legal ramifications, and personal values.

Institutional Obligations

Situation

Julie lives in a small town, 200 miles from the state's institution of higher learning, where she received her bachelor's degree. The closest educational facility is a community college about 15 miles away. This community college offers both on-campus classes at the preparatory level and classes transmitted from the university through the technology of compressed (or interactive) video. Julie would like to continue her education but, as she is the primary care-giver for her invalid mother, she is not able to commute to the university campus.

Question

Does the university have an ethical obligation to meet Julie's educational needs and provide continued course work for her via compressed video?

Response

Establishing and maintaining a continued relationship between the educational institution and the student is an obligation for any university, regardless of where the course work is offered. Indeed, many college and university mission statements typically include outreach programs as an integral part of the university's work. With advancements in distance learning (such as teleconferencing, interactive video) these obligations become much easier for universities to fulfill. Since the technology is available to transmit university classes to the nearby community college, offering these classes to Julie helps fulfill the mission of the university.

For example, the Wyoming State Department of Education recently adopted a state-wide assessment system for science and math. The State Department requested the University of Wyoming to coordinate the training to the state's science and math teachers. Compressed video facilitated the training needs for 82 of Wyoming's teachers.

Discussion

In addition to the mission statement of colleges which provides for outreach programs, a second related ethical concern occurs in the provision of classes through compressed video. Distance learning courses often are offered in an "open enrollment" fashion, allowing admission to all who apply (Zvacek, 1991). Or perhaps more specifically, to what degree must the university be responsible for determining the "readiness" of students to take classes through compressed video? Several research studies have examined the characteristics of successful distance learners. These characteristics include high levels of motivation, self-directedness, organization, and independence (Ehrman, 1990; Gibson, 1985; Moore, 1985; Tift, 1989; Reed and Sork, 1990). Should the university allow only students with these characteristics to enroll?

What obligation, if any, does the university have to prepare students for distance education?

The literature suggests three avenues available to university personnel to encourage student "readiness" for distance learning. The first, continued contact with the student, can be met in a variety of ways including: letters, phone calls, and personal visits (Moore, 1985; Moore, 1992, Tift, 1989). Second, learning opportunities for students to use the technical equipment can easily be incorporated as a small part of each lesson (Gibson, 1985; Tift, 1989). Third, an intermediary or counselor linking the student and the university can provide personal interaction and may be connected to lower dropout rates (Gibson, 1985; Moore, 1985; Tift, 1989).

Course Design

Situation

A large land grant institution has just hired Dr. Jones to teach in the Chemistry Department. Dr. Jones' first teaching assignment includes a freshman course offered via compressed video technology. She is struggling to design effective course delivery.

Question

How can Dr. Jones design her Chemistry course for the best possible teaching and learning?

Response

The design of distance education courses and programs is in many ways similar to the design of conventional educational settings. Instructors may need to address specific aspects of instructional design for distance education. Creative approaches can address concerns such as access to current media materials, opportunities for individualized instruction and critical feedback, plus student to student interactions.

Discussion

One of the challenges of teaching distance education courses is in designing or planning them (Moore, 1985; Wolcott, 1991). While research to date has not yet addressed the issue of which delivery service is best for presenting given content (Tift, 1989), experts in the field have noted that the more interactive a distance education course can be, the better (Moore, 1985; Reed & Sork, 1990; Tift, 1989; Zvacek, 1991). Additionally, course design involves pinpointing course structure ranging from complete learner control to complete institutional control. Distance education courses positively evaluated by learners facilitate learner control and input (Gibson, 1985; Moore, 1985). Other factors to consider in the design of an effective distance education course include flexibility, individual student-identified projects, self assessment, and "real world" application (Gibson, 1985; Taylor & Kaye, 1986; Tift, 1989). See Chapter 10 for additional information concerning assessment and evaluation.

See Chapter 10

Marketing

Situation

Tom is thinking about taking some compressed video business classes at the nearby community college in order to learn more about his job at the bank. Tom read about these classes in a bright, flashy, expensive-looking brochure put out by the university. The brochure listed only classes, nothing about pre-requisites or skills needed for successful completion.

Question

What obligation does the university have to present clearly and completely the requirements of classes and the demands placed on the learner?

Response

The practices governing program and course offerings, as well as the associated marketing of these programs and courses, reflect an issue similar to conventional education. Universities have an obligation to present their courses with as much accuracy as possible, providing the names and phone numbers of people available to answer questions. Extra care must be taken by the university in distance education courses since academic work completed via distance learning may not be considered equivalent to course work completed through conventional means. Universities should provide students with the critical information they need to make appropriate choices for themselves and the completion of their program.

Discussion

Courses offered through distance education should first reflect a need in the community (Tift, 1989). Therefore, an institution's priority should be a needs assessment throughout the state or target area. Marketing a class which reflects the identified need can promote an increased link between an institution and community (Koontz, 1989; Tift, 1989). Knowledge of students, their needs, the competition, and the economic environment influences the marketing of distance learning classes (Koontz, 1989; McNeil, 1985; Young, 1989). Certainly, the best marketing tool is the successful, vocal student who has completed distance education courses (Moore, 1985; Young, 1989).

Management of Offerings

Situation

Dr. Henderson, Dean of the College of Education, has just been awarded a sizable grant to implement distance education courses throughout the state by means of compressed video.

Question

What are some of the management concerns of distance learning course offerings?

Response

Issues related to the management administration of course work through compressed video include personnel selection, finances, marketing, knowledge of the technology, effective delivery of services, and evaluation procedures.

As institutions and organizations handle demands of compressed video and become more flexible in their policies, quality control concerns arise.

Discussion

One of the most important pieces in the delivery of a successful distance learning program is an administrator with a vision (Koontz, 1989). As with conventional education courses, the three important ingredients for success are people, policies, and resources (McNeil, 1985). People must be competent, committed to a distance learning program, and recognize the ways in which distance learners are different from conventional, on-campus learners. Encouragement and support in the form of release time and monetary assistance are essential for faculty who redesign conventional courses. Guidelines must reflect rather than determine the structure of distance education policies, to include policies on enrollment, residency, textbook adoption, and training (McNeil, 1985; Shaeffer, Kipper, Farr, & Muscarella, 1990). Resources must be available for marketing, course development, advertising, publication, and training.

Student/Instructor Interaction

Situation

A student's spouse is hospitalized. Richard, the student at a remote site, is unsure about his ability to complete assignments and attend class in a competent, timely manner during the next two weeks. He would like to visit with the instructor about possible allowances that could be made for his situation.

Question

How can an instructor encourage and facilitate private time with students when spatial separation inhibits face to face interaction? What obligations does an instructor have to monitor emotional states and motivation of students?

Response

Alternate means of communication are of utmost importance when students and instructors cannot interact personally before and after designated class time. To encourage students' ability to communicate, the course syllabus can delineate a variety of means for personal contact. Ideas include: designated office hours for telephone calls from distant students, a toll free telephone number or credit card number, fax number, electronic mail, and a personal letter asking for formative evaluation information about the course. In addition, time for reflection and feedback at the beginning and end of each class session can enhance informal communication and facilitate a climate of trust and caring. Humorous surprises cross-site can assist the camaraderie among all students. By means of proactive strate-

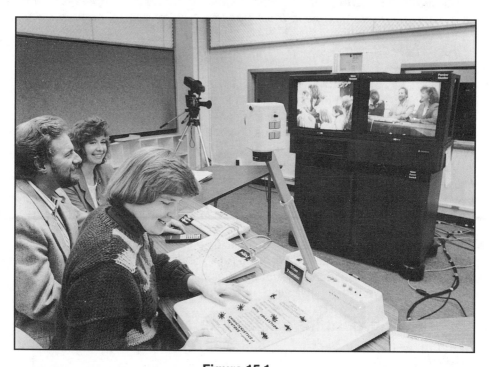

Figure 15.1
Humorous surprises cross-site can allay the sense of depersonalization
among students and instructors

gies, the sense of depersonalization between instructor and students can be allayed.

Discussion

Reed and Sork (1990) question the extent to which instructors must take into account emotional concerns of students. According to Sherry (1991), ethical considerations involve each student's general welfare. The preamble of the American Psychological Association's ethical principles (1989) references the "dignity and worth of the individual" (p. 633). American Counseling Association's (American Association for Counseling and Development) Ethical Standards (1988) emphasize respect for each individual's worth. In keeping with ethical codes of such human service professionals, instructors and administrators need to offer support services and facilitate user-friendly assistance for all involved (Olcott, 1991). Instructors can encourage the growth and development of active learners despite the lack of traditional human contact.

Privacy

Situation

Dr. Brian is teaching a graduate level course entitled *Science and Societal Issues* to classroom teachers in five sites throughout the state via compressed video. After presenting several simulation activities designed to promote discussion and questioning by high school students, Dr. Brian makes the following assignment: "Videotape yourself presenting these activities to your students and any subsequent discussions. Be prepared to share your videotape with your colleagues during our class next week."

Question

By videotaping and sharing this activity with others across numerous sites via compressed video, is Dr. Brian or the individual teachers participating in the class legally or ethically violating any students' right to privacy?

Response

Dr. Brian and the teachers *may* violate the concept of privacy on legal grounds (depending on state laws) and *probably* ethically violate the students' privacy. Privacy is closely related to confidentiality (a topic to be discussed later in this chapter). A solution in this scenario is to have the instructor and the students review ethics codes and state laws related to privacy, and at the very least, have the students and/or their parents sign consent/release forms. Even though this appears to be an innocent and well-meaning educational experience, having numerous individuals see and hear the students behaviors, attitudes, and opinions related to specific issues without their consent is an ethical violation of privacy.

Discussion

No "right to privacy" is specifically described in the Constitution. "The term 'privacy' meshes together complicated concepts from case laws, statutory law, and professional ethics" (Jacob & Hartshorne, 1991, p. 49). Privacy issues are often interwoven with confidentiality issues, and one should become familiar with existing state confidentiality laws.

Figure 15.2
By videotaping and sharing classroom activities via compressed video, is a teacher violating students' rights?

More important, perhaps, is the ethical issue related to privacy and how easily it can be violated in a classroom and ultimately by compressed video. Siegel (1979) defines privacy as "the freedom of individuals to choose for themselves the time and the circumstances under which and the extent to which their beliefs, behavior, and opinions are to be shared (with) or withheld from others" (p. 251). For example, the American Psychological Association ethics code suggests individuals in the profession share clinical information in other professional experiences (professional meetings, classes, workshops, writings, etc.) only with written consent (American Psychological Association, 1989).

Although no mention of privacy is made in the Constitution, the Hatch Amendment, enacted in 1978, provides protection to students and their parents from school actions that intrude on or invade privacy. Although the Amendment's regulations apply only to federally funded programs, current legal opinion views the Amendment as appropriate to general school conduct regarding the privacy issue. To summarize, individuals should give careful thought to legal and ethical implications of the privacy issue prior to using compressed video in an educational environment.

Supervision

Situation

A student teacher videotapes a classroom mathematics lesson and asks for feedback from his distant supervisor. A counselor-in-training videotapes a counseling session and wants help in conceptualization about the case. In both instances, the supervisors watch the videotapes and conduct supervisory sessions via compressed video.

Question

What special considerations may supervision by means of compressed video require?

Response

As always, to ensure the rights and privacy of students, the students and their parents must know when students are being videotaped, for what purpose the tapes will be used, and who will see the tapes. Informed consent and freedom of choice are critical. Therefore, approval for videotaping must be given by parents for minors. Proceeding in accordance with the highest standards possible, a supervisee shares information only with those authorized to receive it. Confidentiality must be maintained with regard to information about students. Consequently, in such situations, compressed video users must check that observers or curious parties do not obtain access to confidential viewing and discussions of such tapes.

Discussion

Students and parents must be informed of the limitations on confidentiality that exist in compressed video, due to possible surreptitious entry into the system. Sherry (1991) emphasizes "the role of the supervisor is an especially crucial one that calls for the highest standards of competence, integrity, and resolve to ensure that the public trust and welfare is duly served." (p. 582). Privacy during communications is to be ensured not only during counseling sessions (Corey, Corey, Callanan, 1993) but during supervision sessions as well.

Confidentiality

Situation

Mrs. Richards is a Special Education classroom teacher. This semester she is a supervising teacher for a student teacher from the university. Instead of the traditional method of a university supervisor observing the student teacher directly in the classroom several times during the semester, contact will occur via compressed video. During the second scheduled compressed video meeting, the student teacher, supervising teacher, and university supervisor discuss a student's academic and adaptive behavior records, including test scores, formal observational data, and anecdotal records. The three are determining what behavior management techniques might best assist the student in the learning process. During the two-way interactive conversation, another remote site makes an unscheduled "appearance" on the network, checking equipment and procedures for their upcoming meeting in one-half hour. They apologize for "eavesdropping" for about three minutes while running a systems test.

Question

Is confidentiality violated on the part of the student?

Response

Yes. Although the three individuals involved are within the limits of confidentiality in what they discussed, confidentiality is "breached" when the unauthorized individuals listened to the conversation.

Discussion

Practitioners have a responsibility to safeguard information, thus protecting their clients' privacy. Waiver forms are necessary to disclose information to others not directly involved (Sheeley & Herlihy, 1986). Practitioners must judiciously choose physical settings for private communications. Although confidentiality is usually a matter of professional ethics, some states could hold an individual liable for a civil breach of confidentiality. Confidentiality should be viewed within society's values, organization's ethical codes, and the individual's interests.

Informed Consent

Situation

Mrs. Ericson and Ms. Mann have completed a college course on the use of compressed video as an educational enhancement tool. They decided to try using the CV equipment recently purchased by their district. Once a week for six weeks the students in Mrs. Ericson's class will teach a social studies lesson to the students in Ms. Mann's class 250 miles away. To demonstrate the success of this unique educational program and innovative technology, they plan to videotape, edit, and make copies of the class sessions for presentations.

Question

Are Mrs. Ericson and Ms. Mann able to implement this project and present results without obtaining consent from all students?

Response

The educators have an ethical responsibility to obtain consent from all individuals involved in this learning situation before videotaping.

Discussion

Practitioners should review and consider The Hatch Amendment, discussed earlier in this chapter.

School actions that may represent significant intrusion on privacy beyond that expected in ordinary classroom activities require parental consent.

Jacob and Hartshorne (1991) state, "Ethical codes and law are consistent in respecting the individual's right to self-determine whether to share private thoughts, behaviors, and beliefs with others. In ethics and law, the requirements for informed consent grew out of deep-rooted notions of the importance of individual privacy" (p. 52).

Taping of classroom activities for educational purposes seems in keeping with Corey, Corey, and Callanan's (1993) statements concerning recording of counseling interviews. As indicated earlier in the chapter, "Clients have a right to be informed about this procedure at the initial session, and it is important that they understand why the recordings are being made, how they will be used, who will have access to them, and how they will be stored" (p. 94).

Data Dissemination

Situation

Mr. Weeks, a special education teacher, wants to conduct an Individual Educational Plan (IEP) meeting via compressed video in order to include university faculty as team members. Narrative records, test data, correspondence, and interview notes are part of student records to be communicated at the meeting.

Question

When utilizing compressed video for data dissemination, what added issues should Mr. Weeks consider?

Response

In order to protect the best interests of the student, Mr. Weeks must inform the student's parents of the purposes, goals, and procedures of the IEP meeting. Security precautions and limitations of compressed video with regard to confidentiality can be explained to the parents. Then, parents must

Figure 15.3
Parents must understand the limitations of compressed video with regard to confidentiality when consulting with a distant professional.

be given a choice to such a manner of consultation with other professionals who can provide services.

Discussion

Protecting the welfare and right to privacy of students are primary obligations of educators. According to American Counseling Association's (American Association for Counseling and Development) Ethical Standards (1988), accurately communicating test results to "appropriate staff members involved in the provision of services" is necessary and appropriate. The circumstances of compressed video bring caution with regard to privacy that must be addressed with concerned parties.

Copyright

Situation

Dr. Alan is currently teaching a College of Education graduate course via compressed video simultaneously to four sites in the state. During the third week of class, she decides to show the students a videotape related to the course content. She borrows the videotape from the University's audio-visual center, shows it to the 35 students, then facilitates student discussion.

Question

By using a single copy of a videotape and transmitting it to four different locations via compressed video, has Dr. Alan violated copyright law?

Response

The answer is "maybe." One cannot transmit copyrighted work without permission, and this scenario is not covered by the "fair use" doctrine. Dr. Alan should have asked the university audio-visual department to check with the company regarding any guidelines on transmission of the videotape. These rights often must be negotiated. Videotapes are sold to schools with a licensing agreement explaining copying and broadcast limitations, as well as public performance regulations.

An instructor can check with the university audio-visual department, refer to the educational film distributor's catalog, or call the company directly to learn of any restrictions in the use of the product. Some companies, like Coronet and Disney, will allow "closed circuit" broadcasts to numerous buildings on campus, but an additional licensing fee may be required for off-campus transmission. The company, Films for the Humanities, allows a broadcasting to numerous sites as long as it is for a university class. Hence the best policy is to check with the copyright owner in each situation.

Discussion

Knowledge of copyright law and its common interpretations as related to the field of education is essential. Professionals must be alert to course cases and new laws in a rapidly changing environment. Specific issues may involve licenses, duplication of software, creation of videotapes with computers, and utilization of scanners (Salpeter, 1992). Users of compressed video face many concerns since CV technology possesses the capabilities of computer, fax, slide (stills), presenter (overhead), and video-tape transmission to numerous sites. Users of CV must not fall into the trap of thinking the current copyright law, on the books for more than ten years, was written only for photocopying or videotape recording and/or duplicating.For additional information, see the list of resources on copyright law included at the end of this chapter.

Copyright law is in effect regardless of the medium used to "share" the product.

Conclusion

Compressed video as an expanding delivery system presents vastly different teaching and learning situations. Rapid technological advances in a complex society demand professionals "maintain and en-hance their consciousness about ethical issues" (Kitchener, 1991, p. 239). As organizations actively promote and participate in compressed video delivery, professionals must protect public trust as well as the interests and welfare of those involved. Conflict of individual and group values in complex circumstances requires reflective use of the core principles of nonmaleficence, beneficence, autonomy, justice, and fidelity. These ethical principles build a framework that facilitates consultation with other professionals. Guided by ethical principles and ethical codes, professionals can identify problems, formulate and critically evaluate possible solutions, then choose a course of action.

References

American Association for Counseling and Development. (1988). *Ethical standards* (rev. ed.). Alexandria, VA: Author.

American Psychological Association. (1989). *Ethical principles of psychologists*. Washington, DC: Author.

Corey, G., Corey, M., & Callanan, P. (1993). *Issues and ethics in the helping professions* (4th ed.). Belmont, CA: Brooks/Cole.

Ehrman, M. (1990). Psychological factors and distance education. *American Journal of Distance Education, 4*(1), 12-24.

Gibson, T.L. (1985). *Heuristics of instructional design for distance education.* Conference report from the Effective Teaching at a Distance Conference, Madison, WI, August 5-6, 1985. (ERIC Document Reproduction Service No. ED 307 847)

Jacob, S., & Hartshorne, T. (1991). *Ethics and law for school psychologists.* Brandon, VT: Clinical Psychology Publishing.

Kitchener, K. S. (1991). The foundations of ethical practice. *Journal of Mental Health Counseling, 13*, 236-246.

Koontz, Jr., F.R. (1989). *Practices and procedures in the administration of ITV Distance Learning Programs at selected institutions of higher education.* Paper presented at the Annual Meeting of the Association of Educational Communications and Technology, Dallas, TX, February 3, 1989. (ERIC Document Reproduction Service ED No. 318 459)

McNeil, D. (1985). *Administration of distance education systems.* Conference report from the Effective Teaching at a Distance Conference, Madison, WI, August 5-6, 1985. (ERIC Document Reproduction Service No. ED 307 847)

Moore, G.R. (1991). Computer to computer: Mentoring possibilities. *Educational Leadership, 49*(3), 40.

Moore, M. (1985). *Adult learning at a distance.* Conference report from the Effective Teaching at a Distance Conference, Madison, WI, August

5-6, 1985. (ERIC Document Reproduction Service No. ED 307 847).

Olcott, D. (1991). Bridging the gap: Distance learning and academic policy. *Continuing Higher Education Review, 55*(1), 49-60.

Reed, D. & Sork, T.J. (1990). Ethical considerations in distance education. *The American Journal of Distance Education, 4*(2), 30-43.

Salpeter, J. (1992). Are you obeying copyright law? *Technology and Learning, 12*(8), 14-23.

Shaeffer, J.J., Kipper, P.R. Farr, C.W., & Muscarella, D.D. (1990). Preparing faculty and designing courses for delivery via audio conferencing. *Mountain Plains Adult Education Association, 18*(2), 11-18

Sheeley, V., & Herlihy, B. (1986). The ethics of confidentiality and privileged communication. *Journal of Counseling and Human Service Professions, 1*(1), 141-148.

Sherry, P. (1991). Ethical issues in the conduct of supervision. *The Counseling Psychologist, 19*, 566-584.

Siegel, M. (1979). Privacy, ethics, and confidentiality. *Professional Psychology, 10*, 249-258.

Strom, S., & Tennyson, W. W., (1989). Developing moral responsibleness through professional education. *Counseling and Values, 34*, 33-34.

Taylor, E. & Kaye, T. (1986). Andragogy by design? Control and self-direction in the design of an Open University course. *Programmed Learning and Educational Technology, 23*(1), 62-69.

Tift, C. (1989). Elements of a successful technology-based distance education program. *Rural Special Education Quarterly, 9*(4), 37-42.

Wolcott, L.L. (1991). *A qualitative study of teachers' planning of instruction for adult learners in a telecommunications-based distance education environment.* (ERIC Document Reproduction Service No. ED 335-023)

Young, H.C. (1989). *The marketing and management of distance education: Challenge of the 1980s and 90s.* Paper presented at the Distance Education Symposium, Edmonton, Alberta, Canada, July 6-10, 1989. (ERIC Document Reproduction Service No. ED 315 060)

Zvacek, S.M. (1991). Effective affective design for distance education. *TechTrends, 36*(1), 40-43.

Additional Information:

Salpeter (1992) details the following sources of copyright information:

Association for Educational Communications & Technology (AECT)
1025 Vermont Ave., NW, Suite 820
Washington, DC 20005
(202) 347-7834
(numerous books on the topic of copyright)

Association for Information Media and Equipment (AIME)
PO Box 865
Elkader, IA 52043
(319) 245-1361
(operates a copyright hotline 1-800-444-4203)

Gary H. Becker
164 Lake Breeze Circle
Lake Mary, FL 32704-6038
(407) 322-0890
(two-part videotape program related to copyright)

National School Boards Association
1680 Duke St.
Alexandria, VA 22314
(703) 838-6722
(Book - *Copyright Law: A Guide for Public Schools*)

Software Publishers Association
1730 M St., NW, Suite 700
Washington, DC 20036-4510
(202) 452-6100

The U.S. Copyright Office
Publications Section
LM-455
Library of Congress
Washington, DC 20559

PART II

Applications and User Profiles

Introduction to Part II

This portion of the book, *Compressed Video: Operations and Applications*, represents a sample of institutions and companies which have been using compressed video. The various reports, profiles, and articles have been written or provided by those people involved in the selection, application, and evaluation of a variety of compressed video systems in a variety of settings. We believe this section to be the core of our publication, because it represents a network of people who know first hand the strengths and weaknesses of this technology. Those who have contributed here have been friendly, cooperative, and involved, and we invite you to peruse their experience and perhaps to even seek them out. Their experience can help us all to better apply this technology and perhaps to prevent some costly mistakes. There are others who have also been in the forefront of compressed video usage who are not included here because of proprietary restrictions, time constraints, or other reasons. We know there are many more examples of compressed video usage, and therefore, we hope to provide a supplement to this publication of additional examples. We would be excited to hear from anyone wishing to contribute their experiences.

The format of Part II is somewhat different than Part I. We have chosen not to edit or adjust the material that was submitted to us since we felt the individual expression of the material best represented those points each author wished to discuss. We have attempted to categorize the submissions. These categories are post-secondary institutions, elementary and secondary education, and government and commercial applications. The number of submissions in each category varies a great deal and is reflective of two things: usage and control. The lower number of submissions in the public school sector could likely be a reflection of low usage of compressed video in comparison to the distance education efforts at the university level. There were many more compressed video applications in the government and commercial sector, but we found a reluctance to discuss these in detail because of security or proprietary reasons in many cases. In Part I of this book, the authors have referred to the profiles included in Part II, however, since we included profiles submitted up until the very last minute, not all of this material was available to authors to examine. The reader should not rely exclusively on material in Part I as an exhaustive reference to Part II.

The profiles and articles in this part of the book span many different rationales, applications and problem solutions. A reader can find material discussing student satisfaction, the linking of separate campuses, equipment specifics and installations, classroom set-ups, course offerings, a variety of planning and decision-making approaches, problems and solutions, and much more in every phase of compressed video usage. Some of the submissions offer detailed information about various specifics of their experience, while others provide a more brief and broader profile of their application. We have included in the appendices two guides (others undoubtedly exist) or manuals for the use of compressed video that we discovered while gathering this material. Permission to reprint them partially or in their entirety was kindly given, and we encourage you to examine those as well as the profiles in Part II.

John Cochenour
October 1992

Again, we want to encourage you to share your own experience by contacting us at the following address:

University of Wyoming
College of Education, Box 3374
Laramie, Wyoming 82071
Voice (307) 766-3146 Fax (307) 766-6668
Barbara T. Hakes
Steven G. Sachs
Cecelia Box
John Cochenour

SECTION I

Post-Secondary Institutions

University of Alabama

Philip M. Turner
Assistant Vice Chancellor for Academic Affairs

526 Ocean City Ave.
Tuscaloosa, AL 35401-1514
voice: (205) 348-9234
fax: (205) 348-3746

When did you start using compressed video?
The InterCampus Interactive Telecommunications System (IITS) became operational in September 1991.

How did you decide to use compressed video as opposed to other telecommunications systems?
We determined that there was a need for two-way video in the applications which we envisioned, and the cost of full band interactive video was beyond our resources. We visited a number of compressed video sites and believed that the quality would suffice for our needs.

Who made the decisions about developing a compressed video network?
The Chancellor, in conjunction with a system-wide committee, made this decision.

Who, why, when, where and how was vendor selection made?
The vendor selection was made by two of the assistant vice-chancellors for Academic Affairs who decided on VideoTelecom, installed through CAE Link, in June of 1991. This selection was made after the vendors were narrowed to three and users of all three vendors equipment were queried. Features and price led to this decision.

What delivery system(s) do you use (i.e. satellite, land line (fiber, T-1, etc.))?
We use T-1 lines.

What are the costs of installation and delivery (monthly, hourly, etc.)?
The equipment comes in turn-key condition, and costs approximately $80,000 per site. We pay approximately $4,000 per month for line charges connecting the sites in Huntsville, Birmingham, and Tuscaloosa. We have leased the lines for three years.

Please describe each application that is presently using the compressed video network. Examples: higher education course delivery, sharing professors/instructors, training and development, video conferencing, think tank sessions, planning, etc.
The IITS is used for the delivery of graduate education, some undergraduate courses, thesis and dissertation proposals and defenses, colloquium, all types of meetings, and other uses.

Describe the facility being used.
The video teleconferencing equipment is housed in regular classrooms in which very little modification has been done.

Who operates the facilities - i.e., technicians, instructors, students, etc.?
The equipment is operated by the faculty and by students who are either work-study or graduate assistants. There is a half-time technician on call at teach site.

(Questions #10 -18 were completed via phone interview because the University of Alabama did not receive written copies of these questions.)

Who schedules the network?
Scheduling is done by the IITS Coordinator.

What are the policies, procedures and priorities used in scheduling the network? Who developed these?
Priority is first given to courses offered by one institution of the university system which is offering a course for another university within the system. Next priority is given for those courses that are unique offerings by one university that would be of interest to another university.

What rate(s) do you use for transmission? Why?
The system is free to those members of the university system.

What peripherals do you have attached to the system and how are they used?
The system is equipped with an Elmo, Pen Pal, and video recorder. In addition, the room is equipped with two computers and a fax machine.

Are you presently, (or do you plan to use) the public switched 56 network for interstate or international communications?
They have no plans to use the public switched 56 network as they utilize a fractional dialer.

Did you conduct a needs assessment? If so, please describe.
A needs assessment was conducted prior to the starting of any course. In addition, students evaluate the course after they have completed it.

If an educational institution, how is teacher education using compressed video?
Teacher education is not conducted per se via the system. They do train teachers in the use of CV and hire a GA at each site to help with training and with glitches in the system.

CALIFORNIA STATE UNIVERSITY

Patricia M. Cuocco
Manager, Media and Telecommunications Support

California State University
P. O. Box 3842
Seal Beach, CA 90740-7842
voice: (310) 985-9429
fax: (310) 985-9400

The CSU is comprised of twenty individual universities with a total enrollment of over 360,000 FTE. It is estimated that by the year 2000, the CSU will have to serve an additional 180,000 FTE. Therefore, interest in all the various distance education technologies is high.

Distance education applications are twofold. The first is from a campus to sites within its own service area (some CSU campuses have serving areas larger than many states). The other is between and among CSU campuses for the purposes of sharing courses. This second application overlays the compressed video signal over the CSU's existing inter-campus T-1 network.

The first use of the compressed video occurred at the Bakersfield campus. Older (pre H.261) CLI Rembrandt codecs are used between the campus and Tehachapi, a town about 45 miles from the campus across a mountain pass which tends to ice over in the winter. Several courses each semester are being offered from the campus to Tehachapi. Transmission is over a dedicated T-1 facility, primarily because fractionalized T-1 bandwidth is unavailable from the local operating company. In any event, older codecs do seem to require the full T-1 for acceptable teaching quality.

CSU Dominguez Hills uses full T-1 and GPT codecs to teach courses at Dominguez High School, in the Compton school district. These are college credit courses offered to high school students in a predominantly minority, inner city area.

CSU Bakersfield and CSU Sacramento also use compressed video on GPT codecs over the CSU's private network, CSUnet, at 384 Kbps. The primary application here is course sharing between the campuses. It is interesting to note that CSU Sacramento is also connected to a four campus microwave network for ITFS and courses can and have been shared between one or more other campuses on the ITFS network by sending the signal either compressed from Bakersfield to Sacramento and then analog ITFS to Fresno, Stanislaus or Chico; or vice-versa.

Several other CSU campuses have applications that would lend themselves to compressed video and are planning to purchase the appropriate technology. Cal Poly, San Luis Obispo has just purchased a CLI Rembrandt VPII system and plans to use it for distance education to sites in their service area. Both CSU Hayward and CSU San Bernardino wish to serve off-site centers with compressed video. This will be done by extending the CSU's network to the off-campus sites and sharing a T-1 line for data, voice, and video services.

Interest in video-conferencing for administrative uses is growing, particularly in light of recent fiscal crises and limited travel budgets. The Sacramento campus has had a connection to the Sprint Meeting Channel ® for over a year. Recently, the local operating company has loaned two CLI Rembrandt VPII equipment with CTX+ software systems to the CSU for a three month pilot project. One has been installed at our Southern California Office of the Chancellor, the other at CSU Sacramento. The intent of the pilot is to test the feasibility of administrative teleconferencing.

Columbia Video Network
Columbia University

Anne McKay
Manager of Operations

Columbia University
510 S. W. Mudd Building
New York, NY 10027
voice: (212) 854-2315
fax: (212) 864-0104

When did you start using compressed video?
1986

How did you decide to use compressed video as opposed to other telecommunications systems?
Users wanted 2-way interactive video; only practical alternative at the time.

Who made the decisions about developing a compressed video network?
Users and top management of the School of Engineering.

Who, why, when, where and how was vendor selection made?
CLI, AT&T, 1986. Most practical alternative at the time.

What delivery system(s) do you use?
T-1

What are the costs of installation and delivery?
Delivery: Paid by users.

Please describe each application that is presently using the compressed video network.
Higher education course delivery: graduate-level engineering courses.

Describe the facilities being used.
2 classrooms equipped with: 2 front cameras, 1 document camera, 1 monitor for incoming video. 4 monitors for in-class students.

Who operates the facilities?
1 technician-supervisor, 10 work-study students.

Who schedules the network?
Dedicated lines.

What rate(s) do you use for transmission? Why?
1.5 mbps. Selected in 1986.

Are you presently using (or do you plan to use) the public switched 56 network for interstate or international communications?
Plan to use 112 locally and interstate in near future.

What hardware model and brand are you using? How is your system configured?
CLI Rembrandt. See above.

Did you conduct a needs assessment? If so please describe.
Possibly, but original decision-makers no longer here.

Other comments or information?
Within the next year we will move away from dedicated two-way T-1 transmission to one-way satellite delivery and two-way transmission at 112 kbps.

The Florida State University Panama City Campus

Wayne Vickers
Director of Instructional Television and Computer Services

P.O. Box 11
4750 Collegiate Drive
Panama City, FL 32405
voice: (904) 872-4750
fax: (904) 872-4199

Using Compressed Video in Long-Distance University Instruction

In December of 1989, the Florida State University Panama City Campus completed installation of a video teleconferencing network dedicated to teaching courses at the university level. The Panama City Campus of FSU is a branch campus dedicated to upper level (junior and senior) and graduate instruction. The campus is located 100 miles southeast of the main campus in Tallahassee. Each semester, 65 to 70 courses are offered in Panama City and 80% of those are taught by full-time faculty from Tallahassee. In developing our system, our desire was not to eliminate instructors traveling the four and a half hour round trip to Panama City. Our ambition was to provide an alternative for instructors whose schedules would not allow the trip. This problem of travel began to limit the courses and program offerings at the branch and was the crux of the investigation into compressed video at FSU.

A commitment by the dean of the Panama City Campus to invest in distance education began our project. The dean and associate dean researched the use of long-distance education at the university level by traveling to various university campuses around the country to observe, first hand, the effectiveness of the medium. After being convinced that the technology was viable for our situation, efforts were made to determine costs and obtain the funding from the provost of FSU.

After comparing the relative cost, quality and availability trade-offs associated with compressed and full bandwidth video, we decided to pursue a compressed video system. The decision for a transmission medium was made after investigating land-based microwave, satellite microwave and installation of a fiber-optic cable. When all three proved too expensive, T-1 compressed video was suggested by our division of telecommunications. With their assistance, we installed a leased T-1 circuit to transmit two links (each at half-T) from Tallahassee to Panama City. One link connects a centrally-located classroom studio on the main campus of FSU to Panama City studio one. The other link connects FAMU/FSU College of Engineering to Panama City classroom studio two.

Selection of the video compressor for our system involved ad hoc research that took into high consideration the student's choice of which compressor delivered a better picture. Our staff had actually selected a GPT Plessy compressor, yet when set up side-by-side with a CLI compressor, students overwhelmingly preferred the CLI equipment. Those two companies were chosen because they were the only two that would allow us to 'test drive' the equipment. Since students are our main customers, we allowed student choice to determine our selection of video compressor.

The classroom studios are designed for either transmission or reception of instruction. In Panama City, two regular classrooms were converted into studios by the addition of extra lighting, cable troughs mounted on the wall, extra ceiling insulation and window coverings. The lighting was supplemented by raising part of the ceiling directly over and in front of the marker board. The section of ceiling was angled so that eight-foot fluorescent fixtures would throw light onto the instructor and board. Eight two-bulb fixtures were installed, four on each side of the board. We have found that combinations of warm-white and cool-white bulbs provide fleshtone colors. Shure Teleconferencing microphones are on the desktops for student use.

Two floor cameras on moveable dollies are used to video the activities in each class. These cameras are mounted on pan-and-tilt heads that allow remote control of the cameras from the control room. Additionally, a camera is permanently mounted from the ceiling pointing down onto the instructor's desk for displaying graphs, books, overhead slides, and to allow the instructor to sit at the desk and write on a notepad. This image is displayed for the originating audience and transmitted to the receiving audience.

Since the main motivation for the system was to deliver long-distance education at the university level, scheduling of courses takes top priority on our system. Applications available on a time available basis include faculty conferences, research meetings, thesis defense, administrative training workshops, administrative meetings, professional organization meetings (IEEE, etc.), ITV scheduling meetings, demonstrations and more. A facility use request form is used to request open times on the system. The forms are reviewed for relevance and impact to the university and then assigned a time and date.

The facilities are operated by a full-time Video-Broadcast Engineering Technologist at each classroom. There is usually a part-time student to help run and coordinate the class session. The Video Technologist is very knowledgeable in audio, video, T-1 transmission equipment, instructional technology and computers. This is the person who knows the ins and outs of the operation of the system.

Our system is consolidated into a three-bay video console and an audio console. The video console has an editor shelf that contains a video mixer, test mixer and controls for moving the cameras. One bay is dedicated to video tape players, one bay to video monitors and the editor shelf, and the last bay contains camera controllers (CCU's), video and audio distribution amplifiers and test scopes. In Panama City, the control room contains the consoles for studio one (main campus) and studio two (engineering building).

Student reaction has been very positive. Limited doctoral research into the effectiveness of the system suggests that courses taught over this system are equivalent to courses taught in live situations. We hope to add a computer interface to allow an instructor to display computer output simultaneously on both campuses. We are also looking to add large-screen technology in the classroom. Currently, there are two 27" monitors located in the room. Students have complained that they cannot see the instructor's writing if they are sitting in the last row of the class.

Our efforts have seen much success in light of our original plan to increase course offerings in Panama City. The system almost totally supports our graduate engineering program and greatly supplements our education and business programs. From our perspective, the technology is the "next best thing to being there" if you can't have live instruction. We plan to continue the project for years to come because of the benefits of closed circuit communications over a long distance. If there is one thing we could recommend for anyone considering video teleconferencing in the classroom, it would be to become familiar with all the options available. Costs are coming down and features are going up, which is always a good situation for resource-constrained institutions.

Maricopa Community College

Janet Whitaker
Director of Instructional Technology

2411 W. 14th Street
Tempe, AZ 85281
voice: (602) 731-8822
fax: (602) 731-8850
E-Mail: whitaker@maricopa.edu

Compressed video was introduced as part of the technology suite in the Maricopa Community Colleges in spring of 1990. Building on a demonstration project in April of 1989 with NEC VisualLink 3000 units that linked two colleges for the month and involved over 50 practice activities, the decision was made to move forward with the purchase of four units in a Phase One pilot for course delivery with the first offerings in spring of 1990.

The Maricopa Colleges, members of the second largest community college district in the United States, are well known as early adopters of technology. The addition of compressed video to enhance the other existing voice, video and data systems was a natural move for us. In 1984 we began a major overhaul of our telecommunications systems with an eye toward as much infrastructure development as needed to move us into the '90s. One of the key components for this development was the installation of a digital microwave network linking ten of our institutional locations: nine colleges and the District Support Service Center. The construction of the multiple T-1 backbone along with purchase and installation of digital PBXs and the rewarding of all the campuses allowed us to meet the existing telecommunications needs, and also allowed a new potential: digital video communications among our colleges.

After the 1989 demonstration project and much discussion with faculty and staff at the colleges, recommendations were made by the Telecommunications Users group to the Information Technology Executive Council to proceed with the Phase One pilot activities. Monies were budgeted and four NEC VisualLink 3000 units were purchased. All four were distributed to the four colleges from whom proposals were received outlining their planned use of, support for, and staff allocations for compressed video.

The codecs, echo cancellors, pad cameras, audio systems and a few necessary cameras were purchased from central telecommunication funds for this pilot project. During the proposal process for participation in this pilot, colleges identified the existing equipment and rooms that would be made available for compressed video applications. This led to some interesting challenges later in the project. For example, not all colleges had equipment of equal technical quality. Therefore image production varies from location to location on the network. This sort of variation has yet to be resolved. Determination of costs for this system is not easy to do. Because we own the network and the equipment, we do not incur additional costs for technical operations. The maintenance and operating costs are part of the overhead of network operations. The original telecommunications upgrades and installations provided the pathways as excess capacity. The equipment has been very stable in terms of reliability and operation. Capital has been our main financial outlay.

In the summer of 1991, we embarked on a major upgrade and addition of three more codecs. We purchased 7 NEC VisualLink 5000 codecs, four of which were placed at the Phase One colleges, two at two of the larger enrollment colleges in the district, and one at the new District Support Services Center. This expanded our network to seven participating institutions on our network. At this time the service was also named Maricopa VCN for Maricopa Video Conference Network. The existing four 3000 models are still here, but are being planned for other activities such as off campus connections and temporary expansion of access to the remaining four colleges in the district.

In addition to the expansion to more sites, we also decided that multi-point connectivity was a requirement to meet the needs of our colleges. Two-site conferencing is "nice," but multi-point is the most desired capability. Multi-point audio teleconferencing had been used in the District since 1982, so linking more than two sites at a time is a natural expectation for our faculty and staff. To solve this problem economically, two staff from the Information Technologies Department researched the use of microcomputer based digital cross-connect technology as a potential solution. Their work led to a "home grown" multi-point control unit that is operational from any computer terminal connected to our data network. Having multi-point control and participation has led to very successful applications of the system.

The first multi-point control unit was implemented using a Digital Access Cross-connect System (DACS). This unit was controlled by one of our VAX computers. At the remote sites, people would connect to the VAX and select the sites to be involved in the conference. The VAX would then determine the appropriate T-1 configuration and transmit commands to the DACS to have it establish appropriate connections for the conference. The use of the VAX permitted multiple conferences to occur simultaneously. It also permitted the controlling site to control which site was the "primary broadcast site" for the conference.

At the start of 1992, we replaced the dedicated DACS with a personal computer system with DACS cards installed in it. With the original DACS, only one site could control what each site was receiving. Now, it is possible for each site to choose which other site they wish to see during a video conference. In addition, the PC has been programmed to always display the current status of the network, so technicians can tell how many video conferences are in progress and which sites belong to which conference.

Applications

The types of activities on VCN are as varied as the people in the system. Our original anticipated use was for shared instruction, either as distributed classes to linked colleges by one originating site or as team teaching projects where groups are separated by distance but participating with faculty from both sites. During Phase One of the project, we experienced both of these arrangements. We have learned that teaching on the network is possible and well received by students. Each of the Phase One colleges originated at least one course or participated in team teaching activities.

Phase Two has led to additional activity because of the network expansion to include the two large colleges, Mesa Community College and Glendale Community College, and the

District Support Services Center. Committees and councils frequently meet on the network for planning activities. In the middle of the instructional day, distinguished visiting lecturers are often scheduled on the network to be shared with remote colleges, thereby increasing the amount of participation by faculty, staff and students in the programs that may be 40 miles away.

The coordinating committee for the network meets monthly to discuss its operation and to develop the inter-college instructional program. This participation has led to an increase from 2 or 3 courses per semester as were offered in Phase One to 8 courses offered in the fall 1992 semester and 10 courses offered in the spring 1993 semester. Additional requests have come from the college community to provide staff development and training. Meetings have been held with the staff development coordinators from the colleges to get them ready for supporting this activity.

An unexpected use of the network has been for technical back-up of satellite programs. In addition to the compressed video network, nine locations have Ku-band and C-band satellite downlinks. During the 1991-92 year, one location had difficulty receiving scheduled programs on their dish. To solve the problem, another site on VCN received the program at their site and retransmitted the signal to the site experiencing technical difficulties. The program was "saved" for the viewers at the remote site.

The most recent request for a new group has been from student government. Each college operates its own student government association. A request came from a student to use VCN as a way to coordinate activities and plans among the colleges, a totally new "connection" for students here. When asked how he found out about the network, the student replied that he saw classes being scheduled this way and thought it also might suit the needs of his organization.

As increasing numbers of faculty, staff and students are exposed to the potentials of video conferencing and the ease of use and the amount of support provided, we are convinced that the demand will far surpass the number of programmable hours.

Facilities and Operation

The Maricopa VCN is actually an institutional network as opposed to a network of video rooms. Transmissions among sites are at the T-1 rates, although the equipment we have allows for fractional T-1 speeds if ever necessary. Signals are received and processed in headends for redistribution on coax broadbands to almost any location on campus. Describing any particular video room is challenging at best.

Some minimum configurations have been identified for interactive participation facilities. All have live bridged audio via telephone for multi-point applications. Microphones are generally hands-free, although one site still uses push-to-talk mics. Speakers are generally built-in as well.

Several monitors are in each room to serve different purposes. One monitor shows the remote sites to the group and one shows the remote sites to the faculty member or group leader. A third monitor is often needed for the local group to see what graphic information is going out over the network. Often this is information that is placed under a pad camera for close-up and hand-written materials. A fourth monitor is sometimes made available as a preview for the faculty member to see what is going to be sent on the network, for example as a way to focus the pad camera before showing to the group.

Camera arrangements also vary. Most sites have two stationary "people" cameras and a pad camera to provide a "chalkboard" function, an overhead projection function and a 3-D magnification function. One of the stationary cameras is set to show groups of participants to remote sites and one is to show the teacher or group leader to remote sites.

Camera switching and network switching adds a level of complexity to the group leader's task list. Practice is needed to think about what is going on locally and to remember to switch to remotes when discussion is taking place and questions are being asked. The amount of support provided for doing this switching is at the choice of the presenter. If he or she wishes to have help in this switching, media support staff are generally provided. However, most instructors request a simple and effective way to handle this switching themselves rather than try to direct technical personnel, particularly during teaching applications. Faculty have expressed a desire to maintain the flow of the process by their own means.

Technical support is provided for set-up and check-out prior to each use of the system. When a portable system is put in place in a new room, the set-up activity is critical. Some sites have developed a video conference cart that includes all the needed components for a more personal video conference capability for meetings. Deans and other executives are more likely to use this type of set-up.

During the program, technicians are "on call" in case of technical failure. In the main, however, all operation is done by the group using the network.

For classes, local program facilitators are available at remote sites. These persons act as support for the students not physically present with the instructor. Their duties include distributing materials, meeting and greeting students in the classroom, liaison for emergencies to campus authorities, and proctoring examinations at instructor request.

Administration

Network scheduling is supported operationally from a central point. Non-instructional event times are requested by group leaders. VCN support personnel check network availability, send a request for participation to the remote sites, arrange for audio teleconference bridge times, receive confirmations from sites and the bridge operators, and then reply to the requester of the scheduled sites and rooms. Requesters are referred to their origination sites for assistance on the use of the rooms, technical operations, special requirements of their activity and logistics support for their event. We also recommend that non-instructional users arrange for one of their group to be remote "leaders and greeters," particularly for the first time the group meets on the network.

Instructional schedules are developed through the VCN Coordinating Committee. This group was established at the beginning of Phase Two to address instructional applications, schedule development, and solutions to logistics issues confronted with distributed classes such as registration process, textbook orders, FTE accounting, cost centers, and library support. Scheduling is one of the main concerns, however, and takes place one year in advance of the actual offering of a class on the network.

An important point regarding priorities of use is that instructional programs take priority over the other uses of the network. Scheduled classes are not "bumped" for non-instructional applications.

Ancillary Support Technologies

The video network is a major component of the network. However it is not the only one. The VCN is actually a system of layered networks: one for voice [audio teleconference bridging via telephone connections], one for video [compressed video transmission via the digital microwave network] and one for data for multi-point control of the system [also via the digital microwave network in the majority of cases]. In our current arrangement, using this layered approach has provided a redundancy of connections so that loss of the microwave system does not halt the event entirely. The audio teleconference can continue until video service is restored. Loss of the audio, however, can mean the total loss of the program. Loss of the data link only stops the switching control of the video signal and does not effect the audio. In addition to the networked activity, other technologies are available for support of programs, including planning and preparation, during delivery, and as supplements to the process.

All sites have access to facsimile machines for sending print materials to other sites in an "on demand" fashion. Fax machines are not part of the video "rooms" however. So, sending materials in advance is the best approach to allow for getting them to support personnel for duplication and distribution to remote participants in a timely fashion.

During programs, some locations have the ability to replay video tapes, record the sessions as they occur, and provide computer graphics display. Each site has taken a different "specialty" of service as the network is developing and as we are discovering the types of services that faculty and general users require for their success.

Another system that is being used for classes is a computer conferencing system called the Electronic Forum. This technology has been very successful over the past two years in support of non-VCN activities. Some faculty have used EF in support of their VCN classes as another way to bridge the distance between their students and allow for continued conversation and exploration outside of the time on the video network. Students are provided computer accounts that allow them to access the EF for posting messages to classmates as a group and also to send electronic mail to individuals, for instance, the instructor. This system can also be used for submitting written assignments electronically from any location.

External Connections

Presently we are operating as a self-contained network with the exception of redistributing other sources such as satellite and videotape programs. Our goals include linking to other networks via land lines or satellite connections. At this time we are concentrating on serving our local audiences and building their skills in using the network. Discussions have been held with institutions in Australia for class sharing opportunities. The international standards in compressed video are solving some of the initial obstacles in these types of connections.

Final Comments

Our experience has shown that solving the technical problems is much easier than solving some of the human ones. Developing interinstitutional trust and cooperation is new to many people. Questions such as why one would *want* to "talk" to another college have been asked. Solutions to the administration of programs and students services are real issues and dilemmas. Issues of fairness and responsibility must be discussed and resolved. The strategy for building awareness and explaining advantages and adjustment requires time and thought and planning. Documents such as user guides and training packages must be developed. All of these activities take energy and commitment and leadership. One person or one team of persons cannot do all of the tasks required. Skills in negotiation, compromise, team building, communication and problem solving are critical for compressed video applications to succeed.

Open-mindedness is also a very valuable asset. It is OK to fail periodically, because it is through failure that some of the most valuable lessons are learned. Faculty and non-instructional users need to know that there are no punishments for trying, only praise. We also must remember that egos need to be checked at the door when beginning an enterprise like this. Only by working together and teaching each other, faculty and students and staff alike, can the potentials of this new networking technology be realized.

Equipment List

PHASE I:
    4 NEC VisualLink 3000 codecs
    4 NEC AEC 400 echo cancellors with microphones
    various 1 chip television cameras
    various preview and viewing monitors
    3 pad cameras with stand
    Phoenix Microsystems 1505 MicroDACS

PHASE II:
    7 NEC VisualLink 5000 codecs
    3 NEC AEC 400 echo cancellors
    386 DOS PC clone Fredericks Engineering DACS PC cards

University of Maryland

Richard N. Rose
Director, TSO System Administration

University of Maryland
330 Metzerott Road
Adelphy, MD 20783
voice: (301) 853-3655
fax: (301) 853-4761

IVN Overview

Through the coordination of the University of Maryland System Office, a 1991-92 pilot project between CBL, UMBC, and the UMCP College of Engineering was implemented using the University's telecommunication infrastructure (UMITS). To date, the project has grown in classes and enrollment and is satisfying the continued political pressure for quality interactive video to strategic areas of the state. Using the Maryland Consortium for Distance Education (IDE) Strategic Plan as a guideline and resource for expansion, IVN will expand to the western and eastern geographic regions of the state, and will eventually interface to national and international compressed video networks. This rapidly growing technology will benefit the UMS and the citizens of Maryland.

To date, class offerings include post graduate curriculums in business, computer science, electrical engineering, and chemistry. Having only been available for two semesters, IVN has transposed into a technologically advanced mechanism for expanding the University's interactive resources throughout the state. In addition to instruction, the IVN system is used for interactive video conferences and group seminars between three sites. While the system has been a monumental success in strategic areas of the state using a point- to-point access, the full potential of IVN has not been realized, as a video switch was not initially purchased for the pilot project and has been manually managed (switched) by UMSA's telecommunications staff. Switching is done throughout the week at specific times.

During the first six months of IVN's existence, several hands-on demonstrations took place among the leaders of the University, including the Chancellor's Council. As a result of these demonstrations and interactive group presentations, the campuses learned that the UMS infrastructure (UMITS) could support additional sites with little effort. It was also learned that there were several campuses academically supporting remote geographic areas of the State with transient faculty. As an example, UMAB has transient educators in all geographic regions and is expecting to enhance their curriculum at Shady Grove. These disciplines will include nursing, llaw, social work and dentistry. Further meetings between the campuses resulted in new knowledge and interests of each other. AEL will be in partnership with FSU; FSU with UMAB; UMAB with UMES and so on. It was easily recognized that IVN could transform current methodologies of teaching into an interactive video network that not only would extend current resources and capabilities more efficiently, but expand the services at those campuses which have professional

have professional disciplines which are needed in the most distant areas. The end result will increase the course offerings, entice more distinguished professors to teach, and provide an interactive video solution which will also take advantage of the latest technologies in personal computer applications, video graphics, remote printing, facsimile, and eventually packet switched networks to LANS and interfacing with multimedia applications.

Response from the campuses was immediate. Campuses began requesting that UMSA coordinate and purchase new equipment for their institutions (see attached). Group purchases for video and ancillary equipment would benefit all with volume and educational discounts, while having a single contact for vendor communication. The equipment bid included video codecs, video switches, and ancillary interfacing equipment. Eventually, an automated reservation system will be purchased which will enable scheduled classes and simultaneous video conferences to be software maintained during peak periods as well as off hours.

Using the consensus-building philosophy which spurred the current IVN pilot system, USMA invited several interested parties together to see if a similar partnership could take place between other remote campuses. Once the meetings took place, a deluge of requests for class scheduling and system purchasing poured in. Based on these requests, UMSA coordinated a system-wide video network purchase between FSU, FSU Hagerstown extension, UMAB, HPEL, Sea Grant College, CARB, and USMA. Some campuses are waiting for the new fiscal year before purchasing, while most, UMAB, FSU, HPEL, Sea Grant, and UMSA, will be making their purchases during May of 1992. With this in mind, UMSA wrote the technical specifications to allow for a six month window for acquisitions. Spread out over two fiscal years, all campuses and State agencies will be able to purchase using this open contract beginning in mid-May, 1992. The response has been overwhelming.

Current IVN Sites

CBL	Chesapeake Biological Lab at Solomon's Island, Maryland
UMCP-Engr	University of Maryland at College Park (Engineering)
UMBC	University of Maryland Baltimore County

Current IVN Courses

ENME 664	ENEE 420	CMSC 420	STAT 464
CMSC 451	MGMT 398F	CHEM 723	ENME631

Campus Committed IVN Sites

FSU	Frostburg State University
FSU	Frostburg State University Extension at Hagerstown
HPL	Horn Point Experimental Lab, Cambridge Maryland
UMAB	University of Maryland at Baltimore
UMSG	University of Maryland Sea Grant at College Park
UMSA	University of Maryland System Administration

System Administration Office of Telecommunications is coordinating the procurement for these campuses and will bill each campus using Journal Vouchers and Stars Charging.

Note: The engineering video codec is on loan by CBL. It is due to move over to the Skinner Building (Sea Grant) in June 1992. This will leave the UMCP College of Engineering School without a video codec. Because the codec was on loan, based on mutual agreements and understandings, CBL has decided that it would be in the best interest of CEES and Sea Grant institutions to move the codec to a site which was more suitable to an interactive environment and which also shared their disciplines of marine biology, biotechnology, toxicology, earth studies, and estuarine studies. The UMCP College of Engineering agreed to provide a video conference room before the fall 1992 semester, but was unable to allocate space. Consequently, the UMCP College of engineering will be without a video codec. After discussing these issues with the Chancellor, it is highly recommended that USMA allocate funds which will provide the ITV Studio with the necessary equipment to continue.

September 1992 Fall Course Offerings

FSU, FSU Extension, CXBL, UMBC, HPEL, Sea Grant, UMUC, UMAB, UMCP College of Engineering:

Social Work	Dentistry	Shock Trauma
Medical School	Pharmacy	Nursing
Law	Statistics	Chemistry
Business	Engineering	MEES
Computer Science	Mechanical Eng.	Physical Therapy Seminars/Conferences

Future Sites

CARB   Center for Advanced Research in Biotechnology, Shady Grove
UMES   University of Maryland, Eastern Shore
SSU   Salisbury State University
DTBC   Downtown Baltimore Center
EIC   External interface connection to peer institutions

Hardware Costs

VideoTelecom Codecs   60 K (Per Site)
VideoTelecom Switch   46 K (Per Site - UMCP and MAB)

Compressed Video at UMSA

The video codecs equipment at UMSA will be used for the Chancellor and staff to participate in Statewide conferences. Because it will not be used on a 24 hour basis, the codec will be used as a backup to other systems around the State. UMSA will have the confidence that the system will have a spare backup codec during a hardware failure.

System Administration Cost

Video Codecs   108K (UMSA and UMCP College of Engineering)
Video Switch   96K (UMAB and UMCP)
TOTAL   104K

Having two video switches allows complete flexibility between the Baltimore - Washington corridor. There are several advantages, reduced T-1 cost, needed redundancy, multiple simultaneous interactive video sessions, extra connections to outside agencies, a direct interface to the future reservation system using switched 56KB service on demand.

UMSA is using the savings from the two Sprint Lines (60K), selling of the VAX 4000's to UMBC (72K), and budgeted telecommunications dollars to pay for two video switches and one video codec. Dollars for the UMCP College of Engineering is not accounted for and is requested out of the Chancellor's discretionary monies.

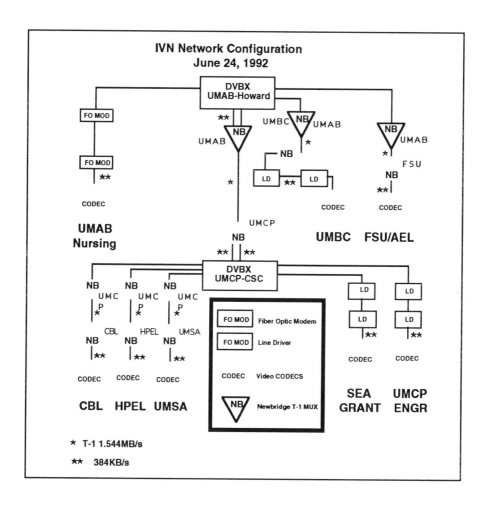

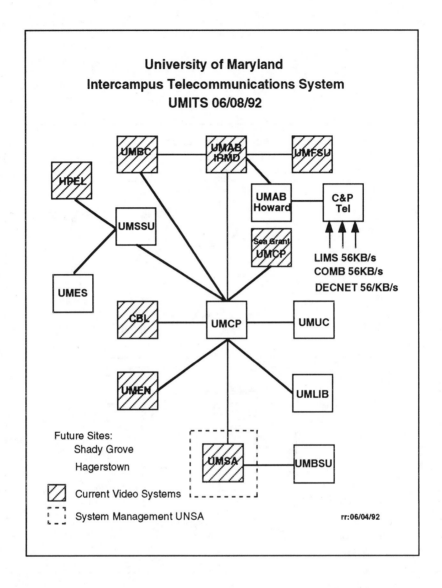

Montana Educational Telecommunications Network: METNet

Janis H. Bruwelheide
Associate Professor, Instructional Technology

Department of Education
College of Education, Health and Human Development
213 Reid Hall
Montana State University
Bozeman, MT 59717
voice: (406) 994-3120
fax: (406) 994-2893
Bitnet: IEDJB@MTSUNIX1
Internet: IEDJB@MSU.OSCS.MON TANA.EDU

What is METNet?

METNet is a far reaching telecommunications network established to address educational opportunity in Montana schools and communities. In 1989 the Montana legislature addressed school equalization issues and provided funding to the Department of Administration to retain consulting assistance. The consultants were asked to conduct a needs assessment and design a telecommunications network through which all Montana organizations and schools could have access to educational resources and move toward implementation of a network plan. The Montana Office of Public Instruction and the Montana University System worked with the Department of Administration and consultants throughout the data gathering period. The final report included the needs assessment and network planning recommendations which built upon efforts of a Task Force on Telecommunications established in 1987.   The report was delivered in June, 1990. The consultants designed a multi-faceted, phased, telecommunications network for Montana consisting of three technology components briefly discussed in the following paragraphs. A 1990 charge identifying long range goals for the Office of the Commissioner of Higher Education reinforced the importance of the report when it identified "increased access to telecommunications, distance learning, and public broadcasting opportunities in concert with other state and private agencies" as a major goal. Since the purpose of this user profile is to describe compressed video networks, more attention will be given to this technology after a brief overview of METNet

The Montana Legislature (HB 30, 1991) established the Montana Educational Telecommunications Network (METNet) "to support education, economic development and government services in the state." The Office of Public Instruction, the Office of the Commissioner of Higher Education, and the Department of Administration are working cooperatively to develop METNet.

There are three components to the METNet: electronic bulletin board, satellite, and compressed video. The first year of the implementation phase, 1991-92, focused on K-12 students and teachers. Efforts were concentrated on implementing multi-technology hardware to enhance existing networks and consisted of installation of satellite dishes, the bulletin board system and the regional 17 sites, some training in BBS use, selection of the compressed video vendor, and installation of four sites. General training and small scale use of the system began in October, 1992.

METNet provides:

~ instructional and education course work for K-12 students, students enrolled in units of the Montana University System, vocational-technical centers, and community colleges;
~ instructional and professional development training for teachers and others involved in education; and
~ telecommunication capabilities to schools, state agencies, subdivisions of state government, and public libraries.

METNet Bulletin Board System (BBS)

Montana educators and individuals interested in Montana education are provided a means to exchange ideas, messages, curriculum guides, lesson plans and other instructional materials through use of computers, telephone lines, and telecommunications software. The general area of educational telecommunications is growing at such a rapid rate that keeping current with new developments will be easier by sharing information through the METNet BBS and inservice training programs. There are 17 K-12 and higher education regional sites for BBS nodes now installed. The METNet BBS utilizes FIDO technology to establish education conferences on both a state and regional level. Each BBS site contains the same statewide conference information and file areas. The Helena server polls or calls each of the remote BBS systems each day to transfer electronic conferences and network mail. This information is updated daily on all METNet BBS servers located throughout the state.

Satellite

Including Star Schools and METNet, 320 satellite downlink sites exist in Montana. There are two uplink sites. A non-METNet funding source is enabling high speed data lines to be developed between the two university system units at Missoula and Bozeman in 1993. These sites will be able to transmit full motion and compressed video communications upon installation of the lines. With the ability to transmit video signals between the two university system units, the Missoula campus will be provided access to the Montana State University satellite uplink facilities. This access will allow more education and information to be uplinked to rural schools and communities.

Compressed Video System

Compressed video is a live, two-way interactive, multi-modal delivery system for education, training, and videoconferencing. Use of compressed video allows students and instructors to send and receive data, voice, and video to other sites with similar capabilities anywhere in the world. Montana has a large land mass with mountainous regions and great distance among schools and higher education institutions.   T-1 lines are plentiful but fiber and ISDN lines are only available in certain areas of the state.   Thus, the consultants recommended a compressed video component for the METNet which would use T-1 lines and the state telephone network.

The Network Environment

The network environment is as follows. The state currently operates an SL-1, ESN private line voice network over digital and analog circuits. Nine major legs of this network are linked by digital T-1 links. The Bozeman-Helena link which crosses between two local access and transport areas (LATA's) is a digital microwave radio system owned by the state of Montana. The other T-1 links are leased. The state also leases analog tie lines to other locations. Nineteen PBX's , Northern Telecom SI-1's, are linked together to form the state telephone network. The network control center is housed in Helena. A Northern Telecom SL-1XT switch with Digital Trunk Interface is installed in the state Capitol Complex. Northern Telecom Electronic Switched Network software which supports alternate routing tables for long distance calls is used by the state network.

Selection Process

The selection team was chosen and work began on specifications and proposal bid requirements in November, 1991, so that timelines for a July equipment installation could be met. The call for compressed video vendor proposals was sent in January, 1992. The bid specification document was approximately 60 pages and it was developed by a representative of the Telecommunications Bureau of the Department of Administration with substantial input from the selection team. The six member selection team was comprised of representatives from the following areas: Office of the Commissioner of Higher Education (Bruwelheide); two technical representatives from the University of Montana and Montana State University; an educational technology expert from the Office of Public Instruction; and two representatives from the Department of Administration. The selection team developed the evaluation documents and point matrix, reviewed all proposals, rated the vendor demonstrations, and summarized rankings of each vendor. Selectors were advised to keep accurate records and maintain confidentiality throughout the entire process. All equipment demonstrations were held during March and April, 1992.   Demonstrations were held in Helena in order to equalize physical conditions. Final selection was made in May and requisite contractual procedures instituted.

Equipment and Sites

Four compressed video codec sites were installed during summer, 1992, and became operational in mid-September. User training began in October. The compressed video system is using inverse multiplexers in a dynamic dialup environment. The equipment company selected was Compression Labs Incorporated (CLI) and the equipment for each site is as follows:

- Rembrandt II VP Gallery units (56-1.544MB/s), CTX Plus, 30 frames per second

- dual 25 inch monitors , Gallery 225

- main camera and auxiliary camera with video routers

- graphics stand
- Coherent Voice Crafter 2000
- auxiliary data ports (for computer, VCR, etc.)

The vendor selected was Whittel who also holds the state telephone contract. Two sites, Helena and Bozeman, were installed using METNet funds. The two remaining sites were installed with higher education funds. Sites selected were: Helena , Bozeman, Missoula, and Billings. The Missoula and Billings sites were selected by the University of Montana in order to deliver an existing MBA project. The Bozeman site was selected based upon the ability to uplink compressed video to the METNet, Star Schools, and existing downlink sites. With uplink facilities, the Billings and Missoula education departments will be provided the opportunity to ship educational programming to Montana downlink sites. The Helena site was selected to develop the technology for compressed video and allow access of the METNet administrative agencies to the technology. All sites identified in the first year are served by the Department of Administration.

Two additional sites are expected to be installed in mid -1993. The METNet advisory group has identified Miles City as a potential site since there is access to existing fiber capabilities in that area. In addition one site will be placed for competitive selection throughout the state. Selection will be based upon ability to provide digital transport, ability to transmit programming, and availability of community partnerships. Additional compressed video sites will be considered depending on availability of funding. The original plan called for a site in every county. Montana has fifty-six counties.

Facilities

The facilities for each site are as follows. The Helena site serves as the center of the network. It houses a multipoint control unit and handles scheduling of the system. Costs are determined by the State Department of Administration also located in Helena, the state capitol. A conference room in the state Capitol building was selected to house the unit. This selection was made due to the benefits of housing the system in a location where legislators and state agencies could see the system in action and use it easily. The room is also dedicated to the system. Existing classrooms were used for the sites at Eastern Montana College in Billings and the University of Montana. Since the classrooms are not dedicated, this act has caused some dissension concerning control of room scheduling. McCall Hall at Montana State University in Bozeman was selected to house the equipment. Several years ago this room was equipped as a low cost studio for teleconferencing and KUSM programs. It has not been used to its potential although installation of the compressed video equipment is expected to increase its use. It is a large room with studio lights and austere furnishings. While not currently used as a classroom, it has been used occasionally by various groups for teleconferencing and "talk" show, interview program, filming. Again dissension has occurred over room scheduling between Helena and Montana State University personnel.

Costs and Financing

The House Bill 30 passed in January, 1991, established a funding mechanism for METNet. The 1991 legislature provided an appropriation of "$450,000, $300,000 from the general fund to the department of administration for each year of the biennium ending June 30,

1993, to be used for the Montana Educational Telecommunications Network *if* $150,000 of the appropriated amount is available in cash or equipment value from federal or other sources. If less than $150,000 of the appropriated amount is available from federal or other funds, the allowable expenditures from the appropriation are reduced proportionately and any remainder of the appropriation must revert to the general fund." The first matching donation of $150,000 was provided by TeleCommunications Incorporated. These funds were used to purchase equipment for METNet, administer the network, and provide some user training.

Transmission costs for the network vary according to the transmission rate and user category (non education or education). The per-hour range is @ $70 for 1/4 T-1 to $170 for full T-1 between two sites. At the time of this report, use has been primarily at the 1/4 T-1 transmission rate. It is cost effective and the quality is acceptable. Training sessions have been conducted at the 3/4 T-1 rate and the quality is very good. The quality at 1/2 T-1 is also good and no blurring occurs. There is a bit of blurring at the 1/4 T-1 rate on hand movements. However, the quality is still good for videoconferencing and class applications unless a lot of motion is required. It is the intent of METNet participants to explore use of the public switched 56 network for international and interstate communications. Several states in surrounding regions have or are in the process of installing compressed video networks.

Applications

At the time of this writing the network has just become operational. One videoconference has been held as have several test demonstrations. An open house to introduce interested parties to the network is scheduled for October 14 and 15. Train-the-trainer session was held September 17 for the colleges and universities. Until that time the network could not be used because contractually the network had not been released to the state. Additional user training is scheduled for late October through mid-November for other state agencies. The Montana State University teacher education faculty are to be introduced to the network via a videoconference and hands-on training on October 30. To date the only coursework being delivered is the MBA degree program between Eastern Montana College in Billings and the University of Montana in Missoula. However, the network is expected to be used by MSU teacher education faculty during winter semester, 1993, and faculty development will be provided as well as support. It is also expected that several educational grant activities such as inservice and videoconferencing will utilize the system. State agencies are planning to use the network for videoconferencing and planning activities.

Policies and Procedures

At the time of this writing METNet has not developed policies, procedures, and priorities documents. Should be fun—

Miscellaneous Information

Prospective network designers would be well advised to explore policies, procedures, and priority statements for use of their network before installing the network. Designers should recommend that the selected sites be officially queried beforehand to describe room and network requirements so there will be no financial surprises and to ensure that all relevant individuals are included in the discussion phase concerning equipment placement and peripheral needs. An omission of this step will lead to misunderstandings and ill feelings which may then impede the process. It is also important to keep and retain accurate records concerning vendor evaluation in the case of dispute and to emphasize confidentiality to the selection team. It is advisable to designate one individual as the primary contact for questions concerning the bid and related information in order to remain consistent. Instructional designers are advised to consider all distance education delivery mechanisms available to users when assisting them in the choice of a technology. Many individuals will be unaware of the options, such as audioconferencing. Faculty development and support are crucial to the success of a program using compressed video.

Murray State University: Center for Continuing Education and Academic Outreach

John P. Hart
ITN Coordinator

Center for Continuing Education and Academic Outreach
Murray, KY 42071
voice: (502) 762-4159

Murray State University began using compressed video for instructional delivery in June of 1990. The decision to use compressed video over other available options was made to avoid having to develop and support the entire delivery infrastructure and to ensure that geographic location would not be a limitation to including a site on the network. By utilizing the public switched telephone network (PSN) we were freed from becoming a communications utility and could concentrate on instructional delivery. These decisions were made by the Dean of Continuing Education Dr. Viola Miller and myself acting as a consultant from another university department. I have extensive experience with electronic communications systems and was asked to help study the options. For the above reasons, I recommended the compressed video system. Other options studied were analog delivery via fiber optic cable and microwave, ITFS and satellite delivery.

We arranged for a six month trial of compressed video in partnership with South Central Bell, BellSouth Foundation and the Tennessee Valley Authority. The trial provided a compressed video link between Murray State University and Paducah Community College some 45 miles away. Paducah made a good test site because we had an extensive history of class offerings via traditional means to provide a baseline for measuring the success of the trial. The trial was so successful that after the first three months, plans were made to expand to a network configuration. One additional community college at Madisonville, and two public school districts were added at that time. Since then, the network has grown to a total of eight sites with plans for an additional nine as well as a connection to the University of Kentucky video network. The purchases were made through standard state bid procedures and the successful vendors were

South Central Bell for the digital equipment and Long Communications Corporation of North Carolina for the classroom linear equipment. In 1991, Murray State University and Digital Equipment

Approximately $80,000 is budgeted annually for line charges and maintenance as well as providing a support staff of two full-time employees and numerous part time employees and student workers.

Currently, a full schedule of upper division and graduate level courses are offered via the network. The community colleges share lower division courses between sites and the public schools share courses to provide an enhanced curriculum to both participants. A joint doctoral program is offered via ITV from the University of Kentucky. Future plans include the provision of advanced placement courses to the public schools on the network and extensive work force development activities. Other applications include student counseling, meetings and demonstrations. Time is also provided for research and development of new applications and technologies.

From the outset, efforts were made to make the classroom atmosphere as user-friendly as possible. The ITN classrooms look very much like traditional classrooms with extra televisions instead of television studios with desks. Much effort was expended in developing camera and monitor placement to mimic the normal lines of sight in a classroom so that students at the distant sites would feel a part of the native classroom. Multiple microphones that are switched through an intelligent audio mixer provide natural sounding audio without the interference of push-to-talk switches. The instructor controls the camera selection with a simple remote control while a student worker takes care of fax transmissions and monitors the operation of the system. Technical assistance is available at all times via a pager to the technical support staff.

The ITN coordinator is responsible for ensuring the successful operation of all portions of the network operation and is personally responsible for the technical infrastructure of the network including all liaison with the phone company and maintenance of the network equipment and software. The coordinator also directs the research and development portion of the operations. Current research and development projects include the development of standards-based desktop videoconferencing and computer network support of classroom instruction. Network scheduling is handled by the assistant ITN coordinator. The assistant coordinator also manages the student assistants and coordinates instructor training. Instructional delivery has the highest priority for use of the network with other uses being scheduled on a basically even footing.

Training of instructors is considered to be the key to success of the Murray State University ITN and a great deal of time is spent with each instructor before they teach their first course. The Continuing Education office pays a stipend to each ITN instructor to develop their first course and provides graphic production services. The high degree of instructor loyalty is credited to this policy as is the success of the classes with students.

In addition to the classroom cameras and microphones, available equipment includes an Elmo Presenter and two VCRs. One of the VCRs is for playback of any tapes the instructor includes in the class presentation. The other is used to record each class session. These tapes are then made available in the library at each site for a period of two weeks following the class. At the end of this period the tapes are recycled. Facilities for slide projection, audio cassette playback and computer LCD panels are available as needed.

At present the system operates at 336 Kbs (384 Kbs less signaling bandwidth) with audio multiplexed in band. The classroom portion of the network will continue to operate at this rate although the desktop video applications will probably use switched 56 Kbs lines for transmission with audio taken out of band. The hardware in use as of this writing is the VideoTelecom CS300 family of codecs running 7.40 software with a 14 port VideoTelecom Digital Video Branch Exchange (DVBX). Plans to upgrade the system to the VideoTelecom MediaMax system are underway and will be completed by August of this year. Channel banks from Telco Systems are used for the D4 communications in most cases with some single and dual port multiplexers used for specific applications.

No needs assessment was conducted specifically for the ITN as the network is considered to be a means to an end and was dictated by our Continuing Education needs assessment that defines our entire role at the University.

Murray State University firmly believes in the use of technological delivery of education as both a means of reaching students placebound by family or job obligations and as a method of preserving a valued rural lifestyle in our area without sacrificing the ability for area residents to obtain a high quality education. We feel that rapid development of similar networks is to the benefit of all concerned.

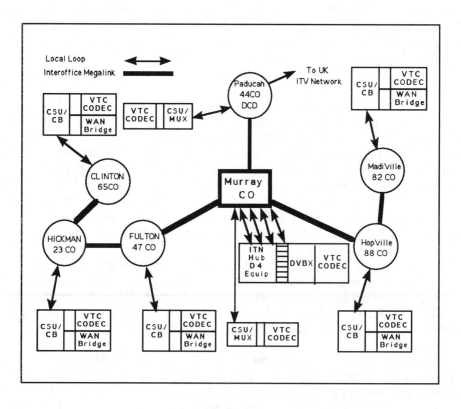

West Kentucky
Interactive Telecommunications Network

Nebraska Educational Telecommunications Commission

William R. Ramsey
Director of Engineering and Technical Services

1800 North 33rd Street
P. O. Box 83111
Lincoln, NE 68501
voice: (402) 472-9333 ext 348
fax: (402) 472-1785

When did you start using compressed video?
The first service commenced April, 1991.

How did you decide to use compressed video as opposed to other telecommunications systems?
Spectrum was available in the NEB*SAT satellite transponder needed to provide interconnection of the Nebraska Public Radio and Television Networks. This transponder could support a number of SCPC digital channels capable of compressed video transmission, but could not support additional channels of full motion video.

Who made the decisions about developing a compressed video network?
The compressed video was an integral part of the NEB*SAT plan which was placed in service in January, 1990, to replace leased microwave interconnection of the public television network. The decision was recommended to the governing board of the Nebraska Educational Telecommunications Commission by management staff.

Who, why, when, where, and how was vendor selection made?
An RFP for a turn-key system was circulated in the fall of the 1990 for the compressed video systems consisting of the satellite antennas, C-band transceivers, modems, and digital codecs. Facilities are interconnected to studio/classrooms either existing or funded separately.

What delivery systems do you use?
Delivery is C-band satellite on transponder 13, Spacenet 3 which is owned by the State of Nebraska.

What are the costs of installation and delivery, etc.?
A C-band satellite terminal consisting of 4.5 meter antenna, a transceiver, codec, modem, etc., installed, is budgeted at $91,000. The cost of maintenance and operation are included in the Commission's overall Engineering budget, and the cost of space segment time is not billed separately since the transponder is owned by the State of Nebraska and used primarily for other service.

Please describe each application that is presently using the compressed video network.
Compressed video is used primarily for instruction and involves both one- and two-way applications and one-to-one and one-to-multiple site situations. The first and largest user is the University of Nebraska Medical Center College of Nursing. Other users are the state and community colleges. Teleconferencing by state agencies and other educational users is a secondary use.

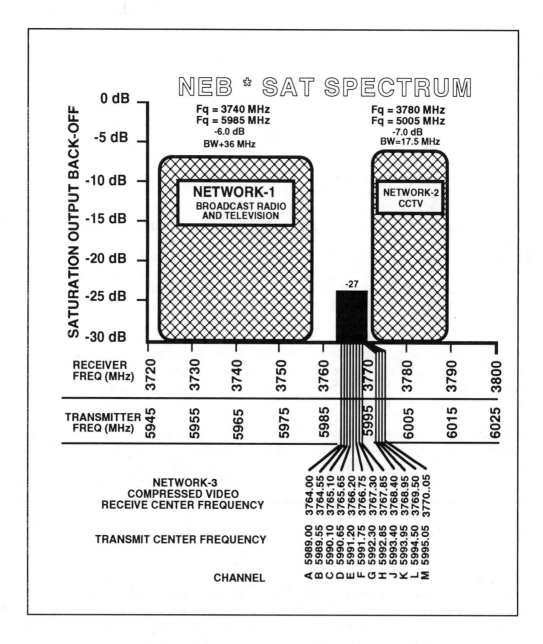

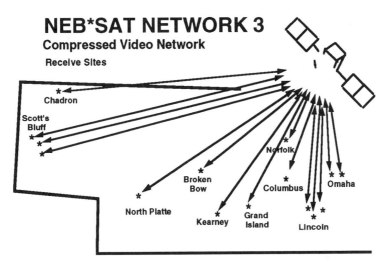

Source: Nebraska Telecommunications Commission

NDSU/Tri-College University Fargo, North Dakota

Ron Stammen

North Dakota State University/Tri-College University
Minard Hall 3215
Fargo, ND 58105
voice: (701) 237-8170

When did you start using compressed video?
The North Dakota Interactive Video Network started operation in the fall of 1990.

How did you decide to use compressed video as opposed to other telecommunications system?
T-1 compressed video was utilized as opposed to other telecommunication systems because it was financially feasible at a ratio of 6-1 over fiber optics. It complied with adult-education features needed to communicate across distances of over 400 miles as it is voice activated for multiple sites utilizing interactivity with two television sets (sending & receiving).

Who made the decisions about developing a compressed video network?
A series of boards and committees involved in the statewide university system, rural health

association, and legislative action helped in establishing the necessary work for the decision making even to occur for developing a compressed video network. The final decision was made by the North Dakota Board of Higher Education.

Who, why, when, where and how was vendor selection made?
Vendor selection information was done by bid via help from consultants.

What delivery system(s) do you use?
North Dakota is one of the first states to create a statewide system that allows multiple video interactive networking which connects two or more sites. The North Dakota Interactive Video Network (ND IVN) is the first step in a long-range plan to connect all corners of the state using contemporary communications technology. It consists of 14 interconnected classroom sites located at universities or colleges in 11 cities. The medium is linked with a compressed video interactive system to all state college/university campuses and the State Capitol. It was constructed during the 1989-1990 school year with the majority of funding through a Federal Rural-Health grant. The furthermost point-to-point distance is 413 miles (Wahpeton to Williston). This video system is a digital system which utilizes codecs to transmit two-way audio and video over leased telephone lines.

What are the costs of installation and delivery?
Costs of the delivery system can be obtained from the ND IVN.

Please describe each application that is presently using the compressed video network.
The system is overloaded during the second year. The Rural Health Association was given top priority. The MBA programs at the University of North Dakota (UND) and North Dakota State University/Tri-College University (NDSU/TCU) were the first overall cohort programs provided with a level 2 priority. Several colleges offered one or several courses as an experiment or occasional outreach services were given level 3 priority. The educational administration programs of both UND and NDSU/TCU were given level 2 priority in February, 1992 as UND provided one course the first two years and NDSU provided ten courses under the priority 3 level. The following table, taken from a published article, provides this level categorization:

Priority	Event Type	Maximum Days before scheduled event
1	Rural Health Project Classes	90
2	Credit Classes for Degree Program	90
3	Other Credit Classes	60
4	Extension programs, other noncredit classes and professional development seminars	59
5	Other programs	59

Table 1
Priorities Established by the North Dakota University System and the Higher Education Telecommunications Advisory Committee (HETAC)
Source: HETAC Program/Policy Subcommittee IVN Meeting - 1/30/91

Events in each priority shown on Table 1 are scheduled on a first-come, first served basis. Degree programs which offer all their credit classes over the network are granted priority 2. The

NDSU/TCU Educational Administration Program has a priority 3 for scheduling purposes and cannot advertise until 60 days before the first meeting date because of the possibility of being canceled due to a lower priority. Events tentatively scheduled prior to other events in the same priority are confirmed after the maximum number of days for that priority has passed.

The following table, taken from a soon-to-be refereed article, provides insight from the contributor's view:

Courses Taught via IVN			Enrollment		
Quarters 1990-91	Number	Course Name	NDSU	On Site IVS	Receiving Instructor
Master Level					
Spring 1991	Ed. 531	Teacher and Student Rights	26	1	Van Berkum
Summer 1991	Ed. 514	History of American Education	27	4	Keogh
Summer 1991	Ed. 539	Secondary School Administration	26	1	Van Berkum
Fall 1991	Ed. 531	Teacher and Student Rights	14	8	Van Berkum
Winter 1990-91	Ed. 534	School Finance	11	7	Stammen
Post-Masters for Credentials and/or Specialist Level					
Fall 1991	Ed. 585	Organization and Administration of Vocational Education	6	6	Stammen
Winter 1990-91	Ed. 586	School Plant Planning and Maintenance	2	10	Stammen
Spring 1991	Ed. 590	Seminar: The Superintendency	4	8	Stammen
Summer 1991	Ed. 596	Organization and Administration of Educational Telecommunication	20	12	Stammen
Spring 1992	Ed. 596	Organization and Administration of Educational Telecommunication	4	15	Stammen

Table 2
Educational Administration Courses taught over IVN Winter 1990-91 through Fall 1991 by Tri-College University

Ten such courses were successfully completed during a one-year period consisting of four quarters, including NDSU/TCU's traditional summer session which includes two 1-week intercessions and two 4-week sessions. The opportunity to initiate this pilot endeavor was taken as soon as permission was granted by the ND IVN governing unit. Consequently, the first course was held during the winter quarter of 1990-91. The last course offering covered in this assessment concluded in the fall quarter of 1991. Table 2 provides the numbers and names of these courses, along with the number enrolled both on the North Dakota State University (NDSU) Campus (the sending site) and the number of students taking courses at the receiving sites in North Dakota. Receiving IVN sites were at Williston, Dickinson, Minot, Bismarck, Bottineau, and Wahpeton.

The courses shown in Table 2 were offered by faculty on regular campus load assignment, except for the last Ed. 596 course which was offered through the sponsorship of NDSU Extension's Continuing Education Service. Further, the following excerpts are taken from this article to summarize action research garnered from these teaching activities.

Innovations

Several innovations have been field-tested during the first four quarters. NSDU/TCU Educational Administration faculty have demonstrated they can elevate ND IVN into the highest form of contemporary distance education technology, explained by Gustafson (1989). Both computer conferencing and computer optical video display has been utilized for demonstration with the NeXT and Macintosh. These technologies have been successfully utilized to project interactive demonstrations with the IVN overhead camera.

Faculty have been using the medium for consulting activities, statewide meetings, and various presentations. Two professors, (Dr. W. Woods and Dr. R. Stammen) were involved in a team project with personnel at the Computer Center to initiate a K-12 grant to satisfy requirements of a successful National Science Foundation grant application for statewide TCP/IP protocol for all colleges and universities in the state system.

This led to the development of SENDIT in 1991. It is a K-12 and Higher Education statewide electronic-mail and forum-conferencing network. The host computer and server is located at the state instructional Computer Center in Fargo, ND. Statewide training is directed by NDSU/TCU educational administration faculty during a three-year period which will end in 1993. Two-thirds of the schools in the state will have had this training by the spring of 1992 ($694,000 has been acquired for this project).

NDSU/TCU Education Administration faculty hold student interaction with SENDIT. This provides ways to discuss matters pertaining to IVN classwork, practicums, field study papers, and advisor duties. Graduate students (practicing school administrators) have demonstrated how to access the library via PALS using SENDIT from rural areas 300 miles from North Dakota State University. This includes accessing libraries nationwide by using SENDIT and Internet access. The IVN has been used to enhance the supervision of the required practicums graduate students are conducting in the field. They have scheduled practicum fairs across the state whereby experiences are shared with a broader range of administrators who would not otherwise travel great distances to attend a meeting of such nature lasting a couple of hours (Van Berkum and Suomala, 1991).

One professor initiated a project in northwest North Dakota connecting six school districts to an interpersonal computing network which utilizes the NeXT Dimension computing technology (Boswell, 1991). Expertise gained in this project prompted experimentation with this technology while teaching over IVN to accomplish the following:
1.   Enlarge (E-Mail) print on the overhead optical camera during demonstrations.
2.   Display digital dimensions shown on the monitor.
3.   Send fax material to save time and avoid noise while teaching. Likewise, material can be sent via fax to this computer for such distribution.
4.   Use interpersonal computing techniques to solve current material and test transmitting problems.

Another professor, Dr. D. Van Berkum, initiated efforts to use the IVN medium for statewide Leadership in Educational Administration Development (LEAD) activities. They held meetings to develop projects serving the practicing school administrators and to conduct Leadership 123 training sessions.

The IVN is utilized by the professors on a monthly basis to coordinate K-12 activities and business for the Southeast North Dakota (SEND) Educational Telecommunication region and the Northwest Telecommunication Consortium. This includes communication with projects involved with North Dakota's Educational Telecommunication Council.

The TCU Provost led the development of a handbook for IVN utilization. It was funded through a Bremer Foundation grant. Resource people from Colorado and Missouri were utilized during the development (TCU Faculty Handbook, 1990). One of the initiatives at TCU is to connect the Minnesota Val-Ed Consortium interactive video system located at Moorhead State University with ND IVN. This would expand services to over one-third of Minnesota.

Recommendations

The data gathered in this assessment focused on research concerning successes and barriers during a one-year phase utilizing the Interactive Video Network (IVN) across North Dakota. Thus, the following recommendations suggest ways to stabilize schedules and assure continuity to NDSU/Tri-College customers (students).

1.   The NDSU/TCU Educational Administration Program needs at least a priority 2 schedule status in order to assure a stable IVN service across the state.
2.   The NDSU/TCU Educational Administration Program must continue to be offered over the statewide Interactive Video Network in order to reach all master-and specialist-level graduate students who are taking advantage of the opportunity.
3.   It is important to utilize experiences and research data obtained during this first phase to develop policies, guideline, goals, objectives, and a visionary statement outlining what is currently directing this active research. This includes incorporating Mody's suggestions to provide an awareness of the IVN media long-term potential.
4.   The extra work taken to utilize IVN be recognized in evaluations and procedures establishing load requirements.
5.   The active research data gathered during this phase at Tri-College University should be immediately utilized to establish research instruments which will yield quantitative results and set the stage for subsequent longitudinal studies.
6.   The NeXT Station computer system should be located at each IVN facility to alleviate data transfer problems and enhance demonstration capabilities for the instructor. The interpersonal computing features provide exemplary features such as the following:
      a.   Provide parity in administering tests by sending an icon document to each IVN that can be immediately printed for each student at that site.
      b.   Serve as a host for local area E-mail and other computer-mediated communications which could support SENDIT and reduce telephone costs.

This system has been used by various statewide groups and a multitude of individual organizations or association sessions on an appointed basis.

Who operates the facilities?
The operation of the facilities is conducted by an engineer who assigns a system operator at each site for whatever session the system is scheduled to be utilized.

Who schedules the network?
Scheduling is accomplished by a network of site coordinators, a state committee, and state director. The schedule is on a list server on the Higher Education Computer Network. The State

Board for Higher Education recently delegated the Outreach Services at the University of North Dakota to take the state directorship starting the 1992-93 school year. This new group is in the process of being oriented for taking over this responsibility.

What are the policies, procedures and priorities used in scheduling the network? Who developed these?
The Higher Education Telecommunications Advisory Committee (HETAC) developed the policies, procedures, and priorities as shown on Table 2 above. A booklet can be supplied which provides this data used for the 1990-92 and 1991-92 school years.

What rate(s) do you use for transmission? Why?
Rates charged for state government, the private sector, or any non-University System entity for using the ND IVN are as follows:
> $125 per hour scheduling the Network
> $10 per hour per site for technical support

Continuing Education classes will continue to pay the $10 per hour site for technical support for courses they sponsor.

What peripherals do you have attached to the system and how are they used?
Peripherals are illustrated in the enclosed outline. They include fax, videorecorder, filmstrip projector, optical viewer, and any computer which instructors desire to attach to auxiliary ports. The NeXT Dimension workstation has been utilized by this instructor to provide a variety of presentations that are currently novel in this regard.

Are you presently using (or do you plan to use) the public switched 56 network for interstate or international communications?
Public switched 56 network is not currently being used by this network. However, plans are underway to utilize the area across the Red River with Moorhead State University and their interactive television system to extend the services for the Tri-College University.

If applicable, what software version are you using?
Procom-plus communications package is the software being utilized to access the DAX port in Bismark or Fargo. TCF scheduling software is used to control the codec settings via the MCU.

What hardware model and brand are you using? How is your system configured?
Hardward brand and model of equipment involved the following:
> CLI Rembrant 11/30 Codec
> Elmo Ev-308 Optic viewer AC120V, 60Hz, 30W
> Panasonic Remote Control Unit WV-7330 and Video Switcher WJ 200RB
> TOA 900 series amplifier A-903-A
> Shure AM Mixer
> System 500 - Sigma Electronic & Desktop SVX-210 Video Switcher
> NEC AEC-400 Acoustic Echo canceller

Did you conduct a needs assessment? If so, please describe.
A needs assessment was conducted by the University system.

Other comments or information?
The North Dakota State University School of Education's educational administration department is providing statewide leadership. This is especially true with programs sponsored by the North

Dakota Educational Telecommunications Council. I am the chairman of the Advisory Committee for this committee.

North Dakota University System

Russell Poulin
Director ND IVN

10th Floor, State Capitol
600 E. Boulevard Ave.
Bismark, ND 58501
voice: (701) 224-2964
fax: (701) 224-2961

When did you start using compressed video?
The North Dakota Interactive Video Network began operation in August of 1990. The network included six sites and one video (multipoint control) switch.

How did you decide to use compressed video as opposed to other telecommunications systems?
Your question implies an either/or choice in the selection of technologies. In the future, I imagine that everyone will have access to the different technologies and the question will become "which is the appropriate technology for this application?"

The following is a description of why we decided to invest in a compressed video network instead of other possible technologies. The major alternative delivery technologies analyzed were phone conferencing, one-way satellite video, and analog two-way video.

Phone Conferencing

North Dakota used (and still uses) phone conferencing. Continuing medical education and meetings have been the primary user of these services. While many applications work very well through audio-only delivery, others are enhanced by including a video element. Addressing rural health needs was a main goal of the grant funding received. The ability to see and demonstrate concepts was considered an important addition to what could be done through phone conferencing alone.

One-Way Satellite

Satellite has the advantage of covering a wide geographic area with relatively little equipment investment as receiving sites. However, there were several disadvantages for the applications we envisioned:

> **Inappropriate Technology for Goals** — One of our major goals is to teach credit classes to specific sites with limited-to-small enrollments. A satellite's

footprint would cover not only all of North Dakota, but also most of the rest of North America. This is technology overkill for a class of twenty students. The temptations of wide delivery areas and cost factors drive usage to courses that enroll hundreds of people. Using one-way satellite for meetings, non-credit seminars, or other low volume uses is cost prohibitive.

Multiple Origination Sites — Each of our campuses has something of value to offer to the others. The expense of an uplink would allow only one origination site. Now each campus has an equal ability to originate programming.

Production Costs — To be effective, one-way video requires a higher level of projection than two-way video. Since interaction is more limited, the presentations need greater attention to television techniques and instruction style. Instruction is more of a performance than with other technologies.

Transmission Costs and Availability — Transmission costs have remained high. Scheduling transponder time is another factor. Often the transponder time is not available at the same time that the room or the instructor is available. Demand for satellite time is going up and there have been considerable writings, of late, on the looming supply problem.

Analog Two-Way Video

During the decision-making process, a group of rural phone cooperatives was very adamant about bidding a fiber optic, analog, two-way video network. This option was rejected for the following reasons:

Cost — the phone cooperatives provided a bid for their proposed solution. To reach the proposed sites, the transmission costs were six times greater than the lowest bid for compressed video. When including the higher start-up costs for compressed video along with the transmission costs, the ratio was 4.5 times greater than the compressed bid. Additional campus cabling costs for fiber optic lines would also have been incurred, and are not figured into the above ratios.

Availability — Due to fiber unavailability in some parts of the state, they also proposed delaying installation for one year while they buried cable.

Flexibility — The analog network was based on a high school model that allows a maximum of four sites to connect at a time. With compressed video, up to 14 sites can be included in a single conference.

The Future — The communications industry is abandoning analog solutions for digital ones. The promise of combining voice, data, and video transmission signals through the use of digital technologies is tremendous. It is better to struggle with the infancy of an emerging technology than the death pangs of the old.

Who made the decisions about developing a compressed video network?
North Dakota had two projects for distance learning that received funding at roughly the same time. The USDA Rural Health Project was a grant obtained jointly by the University of North Dakota School of Medicine and the North Dakota State University Extension Service. The goal of this project was to deliver complete health majors to rural areas. This project was overseen by a Project Management Board.

The North Dakota University System Office received a state legislative appropriation to invest in telecommunications technologies. The goal of this project was to create a network to share courses and knowledge among the campuses. This project was overseen by the Higher Education Telecommunications Advisory Committee.

The two projects soon realized that they could create a greater impact by joining forces. A Joint Technical Subcommittee was formed to research the possibilities. In a joint meeting, the two groups approved the findings of the subcommittee. The North Dakota Board of Higher Education gave a final approval to the project.

Who, why, when, where, and how was vendor selection made?
Who — The Joint Technical Subcommittee set the requirements and technical specifications. Extensive use was made of experts in different audio/video technologies and instructional technology design from different campuses. North Dakota State University was chosen as the bid agent for equipment. Three equipment bids were advertised:

1) For the compression equipment (codecs and switches);
2) For the remaining classroom equipment (cameras, microphones, cables, wires, etc.)
3) For construction of the teaching console and cabinets.

The North Dakota Information Services Division, the state telecommunications agency, advertised a bid for the communications lines.

When — All bids were due in late May, 1990. Bidders had about 60 days to answer the bids. Results were compiled and final decisions made at a meeting on June 14, 1990.

How — The Joint Technical Subcommittee set the requirements and technical specifications before the bid process began. The Subcommittee reviewed the submitted bids, considered the alternatives (especially resulting from substitutions or additions to the bids by vendors), and made a recommendation on each bid. The recommendation was presented at the June 14 meeting. A major change to the recommendation was made at the meeting (two switches instead of one) and the plan was adopted.

Why — The following is a list of reasons for making the selections for each bid:

1) **Compression Equipment** — The Joint Technical Subcommittee created a video tape that each vendor had to run through their compression equipment at 1/4 T-1, 1/2 T-1, and full T-1 transmission speeds. Both sound and video had to be on the tape. The tape was a very important step and was especially helpful to the participants at the June 14 meeting. Bid price was also a major factor. Compression Labs, Inc. was selected as the codec vendor because it: a) had the best audio

handling protocols; b) had the second-best picture quality; c) had the best multipoint control unit; d) had the lowest bid price.

2) **Classroom Equipment** — Todd Communications was chosen because they had the best bid price.
3) **Console Construction** — March and Brother was chosen on the basis of bid price.
4) **Communications Lines** — US West was chosen for intra-LATA communications on the basis of bid price. US Sprint was chosen for inter-LATA communications on the basis of bid price.

What delivery system(s) do you use?

ND IVN uses terrestrial T-1 lines for transmission. In some places, these happen to be fiber optic lines. In most places, normal T-1 lines are used. A pilot project using compressed VSAT satellite for transmission will begin this fall. This option may be used for some connections in the future.

What are the costs of installation and delivery (monthly, hourly, etc.)?

Each new site costs roughly $75,000-80,000 for classroom and transmission equipment. Users are charged $125 per hour.

Please describe each application that is presently using the compressed video network.

Higher education, credit classes comprise about 60-80 percent of the usage in any one month. About half of the courses are part of a complete degree program that is being delivered through the network. The other half of the courses are individual courses that are delivered for a variety of reasons: support of students at a distance for some of their degree requirements, campuses seeking to add opportunities for their students, resource sharing among campuses, campuses trading courses, instructors seeking new markets for favorite courses, general interest courses, and courses fulfilling needs of a specific target group. Meetings are the next largest usage group. From higher education, faculty, presidents, extension service, video network, system-wide councils and others have used it. The following is an incomplete lists of groups that have used the network...

State Agencies

Council of State Employees
North Dakota National Guard
North Dakota Human Services Division
North Dakota Information Services Division
North Dakota Department of Public Instruction

Professional Organizations

North Dakota Bankers Association
North Dakota Conference of Social Welfare
North Dakota Physical Therapy Association
North Dakota Society of CPA's
North Dakota Dietetics Association

Non-Profit Groups

North Dakota Catholic Conference
Northern Lights Council of Boy Scouts

Agriculture

Agriculture Extension Service
North Dakota FFA
Soil Conservation Service

Education Groups

Tech/Prep Project Management Group
Council of College Faculties
SEND (South East North Dakota K-12 Education Technology Group)
North Dakota Adult Education Association
North Dakota Speech and Theatre Association
University of North Dakota Presidential Search Open Meeting
Gifted and Talented Association
Governor's Employment and Training Forum
Displaced Homemakers Advisory Committee

Education Seminars

Continuing Medical Education
Custodial and Office Maintenance
Emergency Medical Technicians
North Dakota Small Business Development Center
North Dakota Association of Realtors

Others

Statewide Meeting with South African Ambassadors
Legal Hearing on Personnel Issue

Non-credit inservice programs are the next largest group of users. The Bankers Association, the Real Estate Association, and the National Guard have held educational programs for their members. The Extension Service has held a number of non-credit workshops for its personnel and for the public.

There have been a few open forums on the network.
 • a legislative hearing on the higher education seven-year plan;
 • learning about or to comment on rules for agriculture programs;
 • comment on Department of Public Instruction Adult Education rules.

Describe the facilities being used.
All but two of the sites are identical in design. There are two monitors and a camera in the front of the room for participants. There are two monitors and a camera above the participants for use by an instructor or presenter in the front of the room. A table microphone is available for every two participants. An echo canceller and controls to adjust each individual microphone level are included. Each room has a VCR, fax machine, slide projector (with video output), and portable overhead presentation camera. The overhead presentation camera can be moved to accommodate left or right handed presenters or other needs of a specific event. Most rooms do not have a computer dedicated to the room. Every room has a jack for accepting analog output from a computer. The design of the rooms leans toward classroom rather than conferencing use. Rooms with windows are discouraged, but most rooms do have windows with blinds. Rooms are continually being improved in terms of acoustic and lighting needs. Special lighting is being installed, "video friendly" backgrounds created, and carpets are being added.

Who operates the facilities-i.e. technicians, instructors, students, etc.?
It was high priority of our design to make the room easy enough for anyone to be trained quickly to operate it, but flexible enough so that a technician can be used. Other networks that we visited required a technician with a great deal of expertise to operate the equipment for the participants. Keeping the controls plain and simple is an important goal for the network. Given that goal, a technician is still required to be in or near every room for every event. The technician has a highly variable amount of participation in the event. The level of participation is determined by the needs of the people using the network. The following are not official definitions, but characterizations of general categories of technician involvement:

- **High Participation.** The technician is in the room at all times and is operating all of the controls. The participants need to learn very little about the operations of the network. This is useful for guest speakers or some instructors who wish to have the additional help at all times.
- **Moderate Participation.** The instructor or meeting chair will operate the switches to choose the camera shots and may perform some other operations (VCR, slides, etc.). The technician is in the room most of the time and concentrates on the audio controls and trouble-shooting, if needed. Many instructors like to have control over the equipment, but wish to have the technician nearby.
- **Low Participation.** The instructor or meeting chair has enough familiarity with the equipment that they can handle most of the operations. The technician is mostly out of the room, but must let participants know where he or she can be reached. The technician usually opens the room, checks the connection and initial equipment settings, waits to see that the event gets started, and then returns for the end of the event.

University of Oklahoma

Kathleen J. M. Haynes and Robert Swisher
School of Library and Information Studies

University of Oklahoma
401 W. Brooks, Room 129
Norman, OK 73109
voice: (405) 325-3921

A Study of the Use of Compressed Video Instruction for Distance Education at the University of Oklahoma School of Library and Information Studies

Some of the material for this chapter was published first in the Journal of Interactive Television (see references).

The master's program of the University of Oklahoma School of Library and Information Studies is one of only 57 programs accredited by the American Library Association in the United States and Canada; it is the only program accredited by the American Library Association in the state of Oklahoma and three contiguous states: Arkansas, New Mexico, and Colorado. The Master's of Library and Information Studies is a 36-hour program of six required courses and six elective courses and is considered the first professional degree. There are opportunities within the course of study for students to specialize in one of four traditional institutional settings (academic, public, school, and special librarianship) or according to function (technical or public services). Students may also focus in an area that reflects unique faculty expertise or materials collections (special collections and rare book librarianship, archives and records management, serials management, biomedical librarianship, etc.).

Embracing both the traditions of the culture of print and the newer nonbook and electronic information technologies, the School's programs are very resource intensive, requiring that graduate students have access to extensive research collections and a wide variety of online and ondisc retrieval systems, as well as, both standard and special purpose microcomputer software.

The library community in Oklahoma is making more demands upon the School to extend curricular and continuing professional education opportunities to students and practitioners at distant sites. The distant site for the University of Oklahoma is The University Center at Tulsa, a consortium of the Oklahoma State Regents for Higher Education. It consists of four publicly funded state universities offering upper division and graduate degree programs in the urban setting of Tulsa, the state's second largest metropolitan area. The consortium was developed nine years ago and has tripled in size over that period. Enrollments for the School at both Norman and Tulsa have steadily increased; the Tulsa enrollment is approximately one-third of the total.

The average Tulsa student takes five credit hours per term at night or on weekends, is employed full time, is 37 years old, female, and has children. The Tulsa graduate students of the

School of Library and Information Studies are typical of this description as well: they are 35 years old, female, married, and employed.

In addition, most of the School's students are more place-bound than the University's traditional campus-resident students.   Several campus-resident students in the School's graduate program on both campuses drive up to two hours to attend class.

Compressed Video

Since the dramatic downturn in the state's economy during the middle 1980's, and its necessary consequences for publicly funded higher education in the state, it was not reasonable to expect that a small professional program at a state university could gain significant new faculty resources to meet an expanding statewide mission. However, the School's faculty thought that more efficient and effective use of its constrained resources could be made for the state if technological solutions were considered.

The faculty identified three technologies that could mitigate distance and time in both the delivery of our graduate curriculum and in our advising and counseling functions: compressed video (the subject of this chapter), modem-based communication and information services (Swisher, Spitzer, Spriestersbach, Markus, and Burris, 1991), and voice-mail messaging.

One means of delivering its program to a statewide audience that has been available since the 1970's is the Oklahoma State Regents for Higher Education Talkback Television System, a full- motion system of one-way video and two-way audio that blankets the state's publicly funded institutions of vocational and higher education and larger public libraries as well—a total of 38 receiving sites. The School's faculty, however, rejected this system for two reasons: one, as a resource intensive program, master's courses could not appropriately be taught wherever the television signal could be received; two, the School's faculty was interested in delivering graduate level instruction with as much student/faculty interaction as possible.

In the fall of 1989, a VideoTelecom Conference System was installed to link the Norman and Tulsa sites of the University of Oklahoma; immediately the School began using it as a means of systematically delivering the graduate program's six required courses each term simulta-neously to a section in Norman and a second section in Tulsa. An existing fiber optic line maintained and scheduled by the Oklahoma State Regents for Higher Education is used to transmit the signals at no cost to the participating institutions. Scheduling time on the Regents system is handled for the School by an office in the University's College of Continuing Education, home of the University's Television and Satellite Services activity.

Because the technology is reversible, and the School's graduate courses are always taught in a once-a-week format, each instructor travels to the Tulsa site (2.5 hours each way) to deliver the class from that end approximately one-third of the time, or five trips per term.

The Tulsa enrollment averages of three courses taught each term (fall, spring, and summer) on compressed video are approximately as large as the Norman enrollments (20 per class in Norman, and 17 in Tulsa). To insure effective on-site instruction, the School paired an instructional facilitator (a locally available practitioner who possesses the master's degree and has experience in the content of the course) with the instructor of each televised course. Training for the facilitators and technicians began during 1990 with brief introductory sessions. Some technicians continued to learn about the system on their own and became adept in using split screen when an instructor used graphics, for example, and following student speakers with the camera during discussions.

The system was purchased and installed in less than six weeks. At the beginning, entire sessions and portions of sessions were interrupted because of technical problems. The primary means of interaction within the telecommunications systems occurs via the voice and data systems, but these systems proved to be the most problematic.

Several changes were made at both sites in an effort to improve the technical quality of the system. A classroom in the School's quarters on the Norman campus was equipped for the fall 1989 term, but it was necessary to shift to one of the University's three full motion (two way video, one way audio) studios the following spring to accommodate other uses of the system. This change was viewed as positive by many of the School's faculty because there would be a trained technician available in the studio's control booth to operate the system, and the studio was located very close to the School's quarters. Different configurations of seating were tried to improve the ability to see and interact with other students. Both ceiling- mounted and tabletop microphones were eventually experimented with to determine which type provided better audio reception at the other end of the system. Speaker levels were adjusted to lessen audio feedback. An expert on classroom environments for instructional telecommunications analyzed both sites and made recommendations. In 1991, the administration of compressed video at the University Center at Tulsa, in coordination with the faculty users at the University of Oklahoma created a handout for students which informed them what was expected of them as active learners in this technological system.

Responding to the School's requirement of better audio, better technical support, and a flexible system configuration that would facilitate a whole range of communication opportunities from operator controlled large classes down through operator-less seminars, committee meetings, and one on one advising between a faculty member and a student, the University administration, in the spring of 1992, authorized the equipping of a second compressed video classroom and the renovation of a University-scheduled classroom in the School's quarters as its location. Operational by the beginning of the fall 1992 semester, the classroom has as its first priority support for the University's efforts at the University Center at Tulsa—direct classroom instruction by the School of Library and Information Studies as well as other Norman-based programs offered at UCT, and indirect support such as telemeetings, teleconferencing, and advising.

The new classroom accommodates 28 students, arranged the three rows of 2 foot by 5 foot tables. Each of the 14 tables holds a goose-necked microphone which is centered on the table. One back corner of the room holds a large technician's console, monitors, faders, pan/tilt/zoom controls, VCR, graphics tablet, codex, phone, etc. The instructor's desk/console, which is not yet complete, holds a copy stand camera and a monitor. Before the end of the current semester, this desk/console area will be raised on a six inch platform, and further equipped with two small monitors as well as a graphics camera input.

The room's floor and walls are carpeted, and impressively "dead" acoustically. Two very large (32 inch) monitors are hung from the room's dropped ceiling, with a set of speaker enclosures (local and far site) by each monitor. The back wall holds a smaller (and therefore less useful) monitor next to the instructor's camera, placed there, clearly, allowing the instructor to more frequently and easily seem to be looking at the students at the far site. The front (student) camera, is located behind and above the instructor (out of typical instructor camera view) and closer to the monitor that is usually programmed to show the far site camera input. Again, this close proximity of a camera to a monitor delivering far site input is meant to facilitate as much intimacy between speaker and other site viewer as possible.

The compressed video system is VideoTelecom's MediaMax with Pen Pal Graphics, a configuration used by all four compressed video partners in the state's higher education user community— Oklahoma State University (Stillwater), University of Oklahoma Health Sciences Campus (Oklahoma City), University of Oklahoma Norman Campus, and the University Center at Tulsa.

Interaction

When the School of Library and Information Studies decided to experiment with compressed video, there was not enough lead time to redesign all the courses or to train the faculty in the use of the technology. Although past research demonstrates that telecommunications is an effective instructional tool, the School was interested in how best to use the technology to create efficient and optimum learning opportunities. The issue of how best to use the media sparks considerable debate. At one end of the spectrum are those who think the media are interchangeable and do not directly influence learning (Clark and Salomon, 1986). Others argue that the media do impact content depending upon the unique attributes of the various media employed (Petkovich and Tennyson,1984). Using an instructional systems design approach in the research design may serve to shed additional light upon the role of media in instruction.

One course became the focus of intensive study with Dr. Connie Dillon, an expert in distance education at the University of Oklahoma. The course, Organization and Description of Materials I, was selected for the study because the instructor uses a variety of interactive and experiential teaching strategies including case study, small group discussion, and problem analysis. One important consideration in the use of instructional telecommunications is the extent to which the technology inhibits the use of interactive teaching strategies, which may ultimately impede higher order learning. It is the interactive attributes of the media that warrant further analysis. A proposal was funded to cover the costs of data gathering and analysis from the University of Oklahoma Research Council. The design of the evaluation provides some insight into questions about how best to use the technology.

If interaction is more problematic in instructional telecommunications, one might assume that the students receiving the instruction at the distance site via telecommunications would not do as well on objectives requiring higher-order learning as the students receiving traditional instruction in a face-to-face mode. The purpose of this research was to examine the impact of telecommunications media upon learning outcomes which are designed based upon level of learning and instructional strategy (Dillon, Haynes, and Price, 1990; Haynes and Dillon, 1991).

The interaction analysis which accompanied two simultaneous observations of both sites indicated that although the distance students interact with the instructor much less than the on-campus students, they interact with the other students at the distance site more. Thus, the distance students seemed to use peer teaching strategies during class, although at times they complained that this kind of interaction interfered with attending to the professor. They also indicated that they believed the on-campus class to be the primary focus of attention.

The students at the distant site behaved much like students in an on-campus class. About one-third of the students actively responded in a large group setting and during small group discussion the quiet students became more involved. Problems with the audio system made the distance students more hesitant to ask questions. Sometimes they appointed a spokesperson whose voice carried well over the audio system. The students indicated that they liked the small group interaction and the practical nature of the course work. Although a site facilitator was available at the distant site, the quantity of student-facilitator interactions in this class was insignificant.

The results of this study indicate that for this group of students, the delivery system did not impact upon learning at any level, suggesting that the problem of interaction at a distance does not impede either lower or higher order levels of learning. An important finding of this research is that negative attitudes expressed by the students toward the delivery system do not appear to affect learning outcomes. Indeed, the negative student attitudes at the distant site may have contributed to student learning. Some evidence for this is presented by Ksobiech and Salomon as cited in Clark and Salomon (Clark and Salomon, 1986) who suggest that students adapt and modify their learning style when the media places different demands upon them.

Student Attitudes

Student attitudes were examined at both the on-campus (Norman) and distant (Tulsa) site using a questionnaire with both open-ended response items and closed-ended response items with order choices using a Likert-type scale (choices of 1-5 with 1 low). The questionnaire, designed by Connie Dillon, was originally used to examine the attitudes of distance students enrolled in courses on the Oklahoma Televised Instruction System. The questionnaire was administered to 11 of the 19 courses delivered to the Tulsa site from fall 1989 to spring 1990. At the end of the fall 1989 term, the questionnaire was distributed to 108 students; 71 were returned, a response rate of 65%. At the end of the spring 1990 term, 156 questionnaires were distributed with a similar response rate.

The content of the open-ended questions were analyzed. Attitudes were grouped by resources directly related to learning, resources indirectly related to learning, and attitudes related to the communication process. Answers were compared between the on-campus site and the distant site.

Resources directly related to learning were significant factors for both negative and positive aspects. At both sites, many students felt that the instructor was the service which helped most in learning the course content. Other factors mentioned were the facilitator and access to the computer lab and the library. Regular visits by the instructor to the distant site were also stated as attributing to the learning of the course content. Further, students at both sites thought the lack of an on-site instructor for each session was a hindrance to learning. At the distant site, access to the computer lab and library was seen as a problem in fall 1989 because these were not open for evening hours after the end of the class. Resources and equipment at each site were often different at the two sites which necessitated different assignments for the distant students.

Resources indirectly related to learning were predominantly a problem for some of the distant students. Advisement and counseling by compressed video was unacceptable to them.

Lack of employment notices and involvement in student activities also seemed to hinder their satisfaction. Technical problem contributed to a lack of student-student interaction between sites and a lack of student-instructor interaction. Attention should be given to the quality and placement of microphones to encourage interaction between the distant and campus site and to allow free movement for the instructor. A copy camera is used at both sites to enlarge material, but the quantity and placement of monitors was not sufficient to see this material well.

Communication between the campuses is not effective. An improved courier service to increase the accessibility of assignments, handouts, and homework transfer is essential. A facsimile machine and an electronic bulletin board are used by the School, but neither was exploited fully. Throughout the 1989-90 period there was no way to fax a handout and have it copied for each student at the distant site without placing a burden on the Tulsa office staff. The distant students thought that feedback about graded assignments was delayed too long.

The School also gathered data about attitudes from fall 1990 to summer 1991 using another questionnaire with closed-ended response items with a similar scale. The students were also asked to rate the courses they attended the previous three terms.

Negative student attitudes related to all the aspects of the compressed video system predominated. Not surprisingly, the fall 1989 term got the lowest ratings; but by fall 1990, the ratings had steadily improved. The highest rating was given for the summer term. The Tulsa students gave higher ratings for the three previous terms than the Norman students. It is evident from the second survey that both Norman and Tulsa students adjusted their attitudes toward the compressed video system over time. The responses in the fall 1990 survey about courses taken in fall 1989 and spring 1990 were higher than when they rated these courses during the actual terms. The reasons for this are unclear, but the comments from students suggest that they were beginning to accept the technology. Also, the changes made to the classrooms and the audio systems may have helped ameliorate the earlier, more negative attitudes.

Ability to See

The quality of the video reception was given the highest score with the Tulsa mean at 3.24 and the Norman mean at 3.27. Questions 1 and 2 dealt with students' ability to see the instructor or facilitator at the other end or students at the other end. The Norman averages were, with one exception, all at the level of 3.0 (average). Tulsa students, however, averaged 3.8.

Ability to Hear

The audio system was ranked as poor for both sites in fall 1989. The audio system got poor marks again in spring 1990 even though transmission was from the remodeled studio. Questions 3 and 4 asked the students' ability to hear the instructor/facilitator at the other end or students at the other end. Both sites gave almost average ratings (Norman = 2.9, Tulsa = 2.7). Question 4, ability to hear students at the other end, offered up the lowest scores. Norman rated this 2.2 (poor) and Tulsa 1.7 (very poor). There is a strong and direct relationship between ability to hear and willingness to continue in the system. Instruction is simply impossible at any level if students cannot hear their instructor.

Other Comments

As noted above, the distance students used peer teaching strategies during class, although at times they complained that this kind of interaction prevented them from participating fully and interacting with the instructor. They saw themselves as distant, separated, and isolated with the on-campus class being the primary focus of attention. When asked about the services that helped them learn, students at both sites listed those most associated with traditional face-to-face learning: instructor, assignments and handouts, and access to library resources. Access to the videotapes of the classes was the only non-traditional help noted. The factors that hindered performance were: poor audio system; slower pace because of the technology; and lack of interaction with the professor.

A majority of the Tulsa students stated they wanted no additional courses offered using the compressed video system. When asked if they would recommend compressed video to a friend, the distance students responded with a mean of 1.81. The Tulsa students in the spring classes also listed the traditional techniques as the most beneficial: professor, lectures, and readings. For factors that hindered performance, they concurred with the fall classes and also listed lack of interaction with other students.

Having a competent technician at each site was cited as a way to improve the system. As in the fall, these students did not want additional courses to be offered through compressed video. When asked if they would recommend compressed video to a friend, they responded with a mean of 1.95.

Faculty Attitudes

Interviews were conducted with each member of the faculty using the compressed video system. Faculty also contributed comments throughout the term on a standard form for reporting system problems. As expected, these interviews reveal a mixture of positive and negative attitudes toward the experience. Delivering courses to Tulsa is part of the normal course load for all full-time faculty, therefore, the opportunity to teach two sections simultaneously saves time and energy. The faculty also like the ability to teach from either end of the system. Other positive comments include having videotapes available for student review and for faculty review of specific methods or student presentations.

Negative comments include the disruption of course content and the loss of time because of technical problems and the need to slow the pace of delivery to fit the system even when it works well. To offset this, more teacher-centered methods are used even by those instructors who prefer learner-centered methods. Most faculty found they had to resort to classroom management techniques that are not usually needed with adult classes.

The autonomy of the classroom is lost because faculty must rely upon support personnel to a degree unheard of in the traditional classroom. While the quality of the technology and technical support are critical factors, technicians must be trained to assume appropriate roles. This is not the same as collaboration with support services to make optimum use of the telecommunications technology. Certainly, exploring the full capabilities of the compressed video system shows promise of improving instructional practice. For example, the technology allows the professor to bring lab experiences into the class, to digitize graphics, and to integrate video into lectures instantaneously. Such features benefit both the on-campus and distance student. Many faculty think the only way the courses are going to work well with the technology is if they are redesigned; release time to work with support staff and funding are necessary to do this.

It is important that faculty development efforts should include education regarding the capabilities and limitations of the technology. The need for a team of experts, with sufficient backup, to support the compressed video project is critical and well documented in the literature. The impact of participation upon the promotion and tenure potential of the faculty is unknown. Faculty are uncertain about the weight these activities will have when promotion and tenure credentials are reviewed by the college and university committees. When instructors teach on compressed video, the evaluations have been consistently lower.

Other departments at the University of Oklahoma are beginning to report the experiences they are having with the compressed video system. A studio at the Health Sciences Center on the Oklahoma City campus is used for courses in nursing. Bircher reports little interaction related to course content, a loss of "all nonverbal and empathic communication", and a "loss of finer vocal nuances: interest, concern, joy, curiosity, etc." (Bircher 1992, p.1). In her experience, the technology "deprives the experienced teacher of the use of his or her expertise [and] reduces him or her to the level of a novice teacher" (Bircher 1992, p. 2).

In summary, the School's experience to date is mixed about the use of this video technology. On the positive side are several features. One, the current arrangement saves 10 days of research time each term for the faculty who are using it. Two, and unexpectedly, we quickly discovered that the system could be used for one-on-one advising during registration periods, allowing Tulsa students to talk to their own faculty advisors in Norman.

On the negative side are problems caused by the steep learning curve of this technically opaque system. Unsatisfactory microphones have forced student-to-teacher and student-to-student audio interaction to be either minimal or artificial and contrived for the class sizes we have: lecturing is facilitated, the unincumbered free flowing interaction of graduate education is not. Also, because of the technical difficulties that had to be solved on-the-fly, our students have lived through some very rough sessions. As a result, they perceive, generally, that they are getting less for their money, though we have evidence to the contrary.

Future Needs

Is compressed video an appropriate technology for distance education? Additional research should focus on the relationship between learning and learner perceptions of the experience. A more practical concern relates to the importance of involving both learners and practitioners in a decision to implement a new delivery system, ensuring that all understand the capabilities and limitations of the media employed. The role of student support groups should be investigated and encouraged. Additional research should examine the role of the distant site facilitator, addressing required competencies and training.

References

Haynes, Kathleen J. M. and Swisher, Robert (1992). "Student and Faculty Attitudes Toward Compressed Video Instruction," *Journal of Interactive Television 1*(1): 55-62.

Swisher, R., Spitzer, K. L., Spriestersbach, B., Markus, T., & Burris, J. M. (1991). Telecommunications for School Library Media Centers. *School Library Media Quarterly 19*(3), 153-160.

Clark, R. E. and Salomon, G. (1986). "Media in Teaching." In M. C. Wittrock (Ed.), *Handbook of Research on Teaching* (3rd ed.) (p. 472). New York: McMillan.

Petkovich, M. D. and Tennyson, R. D. (1984). "Clark's Learning from Media: A Critique," *Educational Communication and Technology Journal 32*:233-37.

Dillon, C., Haynes, K. J. M., and Price, M. (1990). "The Impact of Compressed Video Upon Student Interaction and Learning in a Graduate Library Studies Class." In B. S. Clough (Ed.), *Proceedings of the 9th Annual Conference of Canadian Association for the Study of Adult Education* (pp.125-130). Victoria, British Columbia, Canada: University of Victoria.

Haynes, K. J. M. and Dillon, C. (1992). "Distance Education: Learning Outcomes, Interaction, and Attitudes." *Journal of Education for Library and Information Science 33*: 35-45.

Bircher, Andrea U. (1992). "On the Advent of Compressed- Video Distance Teaching: An Experiential Teacher Perspective," Oklahoma Conference, American Association of University Professors Newsletter May:1-2.

Vermont Technical College

Darrell Thompson and Suzie Wilson
VIT Coordinators

Randolph Center, VT 05061
voice: (802) 728-3391

Vermont Interactive Television

What is Vermont Interactive Television?

Vermont Interactive Television (VIT) is a demonstration project that will link Vermont Technical College in Randolph Center and North Country Area Vocational Center in Newport with interactive television from January 11 to May 1, 1988. This joint project involves the Vermont Department of Education; the Vermont Agency of Economic Development and Community Affairs; New England Telephone; and the Vermont Department of Employment and Training, along with North Country Area Vocational Center and the Vermont State Colleges System, which is made up of Vermont Technical College , Community College of Vermont, Lyndon State College, Johnson State College, and Castleton State College.

What Is Interactive Television?

Interactive Television is an instructional and teleconferencing medium which, via the telephone networks, links two or more locations with two-way audio and visual communication. In other words, people in Newport and Randolph Center will be able to see and hear each other at the same time!

What is the Project's Purpose?

The purpose of the VIT project is to explore the potential of interactive television as part of a new statewide telecommunications system. This will be accomplished by demonstrating its many uses, including delivery of academic courses, workshops, seminars, meetings, and human resource development training programs for businesses, government agencies, non-profit organizations and educational institutions. Simply stated, the system would enable individuals throughout Vermont to meet, exchange ideas, and learn without the necessity of leaving their locale.

How Can I Get Involved?

To define the limits of the system, we are actively seeking as many different uses as possible. If your organization has a potential use for Vermont Interactive Television's diverse applications, we want to talk with you about your ideas.

Northern Virginia Community College

Steven G. Sachs
Associate Dean

Instructional Technologies and Extended Learning
Northern Virginia Community College
8333 Little River Turnpike
Annandale, VA 22003-3796
voice: (703) 323-3371
fax: (703) 323-3392

Compressed video was first used for classes at NVCC beginning in the fall semester of 1990. The equipment was actually delivered in March of 1989 and took almost a full year to install and debug.

The decision to use compressed video was less systematic and more pragmatic than it should have been. NVCC is composed of five campuses, each in different political jurisdictions. Each jurisdiction is served by at least one cable TV system, and sometimes more than one. At least one of our major jurisdictions does not have a campus of its own. In the mid-1980's the largest political jurisdiction, Fairfax County, awarded a cable-TV franchise. NVCC became the headend of one channel at that time, and received funds from the cable company for several projects. One was to equip the headend and studios. A second was to interconnect our campuses. It was thought at that time (by my predecessor) that this would also allow us to interconnect to other cable-TV systems. The original "interconnect" grant from the cable-TV company was not really for money. Instead, it was simply a commitment to interconnect the campuses. My predecessor thought it would be better to have the money (for a plan he had in mind) and negotiated a cash settlement of, I believe, $100,000. An additional $450,000 in funds were obtained from the Virginia General Assembly to complete the interconnection among campuses.

He commissioned several studies over the next year to identify the best strategy for connecting the campuses with ITFS or microwave and found that the need for towers and potential lack of available channels were serious impediments. He also determined that we probably had enough seed money to build an integrated voice-data and video system interconnecting the campuses instead of just a video system. He also became aware of compressed video (by CLI) at about this time—late 1986, early 1987. Work was begun on an RFP for the voice-data-video system. The team working on it involved him, the Director of the NVCC Computer Center, representatives from the college purchasing department, representatives of the state department of information technology, and of the state purchasing department who actually controlled the process and would make the purchase for us. A consulting company familiar with this process was also heavily involved. The package went out for bid in fall 1987 with an opening date in February, 1988.

The package left open the technology that could be used for interconnecting the campuses, compressed video was listed as an acceptable option. The significant feature of the system was that it had to be a completely turn-key operation. The vendor would be responsible for every aspect of installation, training and documentation

While the bids were out, my predecessor left and I inherited the project. Also during this time, we became aware of the compressed video technology from VideoTelecom. When bids were opened, there were only four bidders and all proposed some form of compressed video from a variety of different companies. While we had very detailed selection criteria to evaluate the bids, we also had some informal ideas on what we wanted in a video system. None of the bids looked promising in this regard. The biggest flaws were in the switching systems to allow multi-point transmissions, cost and experience of the vendors. We wrote some new specifications, based on what we had learned from VideoTelecom, and had the vendors rebid that portion during the negotiations. Several came back with VideoTelecom equipment. The main features of VideoTelecom that were significant to us were: their hand-held remote controls, their picture quality at low speeds, their video bridge for multipoint transmission, their software-based system (allowing for easy upgrade) and the relatively low cost for codecs.

Even though we negotiated from February through July, we could not get all parties on either side to reach agreement. Other changes at the college during the Spring forced us to abandon the project. We were left with a problem, though. The money from the General

Assembly had to be spent by June 30, 1989 to interconnect the campuses, and much of the money from the cable-TV system had already been spent on the failed voice-data-video project. Therefore, by fall of 1988 we had to go back out to bid for a video system alone. There was no time to re-think the project so we rebid compressed video since we had some idea of the cost and knew we could bring that in for the funds available. However, this time we could not bid a turn-key system. Instead, we had to bid both the codecs and the video bridge separately. Only after those bids were open could we buy components such as cameras and cables, etc. with the left over money. The college became its own integrator.

In retrospect, there were a lot of things about compressed video we had not thought about and a lot that changed with the technology while we were in the process of bidding and installing the system. For example, we originally planned for a portable system that could be moved from classroom to conference room. However, with the system we bought, there were too many connections to make, the system was too sensitive and the audio was too hard to adjust to make this practical. We did not anticipate the need for our technician to monitor the system. We did not anticipate the high maintenance cost for the codecs and DVBX (as compared to other video equipment and systems). And, we did not anticipate the problems we have had with our computer center that multiplexes our signal onto the college data lines connecting the campuses. Furthermore, our needs have changed in the years between the inception of the system and its installation and use. We have more need for a system that interconnects cable-TV systems and gets us off-campus to other sites than one that interconnects the campuses and can go nowhere else.

The ultimate decision to use compressed video was really made by the Associate Dean, my predecessor, and myself. Because we originally did not bid a video system alone, we received the initial bids for the voice-data-video system from large phone company vendors with the video component as almost an after-thought or aside. Therefore, we never really received well thought out and well presented bids from all the major compressed video manufacturers or from major system integrator. In hindsight, this was too bad. One problem in Virginia, though, is that it is very hard and very time consuming to do a Request-for-Proposals (RFP) where broad system criteria are specified and vendors make proposals for meeting those needs, as compared to Request-for-Bids (RFB) where bids on specific equipment are requested. In the end, time constraints forced us to issue an RFB for codecs that could do certain things and had certain features instead of really having a shoot-out among various companies and strategies.

Our compressed video runs on half of the T-1 lines that currently carry the college data between the campuses. In fact, the college computer center is located directly below our television center. Our DVBX (the video bridge) is connected by thick, multi-line computer cable to multiplexers in the computer center. They take care of transmitting it on the T-1's that connect the center directly with each campus. At three of the outlying campuses, the signal comes off the T-1 through another multiplexer in a phone room and is carried by computer cable to the campus Audiovisual department. It goes through a simple ABCD switch (from our plans to make the system portable) to a classroom. This also made it possible for the system to be set up and tested in the AV department during installation. At the fourth distant campus we had to connect the AV department to the phone room with line drivers due to the distance involved. The line driver also let us use coax cable for the connection. The coax was easier to work with, but the line drivers cost $6,000 per pair.

Overall, the system cost about $550,000 to install. Over the past two years, more than 23 classes have served over 425 students. Dozens of meetings have been held over the system as well. Now that the equipment is out of warranty, it looks like on-going maintenance will run about $15,000 per year. At least $8,000 per year will be the maintenance agreement on the DVBX (video bridge). We could not afford maintenance agreements on the nine codecs. Our biggest surprises with the system are that we need to have at least 2-3 codecs repaired each year and that maintenance costs are so high and fluctuate so frequently. There have been three changes this year alone as the company changes its business plans and strategies. We started with time and materials which usually ranged from $500-1000 per repair. Then it went to a $1,500 flat fee. At that time a maintenance agreement was about $3,000 per codec. Now it is $3,000 flat fee per repair and maintenance agreements are about $2,000 per codec.

We have nine VideoTelecom CS-300 series codecs. One in each of the five classrooms (one per campus) that are the primary sites. We have one in our control room that the technician uses to help set-up and monitor classes and meetings. We have one in another teleconference receive room at our television center that we can use for connecting with the regular classroom at the center when we want to use two sites for testing or training. The other two codecs we use for spares. It was originally planned that we would have one in a second building at our largest campus and one in the central administration building also at that campus. However, we have not been able to get the necessary cabling across the campus. The amount of technician time required in operating the equipment in the first year, and the need to have spare codecs to replace units that break down have discouraged us from this plan.

Each room is equipped with three cameras. Two Panasonic WDVM-5000 cameras with zoom lenses—one focused on the instructor and one focused on the students, plus an Elmo copy stand camera. We use Darome push-to-talk microphones for the students (1 mic for every 2 students). The mics are connected with 2 or 3 in series to in inexpensive Shure mixer. The instructor wears a lavaliere microphone that is also connected to the mixer. We have two TV monitors and a VCR in the back of each room. One monitor shows the video sources in that room. The other shows a remote site. The system uses audio switching or can be set to autocycle showing each remote site on a pre-set time schedule. We take the video signal out of the remote site monitor and run it through an RF-modulator and send an RF signal to one or two TV sets in the front of the room. Students watch these TV sets. The audio also comes out of these TV sets. The instructor switches cameras in the classroom through a hand-held remote control. We have added one more Panasonic camera to the front of each room at a lower angle than the one that currently shows the students. This new camera will be used for meetings when there are only a few participants. Each room also has a simple autodial speakerphone so the instructor can phone the other rooms or call a technician for help. Our back-up system uses the Darome microphones already in place by connecting them to a Darome convener and we just run an audio conference over phone lines. This is being replaced with Polycom Soundstation audioconferencing units with built in microphones, speaker and phone dialing keypad.

The system is managed by our college television center staff. We have a technician who sets up the conferences and provides help by phone or directly over the system. At each remote campus the AV staff provides assistance as needed. Scheduling is done through the Associate Dean's office. In each room, the instructor or the students operate the system—they even have to turn it on if the AV department forgets. (We have everything connected so it is a one-button on system.) The technician at our television center has many other duties, so does not sit and watch every class or meeting once it is set up and appears to be operating well.

West Virginia Northern Community College

Charles A. Julian
Director of Library Services and Distance Education

West Virginia Northern Community College
College Square
Wheeling, WV 26003-3699
voice: (304) 233-5900
fax: (304) 233-5900 - ask for fax machine

Telecommunications System

The foundation of the telecommunications system at West Virginia Northern Community College is an interactive audio, video, and data network linking the central Wheeling campus to the New Martinsville campus, 38 miles to the south. Identical facility configurations at either site enable an instructor to vary the send and remote sites in accordance with the specific requirements for particular courses.

A specially equipped room is utilized on each campus for the telecommunicated instruction. Each room contains three Sony DXC-3000 charge-coupled device color cameras capable of video transmission. One camera is aimed at the instructional console, one camera is aimed at students in the classroom, while the third camera console/teaching lectern consists of the routing switches necessary for the control of video images, two rack-mounted video recorders, the copy stand area, and a black and white videowriter. All outgoing video images, including full-motion videotapes, pass through the videowriter and may be manipulated by instructors.

Video images are viewed by students on four 245 inch color monitors hung from the ceiling. Audio is transmitted via a Shure teleconferencing multi-microphone system utilizing voice-activated microphone/speaker modules hung from the classroom ceiling. The audio teleconferencing system operates in a quasi-duplex mode with rapid, automatic switching between transmit and receive and full interrupt capabilities. The instructor monitors students at the remote site with a Program Receive monitor and is able to view transmitted video images via a console-mounted monitor or a separate monitor hung from the classroom ceiling.

Signals are transmitted via a T-1 wide band telephone line. Video and audio signals are encoded/decoded via two CLI Rembrandt video transmission systems, i.e., codecs. A codec is hooked into the teleconferencing system at each site. The configuration of equipment enables the instructor to fully control video and audio signals transmitted to and received by students. No technicians, producers, or engineers are needed to operate this system — it is entirely instructor-driven.

Six pilot classes with a combined student enrollment of 226 were initially taught. These classes included Anatomy & Physiology II, Advanced BASIC Programming, World Cultures II, Small Business Management, Calculus I, and Simple Health Problems. Currently thirteen classes are taught on the system which has enabled the college to offer sections of courses to students who would not previously have had access to them. Additionally, the most qualified instructor may now teach a course section whether that instructor is based at the Wheeling or New Martinsville campus. Faculty travel will also be hopefully reduced.

Other components of the system include the ability to transmit microcomputer signals and data from one campus to another, the use of facsimile machines to speed the transmission of printed data, and a connection with earth satellite dishes for receipt of externally broadcast signals.

SECTION II

K-12 Schools and Combined Networks

St. Vrain Valley School District, Colorado

Randall W. Donahoo
Director of Information Technology

395 S. Pratt Parkway
Longmont, CO 80501
voice: (303) 772-4113
fax: (303) 776-2562

We use compressed video running 768 kbps on leased T-1 to connect a classroom in our smallest 7-12 school to a classroom in one of our two largest 9-12 schools. Classes are taught in both directions. The courses to be taught each year are determined by the principals of the two schools based upon what their students need and the teachers available to teach those courses. From the time we began in 1991, we have "teletaught" French I and II, calculus, bookkeeping, psychology, and health.

Background

Before installing this system, I studied IFTS, microwave, and cable operator interconnects. Compressed video and T-1 proved to be the only affordable system which met our requirements for a fully interactive video and audio delivery system.

We purchased the VideoTelecom CS350 codecs and most of the video equipment from US West, from whom we also lease the T-1 lines. Buyers should be aware that US West is not really a distance learning vendor. It is a teleconferencing vendor, and company representatives are still learning their own systems. They do not yet understand classroom needs. We've had to make many adjustments in our equipment arrangements, but we knew that would be the case. Generally speaking, the system works well.

Classroom Equipment

Each of our schools is equipped with an Elmo Presenter, a teacher camera, a student camera, two monitors for the teacher to view, two monitors for the students to view, a fax machine with phone, a VHS video cassette recorder, pancake mics, and a microphone mixer. The room at Skyline High School is larger than the room at Lyons High School, so Skyline's requires more microphones.

An innovative media specialist at Lyons has connected both an Apple IIe and a Macintosh to the system at various times for data transmission. Also, the IBM-PC internal to the VideoTelecom equipment can be used for data transmission and "slide show" delivery.

Costs

Our initial capital investment was about $50,000 per school. We pay about $640 per month for the leased T-1 line, even during the summer months when it is unused. Although we could use simply one-half of that line for our distance education delivery, since fractional T-1 is not available to us, we will soon incorporate the use of the other half into our phone and data systems.

Future

It is our intention to expand teleteaching capabilities to all our six high schools. To do so, we'll install a DVBX at a central location and connect all schools there. This will enable us to run classes point to multiple-point. As we expand our compressed video network, we will select vendors via competitive bids and requests for proposals. We may even be able to mix our delivery system using cable and fiber for some portions of the network.

We foresee crossing school district lines in order to connect our schools with other high schools, with a community college, and with a nearby university. We have been working with our BOCES over the past two years to develop connections with other networks in the state.

Support

We have an audiovisual technician in our district service shop who responds instantly to system failures. He has toll-free telephone support from US West, and the support team has slowly developed the knowledge and strategies to actually help us solve problems rather swiftly.

However, teachers really need lots of school-level support too. Someone at each school needs to be familiar with the equipment and its operation so he or she can serve as "first alert" help when something goes wrong. Both the principal and the media specialist at one of our schools have teamed up to fill this need. The other school's teachers still lack real on-site support.

Concerns & Recommendations

1. Don't use a VCR for video delivery over a compressed video system. If possible, deliver a tape to each site instead.

2. Our French teacher has complained about two conditions which are common to compressed video. One, the lip-to-voice sync is important in foreign language instruction, so compressed video presents a handicap for foreign language instruction, in her opinion. Two, don't believe VideoTelecom's promise that the system will not "clip" audio. A louder voice will always clip off a quieter voice, and you can only hear one site at a time. This poses a problem for our French teacher who expects audio over the system to allow simultaneous talking such as goes on in all classrooms, especially in her foreign language classroom.

3. Disparate school schedules create problems. Expect headaches if participating schools are not on the same daily schedule.

The Utah EDNET System

Edward N. Ridges
Associate Director, Utah Education Network

University of Utah
Media Services - Building 002
Salt Lake City, UT 84112
voice: (801) 581-4553
fax: (801) 581-5735

The Utah EDNET system presently consists of 44 sites connected by microwave. The initial charge, which has been completed, was to connect all higher educational institutions within the state. Additionally, several high schools, a correctional facility, and the State Office of Education have all joined the system.

When did you start using compressed video and how did you decide to use compressed video as opposed to other telecommunications systems?
As we now look to the future, we have selected the compressed video as the distribution system of choice. This decision was made both politically and practically. Politically it is felt that the bandwidth required to support an interactive video/data system would result in an upgrade to the existing phone services in some of the rural parts of the state. Thus, the implementation of the compressed video system results in an upgrade of the telecommunications infrastructure in these remote areas. Practically, it makes sense now that the technology has evolved to a satisfactory level, to use existing distribution systems which others will install and maintain, thus eliminating the necessity for EDNET to essentially duplicate, or bypass, some of the commercially available services. When the initial microwave installation was begun, commercial products and distribution systems were not available to provide the required bandwidth.

Who made the decisions about developing a compressed video network?
The decisions relating to the use of compressed video were made jointly by representatives of both EDNET and the planned recipients which now consist of all of the rural high schools in the state of Utah. Our present efforts will result in connections to 57 new sites using the compressed video technology.

Who, why, when, where, and how was vendor selection made?
We are presently in the process of identifying a vendor. We began this process by hosting a nationwide codec shootout. We invited all eight codec vendors to participate in this event and configured the equipment in such a fashion that the evaluators were unable to determine whose codec was being demonstrated. We developed our own tape which included much more action than the standard video conference will include. Over the course of two days, we saw presentations from 7 of the 8 participants. We required the demonstrations to be H.261 compatible and to meet all iterations of the CCITT standards. This effort resulted in a short list of 4 vendors, each of whose products appear to meet our needs. Subsequent to the shootout, several educators approached us with concerns about the picture quality. Consequently, U. S. WEST and VideoTelecom brought in 4 units and installed them in our existing network at three sites and at a new site which is presently unserved by EDNET. We used this equipment for a 2

week period for demonstration, for course work, for actual class work, and for several meetings. We received approval on its future use as an educational delivery system.

Our plans are to use existing telephone services within the state in what we believe is an unique agreement. US WEST, GTE, and the Rural Exchange Carriers of Utah have all agreed to use the same tariffs and provide the same services. As a result, we do not have to negotiate individual agreements with many different telephone providers. Thus, we will end up with a delivery system that includes both the existing full motion broadcast quality microwave system and the compressed video T-1 based delivery system. This network will also include the ability to receive satellite delivered programming, and an ITFS component in the Salt Lake City area.

Costs of Installation and Delivery

We are still in the process of identifying a vendor, making the installation arrangements, and refining the T-1 monthly costs.

The system uses consist of:
University and College level courses
High school classes
Concurrent enrollment courses
Extension/Adult Education courses
Applied technology courses specific governmental agency classes such as Corrections, EMT
    recertification, and teacher certification
Administrative meetings
Occasional one on one interactions for ad hoc events

Describe facilities:
Each of the end sites provides a room in which the "receive site" equipment is installed. The rooms need to be adequate in terms of acoustics, lighting, ambient noise level, and configuration. Because the system has occupied rooms at the end sites which were already existing, we have very few "ideal" sites, but the nature of the technology and the users is forgiving enough that this has not been a serious impediment.

Who operates the facilities?
Each end site has a "site facilitator" who is trained by EDNET to operate the studio equipment. Each end site has at least one backup person for this site facilitator. The overall system is operated from a Technical Operating Center (TOC) in Salt Lake City and is staffed by EDNET technicians 16 hours a day. These technicians assist in configuring the system for particular events, in switching between sites in the case of a multiple site event, and trouble shooting difficulties with the local site facilitator.

Who schedules the network?
The EDNET office in Salt Lake City handles the scheduling process. Anyone who wishes to use the system contacts this office and works out the specifics in terms of times and locations required for their activity. There is a process for resolving conflicting requests. I have attached a copy of the scheduling process. This process was developed by EDNET staff and subsequently ratified by the governing consortium.

What rates do you use?
We have selected the quarter T-1 364 KBS as the speed of choice. This allows a significant portion of the remaining line capacity to be used for data transmission. We anticipate that the data traffic side of the system will be equally as desired as the video teleconferencing capacity.

What peripherals do you have attached?
As we are still in the design phase of the compressed video component, some of this will be speculation. We are planning to have faxes, access to CD ROMS, both IBM and Apple PC capability, some sort of a graphics interface such as the PenPal, an Elmo Presenter, video recorder, and modems as required.

Do you plan to use the public switched 56 network?
We won't initially use the switched 56 network, but will configure one of our HUB sites so that this is an option if required.

What hardware model and brand are you using?
We are just completing the RFP. The vendor, models, and exact equipment compliment will be selected at the conclusion of the proposal evaluation process. We plan on minimum of one camera and one monitor per site - with HUB sites likely to have two or three cameras and multiple monitors.

Did you conduct a needs assessment?
Some preliminary needs assessment work has been completed and a formal needs assessment will be completed by December 1992. The final system configuration will be developed to match the needs identified in this effort. It will be constructed in a modular form so that it can evolve to match the changing needs which the future will bring.

Utah is proud of its distance learning efforts and the opportunities for equality of education that are being provided to its citizens. The cooperation of all involved make this complex endeavor possible and successful.

SECTION III

Government
and
Commercial Users

United American Reporting Services, Inc.

David B. Jackson
Affiliate of LINC

2214 N. Akard, Suite 600
Dallas, TX 75201
voice: (214) 855-5300
fax: (214) 855-1478

When did you start using compressed video?
Our firm started using compressed video in July of 1989.

How did you decide to use compressed video as opposed to other telecommunications systems?
We are a court reporting firm, and we felt it very important that attorneys have the ability to see the person they are interviewing or taking depositions from.

Who made the decisions about developing a compressed video network?
I was among a group of individual reporting firms who made the decision to form a network of court reporting forms offering these services to attorneys.

Who, why, when, where and how was vendor selection made?
Our group of reping firms held a "vendor competition" in Atlanta where we saw presentations made by all three of the major players in compressed video at that time: VideoTelecom, CLI and PictureTel. We chose VideoTelecom because of its range of speeds, computer functionality, quality of compression and price.

What delivery system(s) do you use?
Our network uses Sprint's fiber, T-1 Meeting Channel for its connectivity.

What are the costs of installation and delivery?
Our site here at United American Reporting Services in Dallas has a monthly T-1 access charge of $503.00 per month. Our installation was approximately $2,500.00.

Please describe each application that is presently using the compressed video network.
Our system is currently being used most by corporations in a public room environment. Our efforts to successfully market to attorneys has thus far been somewhat disappointing.

Describe the facilities being used.
We provide a conferencing room environment much like any attorney's office would provide with a console cabinet housing the video equipment.

Who operates the facilities?
We have three people trained in the operation of our equipment. They perform other duties in our business and fill in the video conference area on an as-available basis.

Who schedules the network?
Sprint's Meeting Channel, for the most part, schedules our conference center.

What are the policies, procedures and priorities used in scheduling the network? Who developed these?
Our operating policies are set out in Sprint's guidelines and we follow them in our own private use as well.

What rate(s) do you use for transmission? Why?
Transmission speeds vary according to customer desire. If we are setting up a deposition, however, we attempt to convince the attorneys they need to transmit at 768 kbps. In a deposition environment it is very important to keep lag-time to a minimum as the court reporter is charged with the responsibility of writing down every word said. If the slower speeds are attempted it creates the problem of people talking over each other inadvertently.

What peripherals do you have attached to the system and how are they used?
In our room configuration we attempted to cover every possible need the attorneys may have, which was one of the reasons for selecting the VideoTelecom codec. One of the first questions we received from attorneys we surveyed was: "How do I know there's not someone in the room holding up cue cards?" We installed additional cameras in each room set on the entire room with ability for the attorney at the remote site to select that camera at any time. We also provide in-band fax capabilities so the attorneys can actually "hand" the witness a document. Our center provides time-date generated videoequipment that meets the guidelines set up by the National Court Reporters Association's Certified Legal Video Specialist program, so if need be, a CLVS can come into our room and hook into our system and make a videotape of the witness that can be played in court. Our center provides, additionally, the Pen Pal graphics with a high resolution slide capability and an Elmo document camera.

Are you presently using (or do you plan to use) the public switched 56 network for interstate or international communications?
We are not planning to use Switched 56.

What hardware model and brand are you using? How is your system configured?
We are using VideoTelecom's latest software for its 350 series codec.

Did you conduct a needs assessment? If so please describe.
We did not conduct a needs assessment.

Other comments or information?
I personally feel that videoconferencing will become successful when transmission costs come down considerably and anyone can get anywhere. Right now networks are too pigeon-holed and it is not convenient for users to hook up to the people they need to hook up to.

The ability to see a person while you're discussing a matter is more significant when you've never met that person before. If you are already familiar with a person's appearance and demeanor, a telephone call is pretty strong competition to the videoconference; and the costs and convenience of the telephone puts it over the top in most cases.

We have always felt our application was perfect for videoconferencing. The witness' appearance and demeanor are extremely important in determining credibility. The telephone only on rare occasion is competition for a videoconference in our application. Our competition is the cost of transmission versus travel. If there's the slightest chance a deposition will go longer than three hours, the attorneys would probably be better off having gone in person at today's transmission costs.

Joint Warfare Center

LTC Herb Bruse

Joint Warfare Center
JWC Bldg. 90065
Hurlburt Fld, FL 32544-5000
voice: (904) 884-7720
fax: (904) 884-5316

(In response to our request for information, we received permission to reprint this article from COMMUNICATIONS NEWS - October 1991.)

Joint Warfare Center uses media-conferencing to enhance war games.

The U.S. Military, a recognized leader in developing and implementing cutting-edge technology, several decades ago began harnessing the power of computers to replicate war tactics and maneuvers that its forces employ on land and in the air, sea, and space.

The reasons are obvious: Using war-game simulation software and state-of-the-art computer hardware to train thousands of men and women in the Army, Navy, Air Force, and Marine Corps is often safer, quicker, cheaper, and more practical than deploying them to a field or sea exercise location.

The Joint Warfare Center, an organization that supports the Commander in Chief, Joint Task Forces, and unified and specified commands and services worldwide, has blended advanced videoconferencing technology with war game simulation technology to increase interactive participation to a larger number of individuals engaged in these important training vehicles.

The added benefits to the military--and, thus, the U.S. taxpayer--are cost and productivity savings derived from eliminating large troop deployment.

In 1990, the Joint Warfare Center purchased six PC-based videoconferencing units and a multi-way switching unit (Digital Video Branch Exchange or DVBX) manufactured by VideoTelecom Corp. and sold by CAE Link. To meet the Joint Warfare Center's requirement for portability and durability, VideoTelecom and CAE Link custom-made rugged carrying cases for all of the units.

VideoTelecom, of Austin, Texas, builds systems unique in functionality, graphics and electronic annotation (Pen Pal Graphics). CAE Link, based in Alexandria, Virginia, specializes in selling training equipment and services to the military. These functions, in addition to audio and video capabilities, make up mediaconferencing.

"Videoconferencing works well in conjunction with war-game simulation because exercise participants can see and share data and information in real time, in color and without delay," says Lt. Col. Dennis Foggy, chief, Support Division of the Joint Warfare Center.

"The war-game simulation exercises we support are customized to fit the objectives as determined by the supported Commanders in Chief. When complemented with videoconferencing, as was the case recently with an exercise involving the Senior Service Colleges, technology is employed at its best," says Army Lt. Col. Herb Bruse, information officer for the Joint Warfare Center.

The Senior Service Colleges include the Army War College in Carlisle, Pa.; the Air Force War College in Montgomery, Ala.: the National Defense University in Washington, D.C.; and the Navy War College in Newport, R.I. Thus, these career exposed to the latest in state-of-the-art technology.

Lt. Col. Foggy and Lt. Col. Bruse note the Central Command (CENTCOM) staff benefited from a computer-driven war-game exercise supplemented with videoconferencing systems provided by the Joint Warfare Center immediately prior to their deployment to Operation Desert Shield.

Called Internal Look '90, the exercise involved a myriad of high-level staff officers participating from locations scattered throughout the United States. Videoconferencing connected three of the major locations in Florida-Hurlburt Field, Duke Field, and MacDill Air Force Base near Tampa (25 and 250 miles, respectively, from Hurlburt Field).

The Joint Warfare Center also video-taped the interactive videoconference sessions.

"Using the videoconferencing systems, we, in essence, transported exercise staffs at these geographically dispersed locations and put them in the same room.

"For Internal Look '90, we initially planned to transmit at 768 kb/s, but we found the picture quality at 384 kb/s was more than adequate for our needs and saved us money." says Lt. Col. Bruse.

"We did this non-stop for 10 days without any serious obstacles."

Recently, the Joint Warfare Center mobilized two videoconferencing suites during the Joint Land Air Space and Sea (JLASS) exercise for the Senior Service Colleges.

This exercise lasted 12 days and the videoconferencing sessions ran flawlessly, according to Lt. Col. Bruse.

"Because of the on-base cable restrictions, we transmitted at 256 kb/s for the JLASS exercise with only a minimum sacrifice to video quality," says Lt. Col. Foggy.

"The systems enabled us to interactively display graphics, maps, and drawings; make instantaneous on—screen changes to those documents using the Pen Pal Graphics tablet; capture an image as a slide; share the data between the videoconferencing participants, and make videotape records of briefings and presentations.

"Videoconferencing proved to be a valuable tool that greatly enhanced the information exchange."

U S WEST
Videoconferencing Networks

Laura Simmons-Lewis

US West
1420 - 5th Avenue, Suite 1400
Seattle, WA 98101
voice: (206) 346-8446
fax: (206) 346-8535

U S WEST is one of the seven regional bell operating companies made up of the former Pacific Northwest Bell, Mountain Bell and Northwestern Bell. The U S WEST territory is made up of the 14 western states excluding California and Nevada. Most of our reporting structures and work groups are spread throughout most of the territory, with concentrations of offices in Minneapolis, Denver, Omaha, Salt Lake, Phoenix, Boise, Portland and Seattle. U S WEST provides regulated and unregulated communications products and services: Voice, data, and videoconferencing equipment is sold from our non-regulated company; analog and digital network services on copper and fiber with transmission from POTS to high speed, including frame relay and SMDS are provided from the regulated company.

Three U S WEST Videoconferencing Networks

U S WEST has three interactive videoconferencing networks in use throughout the company. In addition, there is a corporate business television network which is used for informational programming for the company. The videoconferencing networks were established to support sales of this product with demonstrations, trade shows and promotional events; for sales and corporate training; for all types of meetings; to reduce travel expense while increasing communications capabilities; to recover lost productive time spent in transit; and, as a quality of life issue, to help relieve employee stress associated with large amounts of travel.

U S WEST uses, and is a reseller of, VideoTelecom products. Four custom rooms were the first rooms on the general use network; all additional rooms were equipped with fully featured Benchmark 225 systems; transport is dedicated DS1 operating at 384 kbps. With the exception of the four custom rooms and the corporate training classrooms, all systems have been installed in existing conference room with no facilities modifications. Most of these work very well, and some will eventually get lighting and furniture upgrades.

Marketing Network

- 11 rooms with modular units located in 9 states
- 5 more rooms to be added in 1993
- installed in existing conference rooms with no facilities modifications
- full system capabilities

- 1 multiway device
- digital crossconnects in the central office extend port capacity of multiway units with drop-and-insert function
- gateway to general use network

Corporate General Use Network

- 60 rooms in 50 sites in the 14 states
- 80 by fourth quarter 1992
- possibly 120 rooms 1994
- 13 multiway units located in 4 cities operating in tandem
- digital crossconnects in central offices to extend capacities of the multiway units with drop-and-insert function
- gateway to marketing network

Corporate Training Network

- 11 classrooms
- 1 multi way device
- transport provided by general use network

System Management

The general use network has installed mainframe software for scheduling and system management. This is provided to both marketing and corporate training as an internally contracted service.

Teechnical Service Center

To provide technical support for our customers and marketing network, the Technical Service Center was established. Standard services and support include:

- Technical support for customers & the market unit
- 800 number 24 hours/7 days per week assistance
- On-line technicians Monday through Friday 8 TO 5 CST
- After hours call back within one hour
- Attendant screening for customer site locator number and authorized caller
- On line technician provides
    * troubleshooting via analog telephone line
    * coordination of overnight parts replacement when necessary
    * network repair coordination—to interexchange carriers within and outside U S WEST operations area
    * remote software loading and/or remote assistance in on-site loading

Lessons Learned in Establishing Networks

In making this a success story, we learned many things which might be helpful to others who are building networks:

1.   There needs to be close agreement between management of the buyer and the provider of the service regarding interaction with vendor. Roles need to be defined at each level of the installation, from ordering, installation and training to maintenance and Q&A.

2.   Get commitment in the beginning, from the senior management team, to support the project, take the training and to start using the system right away.

3.   Get commitment that all managers and professionals will use the equipment and attend training.

4.   There needs to be positive communication through all the organization's media of these commitments.

5.   There needs to be commitment in terms of budget emphasis on "no travel funds, use videoconferencing instead". After all, it what we *inspect* that happens, not what we *expect*.

6.   Designate a project manager whose job it is to make sure everything happens on schedule and who has the authority to sort out difficulties, roadblocks and territorial issues. The project manager will be invaluable in minimizing these distractions.

    There will be territorial issues around technical operations, installation, conference room selection and administration, scheduling and on-going maintenance for each site on the network. We found that people were reluctant to give up a conference room for videoconferencing because they had to give up availability of that room in their own local schedules. Responding to this need, blocks of hours can be reserved and the room made unavailable for videoconferencing, but when it is designated for videoconferencing use, it is only available through the main scheduler.

    The U S WEST Videoconferencing Network Manager says "the videoconferencing network must be viewed as a whole network. The key to success in managing the network is centralized scheduling; control of the rooms is essential. This is the only way to guaranty no double bookings."

7.   There is a tendency by everyone to over-simplify videoconferencing systems, to underestimate the amount time it takes for installation, training. "After all, it's just a PC; or it's just a VCR or a camcorder". A general rule is that it always takes more time than you expect, from order entry and ship date to installation and cutover. Allow for this in your planning and you will minimize much of it.

8.   Establish a hotline to answer questions and talk users through system operations. Many of the problems we experienced disappeared when the Technical Service Center was established and taking calls. Almost no one reads the directions, they just start plugging in cables as if they knew what they were doing. Then they can't figure out why it won't work. We encourage them to call the hotline to minimize frustrations and get their system running quickly.

9.   To support the videoconferencing network, U S WEST has appointed a room administrator for each site. This person turns on the system, establishes the videoconference connection to the multiway unit and may also be responsible for programming the multiway. The room

administrator also trains meeting participants on system operation and sometimes advises on adaptation of presentation materials.

10. Internal billing may also be desireable in your organization. Develop a formula early on if you need it.

The U S WEST videoconferencing manager developed a productivity formula in order to get some idea of the financial benefits of using video for meetings. His approach if very conservative, but is easily justified

- determine the number of conferences during the period
- determine the number of sites involved in each conference
- compute number of trips avoided
- assumption: for any given conference, at least one attendee at all but the originating site must travel——

For example:
  3 cities = 2 trips of one day avoided
  6 cities = 5 trips avoided
  14 cities = 13 trips avoided

11. A major issue will be adaptation of materials and styles for meetings, classes or any kind of presentation.

Some examples:

U S WEST Corporate Training spent one year adapting material before teaching any course.

A Colorado school district began teaching and then decided to bring in a consultant to help adapt teaching materials and develop contracts with students on appropriate behavior and involvement in the classes. Satisfaction dramatically increased as a result of this work.

At the University of Wyoming, the Extended Studies department coaches instructors on adaptation of materials and styles before the courses are offered. This was very helpful although the instructor I talked with said that she continued making changes as she became more comfortable with the videoconferencing system.

Also at the University of Wyoming, a Director in the College of Education said that you must change what you are doing every three to four or five minutes or the distant students "go into television watching behavior. Their eyes glass over, they kick back, relax and tune out interactivity and just watch the class."

My own experience with a presentation from Seattle to Portland and Denver taught me an important lesson. I expected to be alone in Seattle with three people in the other two locations. It turned out that I had eleven people with me in Seattle. I had positioned myself at the controls, near the videoconferencing equipment, with the people sitting around the table to my left. As I presented, I was either talking to the distant locations with my back to my room, or I was talking to those in my room with my back to the camera and the distant rooms. The people in my room felt comfortable interrupting me with questions, not paying any attention to the distant rooms. The people in Portland and Denver also felt at ease talking among themselves. The result was that the presentation seemed disorganized. In the future, I will give control of the videoconferencing system to someone else and make my presentation from the head of the table where I can see both those in my room and the distant rooms.

CONCLUSION

To determine if videoconferencing at U S WEST is a success , we need to address the original objectives:

- Reduction of travel expense
- Increase communications capability
- Recover productive time being spent in transit
- Restore individual energy and equilibrium—Quality of life/time

Using the measurable criteria of expense reduction, the videoconferencing installation at U S WEST was a huge success. Travel expense was reduced 24%, 1992 vs. 1991, year to date.

Using a testimonial is probably the best way to measure the other objectives. One director in the videoconferencing network group said it best:

> "I had meetings today with ten people in five cities and I still had dinner at home with my family."

His communications capabilities have been expanded, no time is lost in transit, and he feels a great improvement in the area of quality. By all measurements, videoconferencing at U S WEST is a good news success story.

APPENDICES

Appendix A

Guide to Planning Instruction for Compressed Video

Barbara Orde

Preface

"The best delivery system in the world is worthless if you have nothing to delivery" (Baltzer, 1981, p. 8).

A Guide to Instructional Design for the Compressed Video addresses the need for strong instructional planning in order to effectively and efficiently make use of the new technology of compressed video. Every successful lesson/unit/ curriculum is the result of hard work in the areas of planning and execution. The instructor, whether in education or business, spends an inordinate amount of time identifying the group to be taught, stating the objectives to be learned, selecting the appropriate vehicle to deliver the message, delivering the information, and evaluating the results. This publication will aid the novice as well as the experienced designer in creating a well laid out plan of instruction with particular attention to the mode of delivery—in this case, compressed video.

The introduction of new technology into an educational setting or the workplace creates a number of problems. Foremost among them is attitude. More often than not, the introduction of technology creates new routines and responsibilities. This in turn creates apprehension and doubt concerning the care and operation of the new technology. The questions that arise with the advent of any new technology have to be addressed to allay these fears and doubts if change is to be implemented. It is the purpose of this guide to provide ideas that will help users of compressed video to adapt to this technology as well as provide a format for the use of compressed video.

Introduction

Compressed video (CV) is one of the newest technologies of telecommunications. The term itself refers to the condensing of the signal so that it requires less space on the carrier whether it be land line (telephone), microwave, or satellite. A single frame is removed from the transmission at regular intervals. This "compression" allows for cheaper, more compact transmissions.

This capability has enabled technologists to develop the highly sophisticated communication system called compressed video. In addition to real time audio and video capabilities, it may also be "... configured to offer fax capabilities, computer generated graphics, videodisc, connectivity, capturing images and sending them as slides to the remote site, picture-in-picture with the ability for each site to see the other and their own simultaneously" (WCTLN Network

News, p. 4). Some systems also have hand-held remotes, self-diagnostics, and complete camera control.

Compressed video has much to offer. It's unique capability for real time interaction involving video, voice and data transmission allows people in two or more locations can see each other, talk, and send visual and hard copy information back and forth. This efficient, effective, and SWIFT communication is important to many people for many reasons. In education and business people can connect to each other for continuing education or training, planning and management, or other activities that would normally require travel for a face-to-face discussion.

Inservice/Preservice

The key to success in the implementation of any innovation lies in its acceptance. Without a positive outlook, the adaptation will be a struggle.   One way to accomplish this is through matching the strengths and interests of the instructor to the capabilities of the technology. A person who is already interested and willing to try something new, will be a leader and role model for others who may be more hesitant. In addition, an instructor that prefers to use visuals and illustrative materials will naturally be more comfortable with the corresponding features of the compressed video. A few people willing to take the lead will inspire others to follow. Be aware, however, that change can take a long time. For a list of references on "Change," see Exhibit A.

Inservice is the appropriate time to have potential instructors overcome their initial discomfort with a new technology. Be assured, technology anxiety is perfectly normal. Even experienced technicians become a little nervous when confronting something new. Besides using the strategies already mentioned, the person presenting the CV for the first time should pace the learning so a little new information is presented with only a moderate risk of failure, i.e. have students try or learn a single application at a time. Allow time for **successful** practice. This prevents information overload which results in confusion and frustration to the beginner.

W. J. McKeachie explains that curiosity is a primary motivating force. "...people are naturally curious. They seek new experiences, they enjoy learning new things; they find satisfaction in solving puzzles, perfecting skills, and developing competence" (p. 222). The introduction of CV can play on these natural phenomena and make the whole experience enjoyable and less stressful. One way to accomplish this is by relating the features CV has to offer to something practical it can be used for. For example, show how the science teacher can perform an experiment with the presenter and all participants at **both** sites can view it simultaneously.   This should spark curiosity instead of anxiety.

Another strategy is to demonstrate how the common can be presented in a novel way. An example of this would be the familiar use of slides. Slides can be saved and retrieved on the hard drive of some CV systems. The instructor simply saves the images before class time and calls them up later as needed. In order to give new users a feeling of success with some of these and other special functions, let them learn that they can master them on their own with little or no special help. There are many manuals and guides on getting to know these systems. See the "Support Materials" list in Exhibit C for listings.

When first using the compressed video, it is advisable to have a technician present during actual presentations to handle unforeseen problems and offer a degree of security to the novice user. This person can be there as a ready aid in case there is some confusion in using the equipment. He/she may also handle the operation of special equipment such as cameras and lighting as well as aiding in the handling of classroom materials. All this takes the pressure off the beginning user of the compressed video system providing a positive experience and, therefore, a greater likelihood of the instructor using the CV again.

During preplanning speak "...not only to issues of technical training, but also to questions of educational *purpose* and *significance*..." (Callister, 1990, p. 6). The selection of compressed video for a particular presentation needs to be clear. If time and distance are factors, then it is appropriate. For example, can a single guest speaker in one location be shared throughout the state at one time? In addition, is it a significant presentation? Is it meaningful and/or important to those people at the remote sites? Clear justification of the purpose will lead to motivation and enthusiasm for designing and delivering quality instruction. People need to realize the cost benefits in not having to travel, the accessibility of resources in distant locations, and the convenience of immediate feedback and interaction. Once these questions of purpose and significance are answered, the next step is following an instructional design suited to the instructor(s) style and objectives. This process will be elaborated upon further in the section titled "Designing Instruction."

After the lesson is planned, preparations can be made for delivery. An important step here is the "Get acquainted" session. This can be facilitated on the compressed video itself if distance is a problem or in person. Some people have used other methods such as pen-pal letters with pictures and video tape of each classroom. The introductory period serves two purposes: the groups can get to know each other and each others' classroom and, everyone can become familiar with the compressed video. This is important to the instructors training to use CV systems as well as to the students they intend to teach using it. You will be reminded of this later in the guide.

How to use this guide

It is assumed the users of this guide are educators or people who are willing to experiment with innovation. Whether the presenters are university professors or businessmen, this guide will aid in their planning during the introductory period and later. Most educators/instructors follow some plan of organization for their presentations. Therefore, this will not be a lesson on how to be an instructional designer, but only an organizational aid when preparing to use the compressed video. The particular strengths of the compressed video will be introduced and elaborated upon where applicable. This is not a paper on theory and philosophy, but a practical, concise, usable aid for those who wish to keep up with this new communication technology.

The book is in loose-leaf form so that the users may disassemble it for easier photocopying of the pages designated for this purpose. The type is large for easier reading and the wide margins are for note-taking. The small illustrations and sub-topic headings in the margins will help you key in on sections while skimming the guide. Here's to good teaching!

Designing Instruction

"...similarly,...the faculty developer needs a full 'bag of tricks,' as opposed to a set format and preprogrammed approach to the design, development, adaptation and/or evaluation of distance delivered instruction" (Willis, 1990, p.1).

The following instructional design model is offered for your use. You will note it is based on an already existing model by the authors cited. The difference is that this guide leads you through the steps with a series of questions. Some, all, or additional questions may be applicable to your situation. These are simply offered to guide you along the planning process. Reference to compressed video will be made where applicable. A planning checklist is provided for your use in Exhibit F of this Guide.

The ASSURE Model

The ASSURE model is found in Heinich, Molenda, and Russell's *Instructional Media and The New Technologies of Instruction* (1989). The acronym stands for the following: A-analyze learners, S-state objectives, S-select media and materials, U-utilize materials, R-require learner performance and, E-evaluate and revise.

Leslie Moller (Tech Trends, 1991, p. 55) wrote a very good article on using the ASSURE model for distance education. The following is based on his report.

A-Analyze Learners:

1.   How will you gain the attention of the learners? Are the learners motivated ? If not, what are you going to do to motivate them? How will you inform them of the objectives to be learned?

2.   Is there an attitudinal resistance to learning with CV? What can you do to address this problem? How will you take advantage of the curiosity factor mentioned in the "Introduction?" Will you use something familiar in a new way? How will you attain positive affectiveness?

3.   Were previous distance education technologies used? Were they successful? Can you build on a positive or counter a negative?

4.   What reading comprehension level are the learners? Do you need to adjust up or down to compensate?

5.   Do the students have existing prior knowledge? Do you need to provide entry competencies or can you build your objectives on existing knowledge? How will you recall prior knowledge?

6.   What do the students expect from the course? from you? from CV? How do you let them know what to expect?

7.   Does this group have previous experience with the CV technology? What do you need to introduce/review?

8.   Has the time schedule and availability of the CV system been worked out?

9.   What are the ages, ability, and education levels of the students?

S-State Objectives:

1.   State performance objectives.

2.   Is the instruction sequenced from the bottom up? That is, did you start with the simple basic objectives and skills and build on them to reach your final objective? Will you need to stimulate recall of prerequisite learnings? If so, how?

3.   Can CV meet the objectives of the course/lesson?

4.   Does the remote location have the necessary materials or setup to facilitate the teaching of the objectives? For example, if you are doing a demonstration, can everyone see what you are doing? Is the sound adequate to carry on a discussion? Are the physical setups of the local and remote sites suitable for observation and evaluation?

5.   Can you handle breaking into small groups if the objective requires this?

6.   Are facilitators trained and available?

NOTE: If any of the above are critical to meeting your objectives and CANNOT be met, then it is necessary to revise the objectives or choose another media.

S-Select Media and Materials:

1.   Will the particular features of CV enhance your presentation? Is there something you would like to do that CV cannot do? (See Table 1 "Instructional Events," p. 13.)

2.   Will the materials you have chosen be available at the remote site? Do you need to send materials ahead of time?

3.   Are the technical resources available at both ends?

4.   Does the instructor and/or facilitator have the necessary skills to carry out the proposed lesson?

U-Utilize materials:

1.   What is your instructional strategy? Will you use peer tutoring, visiting experts, demonstrations, instructional games, experiments, simulations, slide shows etc.?

2.   How will your chosen materials be used? Do you need an overhead? opaque projector? slide projector? Do the sites have compatible equipment? Is technical help available at one, or preferably, both ends?

3.   What are the time limits?   When should you start, stop and break?

4.   How should the classroom be set up? (i.e., Would a single long table suffice or chairs in a semi-circle?) Is the CV system operational? Do you have to do any prior preparation such as load slides?

5.   Have you arranged a "getting to know you" time? Some suggestions were listed in the "Preservice/inservice" section of this guide. Are all arrangements with the distant sites confirmed?

R-Require learner performance:

1.   How should learner practice be provided? In class? Carried out by the facilitator at the remote site? On their own as independent study?

2.   How will the learners get practice? Will it be visual? Pen and pencil? Spoken?

3.   How will you provide feedback to the students? Will you do it orally, face-to-face on the monitor? Will you fax notes? Will you write notes on the presenter? Will the facilitator at the other end provide the feedback? Will you require something to be done outside of class and later turned in for feedback? Will your responses be via computer, telephone, CV or other?

4.   How can you maximize response levels? Will the distant learners interact with the instructor not being physically present? Do students respond better with a local facilitator?

5.   How will you reinforce proper responses? Do you have a plan for making the new knowledge transferable?

E-Evaluate:

1.   How will the evaluation be done? *Do your test items relate directly to your objectives?* Will you require some type of written or oral report? Will the instructor or facilitator monitor? How will the remote site be handled?

2.   How will consistency in different locations be assured?

3.   How will the instructor respond and how soon?

4.   How will the evaluation information be transmitted to the learner? The logistics problems are the same as in the feedback section.

5.   Did students have any difficulty following instructions? Was this due to limitations of the medium? Did the problem originate from some other source? Will you do a written evaluation of instruction? Of the learning experience?

Other Uses of the Compressed Video

Educational (WCTLN Network News, May, 1991):

Staff development

Inservice programs

Exchanging expert teachers between districts

Collaborative curriculum planning

Receiving credit courses

Bringing an expert scientist or other content person from the UW campus to the district

Engaging students in collaborative learning programs among the districts

Conferencing between sites about a variety of issues and topics

Student conferences or meetings

Student contests in various areas

Career counseling for students with professors at the University talking about different programs

Advising about college programs

Modeling outstanding programs for each other

Providing more opportunities for teachers to meet with each other to improve education in their own programs.

CARL, the online catalog of the University of Wyoming, is accessible through CV enabling groups to search as a class and receive instruction in the use of library catalogs.

Local Uses:

Boy Scout and Girl Scout troops could meet and share learning experiences. This would allow youth to work towards badges not otherwise available locally by utilizing experts at remote sites.

Church groups could conference.

Local business organizations could meet with home offices instead of having to travel.

The Red Cross or other agencies that require recertification and/or other training and use visual techniques could use the CV for their particular forms of continuous education.

Political presentations and discussions could be carried on in many locations without the main speakers having to travel great distances often in adverse weather conditions.

Cautions and Tips

Below are listed a few general cautions and helpful suggestions when applying compressed video:

1.   Make the lesson as concrete as possible so as to insure learning, but enough of a challenge for it not to be boring or beneath their capabilities.

2.   Write your lesson plan first and then select the appropriate media to deliver the message. In the case of CV this would refer to which feature most effectively accomplishes the objectives.

3.   When first using the CV, make full, detailed lesson plans with goals and strategies described. You may also want a technician present during classes.

4.   It is helpful for the instructor to visit the receiving end at the beginning and possible midway through the instruction. This develops group cohesion and a better rapport. A visit at the end of instruction may also be helpful for evaluation feedback.

5.   For complex presentations, use a story board. Plan ahead for each element to be presented, the camera angles involved and special effects.

6.   In any media presentation it is important to organize and test equipment beforehand. With CV also test the equipment at the remote site. This must be done each time.

7.   Arrange rooms in advance so all participants are within the field of view. This is especially important for discussion. Speakers should not have to turn towards the camera. Do the same for the microphone(s). The instructor must remember to face the camera not the projected image of the student at the remote site. When the instructor must move among the class, focus the camera on the class.

8.   Diagrams and writing to be placed beneath the over-head camera should be clear and large enough to read. Visuals made with felt tip pens on light colored paper show up well.

9.   Promote interaction by posing a question and requiring students at both locations to raise their hands (Greenwood & McDevitt, 1987, p. 12). Students are reticent to speak to an image rather than the live person.

10. The instructor must be trained in the use of the equipment.

11. When taking notes on an overhead, be sure your hand does not obscure the students' view.

12. For trouble-shooting tips, see the corresponding handout masters in Exhibit D.

Strategies

Gagne and Briggs' "Instructional Events and the Conditions of Learning They Imply for Five Types of Learned Capabilities" (p. 166) identifies instructional events in the same manner as the ASSURE model. Table 1 below gives a comparison of the two.

Table 1 Comparison of the ASSURE Model and Instructional Events

ASSURE	INSTRUCTIONAL EVENTS
A-Analyze Learners	Gaining attention Stimulating recall of prerequisite
S-State Objectives	Inform learner of objectives
S-Select media and materials	(included in next category)
U-Utilize Materials	Presenting the stimulus material Providing learner guidance
R-Require Learner Performance	Eliciting the performance Enhancing retention and transfer
E-Evaluation	Providing feedback

The second "S" in the ASSURE model (Select Media and Materials) is not recognized as an "Instructional Event" by Gagne and Briggs. However, they do elaborate on this in "Relationships Among Some Components of an Instruction System" (p. 176-177). Refer to these tables when planning your presentation strategies and choosing the media to carry them out.

Also see Wilbert J. McKeachie's "Checklist of Teaching Techniques". After deciding upon the goals and objectives of your instruction, you can use this reference to choose a technique. It serves as a guide to match goals with a particular technique. For example "books" suitable for "knowledge" and "critical thinking" whereas "role playing" teaches "real-life experience" and "develops human relations skill" and "interest."

Some other strategies follow:

1. Learners can submit copies of their work to be shared with other students both local and distant.

2.   Provide a model of procedures for the distant learner to follow. They must know what is expected of them, how to go about meeting expectations, and how to show they have met the learning requirements.

3.   The class can be videotaped for review at a later date, for the use of missing students, or as a resource for homebound students.

4.   The telephone and other media can also be used to supplement instruction.

5.   Visuals can be shared instead of having to make individual copies for each member of the class.

6.   The CV can also be used for training in public speaking, interviewing, leading local groups, etc. McKeachie suggests focusing on a particular skill such as asking questions or eliciting student comments (1978, p. 140).

7.   Give students a chance to undertake tasks on their own to prove they can succeed.

8.   Facial expressions, gestures, animation and vocal intensity can be as important as the words spoken. Be enthused and show it.

9.   Ask a colleague to sit in on a class and give you feedback and suggestions for improvement.

10.   The behavior of the students will be an indication of the effectiveness of the instruction.

11.   Individual conferences with students outside of class will also give you feedback as to individual progress and that of the class as a whole.

12.   Sharing of information via e-mail, electronic file transfers, and artifact exchanges before videoconferencing can enhance your presentations.

13.   Students should be encouraged to participate both mentally and physically whenever possible.

Exhibit D contains copyable materials shared by other institutions. These may be used as is or adapted to your situation.

Evaluation

Feedback

Formative evaluation allows you to significantly improve your goals to meet the needs of your students. This type of feedback is done during instruction and is a means of determining if the instruction is effective. (i.e. Is the objective being learned? Should another approach be tried? Do you need to slow down? Review?) By paying attention to these types of issues before concluding the instruction, you are assured some consistency in the outcomes by adjusting instruction thus enabling the students to better understand and meet your criteria.

Some of these formative evaluation techniques were mentioned previously in the "Strategies" section. However, they will be included here again for quick reference.

Formative Evaluation Techniques

1. Some learning outcomes can check progress. These include: responses such as memorization; recitation or explanations as in paraphrasing; classification, prediction, and decisions where rules are applied; and performance or problem-solving.
2. Individual conferences for personal progress reports.
3. Colleagues can often give invaluable suggestions.

Instruction

McKeachie (1978, pp. 292-295) has a very good suggestion for an evaluation tool. See "Student Perceptions of Learning and Teaching" on the following page. He includes student affectiveness as well at the effectiveness of instruction.

You may also may want to evaluate your planning process. Some points to consider follow:

1. Did you meet the local need or demand?
2. Was the instructional package complete? Should there have been more materials? less? Would another medium instead of— or in addition to—the existing one(s) have been more efficient?
3. Does the material encourage active participation?
4. Is the media component interesting and well-produced?
5. Is the course well-designed with specific learner objectives?
6. How flexible are the course materials?
7. What is the longevity of the materials? What parts are consumable and need regular replacement? What are durable and have a longer life?
8. Did you have/need faculty or content experts to work with students in the subject matter area? (Baltzer, 1981, pp. 9-10)

It is very important that test items reflect the objectives being taught. Have you coordinated these? What types of test items did you choose? Were they effective? Did they measure what they were supposed to based on the objectives? It would be prudent to ask yourself if your expectations were reasonable. Perhaps a colleague could help you with this by reviewing a few test results.

Since your are using compressed video, it would be appropriate to evaluate its performance as a medium and as an instructional tool. Some forms are provided for your use in Exhibit F.

Student Perceptions of Learning and Teaching

Your GPA in all courses: _____   Sex: Male   Female

1-almost never or almost nothing
2-seldom or little
3-occasionally or moderate
If not applicable, leave blank.

4-often or much
5-very often
6-almost always or a great deal

Impact on Students:

1.   My intellectual curiosity has been stimulated by this course.
       Comments:

2.   I am learning how to think more clearly about the area of this course.
       Comments:

3.   I am learning how to read materials in this area more effectively.
       Comments:

4.   I am acquiring knowledge about the subject.
       Comments:

5.   The course is contributing to my self-understanding.
       Comments:

6.   The course is increasing my interest in learning more about this area.
       Comments:

Instructor Effectiveness

7.   The instructor is enthusiastic.
       Comments:

8.   The instructor gives good examples of the concepts.
       Comments:

9.   The instructor goes into too much detail.
       Comments:

10.   The instructor is helpful when students are confused.
       Comments:

11.   The instructor seems knowledgeable in many areas.
       Comments:

Rapport

12. The instructor knows students' names.
Comments:

13. The instructor is friendly.
Comments:

Group Interaction

14. Students volunteer their own opinions.
Comments:

15. Students discuss one another's ideas.
Comments:

16. Students feel free to disagree with the instructor.
Comments:

Difficulty

17. The instructor makes difficult assignments.
Comments:

18. The instructor asks for a great deal of work.
Comments:

Structure

19. The instructor plans class activities in detail.
Comments:

20. The instructor follows an outline closely.
Comments:

Feedback

21. The instructor keeps students informed of their progress.
Comments:

22. The instructor tells students when they have done a particularly good job.
Comments:

23. Test and papers are graded and returned promptly.
Comments:

Notice!!! This scale is different!!!

Student Responsibility

1-definitely false
2-more false than true
3-in between

4-more true than false
5-definitely true
If not applicable, leave blank

24.   I had a strong desire to take this course.
Comments:

25.   I actively participate in class discussion.
Comments:

26.   I try to make a tie-in between what I am learning through the course and my own experience.
Comments:

27.   I attend class regularly.
Comments:

28.   I utilize all the learning opportunities provided in the course.
Comments:

29.   I have created learning experiences for myself in connection with the course.
Comments:

30.   I have helped classmates learn.
Comments:

Overall Evaluation

Indicate your evaluation of characteristics below, using numbers based on the following:

1. Poor   2. Fair   3. Good   4. Very Good   5. Excellent

31.   Rate the instructor's general teaching effectiveness for you.
Comments:

32.   Rate the value of the course as a whole to you.
Comments:

Added Comments Below:

References

Baltzer, J. (1981, October). *Alternative Delivery Systems: A Potential Partnership for Education and Public Broadcasting.* Paper presented at the Conference of the Western Educational Society for Telecommunications, Reno, NV, October .

Callister, T. A. (1990) Computer literacy programs in teacher education *Computers and Education, 14*(1), 6.

Gagne, R. M. & Briggs, L. J. (1979). *Principles of Instructional Design,* New York: Holt, Rinehart and Winston, New York.

Greenwood, A. & McDevitt, M. (1987). *Multiple teaching strategies for use with an instructional telecommunications network.* Paper presented at the Society for Applied Learning Technology.

Heinich, R., Molenda, M. & Russell, J. D. (1989). *Instructional media and the new technologies of instruction* (3rd ed.). New York: Macmillan.

McKeachie, W.J. (1978) *Teaching tips: a guidebook for the beginning college teacher* (7th ed.). Lexington: D.C. Heath and Company.

Moller, L. (1991). Planning programs for distant learners: using the ASSURE Model. *Tech Trends,* 36(1), 55-57.

Staff. (1991, January 14). Capabilities of compressed video systems. *WCTLN Network News,* p. 4.

Staff (1991, May 8). What can districts gain from the compressed video network? *WCTLN Network News,* p.1.

Willis, B. (1990). *Faculty resource guide to distance education: a practical guide to teleconferencing and distance education* (Draft September 1990), Prepared by the Faculty Development Subcommittee of the Western Cooperative for Educational Telecommunications. P. O. Drawer P, Boulder,CO 80301. Pub. No. 00:00:0090:WICHE:00.

Exhibit A - Additional Readings

Bennis, W. G., Benne, K. D. & Chin, R. (1985). *The planning of change* (4th ed.). New York: Holt, Rinehart and Winston.

Carl, D. L. (1991). Electronic distance learning: positives outweigh negatives. *T.H.E. Journal, 18*(10), 67-70.

Dick, W. & Carey, L. (1990). *The systematic design of instruction* (3rd ed.). Harper Collins Publishers.

Diebold, J. (1969). *Man and the computer: technology as an agent of social change.* New York: F. A. Praeger.

English, P. C. (1988). Back-to-school with distance learning. *Community, Technical, and Junior College Journal. 59*(1), 36-38.

Gayeski, D. M. (1991). Software tools for interactive media developers. *Tech Trends, 36*(2), 18-21.

Havelock, R. G. (1982). *The change agent's guide to innovation in education.* Englewood Cliffs, NJ.

Hezel, R. T. (1990, May). *Statewide planning for telecommunication in education.* (Available from The Annenberg/CPB Project, 901 E Street, N. W., Washington, D. C. 20004-2006)

LeBaron, J. (1989). *Kids interactive telecommunications project by satellite (KITES): a telecommunications partnership to empower middle school students.* Lowell, MA: University of Lowell. (ERIC Document Reproduction Service No. ED 315 032)

Lepper, M. R. & Gurtner, J. (1989). Children and computers: approaching the twenty-first century. *American Psychologist.* February 1989, 170-178.

Mullen, R. W. (1990). Laboratory for harnessing television. *Tech Trends, 35*(6), 18-21.

Parker, L. H. (1983). *Teleconferencing in education.* ERIC Digest. Washington, D. C.: National Institute of Education. (ERIC Document Reproduction Service No. ED 254 214)

Reigeluth, C. M. (1983). *Instructional design theories and models: an overview of their current status.* Hillsdale, New Jersey: Lawrence Erlbaum Associates, publishers.

Riddle, J. F. (1990). *Measuring affective change: students in a distance education class.* Greeley, CO: Western Institute of Distance Education. (ERIC Document Reproduction Service No. ED 325 514)

Sachs, S. G. (1991). Teaching thinking skills to distant learners. *Tech Trends, 36*(1), 28-32.

Schamber, L. (1988). *Delivery systems for distance education.* ERIC Digest. (Report No. EDO-IR-88-6). Washington, D. C: Office of Educational Research and Improvement. (ERIC Document Reproduction Service No. ED 304 111)

Trimby, M. J. & Gentry, C. G. (1984). *State of ID systems approach models.* (ERIC Document Reproduction Service No. ED 298 896)

Whiston, T. G., Senker, P., McDonald, P. (1980). *An annotated bibliography on the relationship between technological change and educational development.* Paris: Unesco, International Institute for Educational Planning.

Exhibit B - Glossary

Key technology terms adapted from *Websters' New World Dictionary of Computer Terms* except where other sources are noted.

Affective Domain: Refers to learnings that encompass emotions, feelings, beliefs, attitudes, and values.

Audio echo: Feedback noise that indicates the sound at the other site is too loud.

Carrier: Digital media, including satellite, and land lines such as fiber, microwave, or land lines (WCTLN Network News, Jan., 1991).

Compression: Reduction of the amount of information to accommodate cost effective digital transmission (WCTLN Network News, Jan., 1991).

Connectivity: The ability to add peripherals.

Consistency: Agreement or uniformity of practice.

Delivery System: The means by which the information in the lesson will be transmitted. This could be lecture, film, audio, or compressed video.

Facilitator: Person who aids in instruction or carrying out the class other than the primary teacher.

FAX: An acronym for "facsimile." An equipment configuration that facilitates the transmission of images over a common carrier network.

Graphics: Transmission of still images, usually from a video source, but in some cases PC-generated. Graphics may also include on-screen annotation involving drawing or text.

Information Overload: Presenting a lot of information in a short period of time. Results in low retention, and frustration.

Inservice: Professional training provided before teaching.

Instructional Design Model: A formula for planning instruction. See "Instructional Systems Design."

Instructional Events: Provide the external conditions that are necessary for learning to occur. Some events function in the same way regardless of the type of learning, whereas, other events function differently depending on the type of learning (Gagne & Briggs, 1979, p. 99).

Instructional Objective: Statement of performance to be demonstrated by each student in the class, derived from an instructional goal. phrased in measurable and observable terms (Oliva, 1988, p. 378).

Instructional Strategy: Planning and direction of instruction with regard to timing, organization, and delivery systems.

Instructional Systems Design: Total set of procedures that are followed in planning developing, implementing, and evaluating instruction. The procedures are derived from knowledge of human learning relevant for instruction and from the results of empirical data obtained during tryouts of preplanned instruction (Gagne & Briggs, 1979, p. 99).

Interactive: Communication in which all participating sites have equal capability. Interactive videoconferencing permits all sites to see and hear one another.

Learning Outcome: Observable performance that indicates that a particular capability has been acquired. Learning outcomes are often stated in the form of performance objectives (Gagne & Briggs, 1979, p. 98).

Mute: To turn off microphones.

Preservice: Professional training before teaching.

Prior Knowledge: Previous learning either from formal education or personal experience.

Reboot: To stop and boot the operating system again. Usually occurs by human intervention as a result of a problem. It is similar to "reset" on a home appliance.

Remote Site: The receiving end of a transmission. An outpost in a distributed network.

Telecommunications: The transfer of data from one place to another over communications lines.

Transferability: Applicability to other settings.

Videoconferencing: Communication across long distances with video and audio contact. It may also include graphics and data exchange.

Videodisc: A plastic platter resembling a phonograph record that uses low intensity laser beams to store visual materials that will appear on a monitor.

Exhibit C - Support Materials

Cardinal Rules for Faculty

1.   Send hand outs to the remote site EARLY.

2.   Arrive at the classroom early.

3.   Show SPECIAL attention to remote sites before class, at breaks and after class.

4.   Do not waste class time trying to fix the system if a problem develops. If there is too much audio or, if necessary, MUTE their audio. If there is a major failure or problem, go to the speaker phone (if you have one).

5.   If you experience problems—major or minor—be sure to let the technicians know right after class. DO NOT FORGET TO LET THEM KNOW.

6.   Do not criticize the system to students. They take their lead from you. If there is a problem, let the technicians know so it can be worked out.

7.   Do not offer—and do not plan—to originate the class from different sites. Students signed up to take the class as a teleconference course and that is what it is. When faculty try to ride the circuit, everyone becomes unhappy.

8.   Collect written anonymous feedback (especially from the remote sites) frequently. Summarize it and let students know what they told you and what you will do as a result. This will significantly improve communication with your students.

Adapted from a handout developed by Northern Virginia Community College.

Introduction for Students at Remote Sites

1.   Welcome—Identify the class to be sure they are in the right one.

2.   Explain that the class is being offered by_____ via compressed video.

Compressed video is live two-way television. While we know that everyone would like to be in the classroom with the instructor, that is not always possible. This class, for example, could not be offered at all if it was not for the compressed video system. There would not be enough students.

Another justification for the course may be to meet the needs of students at a distance who desire to take the course but cannot be on campus.

3.   The compressed video system may be turned on for you. However, you may wish to learn this procedure from the technicians before class time. This may have been introduced during preservice training. Be sure you (the remote site) are familiar with the startup and rebooting steps.

4.   There is one other piece of equipment that you should know about. This is the remote control. It is specially designed to operate the equipment. The only three controls you will probably ever use are the MUTE BUTTON, VOLUME BUTTONS and CAMERA BUTTON. The MUTE button turns off the microphones in your room. The VOLUME buttons raise and lower the volume from the TV set. The CAMERA button changes which camera is sending a picture. To use the remote control, just point it at the target control and push the button.

5.   To get the most out of this class there are three simple things you should do:

   a.   Avoid the temptation to chit chat. While the instructor is in another room— and this class is a lot like watching TV— you will bother other students who are trying to listen. We cannot make the system loud enough for everyone to hear if several people in the room are talking at the same time as the instructor.

   b.   Get involved. It is not impolite to interrupt if you have a question or comment. This is a little different than a regular classroom setting where you raise you hand and wait.

   c.   Take advantage of the time right after class to talk with you instructor

Adapted from a handout developed by Northern Virginia Community College.

Personal Resources

from the WCTL Network Advisory Board

State of Wyoming Representatives

ECONOMIC DEVELOPMENT AND STABILIZATION BOARD

Chris Clothier, Ex Officio

Economic Development Representative
Herschler Building, Third Floor-East
Cheyenne, WY 82002
(307) 777-7284 (6419)
FAX # 777-5840

Ann McGowan

Designee
Researcher and Librarian
Herschler Building
Cheyenne, WY 82002
(307) 777-6430

WYOMING EDUCATIONAL MEDIA ASSOCIATION (WEMA)

Chuck Bayne
President
IDP, Commission Chair WEA
Laramie High School Media Lab
1275 N. 11th St.
Laramie, WY 82070
(307) 721-4420

Mimi Gilman
Director
Carbon Co. Instrul. Mat. Ctr.
Carbon Co. School Dist. #2
315 N. 1st St., Box 1530
Saratoga, WY 82331
(307) 326-2395

WYOMING STATE DEPARTMENT OF EDUCATION

Steve King
Data Use Facilitator/ Finan. Mod.
State Dept. of Education
Education Computing Council
Hathaway Building
Cheyenne, WY 82002-0050
(307) 777-6670

Diana Ohman
Super. of Public Instruction
Hathaway Building
Cheyenne, WY 82002-0050
(307) 777-7675
FAX # 777-6234

GOODLAD TECHNOLOGICAL TASK FORCE

John Shea, Librarian
East Elementary School
Converse Co. School Dist. #1
615 Hamilton
Douglas, WY 82633
(307) 358-3502

See **Steve King** above

Valuable Tips for CV Faculty

Before class, as you notice students coming into the remote site(s), be sure to welcome them or chat with them so they feel a part of the class. If there is a site not visible, do not hesitate to ask if anyone is there yet. This will let you acknowledge them and chat with them.

After class, or when you take breaks during class, take some time to give special attention to the remote site(s). Be sure to ask them to stay for a few minutes and let them know that it is a special time for them. If you need a break, take it after the special time devoted to the remote site(s). Do not just ask them if there are any questions. Ask them how they feel about how things are going; give them some choices of something and ask which they would prefer; ask them something to which they have to respond.

At the first class meeting, tell students to let you know if you walk off camera or if they cannot hear you. You might even walk off camera and scold them (slightly) if they do not tell you.

If there is a lot of audio echo, it is the audio at the other site that is too loud. If necessary, have the remote site MUTE their audio.

Audio should always be raised on the TV set.

Adapted from a handout developed by Northern Virginia Community College.

Student Information for the Interactive Compressed Video System

There are several responsibilities you have in helping to make the educational experience be as good as possible:

1. Sit where you instructor can see you. The School's faculty find the lack of personal contact frustrating too. They get more inspired—and their lectures get a lot more interesting to you—if you can see students instead of empty chairs. You must shoulder some of the responsibility of being seen by the other end.

2. Speak clearly, facing a microphone. While facing a camera is important too, it is simply imperative that you be heard by the other end. Let the other end know who you are by announcing your name and raising your hand.

3. Keep background noise down (talking, shuffling paper, etc.). It can have the effect of drowning out what is being said elsewhere in the room. Do not begin to speak when someone else is speaking.

4. Let your instructor or facilitator know right away if the sound or picture quality becomes degraded or disintegrates. This is no time for politeness: you are probably going to miss class content you'll be responsible for later! Bring the problem to someone's attention immediately.

5. When there is no technician in the room, it is important that you leave adjustments to the instructor or facilitator. They will contact a technician if needed. You risk making the situation much worse by "helping" make adjustments.

Adapted from materials produced by the School of Library and Information Studies at the University Oklahoma, Norman, Oklahoma, April 2, 1991.

Exhibit D - Trouble Shooting Guide

Problem	Solution
Audio Echo	Turn down or mute audio at remote site.
Major failure	Use speaker phone
Can't hear at remote site	Check mute on/off switch
Feedback (whine or noise)	Microphone and the person speaking are too close
No connection; video out	Call on phone to site and determine problem
Wrong picture on the screen	Change cameras
Rolling picture, brightness not set correctly	Call a technician
Dark picture	Turn the lights on in the room, if this doesn't help, contact a technician.
Lag when playing a videocassette	Send a tape to the remote site and play at the same time as sending site.
Tracking is off (picture jumps)	Adjust the control on the VCR
Presenter is too dark	Open the aperture

Exhibit E - Planning Checklist

Photocopy this checklist to use in your planning. Ask yourself how you will:

A-Analyze Learners

1. Gain attention (based on age) _____

2. Create positive affectiveness _____

3. Build on or compensate for previous distance education experience _____

4. Adjust for reading comprehension level _____

5. Recall prior knowledge _____

S-State Objectives

6. Build on smaller objectives to reach goal _____

7. Use CV to address objectives _____

8. Use facilitators to meet objectives _____

S-Select media & materials

9. Use special capabilities of CV _____

10. Send materials to remote _____

U-Utilize materials

11. Deliver your message _____

12. Use your materials

13. Set time limits _____

14. Set up the classroom _____

15. Coordinate with the other site _____

R-Require learner performance

16. Provide learner practice _____

17. Provide feedback_____

18. Reinforce proper responses _____

E-Evaluate

19. Directly relate test items to objectives _____

20. Be sure testing is consistent at all sites _____

21. Transmit results and in what time frame _____

22. Evaluate instruction _____

23. Evaluate compressed video use_____

Exhibit F - Evaluation Instruments

Evaluation of Guide

Note: It was necessary to change the format of this guide so that it could become Appendix A of this book. Although the content was unchanged, the type size and page layout were changed substantially.

If you would care to give feedback to the author of this guide, photocopy this page, fill it out and return to:

Barbara J. Orde
4746 E. Skyline Dr. #86
Laramie, WY 82070

1.   Do you like the loose leaf format? Why or why not?

2.   Do you like the split page format? Why or why not?

3.   Is it easy to glance and find subtopics?

4.   Is the print large enough to make it easy to read?

5.   Is the language clear and easy to read?

6.   Is the purpose of the guide well defined?

7.   Is the information accurate and complete?

8.   Does the organization seem logical? Suggestions?

9.   How did you use this guide?
      _____Scan   _____Read entirely   _____Quick reference

10.   Did you have previous compressed video experience?

11.   Have you used the ASSURE model before?

12.   What grade level were you planning for when using this guide?

COMPRESSED VIDEO
STUDENT CRITIQUE

1. What did you like about your first compressed video experience?

2. What did you dislike about your first experience?

3. What did you think of the picture quality of the monitor?

4. What did you think of the sound quality?

5. How do you think compressed video will be useful to you in school?

6. How do you think the overhead and writing pad will be useful?

7. Would you like to do this again? Why or why not?

8. Other comments:

Adapted from materials from Dr. Barbara Hakes, WCTL Network

Compressed Video Survey
(Beginning of Session)

Please answer these questions at the START of the session even if you have answered them before in another session. All information will remain confidential, but we need complete answers in order to use this information to meet the needs of potential users. Thank you!

Today's Date:_____Your name or SSN:_____

Birthdate:_____Circle: Male   Female

Occupation/position:_____ Industry you are in:_____

If student, give name of college major or school:_____

To indicate your feelings, circle **1** for DISAGREE STRONGLY or circle **5** for AGREE STRONGLY. If your are somewhere in between, circle **2,3,4**, as appropriate. Compressed video has been abbreviated "CV."

1. I can think of some advantages to using CV in my job or school setting.

            1   2   3   4   5

    Comments: _____

2. The use of CV could be compatible with my job or school setting.

            1   2   3   4   5

    Comments: _____

3. CV would be a complex system to use on my job or in my school setting.

            1   2   3   4   5

    Comments: _____

4. I have had ample opportunity to try out CV to see how it would work.

            1   2   3   4   5

    Comments: _____

5. I have had ample opportunity to observe CV to see how it would work.

            1   2   3   4   5

    Comments: _____

Please indicate your PRIOR EXPERIENCE with CV by circling the appropriate number.

1   No prior experience..............I have never seen or heard of compressed video.

2   Minimal prior experience.................. I have seen/heard of it, but am unsure.

3   Some prior experience.......................I have used it and feel somewhat familiar.

4   Quite a lot of prior experience.........I have used it in the real world and feel familiar with it.

5   A lot of prior experience......................I use it frequently and feel confident about it.

Any other comments you might make:

From Dr. Barbara Hakes, University of Wyoming, College of Education WCTL-N.

Compressed Video Survey
(End of Session)

Please answer these questions at the END of this session even if you have answered them before in another session. To indicate your feelings, circle **1** for DISAGREE STRONGLY or circle **5** for AGREE STRONGLY. If you are somewhere in between, circle, **2**, **3**, or **4** as appropriate. Compressed video has been abbreviated "CV."

1. If I use CV, I will be able to communicate more effectively.

    1   2   3   4   5

2. I perceive that CV is an economical means to communicate.

    1   2   3   4   5

3. If I use CV, I will gain social status.

    1   2   3   4   5

4. I have seen articles or heard discussions which assure me communication through CV has many advantages over current means of communication.

    1   2   3   4   5

5. I feel that CV is compatible with the existing values of my organization.

    1   2   3   4   5

6. I feel that CV could fill a need of my organization.

    1   2   3   4   5

7. I feel that CV is compatible with the ideas of my organization.

    1   2   3   4   5

8. I could convince my organization to accept CV more quickly if it were given a "catchy" name.

    1   2   3   4   5

9. I feel that CV technology is difficult to understand.

    1   2   3   4   5

10. I feel that CV technology is difficult to use.

    1   2   3   4   5

11. Letting me try out CV technology has proven useful to me.

           1   2   3   4   5

12. Observing CV has reduced my uncertainty about its complexity.

           1   2   3   4   5

13. Observing CV has reduced my uncertainty about its contributions.

           1   2   3   4   5

14. I am aware that many leaders in business and education are adopting CV technology.

           1   2   3   4   5

15. This awareness that others are adopting this technology will influence my decision to adopt CV technology.

           1   2   3   4   5

16. I can think of some advantages to using CV in my current job or school setting.

           1   2   3   4   5

17. The use of CV would be compatible with my job or school setting.

           1   2   3   4   5

18. CV would be a complex system to use on my job or in my school setting.

           1   2   3   4   5

19. I have had opportunities before to try out the use of CV to see how it would work in my job or in my school setting.

           1   2   3   4   5

20. I have had opportunities before to observe the use of CV to see how it would work in my job or in my school setting.

           1   2   3   4   5

Was this experience with CV valuable to you? Why or why not?

From Dr. Barbara Hakes, University of Wyoming, College of Education, WCTL-N

Appendix B

North Dakota Interactive Video Network: A Practical Guide to Teleconferencing and Distance Education (excerpts)

Joseph R. Tykwinski
Russell C. Poulin

NORTH DAKOTA

Interactive Video Network

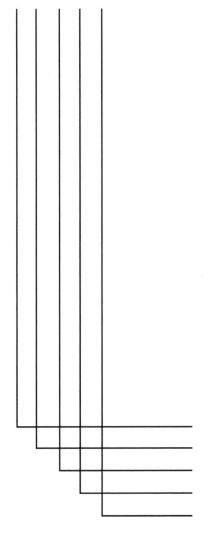

*A Practical Guide to Teleconferencing
and Distance Education*

Joseph R. Tykwinski   Russell C. Poulin

Contents

Chapter 3

Personnel, Management, And Scheduling For IVN

The vitality of the North Dakota Interactive Video Network is dependent on the presenters, instructors, technical support personnel, managers, and policy makers involved. This chapter identifies the role and responsibilities of the people and committees associated with the Interactive Video Network. Included in the last part of the chapter is the procedure for scheduling an IVN Event.

Event Coordinator (Classroom Instructor)

The Event Coordinator is any person wishing to conduct a class, seminar, meeting, or other activity over the Network. The most important person in a successful video activity is the Event Coordinator. That person is the human connection making the technology transparent to the participants. For classes, the instructor assumes this role.

Dependent on the specific activity, the Event Coordinator spends a varying amount of time leading the group. In addition, a successful activity requires behind the scenes preparation in order to bring people and materials together as planned.

For example, an instructor loses some of the freedom normally enjoyed in a class. With students at a distance, the simple task of distributing hand-outs assumes a new complexity. The instructor must plan ahead. Often, diverse resources need to be coordinated to accomplish daily tasks.

Helpful hints for Event Coordinators and classroom instructors:

- **Plan ahead.** Anticipate possible problems before they happen. Give the participants a class syllabus or meeting agenda. Prepare hand-outs early.

- **Pay attention to logistics.** Develop methods to distribute materials to participants at receiving sites. Develop methods for them to send materials to the instructor.

Instructors should perform self assessments by viewing recorded presentations of themselves.

- **Become proficient with the new teaching environment.** Be open to suggestions which may improve teaching effectiveness. Seek further assistance from the Site Coordinator at the local campus.

- **Develop contingency plans.** Technical problems will occur. Create a plan in case these problems occur. Be able to reschedule the meeting or use phone conferencing. Have an alternate lesson plan available at the receiving sites.

- **Make others aware of added responsibilities**. Inform students and other participants about the additional tasks required to conduct an effective event. Inform them of the tips that will make them knowledgeable users of the system.

- **Work closely with the Site Coordinator.** Inform the Site Coordinator of any changes to the event, especially changes in times or number of sites participating. Provide the Site Coordinator with promotional material or other publications describing the event. The Site Coordinator often receives inquiries about events on the Network.

Site Coordinator

The Site Coordinator is the person designated by the campus or site to coordinate on-campus details in classroom scheduling. This person maintains final approval authority for all IVN activities on that campus.

This position provides a key link among the various educational institutions, students, instructors, system scheduling, campus personnel, and users in the community. The Site Coordinator handles the local arrangements for interactive video classes and other events held in the classroom.

Although the Site Coordinators are responsible for a variety of tasks, they may arrange for other people to perform some of these functions. These responsibilities include:

- Serve as contact for scheduling the local classroom.

- Serve as liason between campus personnel and other sites.

- Coordinate with other sites the arrangements required for those sites to receive an event originating from the local site.

- Coordinate with other sites the arrangements required to receive an event originating from another site.

- Serve as liason with the Interactive Video Network Director and the IVN Executive Committee.

- Coordinate IVN efforts with the campus Academic Vice President, Registrar, and Financial Aid Officer.

- Coordinate schedules and assure smooth classroom operation with the Classroom Technical Coordinator.

- Arrange for logistical assistance for classroom participation.

- Provide orientation and training for campus personnel on effective use of the system.

- Serve as a local contact for students and area residents seeking help or information about the Network.

21

- Provide general information about educational programs available through the Network.

- Promote the use of the Network, within campus and system guidelines.

- Monitor marketing material for events originating from the local site.

- Serve as liaison between the campus and the Rural Health Project.

Classroom Technical Coordinator

The Classroom Technical Coordinator is the person designated by the campus (or site) to coordinate on-campus details in classroom maintenance and operation.

The Classroom Technical Coordinator is a faculty or staff member who serves as the local technical contact for the Interactive Video Network. The Classroom Technical Coordinator is not required to know all of the technical details regarding the operation of the communications and classroom equipment, but must be comfortable with audio and video equipment. Further, the Classroom Technical Coordinator needs to be able to make basic adjustments to the equipment and is responsible for daily operation of the interactive video classroom.

When a problem develops in the video classroom, the Coordinator should localize the problem. Is the problem with a piece of equipment (a camera or microphone) in the room? Are the transmission lines working properly? Is the site experiencing power failures? Do the participants not fully understand how to operate the controls? Is there some new, unanticipated problem?

If the solution is within the Coordinator's expertise, the Coordinator fixes it. If the problem is more difficult, the Coordinator seeks assistance from the appropriate source.

Classroom Technical Coordinators share some of the duties of the Site Coordinator. Among those duties, the Classroom Technical Coordinator needs to help assure that classroom technicians or other personnel are in the classroom at scheduled times so that events occur as planned.

22

IVN Strategic Advisory Committee

The IVN Strategic Advisory Committee is comprised of one representative from each campus. It is charged with making strategic recommendations on the programming, scheduling, and training needs of the Network.

The Committee has other duties such as making general planning and policy recommendations regarding the direction of IVN. Additionally, the Committee also:

- Serves as an arbiter in scheduling disputes.

- Promotes use of the system in ways that enhance cooperation and educational opportunities across the campuses.

- Develops a general plan for training instructors and other users in the effective use of the Network.

- Recommends incentive plans to encourage faculty and campuses to participate in IVN usage.

IVN Executive Committee

The Executive Committee is charged with managing the North Dakota Interactive Video Network. The Executive Committee duties include:

- Reviewing and approving of the policies for operating and using the Network.

- Overseeing and approving the expenditure of the Network budget.

- Seeking and approving cooperative agreements with other organizations central to the operation and usage of the Network.

IVN Director

The IVN Director is charged with the day-to-day management of the North Dakota Interactive Video Network. The Director coordinates with Network personnel and committees to maintain operations and to seek ways to improve the delivery of IVN events.

Procedure for Scheduling an IVN Event

1. A person intending to hold an interactive video event contacts the Site Coordinator for their campus. That person becomes the Event Coordinator. The site hosting the event then becomes the Originating Site.

2. The Site Coordinator at the Originating Site determines:
   a. if the event is within campus guidelines for IVN classroom use.
   b. if the local IVN classroom is available.
   c. if the necessary resources are available to hold the event.
   d. if the other sites are available by checking the Master System Schedule.

3. If the other sites are free on the schedule, the Site Coordinator requests the event be held by contacting the IVN Scheduling Coordinator and the Site Coordinators at the other sites. The event is tentatively scheduled.

4. Events are confirmed on the schedule according to their level of priority:
   a. Rural Health Project and classes part of an approved academic program may be confirmed 90 or more days in advance of the first day of the event.
   b. All other academic classes may be approved 60-89 days in advance of the first day of the event.
   c. All other events may be confirmed on a first-come, first-served basis less than 60 days in advance of the first day of the event.

   Event Coordinators may ask the Site Coordinator about the process to confirm events early. Receiving sites retain the right to confirm or deny any event.

5. Upon being notified of event confirmation or denial, the Site Coordinator notifies the Event Coordinator and other campus personnel of the schedule. It is the responsibility of each Site Coordinator to ensure that the event occurs as agreed with the other sites.

6. The Site and Event Coordinators keep in touch as necessary until the event is completed to assure a successful event.

Chapter 6

Preparing And Presenting Visual Aids

Much of what students learn today is acquired through their sense of sight. Putting aside individual learning styles and preferences, the eye is capable of gathering more information in a shorter amount of time than the ear. Furthermore, students will retain the information longer if it is presented in a visual format.

Television is a visual medium. When the interactive video system is used to teach the role of visual aids naturally increases. In order to explore the area of visual aids for television, this chapter is divided into the following sections:

* **Formats for Visual Aids**
* **Design and Layout Criteria for Visual Aids**
* **Presenting Visual Aids**

Formats for Visual Aids

In the Interactive Video Classroom, all visual material needs to be in a video format before it can be displayed on the television monitor. Visual aids that are used in a traditional classroom may or may not be useable in the Interactive Video Classroom. Some of these aids will be useable, but they may need to be reformatted. On the other hand, some new types of visuals which were previously difficult or impossible to display using traditional classroom equipment may be included.

This section will explain the capabilities and list the types of visual material that can be displayed using selected pieces of equipment.

45

- **The Visual Presenter.** This device functions much like an overhead projector. The visual presenter has more capabilities than an overhead projector and the graphics are easier to prepare than transparencies. This device can display photographs, charts, maps, information from books, and small three dimensional objects. All items are displayed in color and they can be magnified using the zoom lens of the built-in camera. Visual aids to be displayed using the visual presenter should be no larger than 9 inches high x 12 inches wide. Larger objects can be displayed by placing them on the instructor's console and using the instructor's camera.

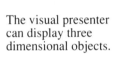
The visual presenter can display three dimensional objects.

- **VCR (Video Cassette Recorder).** Each classroom is supplied with a 1/2 inch VHS player/recorder. This recorder is capable of displaying a quality still frame for short periods of time. Be aware that there are several formats for video tapes including 3/4 inch U-Matic and 1/2 inch Beta. The 1/2 VHS recorder supplied in the main classroom will not play other videotape formats. To play these other formats of video tape, either have the information transferred to the 1/2 VHS format or make arrangements to have the appropriate VCR connected to the classroom system. There is extra space available in the instructor's console to accommodate such added equipment.

- **Slide Transfer System.** This device can be used to display photographic slides. It looks and operates similarly to a traditional slide projector. Some slides will not work well when displayed for television, especially slides that are taller than they are wide. Design and layout criteria for slides and other visuals are discussed in the next section.

46

The instructor's console was designed to accommodate additional equipment quickly and easily. The following pieces of equipment are optional and are not included as standard classroom equipment. The use of additional equipment such as the following items, is encouraged whenever they are available and they can enhance the presentation.

- **Film Transfer System.** This device converts film images to the video format. There are many variations of this device, but the simplest type looks and operates exactly like a regular projector. The only difference is that the projection lens has been replaced by a miniature video camera. Some large film libraries such as the North Dakota State Film Library, may be able to convert certain films to videotape at a minimal cost.

  A film image can be projected to a wall screen or to a rear screen projection unit, and then a video camera can be used to record the image. However, this process does have a disadvantage. Due to the persistence of vision, the human eye does not normally see the shutter; the camera will see it, and the result will be a slight black flicker as the videotape is played. This may be unacceptable; in which case, one of the other transfer techniques described must be used.

- **Microscope Camera.** With this device, anything that can be viewed with a microscope including microscopic organisms and miniature electronic circuits can be projected to a television monitor. Once the "miniature camera" is attached to a standard microscope, the microscope is used in the normal fashion.

- **Videodisc Player.** This device can display everything that a VCR can with additional capabilities. With a videodisc, any point on the disc can be accessed almost instantly without wasting time trying to rewind or fast forward. Points on the disc can be accessed using a bar code reading wand and corresponding labels within lecture notes, or they can be programmed into the videodisc player. The video disc player can also be connected to a computer and the computer can perform the search. Thousands of single frames of still images or slides can be stored on one videodisc. The still images can be displayed for unlimited lengths of time and the picture quality of the images is excellent.

- **Computer.** Recent developments in hardware and software make the computer an exceptionally good tool for generating high quality text and graphics for the video format.

To make a computer useful in the interactive video classroom, the following items need to be included in the computer system.

1. **Presentation Software.** This software is designed specifically for making presentations and should include such features as automatic templates for the background, automatic generation of charts and graphs (just input the data), a simple method of generating text, and the ability to generate several colors.

2. **Color.** The computer should be able to output color images. Some computers may not have a color screen, but they may be able to assign colors to text or other graphic elements and then output color images to the television monitor in the interactive video classroom. A color screen is preferable so that the chosen color combinations can be viewed before they are presented in the classroom.

3. **Video Signal Output**. Most computers cannot output a NTSC video signal unless a special internal video output card or "external box" is added to the computer. If this card contains Genlock, computer generated text or images can be superimposed on top of another video signal.

The computer is also capable of generating high quality digitized sound. It can also connect to many other peripheral devices such as a CD-ROM player or modem. These devises can provide immense on-line resources in the classroom.

- **Character generator**. This device is a specialized piece of equipment that takes on many different forms, it often looks like a small key pad. This device will electronically produce letters and numbers directly on the television monitor. If this device contains Genlock, the characters can be superimposed on top of a video image.

- **Chalkboard or Marlite Board**. These devices are used as they would be in the traditional classroom. However, the design and layout criteria for visual aids that are discussed in the next section must be followed. Not all interactive video classrooms have these boards available because the visual presenter is usually used in their place.

Design and Layout Criteria for Visual Aids

In order to properly select or prepare visual material for a class, it is important to understand the design and layout requirements of video images. Until instructors are familiar with what works and what does not work well on television, they should take time to test the legibility of their visuals before class using the actual classroom equipment if possible. The selected or prepared visual aids must conform to the design and layout criteria within these five areas.

* **Aspect Ratio**
* **Safe Area**
* **Size and Quantity of Letters**
* **Resolution**
* **Contrast and Color**

Aspect Ratio

The aspect ratio of the television monitor is three to four; the picture is always three units high to four units wide. All visual information must be contained within this 3 x 4 aspect ratio. Graphic materials, such as slides, photographs, and flat materials, should be presented in this horizontal area.

Aspect Ratio

49

To quickly determine what portion of an existing photograph, illustration, or other graphic will appear on a television monitor, a video aspect ratio transparency can be used. To make a transparency, the graphic provided on the next page should be enlarged with a photo copier to about 150% of the original size. Then a transparency is made from the photocopy. The transparency is comprised of several rectangular boxes, each one conforming to the video aspect ratio. To use the transparency, the transparency is simply laid on top of a graphic and adjusted to determine if the desired elements of the graphic fit into <u>one</u> of the boxes.

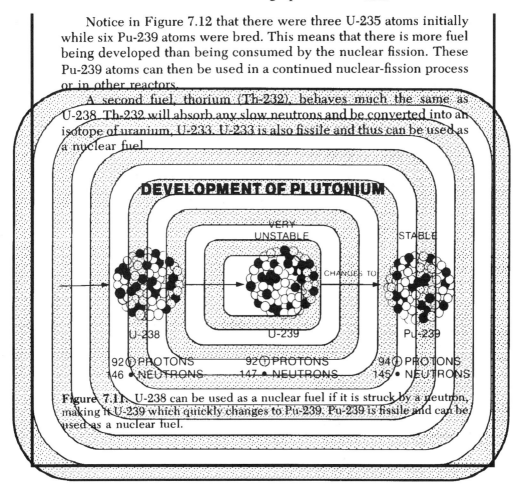

Notice in Figure 7.12 that there were three U-235 atoms initially while six Pu-239 atoms were bred. This means that there is more fuel being developed than being consumed by the nuclear fission. These Pu-239 atoms can then be used in a continued nuclear-fission process or in other reactors.

A second fuel, thorium (Th-232), behaves much the same as U-238. Th-232 will absorb any slow neutrons and be converted into an isotope of uranium, U-233. U-233 is also fissile and thus can be used as a nuclear fuel.

DEVELOPMENT OF PLUTONIUM

VERY UNSTABLE — STABLE — CHANGES TO

U-238 — U-239 — Pu-239

92 PROTONS — 92 PROTONS — 94 PROTONS
146 NEUTRONS — 147 NEUTRONS — 145 NEUTRONS

Figure 7.11. U-238 can be used as a nuclear fuel if it is struck by a neutron, making it U-239 which quickly changes to Pu-239. Pu-239 is fissile and can be used as a nuclear fuel.

A video aspect ratio transparency placed on top of a page from a book. (Page courtesy of <u>Energy Technology: Sources of Power</u>, Schwaller, 1980.) To include all of the graphic in the safe area of the monitor, elements within the largest clear rectangle should be displayed. This would include the illustration description and the last three lines of the main text.

Video Aspect Ratio

Safe Area

The area framed by the camera and displayed on the television monitor is called the scanning area. The safe area is a smaller area contained within the scanning area. (Reference the illustration below.) All pertinent information should be contained within the boundaries of the safe area if it is to be seen on the television monitor. Information outside the safe area can be lost or distorted. The actual size of the safe area, as compared to the scanning area, will depend on the television monitor that is used. As a general guide in determining the safe area, at least a 10% border should be allowed around the inside edge of the scanning area. A more accurate test would be to display the visual aids using the actual classroom equipment and then view the visuals from the back of the student seating area.

Safe Area

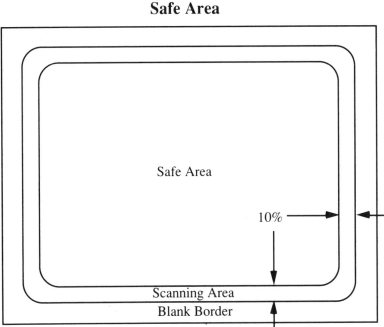

In addition to a 10% border around the safe area, a blank border should be included outside of the scanning area. This blank border allows visuals to be framed quicker because their exact placement under the visual presenter is not necessary.

- The total blank area that should surround the graphic elements on an 8 1/2 x 11 inch sheet of paper is 1 - 1 1/2 inches.

Size and Quantity of Letters

Lettering is the most critical element in many of the visual aids prepared for classroom instruction. Lettering can be used on prepared visuals such as slides, layouts made for use with the visual presenter, and computer generated graphics. Lettering can also be generated in the classroom using less formal methods, such as writing on a blackboard, marlite board, or writing under the visual presenter.

The following guidelines can be used to determine the size and quantity of letters to use regardless of how they are generated. This is true because no matter how big or small the original letters, they are all projected to a television monitor that does not change in size. Of course, lettering for a blackboard needs to be larger than lettering for the visual presenter, and the size of lettering presented with the visual presenter will vary. The appropriate letter size is directly related to the amount the visual is magnified or reduced by the zoom lens of the camera.

- 8 lines of type maximum.

- 50 words maximum.

- The space between lines of type used for television should be one and a half to two times greater than what is recommended for printed materials.

- Use markers, chalk, and printers that yield bold lettering.

- Use printed type styles that are plain and easy to read. Fancy fonts are difficult to read on a television monitor.

Because much of the text material will probably be displayed using the visual presenter, some additional guidelines and hints are listed below:

- A single visual contained on an 8 1/2 x 11 inch sheet of paper should have lettering that is at least 1/4 inch (18 points) high and preferably 3/8 inch (27 points) high or more.

- Most textbook lettering is unusable unless the text is of the above mentioned size, or the pages are divided into three or more columns of text and the text can be enlarged to the above mentioned size.

- The best way to produce large text is to use a computer and a good quality printer such as a laser printer. Satisfactory results can be obtained from a typewriter.

Using a Typewriter to Create Text for the Visual Presenter

The text in the box to the right was created using a typewriter. Each of the three paragraphs represent a single visual to be displayed using the visual presenter.

Six of these paragraphs can be placed on a single 8 1/2 x 11 inch sheet of paper. The paragraphs can be displayed at this small size by magnifying them with the zoom lens of the visual presenter. Another option is to enlarge the paragraphs with a photocopy machine so that each paragraph fits on its own 8 1/2 x 11 inch sheet of paper. As an example, the first paragraph was enlarged 200% with a photo copy machine. The enlarged graphic appears on the next page.

The exact width of typed text columns and the number of lines of type that can be included on a single graphic will depend on the size and style of type the typewriter produces. The design and layout criteria previously explained should be used to determine the appropriate column width and number of lines.

Lettering that is to be displayed using the visual presenter can be created using a type-writer and a photocopy machine.

Place the text in columns that are about 2 inches wide. Use a line spacing of 1 1/2. After about 6 lines of type start a new paragraph.

The final step is to enlarge each paragraph approximately 200% with a photocopy machine. Remember to use colored paper.

54

Lettering that is to be displayed using the visual presenter can be created using a type-writer and a photocopy machine.

Resolution

Just as text needs to be of a simple style and broad stroke, charts and illustrations need to be uncluttered and use broad lines. Thin lines and small details will not produce acceptable results when viewed on a television monitor. Existing graphic material can often be made acceptable by enlarging it with a photo copier and retracing the important lines with a broad marker.

Contrast and Color

The color aspect of video adds realism and interest. Color can be used to focus the viewers attention on an important word, phrase, or a particular area of an illustration.

Video does have some problems handling colors that are highly contrasted (i.e. black lettering on a white background). Very bright colors (i.e. white or florescent green) can cause picture flare and distort other colors within the picture. The best colors to use for video are those in the middle of the color spectrum. For visual aids, a light gray, blue, or pastel background will work best if black lettering is used. If colored lettering is used, yellow letters work well with a variety of background colors, especially light gray or blue. Many combinations of colors will produce pleasing results. Combining highly contrasted colors must be avoided.

Presenting Visual Aids

When teaching in an interactive video classroom, always be aware of what the receiving site students are seeing on their television monitor. This means that instructors need to keep one eye on the overhead monitor at all times, including when they are presenting visual aids.

There are also other reasons why instructors should watch the overhead monitor. When presenting visual aids, it is appropriate to switch to the instructor's camera occasionally to maintain "face to face" contact with the students at the receiving sites. Because the instructor's camera is next to the overhead monitors, it is easy to maintain eye contact when switching from one camera to the next. When watching the overhead monitors or the instructor's camera, it is also easy to glance at the receiving site monitor to view the students at the receiving sites.

When using the visual presenter, watch the overhead monitor and not the visual itself. This will assure the following:

- The visual is properly centered.

- Written material runs horizontally across the monitor. It is legible, and it does not run off the edge of the scanning area. Watching the overhead monitors while writing beneath the visual presenter can be awkward at first, but it is important to master this technique. Lightly ruled paper may be helpful to some instructors.

An instructor watching the overhead monitor while writing beneath the visual presenter.

- The visual is not being blocked by a hand, arm, or head.

- The lens is set at the proper zoom level. If the zoom is too far out, part of the flatbed may be captured by the camera, detail may be sacrificed, and the text may be too small to read. If the zoom is too far in, the students may not see all of the visual, and the text may run beyond the scanning area of the monitor.

Some instructors may choose to use a marlite (dry marker) board or a blackboard on which to write their lecture notes. Be aware of the following disadvantages of using a large wall mounted board.

- The instructor's camera will be used to display the material, so the students will be viewing the instructor's back as they write.

- Due to the resolution of the television monitor, it is necessary to make an extra effort to use very thick lines.

- It is awkward and difficult to write on a large wall mounted board and watch the overhead monitor at the same time. It will take additional practice to be assured that the print is legible on the television monitor, and that it stays within the safe area of the television monitor. A classroom technician may be needed to operate the instructor's camera so that text will be properly framed.

- The design and layout guidelines discussed in the previous section must still be followed. This means that most instructors will not be able to display as many words on the board at one time as they would in the traditional classroom.

A marlite board or blackboard used in the IVN classroom is usually divided into retangular sections adhereing to the 3 x 4 aspect ratio. These sections are captured with the instructor's camera and displayed one at a time. The information contained in each section must adhere to all design and layout guidelines discussed in this chapter.

An alternative to the large board is a small marlite board that can fit under the visual presenter. This type of board does not allow physical self expression in the way a large board would, but it has the advantage of using the visual presenter.

Most of the other visual aids used in the interactive video classroom require no special presentation techniques beyond the traditional classroom techniques. As in the traditional classroom, cue up all visual aids before the class begins.

Appendix C

Task Analysis of the Operation of Certain Control Elements of a Portable Compressed Video System

Dale Smith

Getting Started

1. Turn on the power switch of the control tablet. This switch is located on the front of the tablet next to the power cord. Press the button in and a green light next to the power cord will light.

2. Turn on the Elmo Presenter power switch. It is located on the upper left corner of the presenter.

3. The codec on/off switch is located on the front right side of the unit just below the preview (right) monitor. The switch has a red dot below it. The dot indicates the off position. Press the switch up to turn the unit on.

4. A. If the unit is operating properly, you will note that the preview monitor will show a booting sequence. This sequence will take between one and two minutes.

   B. If the unit does not come up, turn the unit off. Open the door below the preview monitor. There are two on/off switches located on two black boxes. Turn both of these switches on, if they are off, and close the door.

   C. Open the left door below the main (left) monitor. Locate the VideoTelecom Media max. There is an on/off switch located below the 3 1/2" disk drive. If this switch is off, turn it on and make sure that the green light above it comes on. Close the door.

   D. Repeat steps #3 and #4A.

5. Once the booting sequence is complete, the main (left) monitor should show another site or a gray screen and the right monitor will show your camera #1 shot.

Control Tablet Operations

Activating the Tablet

The control tablet is pressure sensitive and by pressing icons on various tablet overlays with an electronic pencil, you will activate functions and control the system.

1. A. Locate the control tablet "Tablet Series A5" overlay. The number is located in the upper right side of the overlay in small print.
    B. Raise the clear plastic sheet that covers the pad and center the overlay. Be sure that the overlay is in the correct position so that the tablet series number is in the upper right corner.

    C. Replace the clear plastic sheet.

2. A. Pick up the electronic pencil which is located in the pen holder on the upper right corner of the tablet. When you use the electronic pencil *always use moderately firm pressure when you press the tablet.*

    (When the instructions are to press, this means to use the electronic pencil to press an icon on the tablet or an area of the tablet.)

    B. Press the "On" icon. The icon is located at the bottom of the overlay. The main monitor will have a brief message indicating "Tablet Series A5 Loaded." The preview monitor will normally show your camera #1 shot.

Displaying Your Site Name

1. In the icon cluster blocks at the top of the overlay, you will see a block noted "Menu" which is located in the second block from the right.

2. Press "Select."

3. You will see a list on the main monitor.

4. Press the "Down" arrow in the menu block, scroll down to "Other Function" and press the "Select" icon.

5. You will see a new list. Scroll to "Site Name."

6. Press the "Select" icon, and you will note that the word "Yes" will appear after "Site Name."

Audio

Setting the Speaker Level

The audio you will set here adjusts the level of your *speaker*, not your *microphone level.*

1. Move to the fourth icon cluster block from the left. It is noted as "Audio."

2. Press either the "+" or the "-" icon. When you press either icon, you will see a number on the main monitor.

3. You can use the "+" icon to raise the number on the screen or the "_" to lower the number. Set the number to "15."

Microphone Operation

1. At all sites, except Laramie 2, touch-to-talk microphones are used.

2. Please do *not* leave the talk buttons on when you are not talking.

Using Preview and Camera

"Preview" feature is used for previewing local cameras only

(When we refer to camera #1, this is physically located beneath the main monitor. You will have control of this camera as indicated in the following instructions.)

1. Locate the icon cluster block noted as "Preview." It is in the icon cluster block just below "Audio" and "Slides."

2. Press preview icon #1. You will see your camera #1 shot on the preview monitor.

3. A. Locate the four directional arrows in the middle of the "Camera Control" area. For our purposes, consider them to be the compass directions of north, south, east and west.

    B. Press the north arrow and watch the screen. You will notice that your camera shot will tilt up.

    C. Press the south arrow and watch the screen. You will notice that your camera shot will tilt down.

    D. Press the east arrow and watch the screen. You will notice that your camera shot will pan to the right.

    E. Press the west arrow and watch the screen. You will notice that your camera shot will pan to the left.

    F. Press the appropriate directional arrows to center the camera shot on you.

4. Locate the six icons at the bottom of the "Camera Control" area.

5. A. The two icons to the lower left are noted as "Zoom."

    B. Press the "In" icon and hold it until the camera stops zooming in. You will notice that your camera shot is a close-up.

    C. Press the "Out" icon and hold it until the camera stops zooming out. You will notice that your camera shot is a distance or long shot.

    D. Press the "In" icon once more and hold it until the camera stops zooming in.

6. A. The two icons in the lower right are noted as "Focus."

    B. Press the "In" icon and watch the screen.

    C. Press the "Out" icon and watch the screen.

    D. You will notice that by pressing the "In" and "Out" icons that the focus on the screen will change.

    E. Using the "In" and "Out" icons, focus your shot.

7. Press "Zoom In" until you have a close-up shot of yourself.

8. A. The two icons in the lower center portion of the "Camera Control" area are noted as "Iris".

    B. Press "Open" and you will see a lighter picture. This allows more light through the iris.

    C. Press "Close" and you will see a darker picture. This allows less light through the iris.

    D. Use the "Iris" icons as needed for adjusting light in the picture.

        (For close-up shots, try to get the person's head about one-third down from the top of the picture.)

        (For long shots of several people, use shots from about waist-level up. This will include any table tops.)

Remember that video is a close-up medium, when someone is talking for an extended period, the camera should be close-up on the individual.

9. You may preview and adjust the camera shot by using icons #2, #3 and #4.

10. Icon #2 is the Elmo Presenter.

11. Icon #3 is for an additional camera which may be used for more flexibility.

12. Icon #4 is intended for use of a VCR, however an additional camera may be placed here.

Using the "Local" Camera Control Area

1. The large icon cluster block that occupies about two-thirds of the left portion of the overlay is noted as "Camera Control." You use this area to set camera #1 shots on the "Preview" monitor.

2. Find the first group of icons under "Camera Control." These are under a subgroup called "Local."

3. Press "Local" icon #1. You will note on the main monitor the message "Sending Camera 1." During the class, anytime that you wish to send the picture of cameras 1, 2, or 3, you must push the camera icon number under "Local."

4. When you press any "Local" icon, the shot will appear on both the main and preview monitors.

5. If you wish to view or set up a shot on a camera different from the one you are sending, press the camera icon of the shot you wish to view under "Preview" and you will see the picture on the preview monitor. When you are ready to send this camera, press its "Local" icon.

If you must adjust a camera #1 shot using the control tablet, this must be done with camera #1 *in preview*.

Using the "Remote" Camera Control Area

The remote camera control area can be used only when there are two sites taking part in the call. This is referred to as a point-to-point call. During the multi-point calls, the remote feature will not work.

1. Find the second group of icons under "Camera Control." These are under a subgroup called "Remote."

2. Press "Remote" icon #1. you will note on the main monitor the message "Remote Camera 1." You may adjust this camera shot by using the camera control features of pan, tilt, zoom, iris and focus.

3. You may select camera #1, #2, #3, or #4 as the camera transmitted from the remote site.

Slides

1. Locate the "Slides" icon cluster block which is in the upper right block of the "Tablet Series A5."

2. A. To save a slide, bring up the image you wish to save on the preview monitor using camera #1, #2, #3, or #4.

    B. Press the "Save" icon which is located in the "Preview" icon cluster block.

    C. You will see a flicker in the preview monitor as the slide is saved. The picture on the main monitor will freeze during this process.

    D. You will be prompted to name the slide on the main monitor. Use either the IBM keyboard at the bottom of the "Draw Area" or the "Tablet Series A5" overlay to type the name of the slide. Press enter.

3. A. To select a slide, press the "Select Slide" icon in the "Slides" block.

    B.   You will see a list of slide names on the main monitor.

    C.   Use the "Up" and "Down" arrows in the "Slides" block to move the arrow on the screen to the slide name you wish to select.

    D.   Press "Select Slide." You will see the slide gradually appear on the preview monitor.

4.   To send the slide to other sites, press the "Send" icon which is located in the "Preview" icon block. The picture on the main monitor will freeze during this process.

5.   For the other sites to view the slide, they must press the "Slide" icon which is located in the upper right corner of the "Draw Area."

See the next section for directions on using the "Draw Area" to annotate.

6.   A.   Once you have sent a slide, then you may use the "Present" section of the "Slides" block.

    B.   If you have slides stored in the order that you wish to present them, use the "Select Slide" method 3 - 5 above for the first slide in your sequence.

    C.   Press the "Fwd." icon in the 'slides' block to advance through your slides. By pressing the "Fwd." icon, the slide will appear on your preview monitor and will simultaneously be sent to the other sites.

    D.   You may also go in reverse order through your slides by pressing the "Rev." icon in the "Slides" block.

    E.   If you must skip forward or back several slides, use the "Select Slide" method covered in 3. A.-D. above because it will take several seconds to go forward or backward through more than one slide.

7.   A.   To delete a slide, press the "Delete" icon in the "Slides" block.

    B.   You will see a list of slides displayed on the main monitor and a message to "Select a Slide to Delete."

    C.   When you have moved the arrow to the slide that you wish to delete, press the "Select Slide" icon.

    D.   The slide will appear on the preview monitor.

    E.   A message will appear on the main monitor asking you if you wish to delete this slide. Move the arrow to "Yes" if you do wish to delete and press "Select Slide." If you do not want to delete this slide, leave the arrow on "No" and press "Select Slide."

8.   To remove the slide list press "Clear List" in the "Slides" block.

The Draw Area

1. Locate the "Draw" area of the tablet.

2. If a slide is sent to you during the class and you are asked to annotate on the slide, you will do so in the draw area.

3. Press the "Slide" icon in the upper right of the draw area. This will allow you to annotate.

4. A. A column will appear to the left on the preview monitor. There are several blocks in this column.

   B. The hide block, if pressed, will cause this column to disappear. To make it reappear, touch area where the block formerly appeared and push the button on the side of the electronic pencil at the same time.

   C. The block which is a solid color can have its color changed by pressing it. This gives you a selection of colors to choose for annotating in the "Draw Area."

   D. The "Line" block is used to select a thin or a thick pencil line by pressing the block.

   E. The "T" block allows you to press it and then press a spot in the "Draw Area" to select where you would like text to begin. Use the IBM keyboard for text with this feature.

   F. The block with the picture of an eraser will allow you to delete portions of the annotation. Just press the block and the electronic pencil may be used as an eraser in the "Draw Area."

   G. When you press the "CLR" block, all annotation will disappear from the preview monitor.

   H. When you press the "WB" block, a whiteboard will appear on the screen.

1. The hand-held remote control allows you to operate the system in a similar fashion as you do with the control tablet.

2. The "Audio" block functions are the same as they are on the control tablet.

3. The "Select Camera" block is used in the same way as "Local" is used in the "Camera Control" of the "A5 Tablet Series." This is for sending camera shots.

4. To be sure that you have control of your site cameras, press the "Local/Remote" button. This is located in the middle of the hand-held remote control. A message will appear on the main monitor. The message will be either "Remote Camera" or "Local Camera." You want "Local Camera."

5. A. To preview a camera shot you must use the "Preview" button which is the third button from the bottom left of the remote control.

B. To locate a camera to preview, you will have to press the "Preview" button until the camera you want is shown on the preview monitor. The camera selection message will also be shown on the main monitor. The "Preview" function will rotate through all of the cameras in order. You may not adjust the camera 1 shot in preview with the remote control. It is necessary to be sending camera 1 and have camera 1 in preview before you can adjust the camera 1 tilt, pan, focus or zoom.

6. A. The "Menu" block is at the bottom of the remote control. The functions are the same as that of the "Menu" functions on the control tablet with certain exceptions.

B. To observe the "Conference Control" menu, press "Option." "Option" shares space with the "Down" button. This button is the last button on the bottom right of the "Menu" block.

C. Once you have accessed the "Conference Control" menu, you may scroll through the choices by using the "Up" and "Down" buttons.

D. When you wish to select one of the "Conference Control" menu choices, move the arrow up or down with the appropriate button. When you have moved the arrow to your choice, press "Execute."

E. Once you have made a choice in the "Conference Control" menu and you wish to see another choice, press "Next" and the menu will reappear.

F. To remove the menu choices from the screen and regain control of the other remote control functions, press "Clear."

Elmo Document Presenter

The Elmo is Sent as Camera #2

1. The buttons used for proper setting of the Elmo are located in the upper portion of the front (top) panel.

2. Set the buttons as follows:

A. Press the "EV-308" button.

B. Set the "Auto/Manu" switch to the "Auto" position.

C. Set the "Nega/Posi" switch to the "P" position.

3. The camera for the Elmo is located at the upper end of the extension arm.

4. To adjust the length of the extension arm, press the button which is located half-way up and on the left side of the arm, and move the upper half of the arm up or down.

5. A. To adjust the angle of the document, stand camera, press the button which is located on the left side of the camera. The camera will only move toward the front of the presenter and it reaches stop points for three positions.

   B. With the button pressed in, you may move the camera from a position pointed straight down to one at a slight angle pointing toward the front of the presenter.

   C. You may also move the camera pointing 90 degrees from the original position.

6. The zoom, focus and iris adjustments are located on the right side of the camera.

Turning Off the System

1. When you are ready to terminate use of the codec, press "Hang-up" in the "Video Call" block.

2. If you are using the hand-held remote control, press the "Hang-up" button in the "Video" section which is located in the upper block.

3. Wait until the message "Connection Idle" appears on the main monitor.

4. Turn off the codec.

5. Turn off the Elmo power switch.

6. Turn off the control tablet power switch.

Appendix D

Videoconference Request Form and Agreement for Video Teleconferencing

State of Wyoming
Department of Administration and Information
Telecommunications Division

VIDEOCONFERENCE REQUEST FORM
7/16/92

CONFERENCE TITLE: _____

SITES: (Designate each participating site by entering the number of attendees expected. Circle the "Host" site).

RKS _____ LAR1 _____ (Classroom Blgd) LAR2 _____ (College of Ed)

CHY _____ CPR _____ RVN ___ PWL _____ SHR _____ GLT _____ TOR ___

Start Date: _____   Stop Date: _____
Start Time: _____   Stop Time: _____
Exclude Date(s): _____

Conference Leader: _____
Phone Number: _____ Fax Number _____

Charge to (circle one):
    X = UW School of Extended Studies
    E = UW College of Education
    U = UW Other Functions (specify): _____
    C = Community College (specify): _____
    D = School Districts (specify): _____
    S = State Government — Budget coding: _____
    O = Other (non-Education of State Government): _____

Please complete the following for correct billing of conference:
Name: _____ Phone: _____
Address: _____
City: _____ Zip_____

REQUESTER SIGNATURE: _____ Phone: _____

AGREEMENT FOR VIDEO TELECONFERENCING
1992-1993

THIS AGREEMENT, made this _____ day of _____, 1992, between the state of Wyoming, Department of Administration and Information, Division of Telecommunications and _____ in which the parties agree as follows:

1. The Wyoming State Network is a digital communications facility which serves the agencies of state government and higher education by transmitting data. The network facilities are leased from various carriers of the telephone industry by the State of Wyoming through the Division of Telecommunications.

2. The Wyoming State Network is managed and controlled by the Division of Telecommunications. The network is further subdivided into various statewide systems which serve 1) the state administrative computer connections 2) the state law enforcement entities 3) the state libraries 4) the community college/university computer connections system and 5) the interactive compressed video system which connects to the Codex equipment purchased by the University of Wyoming through the Education Trust Fund.

3. Because the Telecommunications Division must recover all costs for the network and pay the billing, the final decision for expanding the network rests with the division under legislative authority.

4. This agreement is for all entities of government wishing to schedule the use of the network on a regular basis, commencing September 1, 1992 and extending through July 31, 1993. The priority schedule adopted by the Video Governance Committee will serve as a basic guide for determining availability. The Telecommunications Division may schedule other users of video when the hours available are not covered by a signed agreement.

TERMS AND CONDITIONS OF THE AGREEMENT:

A. This Agreement will be in effect from September 1, 1992 to July 31, 1993. It may, with the mutual approval of the parties, be extended for one additional contract period. The state reserves the right to increase the hourly rates if the agreement is extended.

B. Each party to this agreement shall bear its own risk of loss for liability and neither party agrees to insure, defend and indemnify the other.

C. The parties may from time to time request changes in the scope of this agreement. Such changes which are mutually agreed upon by and between both parties shall be incorporated by written amendment to this agreement.

D. The State of Wyoming and the Telecommunications Division specifically reserve any claims they may have to sovereign immunity as a defense to any action arising in conjunction with this agreement.

E. This agreement is based on a minimum video usage of the Wyoming State Network for video of one hour per week for a period of no less than thirty days and a maximum time not to exceed the duration of one complete academic semester.

F. Cancellations for scheduled usage under this agreement will be charged as follows:

1. If written notice is given to the Telecommunications Division forty-five (45) days or more in advance, there will be no charge.

2. If written notice is given to the Telecommunications Division less than forty-five (45) days but more than fifteen (15) days in advance, a cancellation fee of fifty dollars ($50.00) will be charged.

3. If written notice to cancel is given to the Telecommunications Division less than fifteen (15) days before the scheduled event is to begin, the requesting entity will be willed at the regular hourly rate, less any time subsequently scheduled by another entity.

G. Agreement for course delivery must be signed sixty (60) days before the beginning of the next semester.

H. The hourly rates are as follows:

1. Educational units (elementary, secondary and higher education) will be charged forty dollars ($40.00) per hour for any two-point or multi-point interactive compressed video teleconference scheduled Monday through Friday. The Saturday hourly rate will be charged at sixty dollars ($60.00) per hour for any two-point or multi-point compressed video teleconference. The Sunday and/or holiday rates will be charged at eighty dollars ($80.00) per hour for any two-point video teleconference plus ten dollars ($10.00) per hour for each additional site that is connected.

2. Other governmental (state and local governmental agencies) will be charged fifty dollars ($50.00) per hour for any two-point compressed video teleconference plus ten dollars ($10.00) per hour for each additional site. Saturdays, Sundays and holidays will be charged at the rate of eighty dollars ($80.00) for a two-point connection plus ten dollars ($10.00) per hour for each additional site that is connected.

I. This agreement specifically deals with any video connections over the Wyoming State Network using the existing video system which connects the ten compressed video units at Laramie/University of Wyoming (two units), Cheyenne-Laramie County Community College, Casper-UW Outreach, Rock Springs-Western Wyoming College, Gillette-UW Outreach, Sheridan-Northern Wyoming College, Riverton-Central Wyoming College, Powell-Northwest Community College and Torrington-Eastern Wyoming College.

7   The Division of Telecommunications must approve any planned network expansion. The proportionate costs for network expansion <u>may</u> be applicable to the requesting entity. EXISTING AGREEMENTS WOULD NOT BE AFFECTED.

8.   This agreement has been established between the Wyoming State Government, Department of Administration and Information, Division of Telecommunications and

_____.

SIGNATURES

Appendix E

Needs Assessment

KEY INFORMANT INTERVIEW QUESTIONS
CARBON COUNTY TECH-NET PROJECT

1) Date _____

2) Name of Agency _____

3) Type of Agency
    Government_____ Education_____ Higher Ed_____
    Business/Industry_____ Community_____
    HealthCare_____

4) Number of employees/volunteers working for the agency?
    under 5_____ 5-10_____ 10-20_____
    20+_____ 50+_____

5) Use of Technology
    Staff training and development_____
    Video-conferencing_____
    Providing service to clients_____
    Other_____

THE TECHNOLOGY WOULD LINK RAWLINS, SARATOGA, ENCAMPMENT AND BAGGS TOGETHER VIA COMPRESSED VIDEO, WITH HANNAH AND MEDICINE BOW BEING CONNECTED WHEN DIGITAL CAPABILITIES ARE READY.

6) How would this techology assist your agency?
    Improve communication_____
    Reduce travel costs_____
    Improve service delivery_____
    Other_____

7) If compressed video technology was in place now, what monetary savings would be estimated for this fiscal year?
    under $10,000_____
    between $10,000 - $25,000_____
    over $25,000_____

8) How many hours would have been saved by using compressed video and traveling less/
    under 100_____ between 100 - 250_____
    between 250 - 500_____ over 500_____

9) Would the technology assist your agency or the community in any of the following areas?
    Improve the quality of the community?_____
    Attract more economic development?_____
    Attract professionals to the community?_____
    Reduce the isolation of Carbon County?_____

10) What kinds of special equipment or arrangements would be required for your agency to benefit from the technology?
    Special seating arrangement_____
    Security and privacy concerns_____
    Kitchen facilities_____
    Lab requirements_____
    Other_____

11) During what hours would your agency require the use of compressed video?
    8 a.m. - 4 p.m._____   4 p.m. - 10 p.m._____
    after 10 p.m._____   before 8 a.m._____   weekends_____

12) What time of year would your agency use compressed video?
    spring_____   fall_____   winter_____   summer_____

13) The location of the technology in your community is an important consideration. What criteria would your agency like to see considered in site selection?
    centrally located_____ ample parking_____
    accessable at all hours_____
    capable of seating 10-25 persons_____
    capable of seating 25-50 persons_____
    capable of seating 50-100 persons_____
    other considerations_____

14) Where would your agency prefer the compressed video system to be located in your community?
    elementary school_____   local library_____
    middle school_____   community center_____
    high school_____   higher Ed center_____

15) Are there any other considerations that your agency believes should be addressed as we apply for foundational and governmental financial support?

Appendix F

VIDEO TELECONFERENCING RFP EVALUATION

On a scale of 1 to 10, with 10 being highest or best, rate each evaluation factor for each vendor. To weigh, multiply each score by the weight, put in gray column, and total at the end.
(Replace lower case examples with your own requirements)

	EVALUATION FACTORS	WGT	VENDOR		VENDOR	
4.2	PROPOSAL COMPLETENESS & TECHNICAL SPECIFICATIONS MET Compliance with mandatory requirements, completeness of technical specifications, presentation of proposal, evaluation systems available	30				
4.3	DELIVERY CAPABILITY Within 60 days, CCITT H.261 standard within 6 months, software upgrades provided for two years	10				
4.4	REFERENCES Five furnished and evaluated	5				
4.6	WARRANTY & MAINTENANCE Remote maintenance and cost, local maintenance and cost, response time, telephone support.	20				
4.7	WARRANTY PERIOD Twelve months or greater	10				
4.8	SUPPORT Consulting service with cost, installation of new equipment with cost, training of support personnel with cost, other services	10				
4.10	COMPRESSED VIDEO LOAN EQUIPMENT Available, loan period, returnable to manufacturer, purchased at discount	5				
4.11	PRICE	15				
	SUBTOTAL (weighted scores)					
	COMPARE FINALISTS					
4.9	PERFORMANCE Picture quality, multipoint ability	30				
	TOTAL					

Appendix G

Codec Comparison - A

Manufacturer	Vendor Name:	Vendor Name:
Model		
Transmission Speed	56-768 kbps	
Resolution	256 pixels x 240 lines	
List Price	$35,000 for system (video/voice/ data and all software)	
Audio	.2 to 3.3 KHz	
Echo Cancellation	Standard: Built-in acoustic echo canceller	
Room Controller	Menu control from hand held wireless remote	
Architectur	Software	
Video Graphics 256X240	Standard: includes image capture, hard disk storage, retrieve and forward	
Computer Graphics	Standard: Includes image capture, hard disk storage retrieve and forward	
Computer Capability	Standard: Built-in PC-AT compatible with 20 megabyte hard disk and keyboard; other computer may be added through user RS232 port	
DSU or CSU?		
Will CCITT be Standard or Provided?		

These spread sheets may be extended to list all vendors being considered.

Codec Comparison - B

Manufacturer	Vendor Name:	Vendor Name:
Model	CS300 Series	
Encryption	DES option -- $1,200	
High-resolution Freeze Frame Graphics 512 x 480	Option: 512 pixels x 480 lines; includes image capture, hard disk storage	
Graphics Annotation with Interactive *Electronic Whiteboard*	Option: Included in high-resolution option above; allows interactive text and drawing in several sizes and colors.	
Communications Interface	RS-449/422, V.35 and Dual V.35	
Video	4 NTSC inputs with built-in video switcher	
VCR	Direct connect (1 of 4 video inputs); Play/Record; no time-base corrector required	
Fax	Direct connection to standard Group III Fax machines via RJ-11 phone jack	
Audio-Only Conferencing	Standard RF-11 phone jack for audio conferencing	
Weight	40 pounds (system-excluding cameras and monitors)	
Heat Dissipation	612 BTU/hr (system)	

Multiway Comparison

Manufacturer	Vendor Name:	Vendor Name:
Model	DVBX-8, DVBX, 14	
Name	Digital Video Branch Exchange	
Price	$70,000 for DVBX-8; $90,000 for DVBX-14	
Number of Sites	8 or 14	
Maximum Number of Simultaneous Conferences	7	
Audio	in band	
Conference Control	Voice activated switching, autocycle, dedicated	
User Setup and Control	Included keyboard and monitor, menu-driven user interface	
Communicates Interface	RS-499, V.35, Dual V,35	
Transmission Speed	56-766 KBPS	
Encryption	Option: DEC--$14,100 plus $1,500 per nod	
Weight	80 pounds	

Appendix H

Guidelines For Conducting A Pilot Program To Select A Compressed Video System

Barbara T. Hakes
Director
Wyoming Centers for Teaching and Learning Network
College of Education

Introduction

On April 30, 1991, the College of Education at the University of Wyoming completed a two month pilot project to evaluate the products of compressed video vendors. The Pilot was the culmination of over eighteen months' worth of work. The completion of that pilot yielded several results which we wish to share with other institutions contemplating the use of compressed video.

During the Spring of 1990, the College had determined that it needed to develop new ways to provide greater and more in-depth clinical experiences for students in its teacher education program. This decision was arrived at based on effective schools research and the College's own determination to improve its educational program.

Background

The University of Wyoming is trying to meet the heavy demand for education by teachers located in remote schools which are spread over vast geographic areas. The population density is approximately 4.7 people per square mile. It requires eight hours to drive across the State and as much as two to three hours of flight time to deliver face-to-face programs by more conventional means. The University has been using audio and audiographic teleconferencing and now prepares video taped programs which are mailed out. The six year old, Wyoming, Goodlad, School-University Partnership has been in the process of developing a compressed video network since the Fall of 1989. The network is being designed to provide opportunities for 1) the development of a model to create increased inservice and preservice programs, 2) the infusion of technology at all levels of education and 3) cooperative development and testing of interactive multimedia courseware through the Partnership Schools. Students in the schools will develop their own programs and courses. Course development will be facilitated by teachers and technology. Simultaneous inservice and preservice training will be provided over the network on the use of multimedia systems.

As the State's only four–year institution of higher education, the University of Wyoming has a mandate to serve the residents of Wyoming. Fewer than one–fourth of the state's inhabitants live within reasonable access to the University or its branch facility in Casper. In

Note: This paper was presented at the 1992 convention of the Association for Educational Communications and Technology.

particular, the College of Education, with its laboratory school (The Wyoming Center for Teaching and Learning at Laramie , WCTL-L) and the state's only teacher preparation program, has substantial need to network with the public schools around Wyoming to provide more in-depth and numerous clinical experiences for the students in its teacher education program. By the same token, geographically isolated schools need to network with other schools and the University to provide their students with opportunities for access to equally rich and strong educational programs. As a result, Wyoming's Partnership has created the Wyoming Centers for Teaching and Learning Network (WCTLN).

BACKGROUND

Six years ago, the John Goodlad School-University Partnership (The Partnership) began with six school districts. Since that time, The Partnership has expanded to include the private sector and a total of fourteen school districts. The Partnership now represents over 75% of Wyoming's public school students. In keeping with its goals to institute changes in education, the renewal of schools and the education of educators, the Partnership has been increasingly involved in collaborative efforts. These efforts have resulted in many changes from the mutual development of a new teacher education program at the University of Wyoming to joint ventures between the State's public schools, the University, the State Department of Education and the State's businesses to improve education at all levels. In November of 1990, through its efforts, the Partnership was announced as one of two national pilot demonstration sites for educational reform. The announcement was made at an invitational forum sponsored by Exxon Foundation in Washington, D.C. This national acclaim was the result of a three year study conducted by the Education Commission of the States, the American Association of Colleges of Teacher Education, and the National Center for Educational Renewal.

A major factor contributing to the selection of Wyoming for the national pilot demonstration was the Wyoming Centers for Teaching and Learning Network (WCTLN). The WCTLN is comprised of the fourteen Partnership districts. Ultimately the Partnership districts will become hubs for other schools in their geographic area. Until last year, the Partnership program was networked largely through face-to-face meetings and audio teleconferences. In the fall of 1989, the WCTLN began developing a state-wide computer network to link schools, businesses and the University. The newly adopted teacher education program called for earlier and more in-depth clinical experiences for preservice teachers, inservice programs for practicing professionals, faculty development for College faculty, and improved ways for mentoring and coaching student teachers as well as provide a support system for first and second year teachers. The Partnership felt it was necessary to explore something more than a computer network to meet these needs. These needs, along with others, prompted the WCTLN to explore the feasibility of developing a compressed video network.

A review of the capabilities of Wyoming's state-wide delivery system revealed a combination of carriers including land lines, microwave, and satellite. Additionally, the WCTLN began a preliminary review of compressed video systems which were on the market. This review uncovered a multitude of variables which the Partnership realized it had to assess before it could make an informed decision about which system to select for the WCTLN. As a result , the WCTLN organized a pilot during March-May of 1990 to serve as a national demonstration for the selection of a compressed video system. That pilot is discussed in this paper.

As a result of the pilot, a state-wide committee was selected to receive bids for a state-wide system. The committee consisted of representatives from the University's School of Extended Studies, the WCTLN, the public schools, community colleges and state agencies. In November of 1991, the State selected a vendor and installation of compressed video systems commenced in January of 1992.

HOW THE PILOT BEGAN

During the fall of 1989, the College formed an "Electronic Classroom Committee." This committee met frequently and generated the following list of outcomes it wished to achieve.

• Create a much stronger educational organization at all levels by providing the system for the networking of resources. The system will improve achievement, retention, motivation and educational efficiency.

• Provide preservice, practicing teachers and young people with an opportunity to gain expertise with the integration of electronic media as part of the teaching / learning process.

• Impact other states given the fact that 70% of the College's students leave to go to 41 other states. The College graduates about 300 teachers each year.

• Facilitate cooperative teaching and learning programs between the College and school districts around the State and the nation.

• Provide new opportunities for faculty development and inservice experiences and allow for interaction between teachers who might otherwise have a very limited peer group.

• Facilitate one-on-one delivery for the developmentally disabled.

• Help expand and enrich the curriculum in Wyoming's public schools by delivering content from the University to districts which can not afford to hire teachers for certain areas. Advanced students in Wyoming's high schools could simultaneously take courses with college students at the University.

• Allow the development of a partnership between the, now twelve, Goodlad pilot demonstration sites*, schools in the pilot site states, the University of Wyoming, and Wyoming's public schools. The university laboratory schools at Laramie and Northern Colorado University in Greeley could become a national laboratory school for other teacher education programs.

• Allow the Goodlad Partnership concept to be expanded to include the private sector.

• Provide opportunities for students at various schools to participate in cooperative learning projects.

Actually, this list represents only a few of the outcomes which have since emerged from our meetings and discussions. After the Committee had created this list it began to explore ways in which these outcomes could be facilitated through technology. Based on the fact that many of these outcomes are dependent upon live interactions with children, other teachers and administrators in public schools, and that it was clear that the College needed to be able to conduct these sessions between ordinary classrooms (as opposed to studio-type classrooms); the Committee began researching the potential of live, interactive video systems.

In July of 1990, the College created a new office to coordinate the development of a network to link the fourteen Wyoming School-University Partnership programs. This office was titled the Wyoming Centers for Teaching and Learning Network (WCTL-N). The WCTL-N arranged for a demonstration of the compressed video system which was being installed by the Western Institute for Distance Education at the University of Northern Colorado in Greeley. In considering the various options for transmission of full duplex audio and video interaction, the WCTL-N came to the conclusion that the most cost effective option for Wyoming was compressed video through a land line carrier. The emerging State network in Wyoming consists of a microwave capability which is being used primarily for public broadcast, and a land line network which is being used for data transmission as well as one satellite link with Ft. Collins, Colorado. In July of 1990, the WCTL-N along with The Wyoming School-University Partnership began planning a pilot demonstration project to evaluate the products from various compressed video vendors.

GUIDELINES FOR PLANNING A PILOT

Initially, the WCTL-N obtained information form three vendors, PictureTel, VideoTelecom, and Compression Labs, Inc. It also established an advisory board for the Pilot. (A comprehensive list of and chart of capabilities of compressed video vendors is available in the November, 1991 issue of Via Satellite, pp. 52-55). The location and dates for the pilot were established as March, April and May of 1991, between Laramie and Gillette, Wyoming. These two communities are separated by 250 miles.

INFORMAL SURVEY

The WCTL-N then conducted an informal, random (n=15) telephone survey (Exhibit A) to find out about how other educational institutions had dealt with the following:

1) *How did they select a vendor?*
2) *How were they using their network?*
3) *How many sites did the network include?*
4) *What kind of carrier(s) was being used?*
5) *Who used the network?*
6) *Where were the sites located, e.g. type of facility?*
7) *Had they developed special facilities at each site?*
8) *What level of technical support did they have to maintain?*
9) *Who operated the system at each site?*
10) *What were the transmission costs?*
11) *How much training was required to use the system?*
12) *What vendor did they support?*
13) *The pros and cons of their system.*
14) *What bandwidth did their system require?*
15) *Is the system movable?*
16) *Does it provide remote control of cameras at the other sites?*

This paper discusses the results of this survey and how they helped formulate the guidelines that were used for the Pilot Project. In particular, Steve Sachs of Northern Virginia Community College provided some immensely useful recommendations regarding questions his institution had asked when they selected a vendor. We incorporated those questions in our survey.

SURVEY RESULTS

1) How, and through whom, did they select a vendor?

Five of the respondents indicated their institutions selected the lowest bidder. Six said they based their selection on what colleagues at other institutions had chosen, and four said they purchased equipment from the first vendor that made an institutional proposal. In nine of the institutions, personnel/faculty associated with instructional television and/or outreach made the vendor selection. In the remainder of the institutions committees made the vendor selection.

2) How were they using their network?

All fifteen were using their networks primarily for delivery of courses, and most of the institutions were broadcasting only one way with two institutions using compressed video in a live, two-way mode.

3) How many sites did the network include?

The range in number of sites on an institutional network was three to twenty-two.

4) What kind of carrier(s) was being used?

Some institutions used a combination of satellite, land line and microwave. Other institutions were strictly satellite and some used ITFS transmission.

5) Who used the network?

Primarily, students needing credit for course work. Returning adult learners comprised the majority of each institution's utilization.

6) Where were the sites located, e.g., type of facility?

Fourteen of the institutions located their equipment in television studio-type classrooms which had been augmented with special lighting and acoustics. One institution used "roll around" systems in ordinary classrooms.

7) Had they developed special facilities at each site?

Six of the institutions constructed special television studio-type facilities. Eight placed the equipment in existing television studio facilities and one institution used regular classrooms.

8) What level of technical support did they have to maintain?

All but one institution supported a minimum of one technician at each site. Others supported up to three technicians at each site. One institution simply relied on the vendor's diagnostics.

9) Who operated the system at each site?

Fourteen sites said their systems were largely operated by technicians. One site said the professor teaching the class operated the system.

10) What were the transmission costs?

The response to this question varied widely. Costs per hour ranged from $200 to $40. Costs increased where satellite transmission was involved, and decreased with the use of land lines.

11) How much training was required to use the system?

In institutions using large, television-type studios, substantial training for both technicians and faculty was necessary. At the one institution which utilized ordinary classrooms and a "one button boot" system faculty learned how to use the system in less than an hour. No technical training was required.

12) What vendor did they support?

Nine supported CLI, one supported NEC, one supported GPT, three PictureTel, and one VideoTelecom.

13) The pros and cons of their system.

Each institution liked its system. All but the VideoTelecom institution indicated they had difficulty with maintenance and repair. None of the institutions had really compared their equipment capabilities with systems at other institutions.

14) What bandwidth did their system require?

Range , switched 56 to full bandwidth. Eight institutions used full T-1 bandwidth and the rest were using 384 kbps.

15) Is the system movable?

Only one institution had a moveable system.

16) Does it provide remote control of cameras at the other sites?

Only one institution had this capability.

GUIDELINES

As a result of this informal survey, the following guidelines emerged. Compressed video technology is changing so rapidly it will be important for any institution considering moving into that technology or upgrading their existing system to conduct some thorough research on this topic before investing.

The guidelines are:

1) Conduct a needs analysis.

2) Develop the goals and objectives for the pilot.

3) Send identical invitations to the vendors.

4) Schedule the vendors on a first contact, first scheduled basis for equivalent time periods.

5) You should not be required to rent equipment for the pilot. You should be able to test drive each vendor's system.

6) Make certain all vendors are perfectly clear about the capabilities you need to be able to use.

7) Develop a Project Newsletter to stimulate interest in the pilot and to help educate people about the technology.

8) Schedule a number of face to face meetings to invite people to participate in pilot.

9) Develop support for the pilot which will allow you to invite people to use the system at no charge.

10) Develop media events.

11) Develop evaluation instruments (Exhibit B).

12) Seek knowledge about the technology and assistance from all potential sources.

13) Develop a method for on-line scheduling of the system.

14) Keep vendors updated on pilot.

15) Link the vendors' technical support people with the technicians for the carrier.

16) Schedule time on-line for each vendor to present its product.

17) Maintain a journal.

18) Develop a baseline test. (Exhibit B)

19) Develop parallel resources at the remote site.

20) Identify a Pilot coordinator at each site.

21) Determine how system training will be accomplished for each vendor's product.

22) Make certain that you have an assistant available at each end for each session scheduled.

23) Begin the pilot and be prepared to adjust to a rapidly changing schedule. Make requests of the vendors for peripherals, and hold conversations via long distance with their technicians.

---

*The twelve Goodlad Pilot Sites Are:

California Polytech State University - San Luis Obispo, CA

Wheelock College - Boston, MA

University of Washington, Seattle, WA

University of Miami at Ohio - Oxford, OH

Texas A & M University - College Station, TX

Metro State College - Denver, CO

Winthrop College - Rock Hill, S.C.

University of Wyoming, Laramie, WY.

Montclair State College, Montclair, NJ

Brigham Young University - Provo, UT

University of Connecticut-Storrs, CT

University of So. Maine - Gorham, ME

EXHIBIT A
WCTL-N COMPRESSED VIDEO USERS SURVEY

1.   How many sites are on the network? When was the network installed?

2.   Where are the primary uses of the network?

3.   How and by whom was vendor selection made? If you did not consider multiple vendors, why not?

4.   Describe the facilities being used at the various sites, e.g., are they fixed classroom facilities with installed cameras and audio capabilities?

5.   Describe the level of technical support (human resources) that is required for the network.

6.   Describe the vendor support provided for the system.

7.   What arrangements exist for upgrading the compressed video system? Who can do the upgrades?

8.   If you were planning to install the network today, would you consider other vendors? Which vendors?

9.   What would you change, if anything, about how you selected a vendor?
      What would you change, if anything, about how you installed the network?

10.   Who physically operates the system at each site?

11.   Who pays for the network?

12.   How is the network scheduled?

13.   What capabilities does your system have?
              Remote site camera control?
              Computer Graphics?
              Fax?
              Picture in picture?
              Videodisc?
              Wireless Audio?

14.   How is the audio system configured?

15.   How much and what type of training is provided for system users?

16.   What are the greatest advantages of the system?

17.   What are the greatest disadvantages of the system?

18.   Approximately what did your compressed video system cost? On a per classroom basis for
              a)   compressed video equipment
              b)   classroom remodeling and equipment
              c)   support staff

19.   Do you use you own camera and audio equipment with the system?

20.   With how many sites can your system simultaneously link?

21.   What carrier(s) does your network use?

22.   Other comments or advice you can give us?

23.   Are there other institutions or groups we could contact?

EXHIBIT B
WCTL-N
PILOT PROJECT - BASELINE COMPRESSED VIDEO RATING
Please rate the compressed video vendors listed to the right on the following items:
1 = Low (Very little, No), 3 = High (A lot, Yes)
Put a check in the box if you have made additional comments on the back.

	RATING FACTORS	Vendor:	Vendor:
1	How much technical support is required?	q	q
2	What is the quality of sound?	q	q
3	Does what you see on the monitors meet your needs?	q	q
4	Will the system work well in the locations in which you will be using it?	q	q
5	Will you need to develop special facilities to use the system?	q	q
6	Will the system work well with the group sizes you will be working with?	q	q
7	Will the system require a minimal amount of training for users?	q	q
8	Can the system be operated by the person conducting the meeting or class (e.g. will not require camera people or other technical support operators)?	q	q
9	Will the system work well with the activities that will be taking place at the sites in the network?	q	q
10	Is this system being installed by reputable groups (e.g., States, Universities, Corporations, etc.)?	q	q
11	Is the picture of acceptable quality?	q	q
12	Does the system meet new CCITT Standards?	q	q
13	Is the level of vendor support high in terms of maintenance and warranty?	q	q
14	Is the system complicated to use?	q	q
15	Does the system require more than 1/3 capacity (384 kbps) of a T-1 carrier?	q	q
16	Does the system have the multipoint capabilities needed by the network?	q	q
17	Is the system "movable?"	q	q
18	Does it provide remote control of cameras? If so, is this easily done?	q	q
19	Does the system all for the use of wireless microphones?	q	q
20	Other:	q	q

This survey may be expanded to include the total number of vendors being considered. Other items to be evaluated can be listed.

Appendix I

Biographies of Authors

Cecelia Box is Assistant Professor of Instructional Technology at the University of Wyoming. She previously held the position of Senior Consultant at Anderson Consulting, where she designed, developed, conducted, and evaluated training for a number of major corporations. She also worked as an instructional designer for manufacturing education at IBM. Her instructional design work includes the design of management training and training for highly technical computer systems. Dr. Box earned a bachelor's and a master's degree from Trinity University in San Antonio, Texas; and a doctoral degree from the University of Texas at Austin. In addition to her instructional design work, she has extensive experience teaching in the public schools. Her research interests include visual design, psychological factors in learning, and social change in the learning process.

Mary Alice Bruce is an Assistant Professor of Counselor Education at the University of Wyoming. She completed her undergraduate work in mathematics at Purdue University and received her doctorate from Iowa State University. As a member of a team of university faculty and public school teachers, she has developed and teaches a coaching and mentoring skills course for master teachers via compressed video. Utilizing compressed video, she collaborates with teams of public school faculty to supervise counselors-in-training. In addition, she established ongoing statewide network meetings for school counselors to consult and interact by means of compressed video. Her research interests include brief counseling, childhood depression, distance learning, and supervision of school counselors.

Coleman H. Burton graduated from Cornell University with a bachelor's degree in mathematics. While employed by General Electric's Advanced Electronics Laboratory, he was designated as his department's representative to learn how to program and operate the Laboratory's first computer. What followed was an almost twenty-five year career in computing, with the General Electric Company, the Syracuse University Research Corporation, and finally the University of Missouri. At Missouri, he was the Director of the Computer Network at the time of his career change to telecommunications. In 1983, he was appointed the first Director of University Telecommunications for the University of Missouri System. Since 1983, each of the four campuses of the University of Missouri at Columbia, Kansas City, Rolla, and St. Louis have installed a new campus telecommunications system. A University owned digital network interconnects the four campuses and also connects to a similar network owned by the state of Missouri. This network supports voice, data, and video transmission between all campuses. He has authored several articles on computing and telecommunications, has made numerous presentations at professional meetings, and is the holder of two U.S. patents for error control communications systems.

John Cochenour is an Assistant Professor of Instructional Technology at the University of Wyoming. He also taught at the School of Library and Information Studies, University of Oklahoma and served as the Director of Media at Southern Nazarene University. He has experience as an instructor and trainer in the United States Marine Corps, was the continuing education coordinator at the Oklahoma Department of Libraries, and has been a manager and trainer in the business sector. He has been involved in distance education for several years and has extensive experience in the application of compressed video for instruction. He received his Ph.D. from the University of Oklahoma. He also has a Masters in Library Science and Masters of Education from OU and a B. S. from Oklahoma State University. He has published in the fields of instructional technology, adult education, and library science and presented numerous scholarly papers. His research interests are in distance learning, problem solving, and information use.

Barbara T. Hakes is an associate professor of Instructional Technology at the University of Wyoming. She previously held the position of Instructor of Library Science and Director of Media Services in the College of Education at the University of Idaho. While at Idaho, Dr. Hakes obtained considerable experience with distance education. Upon completion of her master's degree at the Washington State University in Media Management, Dr. Hakes moved to the University of Wyoming where she was hired to serve as director of media services in the College of Education. She served in that capacity for six years, always attempting to bring cutting edge technologies to the faculty and students of the college. She has also taught instructional technology courses in the library/media program. Dr. Hakes completed her doctorate at the University of Iowa in the design of interactive learning systems (interactive videodisc and microcomputers) in 1980. Dr. Hakes returned to Wyoming where she is currently serving as Director of the Wyoming Centers for Teaching and Learning Network and Director of the Wyoming Center for Educational Research. Dr. Hakes served as a member of the National Board of Directors of the Association for Educational Communications and Technology. She was also national president of the Division of Instructional Development of the same association and is a member of Governor Sullivan's State Communications Committee. She has extensive experience in distance education and compressed video. Her research interests include interactive learning systems and lifelong learning. Dr. Hakes has written numerous articles, papers and grants and has presented many papers at national conventions.

Richard T. Hezel is president and owner of Hezel Associates, a communications research company based in Syracuse, New York which specializes in statewide distance education planning. Dr. Hezel has had more than 20 years of experience in telecommunications and education. Prior to establishing Hezel Associates, Dr. Hezel was professor of telecommunications at Syracuse University and at the University of Houston. Dr. Hezel has participated in national workshops and conferences on distance education and telecommunications sponsored by the U. S. Department of Education, the Council of Chief State School Officers, the Annenberg/CPB Project, and the Aspen Institute. In addition, Dr. Hezel has served as a consultant for more than 15 states which are planning statewide educational telecommunications networks.

Landra L. Rezabek is an Assistant Professor of Instructional Systems, College of Education, Florida State University, and a former Assistant Professor and Educational Technology Program Unit Coordinator, College of Education, University of Wyoming. She received her bachelor's degree in English Education from the University of Virginia, her master's degree in Adult Education and Instructional Services from the University of Wyoming, and her Ph.D. in Educational Technology from the University of Oklahoma. She has taught numerous courses in the areas of distance education, instructional design, visual literacy, and educational technology both on- and off-campus. Her distance teaching experiences include the use of audio, audiographic, microwave, videotape, and compressed video delivery systems. Dr. Rezabek has been a junior high and high school English teacher and media specialist as well, and she is interested in the potential for distance delivery systems to support life-long educational opportunities for learners of all ages. Her current areas of interest also include facilitating interaction among distance learners and instructors and the effective use of visuals in distanced teaching and learning environments.

Steven G. Sachs is the Associate Dean for Instructional Technologies and Extended Learning at Northern Virginia Community College. Dr. Sachs is responsible for all distance learning activities at NVCC including: Extended Learning Institute with 3,500 enrollments per semester in over 80 traditional one-way video and print-based courses; their compressed video network connecting the college's five campuses over which are offered 8-10 courses per semester; their television center that provides programs for six local cable-TV systems; and their satellite teleconferencing operations. In addition, he is the chair of the Virginia Distance Education Network Task Force of the 23 member Virginia Community College System which is putting together a state-wide distance education program. He is a past president of the Division for Instructional Development of the Association for Educational Communications and Technology. Among his many publications are: "Teaching Critical Thinking to Distance Learners" (Tech Trends, Jan/Feb 1991); Doctoral Dissertations in Instructional Design and Technology: A Directory of Dissertations 1977-1986 with E.P. Caffarella (AECT, l988); "Microcomputers for Automated Instructional Management" chapter in Educational Media Yearbook, 1986). His convention papers include: "Implementing Large Scale Technology Projects on College Campuses" (AECT, 1991); "Overcoming Service Area Boundaries in Statewide Delivery of Distance Education," "Factors in Choosing a Compressed Video System—The Human Dimension," (AECT 1992). In addition, he is frequently invited to present workshops on characteristics of effective instruction and using new technologies to improve classroom instruction.

Wilhelmina Savenye is an Associate Professor of Learning and Instructional Technology at Arizona State University. She has also taught at the University of Texas at Austin and San Diego State University. She began her career eighteen years ago as a media technician and has been involved in educational technology ever since. She earned her master's and doctoral degrees at Arizona State University, as well as a bachelor's degree in anthropology from the University of Washington. Her experience in instructional design and evaluation includes work in distance education via video, and interactive video and multimedia for military training, training in high-technology companies, high-school science education and guidance, and teacher education. She conducts experimental and qualitative research focusing on how to improve learning through instructional design and interactive multimedia.

Richard A. Shade is an Assistant Professor of Special Education in the College of Education at the University of Wyoming. He earned a bachelors and masters degree in Special Education from Bloomsburg University in Pennsylvania and a doctorate in special Education from the University of Northern Colorado. After teaching gifted and talented students for 13 years in Pennsylvania public schools, he currently teaches various undergraduate and graduate courses in Special Education. He is a member of a team of public school teachers and College of Education faculty responsible for developing and implementing a three year project on the coaching and mentoring of student teachers via compressed video. He has published in the fields of gifted and talented education and teacher education, and has been invited to make numerous presentations at professional meetings. His research interests include gifted education, distance learning, and humor.

Lawrence Silvey is the Executive Director of the Wyoming Institute of Lifelong Learning (WILL) for Business and Industry. He has served in the past as the Human Resource Manager for a Fortune 500 company, Director of Employee Relations, Director of Personnel and Safety,

Industrial Trainer, Safety Supervisor, and Audio/Visual Training Coordinator. He was an Associate Professor of Speech Communication at Montana State University and also taught at the University of Utah, the University of Nebraska at Kearny, Louisiana State University, and Denver University. His educational preparation includes a Ph.D. from the University of Utah, an Education Specialist degree from the University of Wyoming, a Master's degree from Denver University, and a B. A. from Idaho State University. He has published numerous articles and papers, founded the Northwest Communication Association (NCA), and served in a variety of other professional positions. His research focus is in adult education and distance learning.

Paula M. Szulc is Project Coordinator at Hezel Associates. As an educator who has worked in the United States, Japan, and India, Ms. Szulc brings an international perspective to research on educational policy and distance education. With a Master's degree in Television, Radio, and Film in hand, Ms. Szulc is currently working on a doctorate in Instructional Design and maintains a vigilant watch on international developments in distance education. As part of her continuing research on international issues in distance education, Ms. Szulc is eagerly looking forward to investigating first hand the use of telecommunications in Swedish adult education workshops.

Dorothy Jean Yocum is an Assistant Professor in Special Education at the University of Wyoming. She received her doctorate from Oregon State University and Western Oregon State College in 1991. As a part of a three year grant associated with the Video Education Interaction Network (VEIN Project) sponsored by U S West, she is member of a team developing a teacher/ student support network through the technology of compressed video. The purpose of this grant is to develop coaching and mentoring skills in master teachers. Consultation/collaboration and adults with learning disabilities are her research interests.

GLOSSARY

ABCD Switch box   An external device used to switch between two devices; such as, printers, modems, plotters, mice, phone lines, etc. An example of how you use such a box: You plug one phone line in the "C" or common RJ-11 jack. You plug a fax machine into the "A" jack. You plug a modem into the "B" jack. By turning the switch, you can use one phone line for either a modem or a fax. An A/B switch box comes in serial, parallel port versions and RJ-11 phone line versions. There are also A/B/C/D switches to switch between four devices (Newton, 1991).

Analog   An electronic signal described as being continuous in both time and amplitude which is in contrast to a digital signal which is discrete.

Analog Gateway   A means of connecting dissimilar codecs. Incoming digital signal from one type of codec is decoded by a similar codec and converted to analog. The analog signal is then passed to the dissimilar codec, coded, and decoded at the far end. Analog gateways achieve interoperability in a prestandardized environment, but have the disadvantages of degrading video and audio quality and often reducing functionality.

Bandwidth   Amount of transmission capability.

The range of electrical frequencies a device can handle. The amount of bandwidth a channel is capable of carrying tells you what kinds of communications can be carried on it. A wide band circuit, for example, can carry a TV channel. A wide band circuit capable of providing one video channel can also provide 1,200 voice telephone channels (Newton, 1991).

Broadcast   One-way video, usually from a single transmission site to many receiving sites can communicate to the transmitting site on an audio-only basis.

To send information to two or more receiving devices simultaneously--over data communications network, a voice mail, electronic system, a local TV or radio station or a satellite system (Newton, 1991).

Carrier   Digital media, including satellite and land lines such as fiber and microwave.

1. A company which provides communications circuits. Carriers are split into "private" and "common" A private carrier can refuse you service. A "common" carrier can't. Most of the carriers in our industry--your local phone company, AT&T, MCI, US Sprint, etc.--are common carriers. Common carriers

are regulated. Private carriers are not. 2. An electrical signal at a continuous frequency capable of being modified to carry information. It is the modifications of the changes from the carrier's basic frequency that became the information carried. Modifications are made via amplitude, frequency, or phase. The process of modifying a carrier signal is called modulation. A carrier is modulated and demodulated (the signal at the other end) according to fixed protocols. Some of the wideband circuits are also called carriers. T1, which typically has 24- channel PCM voice circuits, is known as a carrier system (Newton, 1991).

CCITT   International Telephone and Telegraph Consultative Committee. An international body that sets worldwide telecommunications standards, such as the Px64 standard being drafted for videoconferencing

One of the four permanent parts of the International Telecommunications Union. It is based in Geneva, Switzerland. It has no power of enforcement, except moral persuasion. CCITT is working on worldwide international ISDN standards (Newton, 1991).

Coder/Decoder A device that encodes incoming analog signal into a digital signal for
Codec   transmission to another codec. The digital signal is decoded into analog format. In videoconferencing, codecs typically code and decode video and audio.

Compression   Reduction of the amount of information to accommodate cost effective digital transmission. For example, sub - T-1 video codecs compress analog signals (roughly equivalent to 90,000 kilobits per second) to digital rates varying from 56 to 1,544 kilobits per second. Different vendors reduce video and audio information in a variety of ways (algorithms), resulting in differences in picture and audio quality and the amount of space their information takes up on a carrier.

Reducing the representation of the information, but not the information itself. Reducing the bandwidth or bits necessary to encode information. Compression saves transmission time or capacity. It also saves storage space on devices such as hard disks, tape drives, and floppy disks (Newton, 1991).

Digital Encryption Standard An algorithm for encrypting (coding) data designed by the
DES   National Bureau of Standards so it is impossible for anyone without the decryption key to get the data back in unscrambled form. The DES standard enciphers and deciphers data using 64 bit key specified in the Federal Information Processing Standard Publication 46. DES is not the most advanced system in computer security and there are possible problems with its use. Proprietary encryption schemes are also available. Some of these are more modern and more secure. The quality of your data security is typically a function of how much money you spend (Newton, 1991).

Digital Encryption Standard. An encryption method defined by the National Bureau of Standards.

Digital   Information contained in the form of O's and 1's for transmission on digital media, including fiber, microwave and satellite. Digital information may include video, audio, graphics and data.

Digital Switch   A means of supporting multiway conferencing in a fully digital network. Digital switches permit multiple users with similar codecs to conference, generally with voice-activated switching. Different vendors offer varying multiway capabilities.

Distance Education   An academic discipline dedicated to an organized system of transferring (delivering) purposive educational information and materials to a receiving individual(s) and/or group(s), for a planned educational experience or result; through a medium (technical, mechanical, electronic, or any other) other than the conventional face-to-face (interpersonal) classroom relationship. There may or may not be immediate two-way communication, and the recipient(s) will not be under the continuous immediate direction of the sender (facilitator or teacher), nor in the same classroom. Progress of the learning individual(s) (receivers) may or may not be monitored and/or evaluated, depending on the existence of any contractual arrangements.

Dual 56   Combination of two 56 kilobits per second lines for 112 kilobits per second video transmission capacity. Dual 56 allows for direct dialing of a videoconference call.

Encryption   Alteration of transmitted information to protect it from unauthorized tapping.

In security the ciphering of data by applying an algorithm to plain text in order to convert it to cipher text (Newton, 1991).

Frames Per Second   Frequency with which video frames appear on a monitor. Broadcast quality video generally consists of 30 frames per second. Full-motion videoconferencing typically offers video in the range of 10-15 frames per second. At very low bandwidths, such as 56 or 112 kilobits per second, the frame rate may be lower.

Full Motion Video   Television transmission where images are sent and displayed in real time and motion is continuous (Newton, 1991).

Full Motion   In compressed video, picture quality that is generally acceptable to users although not of broadcast quality. Typically full-motion video provides 10-15 frames per second.

Full-duplex Audio   Audio that allows remote sites to speak simultaneously without losing audio contact. Full-duplex audio may be provided in a point-to-point or multiplex conference.

Graphics Transmission Transmitting still images, usually from a video source but in some cases PC generated. Graphics may also include on-screen annotation involving drawing or text.

H.221   The   CCITT Px64 standard to communications protocol for videoconferencing.

H.261   The CCITT Px64 standard relating to the video compression algorithm.

Half-duplex Audio   Audio that permits only one site to speak at a time.

In band   Transmission taking place within allocated bandwidth. For example a video call with a total of 768 kilobits per second may allocate 32 kilobits per second for audio, leaving 736 for video.

Interactive   Communication in which all participating sites have equal capability. Interactive videoconferencing permits all sites to see and hear one another.

Interoperability   Communication between dissimilar codecs. The CCITT Px64 standard is designed to permit interoperability.

Integrated Services Digital Network.   A totally new concept of what the world's telephone
ISDN   system should be. According to AT&T, today's public switched telephone network has the following limitations: 1) Each voice line is only 4 kHz, which is very narrow. 2) Most signaling is in-band signaling which is very consuming of bandwidth (i.e. it's expensive and inefficient). 3) The little out-of-band signaling that exists today runs on lines separate to the network (This includes signaling for PBX attendants, hotel/motel. Centrex and PBX calling information.) 4) Most users have separate voice and data networks (which is inefficient, expensive, and limiting). 5) Premises telephone and data equipment must be separately administered from the network it runs on. 6) There is a wide and growing variety of voice, data, and digital interface standards, many of which are incompatible. ISDN's "Vision" is to overcome these deficiencies in four ways: I) By providing an internationally accepted standard for voice, data and signaling. 2) By making all transmission circuits end-to-end digital. 3) By adopting a standard out-of-band signaling system. 4) By bringing significantly more bandwidth to the desk top. An ISDN central office will deliver to the user's office or factory basic ISDN services, also called interfaces (Newton, 1991).

Kilobits Per Second   Measure of rate of digital transmission often abbreviated Kbps.

Microwave   Electromagnetic waves in the radio frequency spectrum above 890 Megahertz (million cycles per second) and below 20 Gigahertz (billion cycles per second). Microwave is a common form of transmitting telephone, facsimile, video and data conversations used by common carriers as well as by private networks. Microwave signals only travel in straight lines. In terrestrial microwave systems, they're typically good for 30 miles, at which point you need another repeater tower. Microwave is the frequency for communicating to and from satellites (Newton, 1991).

Multiplexer or "MUX" A device that permits subdivision of a given bandwidth. For example, a T1 multiplexer may divide a T1 line (1,544 kilobits per second) into two capacities of 768 kilobits per second each. Other multiplexers may divide a line into roughly thirds, or 384 Kpbs.

Electronic equipment which allows two or more signals to pass over one communications circuit. That circuit may be a phone line, a microwave circuit, a through the air TV signal. That circuit may be analog or digital. There are many multiplexing techniques to accommodate both (Newton, 1991).

Multiway Communication between more than two sites. Multiway communication may occur through a digital switch or through an analog gateway.

NTSC North American Standard for analog video format.

North American Television Standards Committee The initials are used to describe the standard method of television transmission in North America. PAL is the name for the format for color TV signals used in West Germany, England, Holland, Australia and several other countries. It uses an interlace format with 25 frames per second and 625 lines per frame. In contrast, the US system uses interlaced scans and 525 horizontal lines per frame at a rate of 30 frames per second. The two systems are not compatible (Newton, 1991).

Out of Band Transmission taking place external to allocated band width. A video call with out-of band audio requires a separate phone line for the audio.

PAL European standard for analog video format.

Pixel Picture element: A measure of resolution for video format.

Pixel picture element Also called a Pel. The smallest unit of a video screen image. The single point in a facsimile transmission (Newton, 1991).

Private Network A series of offices connected together by leased and non-leased phone lines with the switching facilities and transmission equipment owned and operated by the user or the carrier and leased to the user. This is a broad definition. But these days with SDN and other virtual private networks, it's hard to see the difference between using a private network and using the public network except that you hope your private network will be cheaper, better quality, and perhaps offer a little more flexibility in the types

Public Network A network operated by common carriers or telecommunications admin-istrations for the provision of circuit-switched, packet-switched, and leased-lines circuits to the public (Newton, 1991).

Px64   The CCITT's international video standard. A compressed technique used in real-time videoconferencing (Newton, 1991).

Resolution   A measure of sharpness or clarity on a monitor.

Resolution   A measure of the quality of a transmitted image. Beginning with the scan processing in the transmitter and ending with the display and or printing process in the receiver, resolution is a basic parameter of any image transmission system. It affects the design of all its subsystems. In the scanner the resolution is a function of the spot size which the scanner optics and associated electronics look at the scene through which the system can uniquely identify the smallest distance along the scan line. Resolution is measured in picture elements (pixels). The number of picture elements per inch determines the sharpness of what you're transmitting (Newton, 1991).

RS 232   Connectivity from the codec permitting data inputs for transmission from .3 to 19.2 kilobits per second.

RS 449   Another standard data communications connector. This one uses 37 pins and is designed for higher speed transmission. Each signal pin has its own return line instead of a common ground return and the signal pairs are balanced lines rather than a signal referenced to ground. The cable typically uses twisted pairs (Newton, 1991).

                         Transmission interface between the codec and the transmission link that typically connects to a T1 multiplexer. A user RS 449 port may also be available for data transfer.

SECAM   French standard for analog video format.

                         Sequential and memory color TV system adopted by France and most Eastern European and Middle Eastern countries. SECAM uses an 819-line scan picture which provides a better resolution than PAL's 625 line and NTSC's 525. The three systems are not compatible (Newton, 1991).

Standards   Uniform specifications to permit interoperability in videoconferencing.

                         Agreed principles of protocol. Standards are set by committees working under various trade and international organizations (Newton, 1991).

Switched 56   Transmission network at 56 kilobits per second that allows dial up videoconferencing. Because picture quality at 56 K bps is often not acceptable, most dial up videoconferencing takes place on two 56 K bps lines, for a total of 11 K bps .

T-1   Commonly used transmission line for videoconferencing, with a capacity of 1,544 kilobits per second. Some compressed video systems use only 384 Kbps, which means they are using only about 1/3 of the capacity of the T-1. Thus, the remaining 2/3 could be occupied by other users who could help share the costs of the line.

Also spelled T1. A digital transmission link with a capacity of 1,544 Mbps. T-1 uses two pairs of normal twisted wires, the same as you'd find in your house. T-1 normally can handle 24 voice conversations, each one digitized at 64 kbps. But, with more advanced digital voice encoding techniques, it can handle more voice channels. T-1 is a standard for digital transmission in North America. It is usually provided by the phone company and used for connecting networks across remote distances. Bridges and routers are used to connect LANs over T-1 networks. There are faster services available, such as T-2 and T4 but these are not used much. T-1 linkscan often be connected directly to new PBXs and many new forms of short haul transmission, such as shorthaul microwave systems. It is not compatible with T-1 outside the United States and Canada (Newton, 1991).

Transmission Speed Data rate for videoconferencing, usually expressed in kilobits per second.

V.35   Transmission interface between the codec and the transmission link that permits switched 56 connectivity.

Video   The picture portion of a televised presentation. It is an electronic signal composed of moving frames of information and transmitted at a frequency range of 1 to 6 megahertz.

Videoconferencing Communication across long distances with video and audio contact. It may also include graphics and data exchange.

Voice Activated Switching   In multiway videoconferencing, used so that all participating sites automatically see the site which is currently speaking.

VSAT-Very Small Aperture Terminal A relatively small satellite antenna, typically 1.5 to 3.0 meters in diameter, used for transmitting and receiving one channel of cata communications. You see VSATs on top of retail stores which use them for transmitting and receiving instructions for sales, etc. (Newton, 1991).

References

Newton, Harry *Newton's Telecom Dictionary.* Chelsea, Minnesota: Bookcrafters, 1991.

INDEX